THE LEGAL FOUNDATIONS OF INTERPOL

This book is a study of the establishment and development of INTERPOL and its responsibility as an international organisation.

Part I of the book examines how INTERPOL was created as an international organisation without a formally celebrated treaty. It considers the circumstances of INTERPOL's creation and the structure and operations of INTERPOL. This content has been significantly updated in this second edition to reflect the developments within INTERPOL since 2010.

This new edition also includes a Part II, which examines INTERPOL's internal and external law, and situates INTERPOL's assistance to its members in the legal regime of responsibility. It is the first text to undertake this task. Part II draws on the jurisprudence of the Commission for the Control of INTERPOL's Files and the authors' extensive experience before this body to discuss in great detail how an individual can challenge INTERPOL's interventions (including the issuance of red notices) on the basis of the Organization's internal rules. Part II also describes the procedures under which INTERPOL members might challenge INTERPOL's interventions and how an individual can hold INTERPOL responsible for breaches of its external law. Part II is integral for any practitioner or individual seeking to challenge INTERPOL and its actions.

In testing theory against practice, this book aims to contribute to the understanding of international institutional law, whilst also demystifying one of the more enigmatic international organisations of the twenty-first century.

The Legal Foundations of INTERPOL

Second Edition

Rutsel Silvestre J Martha
Courtney Grafton
and
Stephen Bailey

•HART•
OXFORD • LONDON • NEW YORK • NEW DELHI • SYDNEY

HART PUBLISHING
Bloomsbury Publishing Plc
Kemp House, Chawley Park, Cumnor Hill, Oxford, OX2 9PH, UK
1385 Broadway, New York, NY 10018, USA
29 Earlsfort Terrace, Dublin 2, Ireland

HART PUBLISHING, the Hart/Stag logo, BLOOMSBURY and the Diana logo are trademarks of Bloomsbury Publishing Plc
First published in Great Britain 2020

First published in hardback, 2020
Paperback edition, 2022

A catalogue record for this book is available from the British Library.

Library of Congress Cataloging-in-Publication Data

Names: Martha, Rutsel Silvestre J, author. | Grafton, Courtney, author. | Bailey, Stephen, author.

Title: The legal foundations of INTERPOL / Rutsel Silvestre J Martha, Courtney Grafton, and Stephen Bailey.

Description: Second edition. | Oxford, UK ; New York, NY : Hart Publishing, an imprint of Bloomsbury Publishing, 2020. | Includes bibliographical references and index.

Identifiers: LCCN 2020024843 (print) | LCCN 2020024844 (ebook) | ISBN 9781849468046 (hardback) | ISBN 9781509901104 (ePDF) | ISBN 9781509901111 (Epub)

Subjects: LCSH: International Criminal Police Organization. | Law enforcement—International cooperation.

Classification: LCC K3465 .M37 2020 (print) | LCC K3465 (ebook) | DDC 344.05/2—dc23

LC record available at https://lccn.loc.gov/2020024843

LC ebook record available at https://lccn.loc.gov/2020024844

ISBN: HB: 978-1-84946-804-6
PB: 978-1-50994-471-2
ePDF: 978-1-50990-110-4
ePub: 978-1-50990-111-1

Typeset by Compuscript Ltd, Shannon

To find out more about our authors and books visit www.hartpublishing.co.uk. Here you will find extracts, author information, details of forthcoming events and the option to sign up for our newsletters.

This book is dedicated to John RWD Jones QC (in memoriam)

FOREWORD

INTERPOL is a complex and very active organisation, which has so far undeservedly attracted only limited interest among scholars. It was thoroughly analysed by Dr Rutsel Martha, from his privileged position as former General Counsel of INTERPOL, in the first edition, dated 2010, of the present book. The time that has passed since that edition and several new developments, especially with regard to protecting persons affected by INTERPOL's activities, have prompted the publication of the present second edition, which Rutsel Martha co-authors with Courtney Grafton and Stephen Bailey. This edition is supplemented by a new part, which focuses on questions of responsibility and remedies.

The authors devote Part I to the question of whether INTERPOL is to be regarded as an international organisation. This question often still arises because INTERPOL was not established on the basis of a formal treaty. The authors clearly reach an affirmative conclusion, referring first of all to Paul Reuter's opinion, given in 1980 to INTERPOL's Secretary General, that a treaty establishing an international organisation may be informal, consisting in the case of INTERPOL in the convergence of wills of Member States with regard to its 1956 Constitution (Chapters 2 to 5). The authors add further arguments in favour of the nature of INTERPOL as an international organisation (Chapter 6). What seems to me most significant is the way the Organisation operates when it acts in the international community. INTERPOL does not generally conduct itself as a common organ of its Member States, but rather as an independent entity.

Some of the questions concerning whether certain activities may be attributable to the Organisation are raised by the ambivalent nature of the National Central Bureaux ('NCBs'). These are listed among the organs of INTERPOL in Article 5 of its Constitution, but are part of the structure of the respective States and often act without being bound by the internal rules of the Organisation, for instance, when responding to the information in a diffusion. According to the authors, 'NCBs are not to be regarded as part of INTERPOL other than for the purposes defined in the INTERPOL Constitution' (Chapter 7). This criterion may give rise to uncertainties about its implications; moreover, it may be difficult to apply when an act addressed to an NCB is not binding under the rules of the Organisation. However, a distinction between activities of NCBs attributed to the respective States and those attributed to INTERPOL appears to be justified.

Since INTERPOL deals with many sensitive cases, it risks making mistakes or accepting requests originating from a biased State that are in breach of the human rights of the persons concerned. An important feature, which is appropriately analysed in the book (Chapters 8 and 9), consists in the possibility for an aggrieved individual to resort to an internal mechanism of review, the Commission for the Control of INTERPOL's Files ('CCF'), whose Statute, entered into force in 2017, has been designed to provide a quasi-judicial process. Members of the CCF are elected by the General Assembly and the Commission is (relatively) independent. Applications may be made to the CCF for 'access to, or correction and/or deletion of, data processed in the INTERPOL Information System' (Article 28(1)(b) of the CCF Statute). Decisions of the CCF are 'binding on the Organization and the applicant' (Article 38(1) of the CCF Statute). However, internal remedies available to individuals are still not fully adequate, in particular, with regard to reparation of wrongful harm that individuals may have suffered.

Individuals aggrieved by INTERPOL's activities sometimes resort to national courts. In most cases they fail because of lack of personal jurisdiction with regard to the respondent or because of INTERPOL's jurisdictional immunity. Article 24 of the Headquarters Agreement between INTERPOL and France provides for arbitration of disputes between INTERPOL and a private party, but only if the 'origins' of the dispute do not 'lie in the application or interpretation of the Organization's Constitution or its appendices': a provision of which the authors advocate a liberal construction, based on a distinction in the cause of action (Chapter 12). This approach may not be altogether to the individuals' benefit, since the Organisation's claim to jurisdictional immunity will be strengthened when there is an alternative remedy.

For disputes among members of INTERPOL, Article 135 of the Rules on the Processing of Data provides a role for the Executive Committee and 'if necessary' the General Assembly in view of a political settlement. The traditional reluctance to accept third-party dispute settlement applies also to disputes between INTERPOL and its members. Such disputes may arise with regard to an alleged breach by the Organisation of one of its obligations under international law. This could occur, for instance, with regard to aid or assistance given by the Organisation to a State committing an internationally wrongful act. The possibility of invoking INTERPOL's international responsibility in this set of circumstances is very limited if one reads Article 14 of the ILC Draft Articles on the Responsibility of International Organizations in light of its commentary, according to which, for responsibility to arise, the Organisation must have 'intended, by the aid or assistance given, to facilitate the occurrence of the wrongful conduct' (Chapter 11).

On all the questions here briefly mentioned and on many others the present book provides an extraordinary wealth of materials, accompanied by a consistently clear analysis.

Giorgio Gaja
April 2020
Judge of the International Court of Justice
Former Special Rapporteur on the topic of the Responsibility of International Organizations at the International Law Commission

PREFACE TO THE SECOND EDITION

Since the first edition of this book appeared in 2010, INTERPOL's internal rules and the general international law pertaining to the operations of international organisations have undergone significant developments, particularly in light of changing attitudes towards the responsibility of international organisations. In preparing the second edition it thus became necessary, while retaining the broad character of the work, to expand the book. Part Two of this book, an addition to the first edition, has benefitted from the authors' extensive experience advising on matters concerning INTERPOL and representing clients before the Commission for the Control of INTERPOL's Files, the internal body tasked with ensuring that the processing of personal information by the Organization is in compliance with the Organization's rules.

The changes to INTERPOL's internal rules principally arise from (1) the adoption in 2012 of INTERPOL's Rules on the Processing of Data, (2) the adoption in 2016 of the Statute of the Commission for the Control of INTERPOL's Files, and (3) the re-constitution of the Commission for the Control of INTERPOL's Files, which is functioning increasingly like a quasi-judicial body.

The general international law pertaining to the operations of international organisations has come to the fore following the adoption in 2011 of the Draft Articles on the Responsibility of International Organizations by the International Law Commission. The adoption of the Draft Articles provided an impetus for further critical discussion and appraisal of the policies and practices of international organisations. It also intensified the debate on the responsibility of international organisations, particularly as regards their responsibility towards private parties.

In the case of INTERPOL, as its interventions continue to increase exponentially in volume, it has attracted vociferous criticism. At the same time, the Commission for the Control of INTERPOL's Files has generated a body of jurisprudence that invites and enables analysis and discussion of the application of international law to the operations of international organisations.

The significant expansion of the book to reflect and discuss the foregoing developments has not detracted from the fact that this book is not a constitutional manual on INTERPOL. It remains a study of the birth and development of an international organisation from the perspective of general international law.

Finally, the authors are indebted to a number of people who assisted with this edition, including Sheetal Balakrishnan, Giulio Calcara, Marija Đorđeska, Mariam Ghazaryan, Myron Phua, Naomi Sirrs, Dhruv Sharma and Kit de Vriese. Needless to say, any errors in law or exposition are entirely our own. We have endeavoured to state the law as at 31 January 2020 (although some later developments have been incorporated at proof stage).

RSJM, CG, SB
London, 2 April 2020

CONTENTS

ABBREVIATIONS

ABHCO	Arab British Helicopter Company
ACHPR	African Charter on Human and Peoples' Rights
ACHR	American Convention on Human Rights
AFIS	Automated Fingerprint Identification System (INTERPOL)
AMIA	Asociación Mutual Israelita Argentina
AOI	Arab Organization for Industrialization
ArCHR	Arab Charter on Human Rights
ARS	Articles on the Responsibility of States for Internationally Wrongful Acts
ATCSA	Anti-Terrorism, Crime and Security Act 2001 (UK)
BIS	Bank for International Settlements
BKA	Bundeskriminalamt (DE)
CARICOM	Caribbean Community
CAT	Committee Against Torture (UN)
CCC	Command and Coordination Centre (INTERPOL)
CCF	Commission for the Control of INTERPOL's Files
CCLEC	Caribbean Customs Law Enforcement Council
CFATF	Caribbean Financial Action Task Force
CJEC	Court of Justice of the European Communities
CJEU	Court of Justice of the European Union
DARIO	Draft Articles on the Responsibility of International Organizations
DEA	Drugs Enforcement Agency (US)
DVI	Disaster Victim Identification
EAW	European Arrest Warrant

EC	European Community
ECB	European Central Bank
ECCB	Eastern Caribbean Central Bank
ECHR	European Convention on Human Rights
ECOSOC	Economic and Social Council (UN)
ECOWAS	European Community of West African States
ECSRC	Eastern Caribbean Securities Regulatory Commission
ECtHR	European Court of Human Rights
EDPS	European Data Protection Supervisor
ESA	European Space Agency
EU	European Union
Europol	European Union Agency for Law Enforcement Cooperation
FARDC	Armed Forces of the Democratic Republic of the Congo
FBI	Federal Bureau of Investigation (US)
FIND	Fixed INTERPOL Network Database (INTERPOL)
GATT	General Agreement on Tariffs and Trade
GDPR	General Data Protection Regulation (EU)
HRC	Human Rights Committee (UN)
iARMS	Illicit Arms Record and Tracing Management System (INTERPOL)
IATA	International Air Transport Association
IBIN	INTERPOL Ballistic Information Network (INTERPOL)
ICC	International Criminal Court
ICCPR	International Covenant on Civil and Political Rights
ICJ	International Court of Justice
ICPC	International Criminal Police Commission
ICPO	International Criminal Police Organization
ICRC	International Committee of the Red Cross
ICTR	International Criminal Tribunal for Rwanda

ICTY	International Criminal Tribunal for the former Yugoslavia
IDI	Institut de Droit International
IFAD	International Fund for Agricultural Development
IFRC	International Federation of Red Cross and Red Crescent Societies
IGO	Intergovernmental organisation
ILA	International Law Association
ILC	International Law Commission
ILOAT	Administrative Tribunal of the International Labour Organization
IMEST	INTERPOL Major Event Support Team (INTERPOL)
IMF	International Monetary Fund
INTELSAT	International Telecommunications Satellite Organization
INTERPOL	International Criminal Police Organization
IPU	Inter-Parliamentary Union
IRPD	INTERPOL's Rules on the Processing of Data
IRT	Incident Response Team (INTERPOL)
ISAP	INTERPOL Strategic Advisory Panel
ISIL	Islamic State in Iraq and the Levant
ITO	International Trade Organization
MIND	Mobile INTERPOL Network Database (INTERPOL)
NATO	North Atlantic Treaty Organization
NCB	National Central Bureau (INTERPOL)
NGO	Non-governmental organisation
OECS	Organisation of Eastern Caribbean States
OSCE	Organization for Security and Co-operation in Europe
PCA	Permanent Court of Arbitration
PCIJ	Permanent Court of International Justice
PRC	People's Republic of China

RCI	Rules on the Control of Information and Access to INTERPOL's Files
RIPC	Rules on International Police Cooperation (INTERPOL)
RPI	Rules on the Processing of Information for the Purposes of International Police Cooperation
SAD	Stolen Administrative Documents Database (INTERPOL)
SIAC	Special Immigration Appeals Commission (UK)
SLTD	Stolen and Lost Travel Documents Database (INTERPOL)
TRAP Act	Transnational Repression Accountability and Prevention Act of 2019 (US)
UDHR	Universal Declaration of Human Rights
UN	United Nations
UNCAC	United Nations Convention Against Corruption
UNCAT	United Nations Convention Against Torture and other Cruel, Inhuman or Degrading Treatment or Punishment
UNCTOC	United Nations Convention against Transnational Organized Crime
UNESCO	United Nations Educational, Scientific and Cultural Organization
UNIDO	United Nations Industrial Development Organization
UNTS	United Nations Treaty Series
USSR	Union of Soviet Socialist Republics
VCLT-IO	1986 Vienna Convention on the Law of Treaties between States and International Organizations or between International Organizations
VCLT	1969 Vienna Convention on the Law of Treaties
WHO	World Health Organization
WTO	World Trade Organization

TABLE OF CASES

COMMISSION FOR THE CONTROL OF INTERPOL'S FILES

Introduction

During the twentieth century, international law, it seems, really came of age.[1] International organisations certainly contributed to that, and, in their own right, they are a striking feature of that period.[2] However, the emergence of international organisations on the international legal plane posed numerous challenges for the generally accepted assumptions of international law; their acceptance as subjects of international law meant that the monopoly of the State disappeared.[3] With its observation in *Reparation for Injuries* that the subjects of law in any legal system are not necessarily identical in their nature or the extent of their rights,[4] the International Court of Justice ('ICJ') set the stage for a theory of subjects of international law which feeds the view that the contemporary global system should be called a 'complex conglomerate system'.[5]

The International Criminal Police Organization ('INTERPOL' or the 'Organisation') was created in 1923 as the International Criminal Police Commission to provide an organised and coordinated response to the demand for international police cooperation. The current Constitution of INTERPOL came into force on 13 June 1956. Despite the fact that the INTERPOL Constitution and the process through which it came into force assemble all the elements that justify its qualification as an international agreement of the same standing as the constituent instruments of other international organisations, the legal character of the

[1] See: Gross, L, 'The Peace of Westphalia, 1648–1948' in Gross, L (ed), *Selected Essays on International Law and Organization* (New York, Transnational Publishers, 1993) 1–21. See also: Lauterpacht, E (ed), *International Law: Being the Collected Papers of Hersch Lauterpacht*, Vol 2, Part I (Cambridge, Cambridge University Press, 1975) 487–533.

[2] The twentieth century has been described as 'the era of the establishment of international organisations' (Claude, IL, *Swords into Plowshares: The Problems and Progress of International Organization*, 2nd edn (New York, Random House, 1961) 43).

[3] The object of the constituent instrument of an international organisation is to create a new subject of law endowed with certain autonomy to which the parties entrust the task of realising common goals (*Legality of the Use by a State of Nuclear Weapons in Armed Conflict* (Advisory Opinion) [1996] ICJ Rep 66, para 19).

[4] *Reparation for Injuries Suffered in the Service of the United Nations* (Advisory Opinion) [1949] ICJ Rep 178.

[5] Mansbach, RW, Ferguson, YH and Lampert, DE, *The Web of World Politics: Nonstate Actors in the Global System* (Englewood Cliffs, Prentice-Hall, 1976) 32. Seidl-Hohenveldern speaks of 'the widening of the notion of subjects of international law' (*International Economic Law*, 3rd revised edn (Dordrecht, Kluwer Law International, 1999) 9–11). See also: Cassese, A, *International Law*, 2nd edn (Oxford, Oxford University Press, 2005) 134–35.

INTERPOL Constitution is regularly questioned or misunderstood.[6] An example can be found in Professor Anne-Marie Slaughter's elaboration of her vision of a disaggregated world order. Slaughter notes that the 'core' of her vision is 'a concept of an international order in which the principal actors are not states, but parts of states; not international organisations, but parts of international organisations. Those parts … link up with one another around the world'.[7] In Slaughter's vision, those 'parts of states' serve to 'expand state power'.[8] Slaughter invokes INTERPOL as a positive example of horizontal cooperation between 'parts of states' (ie, between police bodies). In so doing, she comments that it is 'remarkable' that INTERPOL, 'the second largest international organization after the United Nations' ('UN'), 'was not founded by a treaty and does not belong within any other international political body'.[9] But is it correct to suppose that INTERPOL was not founded by a treaty?

This question brings to the fore the legal and administrative process by which international organisations are created. In general, the legal process of creation or incorporation 'abounds with fictions and abstractions'.[10] These fictions and abstractions are normally taken for granted in considering whether a natural person is a legal subject and hardly call for reflection. However, when it comes to entities which owe their existence to public international law, the situation changes: the international community has no prescribed legal and administrative process of incorporation.[11] Therefore, an international organisation must legitimise its existence, its powers, its independence, etc, by reference to, and interpretation of, its constituent instrument in the context of general international law. In most cases, there exists a formal and solemnly concluded multilateral treaty comprising the constituent instrument of the organisation. In the case of INTERPOL, there is, on the one hand, the absence of a formal and solemnly concluded multilateral treaty establishing an international organisation and, on the other hand, the presence of indices of an international legal person. INTERPOL shares this particularity with other international organisations, such

[6] See: Riegel, R, 'Internationale Bekämpfung von Straftaten und Datenshutz' (1982) 37 *JuristenZeitung* 312–19 at 316. See also: Anderson, M, *Policing the World: INTERPOL and the Politics of International Police Cooperation* (Oxford, Oxford University Press, 1989) 57–73; den Boer, MGW, 'Internationale Politiesamenwerking' in Fijnaut, CJC, Muller, ER and Rosenthal, U (eds), *Politie: Studies over haar werking en organisatie* (Alphen aan den Rijn, Samsom, 1999) 577–626; Sjöcrona, JM and Orie, AMM, *Internationaal Strafrecht vanuit Nederlands perspectief*, 3rd edn (Deventer, Kluwer, 2002) 217, 270, 348.

[7] Slaughter, A-M, *A New World Order* (Princeton, Princeton University Press, 2004) 162.

[8] Ibid, 266–71.

[9] Ibid, 56.

[10] Riphagen, W, 'The Second Round of Treaty Law', in Capotorti, ED et al (eds), *Du Droit International au Droit de l'Integration: Liber Amicorum Pierre Pescatore* (Baden-Baden, Nomos, 1987) 565–81 at 565. See also: Verzijl, JHW, *International Law in Historical Perspective*, Part I (Leiden, Sijthoff, 1969) 1.

[11] Crawford, J, *Brownlie's Principles of Public International Law*, 9th edn (Oxford, Oxford University Press, 2019) 512–13.

as the Inter-Parliamentary Union ('IPU'),[12] the Organization for Security and Co-operation in Europe ('OSCE')[13] and the Organization for Petroleum Exporting Countries.[14] It therefore becomes necessary to identify and qualify the legal act which created INTERPOL. Is it accumulated international practice accepted as law,[15] or a unilateral act of another international organisation,[16] or an agreement under international law? The view held by the authors and expressed in this book is that the INTERPOL Constitution is an agreement between subjects of international law governed by international law which created a new subject of law possessing its own international legal personality.

The first purpose of this book (Part I) is to substantiate this view. Accordingly, some preliminary remarks relating to the definition of an international organisation are set out in Chapter 1. Chapters 2 to 5 are premised on the theory of validity of international juridical acts,[17] ie, irrespective of the form in which the intention to establish an international organisation is expressed, the legal act which gives effect to this intention must not (1) lack an appropriate object, (2) suffer from a lack of volition or defaults in the expression of wills, (3) be undertaken by an entity or person which lacks capacity, or (4) contain any essential faults of form.[18] It seemed logical to the authors to organise Chapters 2 to 5 broadly in the sequence of these conditions of validity. Chapter 2, therefore, considers whether extrajudicial international police cooperation can be considered an appropriate object and provides an overview of how the rule of law operates in an informal context.[19] The task in Chapter 3 is twofold: first, to

[12] See: 'The international legal personality of the Inter-Parliamentary Union (IPU), its status as an international organisation in international law and the legal implications of such status for the IPU's relations with governments and other international organisations', Joint Legal Opinion of Brownlie, I and Goodwin-Gill, GS (31 May 1999).

[13] See: Akande, D, 'International Organizations' in Evans, M (ed), *International* Law, 5th edn (Oxford, Oxford University Press, 2018) 227–58 at 250.

[14] Ibid.

[15] Eg, as was the case with the Pan-American Union, the predecessor of the Organization of American States.

[16] Eg, the UN Industrial Development Organization was established by a unilateral act of the UN General Assembly.

[17] See: Verzijl, JHW, *International Law in Historical Perspective,* Part VI (Leiden, Sijthoff, 1973) 66–81. Part I could have considered the question of validity through the prism of the 1969 Vienna Convention on the Law of Treaties ('VCLT'). However, the VCLT did not enter into force until 27 January 1980, almost 24 years after the INTERPOL Constitution came into force. Even then, it is difficult to assert that Article 42 of the VCLT and the various grounds for invalidity in the VCLT were customary law at the time of the conclusion of the VCLT (see the scepticism of Kohen, M and Heathcote, S in 'Invalidity, Termination and Suspension of the Operation of Treaties' in Corten, O and Klein, P (eds), *The Vienna Convention on the Law of Treaties: A Commentary*, Vol 2 (Oxford, Oxford University Press, 2011) 1018. The authors of this book have, therefore, adopted an analysis that better reflects the legal situation as it stood in 1956 and which is not limited to treaties but has a wider scope.

[18] See: Verzijl, JHW, *International Law in Historical Perspective*, Part VI (Leiden, Sijthoff, 1973) 66–81. See also: Guggenheim, P, 'La validité et nullité des actes juridiques international' (1949) 74 *Recueil des Cours* 195–268.

[19] 'The political arena provides a conundrum of policies that shape the environment in which law enforcement takes place. We must distinguish between the formal and informal environments which

determine whether the meeting of wills reflected in the INTERPOL Constitution can be attributed to the countries of the participating police bodies, and second, to determine whether these countries can be deemed to have expressed their consent to be bound by the INTERPOL Constitution. Chapter 4 considers whether the concurrence of wills reflected in the INTERPOL Constitution is attributable to two or more subjects of international law. Chapter 5 discusses the informal nature of the INTERPOL Constitution. Chapter 6 then considers the governing law of the INTERPOL Constitution, and Chapter 7 answers the question of whether the INTERPOL Constitution purports to create, and has actually created, a new subject of law with a distinct will (*volonté distincte*) that bears rights and duties derived from international law. Part I concludes that INTERPOL is an international organisation.[20]

The second purpose of this book (Part II) is to examine INTERPOL's internal and external law and situate INTERPOL's assistance to its members in the legal regime of responsibility. This part of the book is especially relevant in light of the continued criticism of the Organisation when it assists its members[21] and the various responses from States and organisations addressing the perception that INTERPOL is being abused by certain members.[22] One such response can be found in the introduction of the Transnational Repression Accountability and Prevention Act of 2019 ('TRAP Act') to the United States Congress. Its aim is to counter efforts by foreign governments to pursue, harass, or otherwise persecute individuals for political and other unlawful motives overseas. The TRAP Act is premised on six findings, one of which states that:

> [s]ome INTERPOL member countries have used INTERPOL's databases and processes, including Notice and Diffusion mechanisms and the Stolen and Lost Travel Document Database, for activities of a political or other unlawful character and in violation of

are both at play in international police cooperation' (Lemieux, F, 'The nature and structure of international police cooperation: an introduction' in Lemieux, F (ed), *International Police Cooperation: Emerging Issues, Theory and Practice* (Portland, Willan Publishing, 2010) 1–22 at 7).

[20] For an analysis of the juridical nature of the OSCE, see: Bertrand, C, 'La nature juridique de l'organisation pour la sécurité et la coopération en Europe' (1998) 102 *Revue Générale de Droit International Public* 365–406.

[21] Eg, Lemon, E, 'Weaponizing Interpol' (2019) 30 *Journal of Democracy* 15–29; Peel, M, 'Is Interpol being manipulated by authoritarian regimes?' *Financial Times* (19 November 2018).

[22] Eg, see responses from: (1) the European Parliament (Rasmus RH, Suter, D and Ivan-Cuco, G, 'Study: Misuse of Interpol's Red Notices and Impact on Human Rights: Recent Developments' requested by the European Parliament's Subcommittee on Human Rights, Document No PE 603.472 (January 2019); 'Letter from six Members of the European Parliament to the EU High Representative and the European Commission' (26 November 2013)); (2) the Parliamentary Assembly of the Council of Europe (Committee on Legal Affairs and Human Rights, 'Accountability of International Organisations for Human Rights Violations', Document No 13370 (17 December 2013); 'Abusive Use of Interpol System: The Need for more Stringent Legal Safeguards', Motion for a Resolution, Document No 13566 (2 July 2014)); and (3) the Parliamentary Assembly of the OSCE ('Baku Declaration and Resolutions adopted by the OSCE Parliamentary Assembly at the 23rd Annual Session', Document No AS (14) DE (28 June – 2 July 2014)).

international human rights standards, including making requests to INTERPOL for interventions related to purported charges of ordinary law crimes that are fabricated for political or other unlawful motives.[23]

This finding seems misguided because it wrongly implies that INTERPOL is a passive entity used by its members without the ability to express its own will.[24] That is clearly not true. INTERPOL regularly rejects applications from members requesting it to issue red notices against wanted persons,[25] and it cancels active notices found to be non-compliant with the Organisation's rules. Needless to say, because INTERPOL is an international organisation, its interventions are attributable to the Organisation, not to the member that receives its assistance.[26] Accordingly, if any entity needs to be held accountable for unwarranted and unlawful interventions by INTERPOL, it should be INTERPOL itself, in accordance with either its internal rules or the relevant rules of international law concerning the responsibility of international organisations. Part II of this book is dedicated to these issues. Chapter 8 is concerned with the internal law of the Organisation, with a particular focus on the substantive provisions that regulate the processing of data by the Organisation. It also draws on the jurisprudence of the Commission for the Control of INTERPOL's Files ('CCF' or 'Commission') and the authors' experience before the CCF to discuss how an individual might challenge INTERPOL's interventions (including the issuance of red notices) on the basis of the Organisation's internal rules. Chapter 9 sets out the procedural mechanisms that an individual or entity must rely on to challenge data processed in the INTERPOL Information System. Chapter 10 considers how INTERPOL members can resolve institutional disputes that arise in connection with the application of INTERPOL's data processing rules. Finally, Chapter 11 discusses the external law and responsibility of INTERPOL, and Chapter 12 considers the principal mechanism through which INTERPOL can be held responsible for breaches of its external law.

[23] 116th Congress (2019–2020), s 2483.

[24] See, eg, the hearing held by the United States Commission on Security and Cooperation in Europe ('Helsinki Commission') on 'Tools on Transnational Repression: How Autocrats Punish Dissent Overseas' to address the concern that 'autocrats often turn to [INTERPOL] to file bogus criminal claims … This abuse of INTERPOL Red Notices and Diffusions enables autocratic governments to harass and intimidate their opponents thousands of miles away, even within free and democratic society' (held on 12 September 2019 at Canon House in Washington, DC).

[25] Eg, the National Central Bureau in India requested a red notice against the former Indian Premier League Chairman. However, after engaging with the Enforcement Directorate in India and legal counsel for the individual, INTERPOL decided not to publish the requested red notice on the basis that the processing of his data would not conform with its internal rules ('Interpol shuts door on ED for Red Corner Notice against Lalit Modi', *The Times of India* (28 March 2017)). See also: Estlund, M, 'You Can't Always Get What You Want: INTERPOL's Rejection of Red Notice Requests', *Red Notice Law Journal* (9 October 2011).

[26] See: Second report on responsibility of international organizations by Special Rapporteur Gaja, UN Doc A/CN.4/541 (2 April 2004).

In concluding this Introduction, we note that, quite apart from the elucidation of the legal foundations of INTERPOL and the laws that bind the Organisation, the book aims to provide a valuable case study on the creation of an international organisation and the responsibility of international organisations. In testing theory against practice, the book hopes to contribute to the understanding of international institutional law, whilst also demystifying one of the more enigmatic international organisations of the twenty-first century.

PART I

1

The Concept of International Organisations

As stated in the Introduction, unlike domestic legal systems, the international community has no prescribed legal and administrative process of incorporation of international organisations. This contributes to the divergence of views that exists with regard to the very concept of an international organisation, its definition and the legal requirements for its existence. The lack of consensus concerning the concept of an international organisation is particularly evident in the work of the International Law Commission ('ILC') and the resulting multilateral agreements containing provisions referring to international organisations. The ILC had deliberately abstained from adopting a definition of "international organisation" 'in order to avoid starting interminable discussions on theoretical and doctrinal questions, on which there were conflicting opinions in the Commission and the General Assembly, as was only natural'.[1] Instead, Article 2(1)(i) of the 1969 Vienna Convention on the Law of Treaties ('VCLT') and Article 2(1)(i) of the 1986 Vienna Convention on the Law of Treaties between States and International Organizations or between International Organizations ('VCLT-IO') employ a minimalist and rather tautological definition according to which '"international organization" means an intergovernmental organization'.[2] According to the ILC's interpretation in 2002, the meaning of the term 'intergovernmental organizations' was to be understood as 'organizations that States have established by means of a treaty or, in exceptional cases (such as that of [the Organization for Security and Co-operation in Europe ('OSCE')]), without a treaty'.[3]

In the context of codifying the principles of the responsibility of international organisations, the definition of an international organisation was gradually elaborated, reflecting various aspects of the accepted notion of international organisations. The initial proposal by Giorgio Gaja, the Special Rapporteur on

[1] '1925th meeting – 15 July 1985' in *Yearbook of the International Law Commission* (1985) Vol I, 284.

[2] VCLT (adopted on 23 May 1969, entered into force on 27 January 1980) 1155 UNTS 331; VCLT-IO (adopted on 21 March 1986, not yet in force). This was also the definition adopted in the Vienna Convention on the Representation of States in their Relations with International Organizations of a Universal Character (adopted on 13 March 1975, never entered into force) UN Doc A/CONF.67/16.

[3] 'Report of the Commission to the General Assembly on the work of its fifty-fourth session' in *Yearbook of the International Law Commission* (2002) Vol II, Part Two, 94, para 469.

the responsibility of international organisations, suggested that an international organisation should be referred to as 'an organization which includes states among its members insofar as it exercises in its own capacity certain governmental functions'.[4] The definition offered by the ILC Working Group, however, was more in line with traditional approaches; it referred to an international organisation as 'an organization established by a treaty or other instrument governed by international law and possessing its own international legal personality distinct from that of its members'.[5] It also clarified that international organisations 'may include as members, in addition to States, other entities'.[6] With the deletion of the phrase 'distinct from that of its members', this definition was accepted by the ILC in the text of the Draft Articles on the Responsibility of International Organizations in 2011 ('DARIO'). Article 2(a) of the DARIO reads as follows:

> 'international organization' means an organization established by a treaty or other instrument governed by international law and possessing its own international legal personality. International organizations may include as members, in addition to States, other entities.[7]

The ILC does, however, note that while this definition is considered appropriate for the purposes of the DARIO, it is not intended as a definition for all purposes.[8] A largely similar definition can be found in the work of the International Law Association ('ILA') on the accountability of international organisations. The ILA Committee on the Accountability of International Organisations speaks of 'intergovernmental organisations in the traditional sense, ie, created under international law by an international agreement amongst States, possessing a constitution and organs separate from its Member States'.[9] The difference in the definitions might be attributed to the fact that the possession of organs is clearly an inherent element of being an organisation, so it is implicitly included in the ILC's definition of international organisations.

[4] First Report on the Responsibility of International Organizations by Special Rapporteur Gaja, UN Doc A/CN.4/532 (26 March 2003) 115, para 34. For a critical analysis on the approach of the ILC, see: Brownlie, I, 'The Definition of "International Organization" in the International Law Commission's Current Project on Responsibilities of International Organizations' in Ragazzi, M (ed), *International Responsibility Today: Essays in Memory of Oscar Schachter* (Leiden, Martinus Nijhoff Publishers, 2005) 355–62.

[5] 'Report of the Commission to the General Assembly on the work of its fifty-fifth session', *Yearbook of the International Law Commission* (2003), Vol II, Part Two, 18, fn 24

[6] 'Report of the Commission to the General Assembly on the work of its fifty-fifth session', *Yearbook of the International Law Commission* (2003), Vol II, Part Two, 18.

[7] 'Draft articles on the responsibility of international organizations, with commentaries' in *Yearbook of the International Law Commission* (2011) Vol II, Part Two, 49.

[8] Ibid, Commentary to Art 2, para 1.

[9] ILA, 'Accountability of International Organisations: Final Report' (Berlin, 2004) 4. The existence of separate organs allows international organisations to be differentiated from mere international agreements.

Despite the absence of a prescriptive definition of international organisations under general international law, there is considerable consensus, or at least a converging opinion, on the constitutive elements of international organisations.[10] In scholarly writings, international organisations are typically defined as legal entities created by (mostly) States, usually on the basis of a treaty with at least one organ able to express a will distinct from that of its members, possessing its own international legal personality and entrusted to fulfil some common, typically public or governmental, tasks:

> … to qualify as an international organisation, it must have the following characteristics:
>
> its membership must be composed of states and/or international organisations;
>
> it must be established by treaty or other instrument governed by international law, such as a resolution adopted in an international conference;
>
> it must have an autonomous will distinct from that of its members and be vested with legal personality; and
>
> it must be capable of adopting norms (in the broadest sense) addressed to its members.[11]

However, within this general definition exist substantial doctrinal debates. It is, for instance, sometimes debated whether the existence of a will distinct from that of its members (*volonté distincte*) should be '[t]he basic criterion for distinguishing an international organisation from other entities'[12] or whether it is evidence of the existence of an international organisation.[13] A debate also exists as to whether international legal personality is objective or derived from the will of members to confer such personality.[14] Similarly, opinions differ as to whether the fulfilment of

[10] Schermers, HG and Blokker, NM, *International Institutional Law: Unity within Diversity*, 6th revised edn (Leiden, Brill Nijhoff Publishers, 2018) 25–7.

[11] Sands, P and Klein, P (eds), *Bowett's Law of International Institutions*, 6th edn (London, Sweet & Maxwell, 2009) 15–6 (footnotes omitted). See also: Reinisch, A, *International Organisations in National Courts* (Cambridge, Cambridge University Press, 2004) 7–8.

[12] This was the view of ILC member Lacleta Muñozv as stated in '1925th meeting – 15 July 1985', *Yearbook of the International Law Commission* (1985) Vol I, 296.

[13] The Institut de Droit international ('IDI') on the advice of Rapporteur Higgins subscribed to this view in Article 2(b) of its draft resolution concerning the legal consequences for Member States of the non-fulfilment by international organisations of their obligations towards third parties: '[t]he existence of a *volonté distincte*, as well as capacity to enter into contracts, to own property and to sue and be sued, is evidence of international legal personality' (Draft Resolution of October 1994 (1995) 66–I *Annuaire de l'Institut de Droit International* 465). However, in its 1995 resolution, the IDI eschewed this discussion and limited itself to considering the 'issues arising in the case of an international organisation possessing an international legal personality distinct from that of its members' (Art 1). See: Higgins, R, 'The Legal Consequences for Member States of the Non-fulfilment by International Organisations of their Obligations toward Third Parties – Preliminary Exposé and Draft Questionnaire' (1995) 66–I *Annuaire de l'Institut de Droit International* 249–89 at 252–57.

[14] Contrast the approach of Seyersted, F, *Objective International Personality of Intergovernmental Organizations* (Copenhagen, Krohns Bogtrykkeri, 1963) with that of Schermers, HG and Blokker, NM, *International Institutional Law: Unity within Diversity*, 6th revised edn (Brill Nijhoff Publishers, 2018) 1029–30.

public, governmental or sovereign tasks is a requirement, since some international organisations perform functions that are difficult to classify in such terms (eg, the Organization of the Petroleum Exporting Countries), but it is undisputed that they are international organisations.[15]

Notwithstanding these debates, it is clear from the work of the ILC, the ILA, the IDI and various academic writers that two elements are deemed crucial for the qualification of an entity as an international organisation. One is that its membership comprises States or other subjects of international law,[16] such as existing international organisations. The latter is evidenced by the membership of the European Union in a number of international organisations, among them the World Trade Organization.[17] The second (related) requirement is the need for an act of establishment on the basis of a treaty or other international instrument. These two criteria help to distinguish international organisations from other entities operating internationally and set up on the basis of, and governed by, national law, such as non-governmental organisations, transnational corporations or multinational enterprises.[18]

Constituent instruments of international organisations have been described as conventions, charters, constitutions, statutes, articles of agreement, etc. It is also accepted that international organisations can be founded by implicit agreement, which might be expressed through parallel domestic legislation, such as the Nordic Council, which was established by decisions of the parliaments of Denmark, Iceland, Norway and Sweden,[19] or by a resolution adopted during an inter-State conference, such as the UN Relief and Works Agency for Palestine Refugees in the Near East.[20] The picture that emerges from these examples is that, as long as the constituent act can be interpreted as an expression of the will to create an international organisation, even though achieved through an agreement in highly simplified form, the requirement of establishment by international agreement will be fulfilled.[21] It can, therefore, be said that the requirement that an international

[15] Joelson, MR and Griffin, JP, 'The Legal Status of Nation-State Cartels Under United States Antitrust and Public International Law' (1975) 9 *International Lawyer* 617.

[16] Note that, increasingly, public–private partnerships that comprise States and international organisations as well as non-governmental entities are being established.

[17] See: Marrakesh Agreement Establishing the World Trade Organization providing for the European Communities as original member of the World Trade Organization (adopted on 15 April 1994, entered into force on 1 January 1995) 1867 UNTS, Art XI(1).

[18] See: Amerasinghe, CF, *Principles of the Institutional Law of International Organisations*, 2nd edn (Cambridge, Cambridge University Press, 2005) 66–104 and Wallace, CD, *Legal Control of the Multinational Enterprise–National Regulatory Techniques and the Prospect for International Controls* (The Hague, Nijhoff Publishers, 1982) 1–5.

[19] Cameron, I, 'Nordic Cooperation' in *Max Planck Encyclopedia of International Law* (online edn, 2009).

[20] Schermers, HG and Blokker, NM, *International Institutional Law: Unity within Diversity*, 6th revised edn (Leiden, Brill Nijhoff Publishers, 2018) 46.

[21] See: Seidl-Hohenveldern, I, *Corporations in and under International Law* (Cambridge, Grotius Publishers, 1987) 75.

organisation be established by treaty does not necessarily mean establishment by formal treaty.[22]

This aligns with the general position that any legally valid written agreement under international law, by whatever name, may qualify as a treaty in the generic sense of the VCLT.[23] It may also be that the establishment of an international organisation is not in written form, so the agreement falls outside the scope of the VCLT but is nevertheless a treaty under international law.[24] Indeed, with specific references to the constituent instruments of international organisations, many academics have made it clear that the founding instrument of an international organisation does not need to be a formal treaty. For instance, after studying various examples, Barberis concludes:

> *[t]outefois, dans tous les exemples cites, bien qu'il n'y ait pas de traite formelle ou que celui-ci n'ait pas existe lors de la création de l'organisation internationale, il a eu sans aucun doute possible accord de volontés entre les États qui sont à l'origine de la constitution de l'organisation.*[25]

Similarly, Amerasinghe speaks of 'establishment by some kind of international agreement'.[26] Klabbers distinctly states that, whether the organisation is created by treaty or some other legal act, '[t]he importance of this characteristic … is above all to indicate that the creation of an international organisation is an intentional act'.[27] The ILC has also endorsed the view that international organisations do not need to be established through a formal treaty but may be set up by an informal or even implicit agreement governed by international law. The ILC expressly acknowledged that 'forms of international cooperation are sometimes established

[22] Schermers, HG and Blokker, NM, *International Institutional Law: Unity within Diversity*, 6th revised edn (Leiden, Brill Nijhoff Publishers, 2018) 41. See also: Bekker, PH, *The Legal Position of Intergovernmental Organisations: A Functional Necessity Analysis of their Legal Status and Immunities* (Dordrecht, Martinus Nijhoff Publishers, 1994) 39.

[23] VCLT, Art 2(1)(a).

[24] VCLT, Art 3: '[t]he fact that the present Convention does not apply to international agreements concluded between States and other subjects of international law or between such other subjects of international law, or to international agreements not in written form, shall not affect:

(a) the legal force of such agreements;
(b) the application to them of any of the rules set forth in the present Convention to which they would be subject under international law independently of the Convention;
(c) the application of the Convention to the relations of States as between themselves under international agreements to which other subjects of international law are also parties'.

[25] 'However, in all the examples cited, although there was no formal treaty or it did not exist during the creation of the international organisation, there was without any doubt a concurrence of wills between the States at the origin of the constitution of the organisation' (authors' translation) (Barberis, JA, 'Nouvelles questions concernant la personnalité juridique internationale' (1983–I) 179 *Recueil des Cours* 145, 217). See also: Seyersted, F, *Common Law of International Organizations* (Leiden, Martinus Nijhoff Publishers, 2008) 46–52.

[26] Amerasinghe, CF, *Principles of the Institutional Law of International Organisations*, 2nd edn (Cambridge, Cambridge University Press, 2005) 10.

[27] Klabbers, J, *An Introduction to International Institutional Law*, 2nd edn (Cambridge, Cambridge University Press, 2012) 10.

without a treaty', such as the OSCE or the Pan American Institute of Geography and History.[28] It is for this reason that the DARIO defines an international organisation as including those organisations established by any 'other instrument governed by international law'.[29]

In conclusion, it seems justified to say that, for an international organisation to exist, its constituent instrument ought to be an international legal instrument of some sort which not only satisfies the criteria for validity of an international legal act[30] but also is governed by international law and contains an expression of an intention to create a subject of international law.

[28] 'Draft articles on the responsibility of international organizations, with commentaries' in *Yearbook of the International Law Commission* (2011) Vol II, Part Two, 49, Commentary to Art 2, para 4.

[29] 'Draft articles on the responsibility of international organizations, with commentaries' in *Yearbook of the International Law Commission* (2011) Vol II, Part Two, 49, Art 2(a).

[30] As delineated in the Introduction.

2

The Object of the Organisation

In the Introduction, we noted that the legal act which gives effect to the intention to establish an international organisation must have, inter alia, an appropriate object. The appropriateness of the object must be considered in light of the principle reflected in Article 53 of the 1969 Vienna Convention on the Law of Treaties ('VCLT'), which states that '[a] treaty is void if, at the time of its conclusion, it conflicts with a peremptory norm of general international law'.[1] A peremptory norm of general international law is a norm accepted and recognised by the international community of States as a whole as a norm from which no derogation is permitted and which can be modified only by a subsequent norm of general international law having the same character.[2] It can be inferred from the foregoing that, for the constituent act of an international organisation to be valid, the object of the organisation must not conflict with a peremptory norm of general international law.

As will become clear in the following paragraphs, the field of extrajudicial international police cooperation is fraught with issues concerning the protection of the fundamental rights and freedoms of individuals. This gives rise to concerns about the propriety of extrajudicial international police cooperation and casts doubt on the legitimacy of any organisation that purports to promote it.[3] Although not all of those issues can be said to arise at the level of *jus cogens*, as will be seen below, both the creators of the International Criminal Police Organization

[1] VCLT (adopted on 23 May 1969, entered into force on 27 January 1980) 1155 UNTS 331, Art 53. The language of Article 53 of the Vienna Convention on the Law of Treaties between States and International Organizations or between International Organizations (adopted on 21 March 1986, not yet in force) is identical to the language of Article 53 of the VCLT.

[2] Dörr, O and Schmalenbach, K (eds), *Vienna Convention on the Law of Treaties: A Commentary*, 2nd edn (Berlin, Springer Nature, 2018) 994–95. We use the phrases 'peremptory norms of general international law' and '*jus cogens*' interchangeably.

[3] On the notion of extrajudicial international police cooperation, see: Ciampi, A, *L'assunzione di prove all'estero in materia penale* (Padova, CEDAM, 2003) 338–53; Balzer, AJ, 'International Police Cooperation: Opportunities and Obstacles' in Pagon, M, (ed), *Policing in Central and Eastern Europe: Comparing Firsthand Knowledge with Experience from the West* (Ljubljana, College of Police and Security Studies, 1996); Vermeulen, G, 'Pre-Judicial (Preventative) Structuring of International Police Action in Europe' in Pagon, M (ed), *Policing in Central and Eastern Europe: Comparing Firsthand Knowledge with Experience from the West* (Ljubljana, College of Police and Security Studies, 1996); Karanja, SK, *Transparency and Proportionality in the Schengen Information System and Border Control Co-Operation* (Leiden, Martinus Nijhoff Publishers, 2008) 399; and Schöndorf-Haubold, B, 'The Administration of Information in International Administrative Law: The Example of Interpol' (2008) 9 *German Law Journal* 1719–52.

('INTERPOL' or the 'Organisation') and its participants have consistently sought to ensure that the Organisation's aims and activities are legitimate under international law, and, more particularly, that they are consistent with fundamental rights and freedoms.

Lawrence is of the view that, to be effective, an international organisation must (1) be given an appropriate mission, (2) be given the means to accomplish its mission, and (3) be viewed as legitimate when carrying out its mission.[4] However, judicial bodies are often sceptical of the legitimacy of extrajudicial international police cooperation, as reflected in the attitude of the Court of Appeal of Dakar in the *Orsini* case. In this case, Orsini, a French national, had been provisionally arrested in Dakar pending extradition to the United States during a layover of a flight from Buenos Aires, Argentina to Nice, France. The arrest took place at the request of the INTERPOL National Central Bureau ('NCB') in Washington, DC. The Court of Appeal of Dakar considered that the provisional arrest was unlawful because, inter alia, it did not consider a request from INTERPOL for the arrest and extradition of a person tantamount to a request emanating from the judicial authorities of the requesting State.[5] It came to this conclusion without considering either the constituent instrument of INTERPOL or the role and function of INTERPOL's notices system. The Court's approach is illustrative of the Organisation's continued struggle with legitimacy. This struggle directly relates to the permissibility of extrajudicial international police cooperation under international law. Thus, it is necessary to pose the question: is the promotion of extrajudicial international police cooperation an appropriate object for an international organisation under international law? Only if the answer to this question is affirmative, can that area of activity validly lend itself as the main objective of an international organisation. Admittedly, appropriate object is a vague concept. As discussed above, an international organisation may be set up for any purpose that does not violate *jus cogens*. If the international organisation violates other rules of international law, it bears responsibility. The focus here, however, is whether an organisation can be set up to promote an activity that, by its nature, could lead to violations of international law, in particular, international human rights law.

Police authorities regularly confront the conflict between the inherently territorial nature of police enforcement under international law and the need to manage transnational elements of crime, for instance, in the gathering of intelligence or evidence, the conduct of interrogations, searches and seizures, and the apprehension of suspects or fugitives. The options available to the police are varied, ranging from undertaking unilateral actions in foreign territory,[6] to arranging informal

[4] Lawrence, RZ, 'International Organisations: The Challenge of Aligning Mission, Means and Legitimacy' (2008) 31 *World Economy* 1455–70.

[5] *Orsini*, Court of Appeal of Dakar, Senegal (23 August 1975) 73 ILR 661.

[6] See: Ronzitti, N, 'The Legality of Covert Operations Against Terrorism in Foreign States' in Bianchi, A (ed), *Enforcing International Law Norms Against Terrorism* (Oxford, Hart Publishing, 2004) 17–24.

operations with local police authorities, to using more formal channels for mutual legal assistance in criminal matters. What are the considerations that motivate the police to opt for one or the other type of extraterritorial operation? Could it be that recourse to unilateral actions occurs out of ignorance of multilateral options? Or does it occur because of the distrust of the local police authorities or other relevant departments, or after attempts to set up a cooperative operation fail? Regardless of the motivation, police authorities are aware that their extraterritorial operations may be examined before a competent court. As such, they are especially focused on how an extraterritorial operation will be perceived under judicial scrutiny. To this end, a practical but legal question that police authorities have to answer when considering extraterritorial enforcement operations is: what are the consequences of a violation of international law before either the national or international court or tribunal that would consider the case, or the relevant international human rights body?

This chapter first discusses whether or not extrajudicial international police cooperation is an appropriate object, bearing in mind the presumptive freedom of action of sovereign States and its resultant implications on the forms and formalities of police cooperation. Thereafter, we turn to the issue of the attribution of police enforcement cooperation to the State and the perceived exclusivity of extradition agreements and mutual legal assistance treaties.

I. Is Extrajudicial International Police Cooperation an Appropriate Object?

The question of the appropriateness, or legitimacy, of extrajudicial international police cooperation is not new. *The Savarkar Case* between France and Great Britain was the first (and probably the only) case where a tribunal was established under international law at the Permanent Court of Arbitration ('PCA') to settle an inter-State dispute concerning police cooperation.[7]

The facts leading to *The Savarkar Case* commenced on 29 June 1910 with a letter from the Commissioner of the Metropolitan Police in London to the Director of General Security (*Directeur de la Sûreté générale*) at the Ministry of the Interior in Paris. The letter stated that Vinayak Damodar Savarkar, an Indian revolutionary (*un révolutionnaire hindou*), was being sent back to India from England to face charges for abetment of murder and that he would be on the steamship *Morea*, which would call at the port of Marseilles on either 7 or 8 July of that year. Conscious of the territorial limitations of police enforcement powers, the Commissioner invited his French counterpart to take all the necessary precautions to guard against the occurrence of any incident during Savarkar's passage through

[7] *The Savarkar Case (France v Great Britain)* (Award of 24 February 1911) XI RIAA 243.

Marseilles. By a letter dated 9 July 1910, the Director of General Security replied to the Commissioner's letter, stating that he had given the necessary instructions at a domestic level to guard against the occurrence of any incident onboard the *Morea* at Marseilles, and that all necessary precautions would be taken in order to ensure Savarkar's imprisonment while the ship was in French waters. In the meantime, upon reaching the Marseilles port, Savarkar escaped. He swam to the wharf but was chased by the crew and arrested by a brigadier of the French port police. Acting under the mistaken belief that Savarkar was a member of the crew, the brigadier brought him back and turned him over to the British authorities onboard the *Morea*. The next morning the ship left Marseille with Savarkar onboard. Upon being apprised of the facts, the French Government protested the manner in which Savarkar had been returned to British custody and demanded his restitution to France on the grounds that his delivery to British authorities amounted to defective extradition. The British Government countered that, according to the arrangements made with the French authorities prior to Savarkar's arrival in Marseilles, the brigadier had been obligated to prevent his escape. The French Government was not satisfied with this response. It argued that the brigadier was mistaken as to his duties and Savarkar could only be recovered by the British if they took appropriate legal proceedings for his rendition. This dispute was initiated before the PCA in 1910, and the final award was issued in 1911. The tribunal held that since there was a pattern of collaboration between the two countries regarding the possibility of Savarkar's escape in Marseilles, and since there was neither force nor fraud in inducing the brigadier to return Savarkar to the British authorities, the British Government did not have to restore Savarkar to the French Government for the latter to hold extradition proceedings.[8] On the other hand, the tribunal also observed that there had been an 'irregularity' in Savarkar's arrest and delivery to the British authorities.[9]

What is to be noted from the facts of *The Savarkar Case* is the practicality, informality and speed with which the collaborative arrangement was set up and how it operated effectively in practice. From the point of police efficiency and cooperation, it cannot be contested that the arrangement worked smoothly and achieved its objective. The fact that this led to an inter-State dispute before an international tribunal explains why the police, when contemplating cooperation, may not welcome the involvement of international lawyers and diplomats. It would seem that international lawyers and diplomats, on the one hand, and the police, on the other hand, are concerned with very different matters. In the above case, while the police saw a successful operation, lawyers and diplomats saw a violation of the rules of international law (or at the very least, a mistaken surrender) that necessitated Savarkar's return to France. The legal mindset that presumably underscored the French Government's decision to litigate was one that

[8] *The Savarkar Case (France v Great Britain)* (Award of 24 February 1911) XI RIAA 243 at 254–55.
[9] Ibid, 254.

regarded formal extradition as the only approach to police cooperation, such that when a criminal who has escaped into the territory of another country is erroneously handed over by the local police, the extraditing country can demand the return of that fugitive. Careful reading of *The Savarkar Case* award reveals that the tribunal also shared this view, but found that the special circumstances of the case, including the mistake committed by the French brigadier, meant that France could not prevail in its demand.[10] This may explain why the International Law Commission ('ILC'), in its commentaries to the Draft Articles on Responsibility of States for Internationally Wrongful Acts, included *The Savarkar Case* in the list of cases illustrating how consent of the aggrieved State can constitute a circumstance precluding wrongfulness.[11]

In *The Savarkar Case*, the award itself, the arguments raised by the parties, and the comments on, and the interpretation of, the award reveal the difficulties involved in considering police cooperation from the point of view of international law. These uncertainties include, but are not limited to, (1) the legal qualification and imputability to the State of arrangements for enforcement cooperation established by the police with their foreign colleagues, (2) the permissibility of police enforcement cooperation without adherence to the formalities of extradition or other existing formal arrangements of mutual legal assistance, (3) the admissibility in court of information obtained by police through the international police cooperation network, and (4) the need for the police to ensure international mutual legal assistance at a pace and with a reach that cannot be provided under the established mutual legal assistance treaties or the international body established to facilitate such cooperation.

II. The Presumptive Freedom of Action of Sovereign States[12]

In the *Lotus* case, the Permanent Court of International Justice ('PCIJ') was confronted with a clash between two opposing views on the nature of international law. Simply put, one view held that sovereign States are only allowed to act within the expressly permitted rules of international law, whereas the other view held that

[10] Ibid, 254. See also: Jennings, R and Watts, A (eds), *Oppenheim's International Law*, 9th edn, Vol I (Harlow, Longman, 1992) 953; Von Glahn, G, *Law Among Nations: An Introduction to Public International Law*, 4th edn (New York, Macmillan, 1981) 262; Brownlie, I, *Principles of Public International Law*, 6th edn (Oxford, Clarendon Press, 2003) 314.

[11] See: 'Draft articles on Responsibility of States for Internationally Wrongful Acts, with Commentaries' in *Yearbook of the International Law Commission* (2001) Vol II, Part Two, 73, Commentary to Art 20, para 8. See also: Cassese, A, *International Law*, 2nd edn (Oxford, Oxford University Press, 2005) 253; Dinh, NQ, Daillier, P and Pellet, A, *Droit International Public*, 7th edn (Paris, Générale de Droit et de Jurisprudence, 2002) 480.

[12] Title borrowed from: Lauterpacht, H, *The Development of International Law by the International Court* (Cambridge, Grotius Publishers, 1958) 359–67.

sovereign States must be presumed to enjoy freedom of action, unless an express rule of international law determines otherwise.[13]

The *Lotus* case concerned a criminal trial which was the result of a collision between the SS *Lotus*, a French steamer, and the *SS Boz-Kourt*, a Turkish steamer, on the high seas. As a result of the accident, eight Turkish nationals on board the *Boz-Kourt* drowned. The issue at stake was whether Turkey had jurisdiction under international law to try the French officer who was on watch duty at the time of the collision. The French Government contended that the Turkish courts, in order to exercise jurisdiction, should be able to trace a basis for such jurisdiction under international law. The Turkish Government, by contrast, took the view that it was allowed to exercise jurisdiction in the absence of any conflict with a principle of international law. The Court was divided (6–6), with its President casting the decisive vote:

> [i]nternational law governs relations between independent States. The rules of law binding upon States therefore emanate from their own free will as expressed in conventions or by usages generally accepted as expressing principles of law and established in order to regulate the relations between these co-existing independent communities with a view to the achievement of common aims. Restrictions upon the independence of States cannot therefore be presumed.[14]

Lauterpacht rightly pointed out that this passage means, in effect, that when, with the help of all the sources of international law (treaties, custom and general principles of law), no clear rule imposing a limitation on a sovereign State's freedom of action can be found, no such limitation may be presumed.[15] The *Lotus* principle is, therefore, primarily relevant when considering whether there is international legal regulation of the relevant subject matter. Once it is established that the relevant subject matter is regulated by an international rule, that rule dictates the permissibility of behaviour, as confirmed in the *Wimbledon*[16] and *Lake Lanoux* cases.[17] In practice, this means that if the legal validity of a State's action is challenged in terms of its consistency with a governing rule of international law (eg, a human rights obligation), that State must show either that the action is justified under that rule (eg, compliant with the relevant human rights norm) or that the action is in a field that international law does not purport to regulate.[18] Thus, despite the criticism levied against the *Lotus* principle in some

[13] *Case of the SS Lotus (France v Turkey)* (Judgment) [1927] PCIJ Rep Series A No 10, 19.
[14] Ibid, 28.
[15] Lauterpacht, H, *The Development of International Law by the International Court* (Cambridge, Grotius Publishers, 1982) 360–61.
[16] *Case of the SS Wimbledon (United Kingdom, France, Italy and Japan v Germany)* (Judgment) [1923] PCIJ Rep Series A No 1, 29–34.
[17] *Affaire du lac Lanoux (France v Spain)* (Award of 16 November 1957) XII RIAA 281–317.
[18] Fitzmaurice, G, *The Law and Procedure of the International Court of Justice*, Vol I (Cambridge, Cambridge University Press, reprint 1995) 138–48.

doctrinal quarters, the principle has proved to function adequately as a paradigm for the interaction between legal regulation and the freedom of action of sovereign States.[19]

III. The Indifference with Regard to Form and Formalities

The principle of presumptive freedom of action of sovereign States has a favourable consequence for extrajudicial international police cooperation, and, thus, for the question of whether the promotion of such cooperation can be an appropriate object of an international organisation. To explain this, we refer to Deflem, who notes that, throughout the nineteenth century, attempts to promote international police cooperation on a broad, multilateral scale were mostly organised at the formal inter-governmental level rather than at the administrative level of police institutions. As international law expanded, so too did formal agreements between governments in respect of police cooperation. However, such inter-governmental accords typically failed to provide a basis for practical cooperation between police authorities. Deflem therefore argues (based largely on the way INTERPOL has been developed) in favour of the bureaucratisation theory of international police cooperation, ie, that police authorities must be sufficiently autonomous from the political dictates of their sanctioning governments to devise objectives and the means for international police cooperation independently.[20]

The Savarkar Case supports this argument. The two police authorities concerned agreed on and executed a practical arrangement to ensure that the detainee did not escape while in transit in France. Yet, the French Government appeared not to have considered this arrangement as an agreement under international law. The French Government was not the only one who held this view. For instance, Anzilotti was adamant that the exchange of letters between the two police chiefs did not constitute an agreement under international law not only because of the lack of competence and the lack of a clear undertaking of an obligation to arrest Savarkar, but also, and above all, because a consensus between the two governments could not be established in this fashion.[21]

[19] Orakhelashvili, A, *The Interpretation of Acts and Rules in Public International Law* (Oxford, Oxford University Press, 2008) 36–43.

[20] Deflem, M, *Policing World Society: Historical Foundations of International Police Cooperation* (New York, Oxford University Press, 2002) 17–23. See also from the same author: 'Wild Beasts without Nationality: The Uncertain Origins of Interpol, 1898–1910' in Reichel, P (ed), *The Handbook of Transnational Crime and Justice* (Thousand Oaks, Sage Publications, 2005) 275–85 at 276.

[21] Anzilotti, D, *Scritti di Diritto Internazionale Publico*, Vol II (Padova, CEDAM, 1957) 213–14: '*Escludiamo, prima di tutto, l'esistenza di un accordo fra i due governi, in forze del quale possa ritenersi autorizzato, e quindi legittimo, l'arresto di Savarkar eseguito dall'agente della polizia francese. Come*

However, with due respect to this eminent late jurist, the present authors beg to differ. With reference to the issue of form, following the *Lotus* principle, States must be presumed to be free to choose any form they would like for establishing international agreements, unless a rule of international law prescribes otherwise. Accordingly, and as discussed in Chapter 5, it is generally accepted that international law itself prescribes neither form nor procedure for the making of international undertakings.[22] In 1961, this position was confirmed by the International Court of Justice ('ICJ') in *Temple of Preah Vihear (Cambodia v Thailand)*.[23] It should, therefore, be of no surprise that international legal acts can also take the form of oral communications, a telegram, a radio announcement, a telephonic communication, a symbolic or tacit act,[24] joint communiqués,[25] minutes of a meeting,[26] and even emails.[27] By the same logic, communications between police authorities requesting and acceding to mutual legal assistance can be regarded as legal acts constituting an agreement within the meaning of international law provided the criteria for validity are met.[28]

On a daily basis, thousands of messages are exchanged between police authorities through INTEPOL's communication channels, among others, where the police authorities of one country ask for and receive assistance in respect of the locality of persons of interest, as well as identifiers, such as DNA profiles, telephone numbers, IP addresses, email accounts, social media accounts, fingerprints, photographs, passport numbers, etc. These messages can also contain requests for assistance similar to that in *The Savarkar Case*, especially where persons in police custody are transported via third countries. The Command and

vedremo fra un momento, le lettere scambiate fra il capo della polizia di Londra e il direttore della sicurezza generale a Parigi, a parte ogni questione di competenza, non permettono di ritenere che il governo francese assumesse l'obbligo di cooperare alla detenzione di Savarkar; ma, in ogni caso, un accordo di tal genere rimane ecluso perchè non potè sopra di esso formarsi il consenso delle due parti.' ('First of all, we exclude the existence of an agreement between the two governments, under which the arrest of Savarkar by the French police officer could be considered authorised, and therefore legitimate. As we will see in a moment, the letters exchanged between the London police chief and the director of general security in Paris, apart from any matter of competence, do not allow a belief that the French government assumed the obligation to cooperate in Savarkar's detention; but, in any case, such an agreement remains excluded because the consent of the two parties could not have formed over it' (authors' translation)).

[22] McNair, A, *The Law of Treaties* (Oxford, Clarendon Press, 1961) 6.

[23] *Case concerning the Temple of Preah Vihear (Cambodia v Thailand)* (Preliminary Objections) [1961] ICJ Rep 17. See also: *Aegean Sea Continental Shelf (Greece v Turkey)* (Judgment) [1978] ICJ Rep 3, para 96.

[24] Verzijl, JHW, *International Law in Historical Perspective*, Part VI (Leiden, Sijthoff, 1973) 80–1.

[25] *Aegean Sea Continental Shelf (Greece v Turkey)* (Judgment) [1978] ICJ Rep 3, para 96.

[26] *Maritime Delimitation and Certain Territorial Questions Between Qatar and Bahrain (Qatar v Bahrain)* (Jurisdiction and Admissibility) [1994] ICJ Rep 112, para 25.

[27] Aust, A, *Modern Treaty Law and Practice*, 2nd edn (Cambridge, Cambridge University Press, 2007) 16–7.

[28] See: Jacqué, J-P, 'Acte et norme en droit international public' (1991-II) 227 *Recueil des Cours* 372–74, who proposed to define the concept of an international legal act as a procedure or transaction governed by public international law which purports to produce consequences that have legal effect. For a more extensive discussion of the validity of international acts, see the Introduction.

Coordination Centre of INTERPOL's General Secretariat ('CCC'), which works on a 24/7 basis, monitors these exchanges and intervenes wherever necessary to ensure addressees follow up on such requests. This form of cooperation, often referred to as 'informal' cooperation, cannot be considered as operating beyond the realm of the law regulating the relations between States. In certain circumstances, these exchanges can constitute a multitude of 'unilateral' agreements, which are executed once a response is provided to the request. Such an operational approach is required in the day-to-day reality of international relations in the area of international police cooperation.

IV. Attribution of Police Conduct

As mentioned above, one of the principal reasons for Anzilotti to deny the existence of an international agreement in the exchange of letters between the British and French police in *The Savarkar Case* is because he questioned the competence of the police authorities to engage their respective countries internationally. Here again the *Lotus* principle becomes relevant. Does international law contain rules that exclude the possibility that police can engage their countries internationally? In *The Savarkar Case*, the British considered that the two police chiefs acted in a representative capacity of the two countries. France disagreed.

In the *Church of Scientology in the Netherlands Foundation et al v (1) Herold and (2) Heinrich Bauer Verlag*, the District Court of Amsterdam held that the Chief of the Federal Office of Criminal Investigation could not be held personally responsible for acts of international police cooperation because those acts were in pursuance of State functions and were therefore performed in his official capacity and not as a private person.[29] Similarly, in *Perez et al v The Bahamas*, the United States ('US') District Court of the District of Columbia refused to consider police enforcement in the territorial sea of the Bahamas as a 'commercial activity' within the meaning of the Foreign Sovereign Immunities Act of 1976,[30] as affirmed by the US Court of Appeals.[31] This is consistent with the dictum of the US District Court for the Eastern District of New York in *Harris v VAO Intourist*:

> [a]s it is used in section 1605(a)(2), 'commercial activity' is meant to distinguish activity which results from what in our society would be termed governmental, public or sovereign enterprises e.g., running police departments or parks from those resulting from acts of foreign state agencies acting in what we would deem a commercial capacity e.g., operating hotels or cruise ships.[32]

[29] *Church of Scientology in the Netherlands Foundation et al v (1) Herold and (2) Heinrich Bauer Verlag*, District Court of Amsterdam (4 June 1980) 65 ILR 380–82.

[30] *Perez et al v The Bahamas*, (Judgment of 25 January 1980) 482 F. Supp. 1208 (D.D.C. 1980); 63 ILR 350–53.

[31] *Perez et al v The Bahamas*, (Judgment of 28 April 1981) 652 F.2d 186 (D.C. Cir. 1981); 63 ILR 601–03.

[32] *Harris v VAO Intourist et al*, 481 F. Supp. 1056 (E.D.N.Y. 1979); 63 ILR 318–19.

These cases suggest that the State is responsible for the acts of the police.[33] It therefore follows, as a matter of logic, that when government representatives establish an international organisation to pursue objectives that can be qualified as *acta iure imperii*,[34] such an organisation is necessarily of an intergovernmental nature. Accordingly, as police functions are by their nature governmental, international police cooperation through INTERPOL is an inter-governmental activity.

It can also be inferred from several domestic judicial decisions involving police cooperation via INTERPOL that, in the law of State immunity, the actions of police officers in the exercise of police powers can be attributed to the State on whose behalf they act. For example, in *Church of Scientology v Director of Scotland Yard*, the claimant sought an injunction against Scotland Yard for releasing a report on the Scientology movement accusing it of dishonest acts detrimental to its members. This report was circulated to the German Federal Office of Criminal Investigation (*Bundeskriminalamt*) through INTERPOL and transmitted to all of its offices of criminal investigation. The Federal High Court (*Bundesgerichtshof*) dismissed the action on the basis that the acts of Scotland Yard and its director involved the exercise of governmental authority of the United Kingdom ('UK') and were not performed by the director in a private capacity.[35] Similarly, in *Schmidt v Home Secretary*, the Supreme Court of Ireland decided that the Commissioner of the Metropolitan Police and an individual agent of the Metropolitan Police were entitled to rely on the sovereign immunity of the State on whose behalf they acted.[36]

In light of these cases and the principle of freedom of action of sovereign States, when can it be said that chiefs of police or police departments engage their countries in the context of international police cooperation? This question is more closely examined in Chapter 3. Suffice it to say at this juncture that much depends on the nature of the acts. Thus, police officers who come together only for social purposes cannot be presumed to perform *acta iure imperii*,[37] and, accordingly, those acts cannot be attributed to their governments. On the other hand, when police bodies of the world come together to perform police tasks, as in the case of INTERPOL, these acts are *acta iure imperii* and, therefore, attributable to the governments of the police bodies involved.

[33] United Nations ('UN') Human Rights Committee ('HRC'), *Suarez de Guerrero v Columbia*, Communication No 45/1979, UN Doc CCPR/C/15/D/45/1979 (31 March 1982).

[34] Seidl-Hohenveldern, I, *Corporations in and under International Law* (Cambridge, Grotius Publishers, 1987) 2–3.

[35] *Church of Scientology v Director of Scotland Yard*, Federal Court of Justice (Judgment of 26 September 1978) *Neue Juristische Wochenschrift* (1979) 1101.

[36] *Schmidt v Home Secretary of the Government of the United Kingdom*, Supreme Court of Ireland (Judgment of 24 April 1997) [1997] 2 IR 121.

[37] Eg, the International Police Association based in Virginia assists individual police officers in their private capacity, and its aims include the development of cultural relations among its members and a broadening of their general knowledge and professional experience.

V. Non-Exclusivity of Mutual Legal Assistance Arrangements

The attitude of the French Government in *The Savarkar Case* and the Court of Appeal of Dakar in the *Orsini* case might be explained by the perceived exclusive nature of extradition treaties. However, one of the manifestations of the presumptive freedom of action of sovereign States is their freedom of choice with regard to the modes of assistance or cooperation with other States in criminal matters. Therefore, in the absence of any mandatory rule of international law or a previous legal undertaking that states otherwise, States can determine, on a case-by-case basis, the conditions, mode and the nature of assistance. In other words, the principle of *electa una via, non datur recursus ad alteram* (ie, where a route is chosen, no recourse to another is given) does not apply.[38] Only if a governing rule of international law expressly excludes alternative modes for assisting or cooperating with other States in criminal matters, would a State not be free to determine the nature of its assistance. Although the tribunal in *The Savarkar Case* failed to apply this principle, Brownlie acknowledged that, in the circumstances of *The Savarkar Case*, 'no general rule forbids surrender, and this is lawful unless on the facts it constitutes complicity in conduct harmful to human rights or in crimes under international law'.[39]

This question of whether a State could exercise freedom of choice with regard to the mode of police cooperation with another State was central to the dispute in *US v Alvarez-Machain*.[40] In this case, the US Supreme Court examined whether the extradition treaty between the US and Mexico should be interpreted so as to include an implied term prohibiting prosecution where the defendant's presence is obtained by means other than those established by the treaty. Alvarez-Machain had been forcibly kidnapped from Mexico in 1990 and brought to the US, where he was arrested by officials from the US Drugs Enforcement Agency ('DEA') and indicted. He moved for an application to dismiss the indictment, claiming that his abduction constituted outrageous government conduct and that the District Court lacked jurisdiction to try him because he was abducted in violation of the extradition treaty between the US and Mexico. The US District Court held that it did lack jurisdiction on this basis. It discharged Alvarez-Machain and ordered that he be repatriated to Mexico. The US Court of Appeals affirmed the dismissal of the

[38] On the principle of *electa una via non datur recursus ad alteram*, see: Ciubanu, D, *Preliminary Objections Related to the Jurisdiction of the United Nations Organs* (The Hague, Nijhoff, 1975) 92–101.

[39] Brownlie, I, *Principles of Public International Law*, 6th edn (Oxford, Oxford University Press, 2003) 313. Note that this assertion seems at odds with the same author's qualification of the surrender of Savarkar as a 'mistaken surrender' at 314.

[40] *US v Alvarez-Machain*, 504 U.S. 655 (1992). See also: Semmelman, J, 'United States v Alvarez-Machain' (1992) 86 *American Journal of International Law* 811–20.

indictment and the repatriation, relying on its decision in *US v Verdugo Urquidez*,[41] in which it had held that the forcible abduction of a Mexican national with the authorisation or participation of the US violated the purpose of the extradition treaty between the US and Mexico. It held so despite the fact that the extradition treaty did not expressly prohibit such abductions. In *US v Alvarez-Machain*, the US Supreme Court disagreed precisely on this point:

> [i]n sum, to infer from this Treaty and its terms that it prohibits all means of gaining the presence of an individual outside of its terms goes beyond established precedent and practice. In *Rauscher*, the implication of a doctrine of specialty into the terms of the Webster-Ashburton treaty, which, by its terms, required the presentation of evidence establishing probable cause of the crime of extradition before extradition was required, was a small step to take. By contrast, to imply from the terms of this Treaty that it prohibits obtaining the presence of an individual by means outside of the procedures the Treaty establishes requires a much larger inferential leap, with only the most general of international law principles to support it. The general principles cited by respondent simply fail to persuade us that we should imply in the United States-Mexico Extradition Treaty a term prohibiting international abductions.[42]

Despite much of the criticism of the judgment's clear failure to consider the application of human rights (discussed in the next section) to the procedure through which Alvarez-Machain was obtained, the analysis of the US Supreme Court on the specific issue of whether an extradition treaty should be interpreted so as to exclude alternative forms of rendition merits consideration.

The non-exclusivity of mutual legal assistance arrangements is indeed of eminent importance for police authorities when dealing with the issue of international police cooperation. Day-to-day international police cooperation occurs under the presumption that, unless a rule of general or particular international law dictates otherwise, police bodies are free to cooperate with one another through the means deemed most appropriate for the case at hand. What was true in 1910 in *The Savarkar Case* about the need for speedy, flexible and operationally-oriented arrangements is still valid and perhaps even more relevant today. For instance, in 2002, Elston and Stein examined the issue of international cooperation in respect of online identity theft investigations and concluded that the current structure of international mutual legal assistance is simply too slow and cumbersome for the digital age.[43] In 2004, the Convention on Cybercrime ('Budapest Convention') entered into force,[44] but critics such as Elston and Stein remain of the view that

[41] *US v Verdugo-Urquidez*, 494 U.S. 259 (1990). See also: Soltero, C, 'U.S. v Verdugo-Urquidez (1990) and limits to the applicability of the bill of rights geographically and as to only the people' in Soltero, CR, *Latinos and American Law: Landmark Supreme Court Cases* (Austin, University of Texas Press, 2006) 145–56.

[42] *US v Alvarez-Machain*, 504 U.S. 655 (1992), 668.

[43] Elston, MJ and Stein, SC, 'International Cooperation in On-Line Identity Theft Investigations: A Hopeful Future but a Frustrating Present', 16th International Conference of the International Society for the Reform of Criminal Law (Charleston, 6–10 December 2002).

[44] Convention on Cybercrime (signed on 23 November 2001, entered into force on 1 July 2004) ETS 185.

the promise of this Convention will not be fulfilled if it is implemented largely (or exclusively) through the existing, slow, cumbersome mutual legal assistance treaty process. Electronic evidence is ephemeral, and the delay inherent in the current structure significantly lessens the chance that this evidence will be obtained and cyber criminals caught. A similar scepticism (at least in part) is also discernible in a report prepared at the request of the UN Office on Drugs and Crime on international cooperation in the prevention, investigation, prosecution and punishment of fraud, and the criminal misuse and falsification of identity and related crimes.[45] One of the major challenges identified in the report is the speed with which both formal assistance and informal cooperation is provided amongst States.[46] The digital age demands a system that can connect prosecutors and investigators with their counterparts quickly so that evidence is not lost due to delay.[47] To this end, the European Union ('EU') and the Council of Europe created a joint project in 2013, Global Action on Cybercrime, to strengthen the capacities of States worldwide to apply legislation on cybercrime and electronic evidence and to enhance their abilities for effective international cooperation in this area in line with the Budapest Convention.

VI. The Obligation to Cooperate

It can hardly be said that any rule of international law imposes positive obligations on States to seek international police cooperation from other States when dealing with transnational crimes. Thus, very little can be said at present on the issue, except in scenarios of positive undertakings given by a country to provide law enforcement assistance to other countries when requested.

A. The Duty of Due Diligence in Policing

As a preliminary matter, can it be said that police can be responsible for a failure to exercise due diligence in the context of international policing?[48] If there is such a responsibility, then it is easy to imagine why it would be useful to have an international organisation whose task includes the facilitation of such cooperation. The revelations in 2004 by Michel Fourniret (dubbed the 'Ogre of the

[45] See: Economic and Social Council, 'Results of the second meeting of the Intergovernmental Expert Group to Prepare a Study on Fraud and the Criminal Misuse and Falsification of Identity Report of the Secretary-General', Document No E/CN.15/2007/8/Add.3 (31 January 2007).

[46] Ibid, 14–5.

[47] Elston, MJ and Stein, SC, 'International Cooperation in On-Line Identity Theft Investigations: A Hopeful Future but a Frustrating Present', 16th International Conference of the International Society for the Reform of Criminal Law (Charleston, 6–10 December 2002).

[48] See: Barnidge, RP, 'States' Due Diligence Obligations with regard to International Non-State Terrorist Organizations Post-11 September 2001: The Heavy Burden that States Must Bear' (2005) 16 *Irish Studies in International Affairs* 103–25.

Ardennes' after the forested border region between France and Belgium where many of his confessed murders occurred) may serve to explore this question. By his own admission, Fourniret had killed nine people, mostly young women and girls, and was convicted and sentenced to seven years' imprisonment in 1987 by a French court for rape and indecent assault of minors. He was, however, freed after a few months because of time already spent in custody. Subsequently, he moved to Belgium and was given a job as a school supervisor without any investigation conducted by the Belgian authorities about his past record. He was later rearrested in Belgium for the abduction of minors and sexual misconduct after being identified by a 13-year-old girl who was bundled into his van after asking for directions. Fourniret confessed after his wife gave information to the police, apparently fearing a conviction similar to the 30-year sentence handed down to the spouse of the convicted paedophile and murderer, Marc Dutroux.

Can it be said that either France or Belgium failed to exercise due diligence, and, if they had exercised such diligence, could his subsequent crimes have been prevented? The answer to this question depends on whether it can be said that States have a responsibility to forewarn other States about individuals that present a potential threat. An affirmative response would mean that States should not only be mindful about protection of their own citizens, but should also warn others about potential threats. The *Corfu Channel* case may provide a foundation for developing such an argument. In that case, the ICJ considered that the duty to notify others about dangerous circumstances is grounded on a 'general and well-recognized principle, namely: elementary considerations of humanity'. It held that 'every State has an obligation not to allow knowingly its territory to be used for acts contrary to the rights of other States'.[49] Indeed, INTERPOL operates on the belief that the best way to provide homeland security for any one country is to prevent transnational criminals or terrorists from entering a country's borders in the first place by working together, and thereby enhancing the likelihood of detection, detention and apprehension. The practical implication is that countries have to ensure that they communicate all potentially relevant information to other countries and update international police databases in a systematic and comprehensive fashion.

There is also an element of due diligence inherent in the principle of *aut dedere aut judicare* (ie, the obligation to extradite or prosecute),[50] which was the subject of a 2014 study carried out by the ILC.[51] For a wanted person to be arrested and for the decision-making process with regard to either extradition or

[49] *Corfu Channel (United Kingdom of Great Britain and Northern Ireland v Albania)* (Judgment) [1949] ICJ Rep 35.

[50] See: Bassiouni, MC and Wise, EM, *Aut Dedere Aut Judicare: The Duty to Extradite or Prosecute in International Law* (Dordrecht, Martinus Nijhoff Publishers, 1995).

[51] 'The obligation to extradite or prosecute (*aut dedere aut judicare*)' in *Yearbook of the International Law Commission* (2014) Vol II, Part Two, 91.

prosecution to be triggered, countries must know whether a person is wanted for arrest. Although the EU has created the European Arrest Warrant, a global arrest warrant remains beyond reach for the moment. However, this does not preclude countries from sharing, on a worldwide basis, information about wanted persons. Former INTERPOL Secretary General Noble went as far as arguing that countries must ensure that data about persons wanted for terrorism or other serious crimes and considered dangerous are stored immediately in international databases.[52] This transnational cooperation is the cornerstone of international policing. To this end, INTERPOL has a tool which is at the disposal of police authorities of all members: INTERPOL can, at the request of any member, issue an INTERPOL red notice.[53] In essence, the red notice advises police worldwide that a certain person is wanted and requests members to apprehend the wanted person on behalf of the requesting country. The red notice contains identifying information on the wanted person, such as a physical description, a photograph or fingerprints, and judicial information about the crime for which his arrest is wanted. Thus, it is arguable, in the context of the principle of *aut dedere aut judicare*, that due diligence requires all countries to stop the person against whom an INTERPOL red notice has been issued to help prevent the commission of further serious crimes that could pose a danger to the life and well-being of the community. More broadly, the foregoing suggests that certain due diligence obligations may bear upon the freedom of action of States in matters of international police cooperation. It is, therefore, not difficult to envisage, as a corollary to this conclusion, an international organisation – like INTERPOL – with the objective of promoting and facilitating the discharge of any such due diligence obligations.

B. Conventional Undertakings to Cooperate in Police Enforcement Matters

The argument in favour of enhanced extrajudicial international police cooperation is further supported by the various treaties that contain an obligation to cooperate in the field of law enforcement, for example, through investigative assistance or information exchange.[54] Such general undertakings to cooperate curtail the freedom of action of the contracting parties in respect of the prevention and suppression of the crimes covered by the concerned treaty. Typically, the parties undertake to

[52] Noble, RK, Secretary General of INTERPOL, 'Prosecuting Terrorism: The Global Challenge' (Speech at the NYU Center on Law and Security, Florence, 4 June 2004).

[53] NCBs can also circulate informal requests worldwide through INTERPOL's channels (ie, 'diffusions').

[54] See for instance: UN Convention against Transnational Organized Crime (adopted on 15 November 2000, entered into force on 29 September 2003) 2225 UNTS 209 ('UNCTOC'), Art 18; Convention on Mutual Administrative Assistance in Tax Matters, as amended by the 2010 Protocol (signed on 25 January 1988, entered into force on 1 April 1995) 3014 UNTS, Art 1.

afford one another the widest measure of mutual legal assistance in investigations, prosecutions, and legal proceedings.[55] More specifically, they may pledge to cooperate closely with one another, consistent with their respective domestic legal and administrative systems, with a view to enhancing the effectiveness of law enforcement action to suppress the commission of the relevant offences.[56] Paragraph 2 of UN Security Council Resolution 1373 (2001) adopted under Chapter VII of the UN Charter imposes a similar obligation with regard to criminal investigations or criminal proceedings relating to the financing or support of terrorist acts, including assistance in obtaining evidence.[57]

In some instances, treaties contain specified directives on the measures that the parties are required to adopt to give effect to the duty to cooperate. This is the case with Article 48(1)(a) of the UN Convention against Corruption and Article 9(1)(a) of the UN Convention against the Illicit Traffic in Narcotic Drugs and Psychotropic Substances, each of which provides that the States parties shall, in particular, take effective measures to enhance and, where necessary, establish channels of communication between their competent authorities, agencies and services to facilitate the secure and rapid exchange of information concerning all aspects of the offences covered by these Conventions. Similarly, Article 8 of the Inter-American Convention against Terrorism requires the States parties to work closely with one another to enhance the effectiveness of law enforcement to combat the offences set out in the international instruments listed in the Convention. In this context, the States parties are obligated to establish and enhance, where necessary, channels of communication between their competent authorities in order to facilitate the secure and rapid exchange of information concerning all aspects of the offences listed in the Convention. It must be noted, however, that conventional provisions often stipulate that such an obligation exists by reference to the domestic laws of each State party by providing that States parties shall cooperate closely with one another, consistent with their respective domestic legal and administrative systems.[58]

[55] UN Convention against the Illicit Traffic in Narcotic Drugs and Psychotropic Substances (adopted on 20 December 1988, entered into force on 11 November 1990) 1582 UNTS 95, Art 7(1); European Convention on Laundering, Search, Seizure and Confiscation of the Proceeds of Crime (signed on 8 November 1990, entered into force on 1 September 1993) 2569 UNTS 91, Art 7(1); UN Convention against Corruption (adopted on 31 October 2003, entered into force on 14 December 2005) 2349 UNTS 41 ('UNCAC'), Art 25(1); UNCTOC, Art 18(1); Inter-American Convention against the Illicit Manufacturing of and Trafficking in Firearms, Ammunition, Explosives and Other Related Materials (adopted on 14 November 1997, entered into force on 1 July 1998) 2029 UNTS 55, Arts 13–14.

[56] UN Convention against the Illicit Traffic in Narcotic Drugs and Psychotropic Substances (adopted on 20 December 1988, entered into force on 11 November 1990), 1582 UNTS 95, Art 9(1).

[57] UN Security Council Resolution 1373, 28 September 2001.

[58] UNCAC, Art 48; UN Convention against the Illicit Traffic in Narcotic Drugs and Psychotropic Substances (adopted on 20 December 1988, entered into force on 11 November 1990) 1582 UNTS 95, Art 9(1); UNCTOC, Art 27(1); Inter-American Convention against Terrorism (signed on 6 March 2002, entered into force on 7 October 2003) OAS Treaty A-66 (2003) 42 ILM 19, Art 8; Inter-American

The ICJ in *Djibouti v France* ruled on a comparable provision in a bilateral agreement on mutual legal assistance in criminal matters. Its judgment contains some indications about the scope and reach of these provisions.[59] Djibouti claimed that Article 1, as elaborated in Article 3(1), of the Convention concerning judicial assistance in criminal matters between France and Djibouti of 27 September 1986 ('1986 Convention') placed France under an obligation to execute an international letter rogatory. Article 1 provides that '[t]he two States undertake to afford each other, in accordance with the provisions of this Convention, the widest measure of mutual assistance in proceedings in respect of offences the punishment of which, at the time of the request for assistance, falls within the jurisdiction of the judicial authorities of the requesting State'. Article 3(1) of the Convention provides, '[t]he requested State shall execute in accordance with its law any letters rogatory relating to a criminal matter and addressed to it by the judicial authorities of the requesting State for the purposes of procuring evidence or transmitting articles to be produced in evidence, records or documents'.

In dismissing Djibouti's contention, the Court observed that the obligation to execute international letters rogatory under Article 3 of the 1986 Convention was to be realised in accordance with the procedural law of the requested State. Accordingly, while France had to ensure that the procedure for assistance was put into motion, such process did not guarantee the outcome, ie, the transmission of the file requested in the letter rogatory.[60] It further pointed out that under Article 2(c) of the 1986 Convention, France may refuse a request for mutual legal assistance if it considers that execution of the request is likely to prejudice its sovereignty, its security, its public order or other essential interests. The Court recalled that the investigating French judge did state the grounds for her decision to refuse the request for mutual legal assistance, explaining why transmission of the file was considered to be 'contrary to the essential interests of France', in that the file contained declassified 'defence secret' documents, together with information and witness statements in respect of another case in progress.[61] The Court found that the reasons given by the judge fell within the scope of Article 2(c) of the 1986 Convention. The Court accordingly held that France was not under an obligation pursuant to Article 3 to transmit the requested file to Djibouti.[62] It seems, therefore, that the general undertaking to provide the widest measure

Convention against the Illicit Manufacturing of and Trafficking in Firearms, Ammunition, Explosives and Other Related Materials (adopted on 14 November 1997, entered into force on 1 July 1998) 2029 UNTS 55, Arts 13 and 17(1); European Convention on Laundering, Search, Seizure and Confiscation of the Proceeds of Crime (signed on 8 November 1990, entered into force on 1 September 1993) 2569 UNTS 91, Arts 9, 18(1)(a) and 18(2).

[59] *Certain Questions of Mutual Assistance in Criminal Matters (Djibouti v France)* (Judgment) [2008] ICJ Rep 177.

[60] Ibid, para 123.

[61] Ibid, para 147.

[62] Ibid, para 202.

of mutual assistance does not necessarily mean that assistance is necessarily due, whenever requested. While the Court was certainly correct in its construction of the treaty provisions, it would have been helpful to include a more thorough consideration of the general principle that States must give effect to their treaty obligations in good faith, and that exceptions have to be interpreted restrictively, with the burden of proof resting on the party invoking the exception.

Be that as it may, the conventional undertaking to cooperate in police matters further highlights the expedience and accessibility offered by an international organisation facilitating such cooperation. As will be explained below, the recognition of the condition of compliance with national law in international police cooperation proves the foresight of the architects of INTERPOL when they articulated the aims of the Organisation.

VII. Permissibility of Police Cooperation without the Formalities of Extradition or Mutual Legal Assistance Treaties

A. Balancing Law Enforcement Needs and Fundamental Rights

Needless to say, when a wanted person is to be transferred from one State to another for the purposes of criminal prosecution or enforcement of a sentence, extradition is the appropriate procedure. However, the cumbersome nature of extradition procedures may often be at odds with the need for speedy police enforcement operations. This becomes more complicated when no extradition treaty exists between the relevant States. Therefore, in practice, States may, and often do, resort to other forms of repatriating persons or obtaining jurisdiction over them. Measures such as deportation or expulsion may constitute alternatives to extradition. The requested State may also simply surrender the wanted person without going through an extradition process. In other cases, foreign agents operate with the acquiescence of, or in collaboration with, the authorities of the requested State, for example, on the basis of ad hoc security cooperation agreements. Given the freedom of action of sovereign States,[63] disguised extradition and simple surrender procedures are not per se illegal under international law in the absence of an express prohibition, but certain aspects may nonetheless infringe specific rules of international law, in particular, certain human rights provisions.[64] Inherent in

[63] See: *Case of the SS Lotus* [1927] PCIJ Rep Series A No 10, 19.

[64] Bassiouni, MC, *International Extradition: United States Law and Practice*, 4th edn (Dobbs Ferry, Oceana Publications, 2002) 183–248. See also: *Harksen v President of the Republic of South Africa and others*, 2000 (2) SA 825 (CC).

the architecture of international police cooperation is a search to reconcile the demands of the general interests of the community with the need to protect an individual's fundamental rights. In *Soering v UK*,[65] the European Court of Human Rights ('ECtHR') noted as follows in this regard:

> [a]s movement about the world becomes easier and crime takes on a larger international dimension, it is increasingly in the interest of all nations that suspected offenders who flee abroad should be brought to justice. Conversely, the establishment of safe havens for fugitives would not only result in danger for the State obliged to harbour the protected person but also tend to undermine the foundations of extradition. These considerations must also be included among the factors to be taken into account in the interpretation and application of the notions of inhuman and degrading treatment or punishment in extradition cases.

The responsibility to ensure this reconciliation rests with both the requested and the requesting State. In general, this means that the rules established by treaties in force concerning mutual legal assistance in criminal matters are relevant for determining whether the arrest was lawful, but the fact that a wanted person has been handed over as a result of informal (spontaneous) cooperation between States does not, in itself, make the arrest unlawful, provided it is in consonance with applicable human rights norms.

B. Extrajudicial Surrender of Wanted Persons

The freedom of action of States to surrender a wanted person to the requesting State can best be explained by starting from a State's right to expel an alien from its territory, which is uncontested in international law, as is evidenced by State practice and the jurisprudence of international courts and tribunals, including human rights bodies.[66] Indeed, in the *Boffolo case*, the Italian-Venezuelan Mixed Claims Commission stated that a general power to expel foreigners, at least for cause, cannot be doubted.[67] Similarly, the Belgian-Venezuelan Mixed Claims Commission held that the right to expel foreigners from, or prohibit their entry into, a State is generally recognised.[68] Likewise, the ECtHR has acknowledged the concern of the contracting States to the European Convention on Human Rights ('ECHR')

[65] *Soering v United Kingdom* [1989] Series A No 161, para 89. See also: *Öcalan v Turkey* [2003] ECHR 125, para 90. For a discussion, see: Van der Wilt, HG, 'Après Soering: The Relationship Between Extradition and Human Rights in the Legal Practice of the Netherlands, Germany and the United States' (1995) XLII *Netherlands International Law Review* 53–80.

[66] See for a comprehensive overview: UN Secretariat, 'Expulsion of Aliens: Memorandum by the Secretariat', UN Doc A/CN4/565, 10 July 2006. See also: 'Text of the draft articles on the expulsion of aliens' in *Yearbook of the International Law Commission* (2014) Vol II, Part Two, 22.

[67] *Boffolo case*, Mixed Claims Commission Italy–Venezuela (Award of 1903) X RIAA 528, 531–32.

[68] *Paquet case*, Mixed Claims Commission Belgium–Venezuela (Award of 1903) IX RIAA 323, 325.

to maintain public order, in particular, by exercising their right, as a matter of well-established international law and subject to their treaty obligations, to control the entry, residence and expulsion of aliens.[69]

This means that, subject to limitations and conditions resulting from general or particular international law (discussed below), States are empowered to expel a person to the requesting State using their right to control entry and permanence of non-nationals to their territory. In that sense, extradition is merely one of the various means through which a State may exercise its territorial powers. Gaja is, therefore, right in pointing out that extradition may be considered a subcategory of expulsion to which particular rules apply:

> [e]xtradition generally occurs on the basis of a judicial and/or administrative measure and takes the form of forcible deportation of an individual to another State. Moreover, extradition serves a specific purpose, that of bringing a person to trial or making a convicted person serve his or her sentence. Finally, it is necessarily directed towards a specific State, which requested that the person be handed over. When all these features are present with regard to a measure which is nevertheless defined by the State that takes it as expulsion rather than extradition, the measure is considered a 'disguised extradition' and comes to some extent under the special regime pertaining to extradition.[70]

Some scholars seek to make a distinction between extradition and expulsion on the basis that the concepts are distinct in purpose: the object of extradition is to restore a fugitive criminal to the jurisdiction of a State which has a lawful claim to try or punish him for an offence, whereas the object of expulsion is to dispose of an undesired alien:[71]

> [i]nternational law distinguishes between expulsion and extradition. Expulsion is an administrative measure in the form of a government order directing an alien to leave the territory; it is often used interchangeably with deportation. Extradition is 'the delivery of an accused or a convicted individual to the state where he is accused of, or has been convicted of a crime, by the state on whose territory he happens for the time to be'.[72]

However, as shown by Jennings and Watts, this distinction is not normative but rather descriptive, and considerations of convenience and politics may influence the choice of recourse to one means or the other.[73] This distinction on the basis

[69] *Moustaquim v Belgium* [1991] ECHR 3, para 43. See also: *Vilvarajah and others v United Kingdom* [1991] ECHR 47, para 102; *Chahal v United Kingdom* [1996] ECHR 54, para 73; *Ahmed v Austria* [1996] ECHR 63, para 38; *Boughanemi v France* (1996) 22 EHRR 228, para 41; *Bouchelkia v France* [1997] ECHR 1, para 48; *HLR v France* [1997] ECHR 23, para 33.

[70] Gaja, G, 'Expulsion of Aliens: Some Old and New Issues in International Law' (1999) *3 Cursos Euromediterráneos Bancaja de Derecho Internacional* 283–314 at 292.

[71] Shearer, IA, *Extradition in International Law* (Manchester, Manchester University Press, 1971) 76–7.

[72] Lambert, H, *The Position of Aliens in Relation to the European Convention on Human Rights* (Strasbourg, Council of Europe Publishing, 2007) 44, fn 155.

[73] Jennings, R and Watts, A (eds), *Oppenheim's International Law*, 9th edn, Vol I (Harlow, Longman, 1992) 940–62. See also: UN Secretariat, 'Study on Expulsion of Immigrants', UN Doc ST/SOA22 and

of purpose is also rarely observed at the level of operational cooperation between police authorities, which explains the wide and interchangeable use of both means in international police cooperation.

No matter the terminology, the human rights obligations which a State is required to observe when it expels a foreigner are not uniform. Two general types of protection are identifiable: (1) substantive protection against expulsion to a country where the person would face grave human rights violations and (2) procedural safeguards during expulsion procedures.[74] In respect of the latter, expulsions are generally only permissible where certain conditions are met. First, the decision to expel must be reached 'in accordance with the law'. Second, the person concerned must be allowed to submit the reasons against his expulsion and to have his case reviewed by, and be represented for the purpose before, a competent authority (except where compelling reasons of national security otherwise require).[75] In *US v Alvarez-Machain*,[76] discussed above, the US Supreme Court did not engage with the human rights obligations of the US. Its approach is in stark contrast with the approach of the House of Lords of the UK in *Ex parte Bennett*.[77] This is perhaps attributable to a difference in attitude on the role of the judiciary in reconciling law enforcement needs and fundamental rights. In *Ex parte Bennett*, the House of Lords held (4:1) that where a process of law is available to return an accused to the UK through extradition procedures, an English court should refuse to try the accused if he has been forcibly brought within its jurisdiction in disregard of those procedures through an alternative process to which the police, the prosecution, or other executive authorities were a knowing party. It is noticeable that in *Ex parte Bennett* the decision of the House of Lords was based on the assumption that only a formal extradition procedure can guarantee the rights of the wanted person; the use of the term 'kidnapping', without any consideration of the lawfulness of the arrest in the surrendering State by the local police, reinforces this assumption. The House of Lords considered, therefore, that the High Court could stay the prosecution and order the release of the accused if it was satisfied that the accused was brought within its jurisdiction in disregard of extradition procedures. Thus, unlike the US Supreme Court in *US v Alvarez-Machain*, the House of Lords looked at extradition procedures as a means to protect the fundamental rights of individuals in the context of international police cooperation.

Corr 2 (replaces Corr 1) (10 August 1955), para 3; Kälin, W, 'Aliens, Expulsion and Deportation' in Bernhardt, R (ed), *Max Planck Encyclopedia of Public International Law*, online edn (Oxford, Oxford University Press, 2012).

[74] See generally: Office of the UN High Commissioner for Human Rights ('OHCHR'), 'Expulsion of aliens in international human rights law', OHCHR Discussion Paper (Geneva, September 2006).

[75] See: International Covenant on Civil and Political Rights (adopted on 16 December 1966, entered into force on 23 March 1976) 999 UNTS 171 and 1057 UNTS 407 ('ICCPR'), Art 13. See also: International Convention on the Protection of the Rights of All Migrant Workers and Members of Their Families (adopted on 18 December 1990, entered into force on 1 July 2003) 2220 UNTS 3, Art 22; Arab Charter on Human Rights (adopted on and entered into force on 15 September 1994) Art 26.

[76] *US v Alvarez-Machain*, 504 U.S. 655 (1992).

[77] *R v Horseferry Road Magistrates' Court (Ex parte Bennett)* [1994] 1 AC 42 (HL).

However, two cases decided under Article 5 of the ECHR (ie, the right to liberty and security of person) favour the proposition that arrest and deportation by police outside a formal extradition process is not, per se, unlawful unless it contravenes the suspect's rights. In *Bozano v France*, Bozano had been sentenced to life imprisonment in Italy for murder and was living in France under a false identity when he was arrested.[78] Italy applied for his extradition under a bilateral treaty, but a French court ruled against extradition on the basis that the Italian trial *in absentia* was incompatible with French policy, so the extradition request was rejected. The French Minister of Interior then executed an order requiring Bozano to leave French territory. Bozano refused but was immediately escorted to Switzerland by the French police. In Switzerland, he was extradited to Italy under the European Convention on Extradition. The ECtHR recognised the principle that all transfers, whether described as expulsion, extradition, deportation or otherwise, need to comply with the minimum procedural guarantees prescribed under domestic and international law. The Court determined that legal procedures affect not only the validity of the transfer, but also the legality of holding the individual in detention for the purpose of removal. The Court held that a deprivation of liberty had occurred under Article 5(1) of the ECHR on the basis that the French authorities had prevented Bozano from making any effective use of the remedies available to him.[79]

The case of *Öcalan v Turkey*[80] deals with a situation comparable to that in *Ex parte Bennett*, where the wanted person was surrendered to the requesting State in an extraterritorial collaborative operation. Öcalan was the subject of seven arrest warrants issued by the Turkish courts and an INTERPOL red notice published at the request of the INTERPOL NCB in Turkey. He was accused of funding an armed gang in order to destroy the integrity of the Turkish State and of instigating terrorist acts resulting in loss of life. On 9 October 1998, he was expelled from Syria, where he had been living for many years. From there he went to Greece, Russia, Italy and then again to Russia and Greece before going to Kenya, where he resided with the Greek Ambassador. On 15 February 1999, Kenyan officials went to the Greek Embassy to take the applicant to the airport. The Greek Ambassador said that he wished to accompany the applicant in person to the airport and a discussion between the Ambassador and the Kenyan officials ensued. In the end, the applicant got into a car driven by a Kenyan official. On the way to the airport, the car in which the applicant was travelling left the convoy and, taking a route reserved for security personnel in the international transit area of Nairobi Airport, took him to an aircraft in which Turkish officials were waiting. The applicant was arrested after boarding the aircraft and flown to Turkey. Öcalan argued before

[78] *Bozano v France* [1987] Series A No 111.

[79] Ibid, para 60. Article 5(1) requires, similar to all international human rights instruments, that any deprivation of liberty must be 'in accordance with a procedure prescribed by law' and fall within one of the cases set out in Article 5(1)(a)–(f).

[80] *Öcalan v Turkey* [2003] ECHR 125, para 90.

the First Section of the ECtHR that his arrest was unlawful because the operation carried out in Kenya violated that country's sovereignty. The First Section found that the applicant's arrest and detention had complied with orders that had been issued by the Turkish courts 'for the purpose of bringing him before the competent legal authority on reasonable suspicion of having committed an offence' within the meaning of Article 5(1)(c) of the ECHR. Moreover, it had not been established beyond all reasonable doubt that the operation carried out in the instant case, partly by Turkish officials and partly by Kenyan officials, amounted to a violation of Kenyan sovereignty and, consequently, of international law. It followed that the applicant's arrest and detention were to be regarded as having been in accordance with 'a procedure prescribed by law' for the purposes of Article 5(1) of the ECHR.[81] The case was referred to the Grand Chamber of the Court,[82] which confirmed the judgment of the First Section. Citing the case of *Stocké v Germany*,[83] the Grand Chamber accepted that an arrest made by the authorities of one State on the territory of another State, without the consent of the latter, affects the person's individual rights to security under Article 5(1). In a significant statement concerning the general principles that apply to the questions posed, the Grand Chamber held that:

> [t]he Convention does not prevent cooperation between States, within the framework of extradition treaties or in matters of deportation, for the purposes of bringing fugitive offenders to justice, provided that it does not interfere with any specific rights recognised in the Convention. …
>
> As regards extradition arrangements between States when one is a party to the Convention and the other is not, the rules established by an extradition treaty or, in the absence of any such treaty, the cooperation between the States concerned are also relevant factors to be taken into account for determining whether the arrest that has led to the subsequent complaint to the Court was lawful. The fact that a fugitive has been handed over as a result of cooperation between States does not in itself make the arrest unlawful and does not therefore give rise to any problem under Article 5. …
>
> Irrespective of whether the arrest amounts to a violation of the law of the State in which the fugitive has taken refuge – a question that only falls to be examined by the Court if the host State is a party to the Convention – the Court requires proof in the form of concordant inferences that the authorities of the State to which the applicant has been transferred have acted extra-territorially in a manner that is inconsistent with the

[81] Ibid.

[82] Under Article 43 of the ECHR, within three months from the date of a Chamber judgment, any party to the case may, in exceptional cases, request that the case be referred to the 17-member Grand Chamber of the Court. In that event, a panel of five judges considers whether the case raises a serious question affecting the interpretation or application of the ECHR or its Protocols, or a serious issue of general importance, in which case the Grand Chamber will deliver a final judgment. If no such question or issue arises, the panel will reject the request, at which point the judgment becomes final. Otherwise, Chamber judgments become final on the expiry of the three-month period or earlier if the parties declare that they do not intend to make a request to refer.

[83] *Stocké v Germany* [1991] Series A No 199.

> sovereignty of the host State and therefore contrary to international law. … Only then will the burden of proving that the sovereignty of the host State and international law have been complied with shift to the respondent Government. …[84]

The ECtHR, in the latter part of the judgment, seems to apply a less restrictive test than the House of Lords in *Ex parte Bennett*, but one which would render the approach of the US Supreme Court in *Alvarez-Machain* unacceptable in any of the States that are party to the ECHR.

The judgment in *Mohamed v President of the Republic of South Africa*,[85] rendered by the Constitutional Court of South Africa, also favours the proposition that arrest and deportation by police outside a formal extradition process is not per se unlawful unless it contravenes the suspect's rights. Mohamed, a Tanzanian national, entered South Africa on a forged passport. He applied for refugee status under the assumed name. The deceit was discovered by an agent of the US Federal Bureau of Investigation ('FBI') who recognised him on the basis of an INTERPOL red notice as a suspect in bomb attacks on US embassies in Nairobi and Dar es Salaam. Thereafter, a collaborative process between the South African police authorities and the US law enforcement authorities resulted in his arrest and interrogation. He admitted that he had taken part in the preparation of the bombing in Dar es Salaam. In the meantime, he was indicted in the US District Court for the Southern District of New York, along with 14 others, and allegedly expressed the wish to be removed to the US. He was subsequently taken from South Africa to the US to face a criminal trial for the Dar es Salaam bombing. Because he was surrendered to the US without a condition that he should not be subject to the death penalty, the US District Court accepted that he was 'death eligible'. While in New York and facing the capital charges, Mohamed launched an application in the South African courts seeking an order to declare his deportation unlawful on the grounds that it was in fact a disguised extradition and because the South African authorities had not stipulated that, as a condition of his removal, the US authorities would not seek, or carry out, the death penalty. The South African Constitutional Court ruled in favour of Mohamed, holding that Mohamed had been unlawfully removed from South Africa. The Court held that the distinction between deportation and extradition was not relevant in the present case because the South African Constitution required South Africa to avoid being a party, whether directly or indirectly, to the imposition of cruel, inhuman or degrading punishment, including the death penalty, no matter the method. For that reason, South Africa's decision to deport Mohamed to face the death penalty was a violation of Mohamed's right to life and his right not to be subjected to cruel or unusual punishment. However, his request to the South African Constitutional Court to order the South African Government to request the US to refrain from executing

[84] *Öcalan v Turkey* [2005] ECHR 282, paras 86, 87 and 90.
[85] *Mohamed and another v President of the Republic of South Africa and others*, 2001 (3) SA 893 (CC).

him was rejected; the Court instead ordered that a copy of the judgment be transmitted to the US District Court. Based on this transmission, and considering that the conviction was based on a voluntary confession and mitigating circumstances were at play, the US jury sentenced Mohamed to life imprisonment.[86]

The reasoning in this decision was echoed in *Roger Judge v Canada* by the HRC.[87] The HRC, which is responsible for interpreting the ICCPR, has stated clearly that a State's international human rights obligations do not end at its borders.[88] In *Judge v Canada*, while interpreting Article 6 of the ICCPR, which guarantees the right to life in the context of extradition, the Committee noted that 'for countries that have abolished the death penalty, there is an obligation not to expose a person to the real risk of its application'.[89] In that sense, the Constitutional Court of South Africa was correct in declaring that surrendering Mohamed to the US without assurances against the imposition of capital punishment was a violation of his rights.

The Supreme Court of the UK considered a related question in July 2019 in the case of *Elgizouli v Secretary of State for the Home Department*. The appellant's son was alleged to have been one of a group of British terrorists operating in Syria (colloquially known as 'The Beatles' due to their English accents), who was involved in the murder of US and British citizens. In June 2015, the US made a mutual legal assistance request to the UK in relation to an investigation into the activities of that group. The UK Home Secretary at the time requested an assurance that the information would not be used directly or indirectly in a prosecution that could lead to the imposition of the death penalty. However, the US would only provide an assurance that the information would not be used directly in a trial that could lead to the death penalty. In June 2018, after extended bilateral discussions between former UK Home Secretary Sajid Javid and former US Attorney General Jeff Sessions, the UK provided the information to the US without requiring any assurances whatsoever. The appellant challenged that decision by way of judicial review. Her claim was dismissed by the Divisional Court.[90]

On appeal the Supreme Court of the UK answered, inter alia, the following question: is it unlawful for the Secretary of State to exercise his power to provide mutual legal assistance so as to supply evidence to a foreign State that will facilitate the imposition of the death penalty in that State on the individual in respect of whom the evidence is sought? Judgment was handed down by the Supreme Court

[86] *US v Bin Laden*, 156 F. Supp. 2d. 359 (S.D.N.Y. 2001). See also: Givelber, D, 'Innocence Abroad: The Extradition Cases and the Future of Capital Litigation' (2002) 81 *Oregon Law Review* 161, 164.

[87] HRC, *Judge v Canada*, Communication No 829/1998, UN Doc CCPR/C/78/D/829/1998 (13 August 2003).

[88] HRC, 'General Comment 31: The Nature of the General Legal Obligation Imposed on States Parties to the Covenant', UN Doc CCPR/C/21/Rev.1/Add. 13 (26 May 2004), para 10; *López Burgos v Uruguay*, Communication No R.12/52, UN Doc CCPR/C/13/D/52/1979 (29 July 1981) para 12.3.

[89] HRC, *Judge v Canada*, Communication No 829/1998, UN Doc CCPR/C/78/D/829/1998 (13 August 2003) para 10.4.

[90] *R (El Gizouli) v Secretary of State for the Home Department* [2019] EWHC 60 (Admin).

of the UK on 25 March 2020.[91] The majority of the Justices answered the foregoing question with a 'no': they were of the view that the common law has not evolved to recognise a principle prohibiting the provision of mutual legal assistance that will facilitate the death penalty.[92] Lord Kerr answered the foregoing question with a 'yes'. Lord Kerr underlined the steadfast opposition by successive UK governments to the imposition of the death penalty in any circumstances, and the related long-standing policy not to provide mutual legal assistance unless death penalty assurances are received.[93] He noted that the common law is not immutable but develops over time to reflect the changing values of society.[94] Lord Kerr summarised six factors favouring recognition of the common law principle in question:[95] (1) the Bill of Rights 1688; (2) British contemporary values; (3) the jurisprudence of the ECtHR;[96] (4) EU law;[97] (5) the fundamental illogicality of, on the one hand, refusing to extradite or deport individuals for trial in a foreign State where there is a risk of the imposition of the death penalty, without requisite assurances, and, on the other hand, facilitating such a trial when precisely the same outcome is in prospect without demanding assurances; and (6) the jurisprudence of the Judicial Committee of the Privy Council. For present purposes, it is not necessary to engage further with *Elgizouli*, save to note that, if the common law recognises that it is objectionable to be complicit in exposing an individual to the risk of execution by extraditing him, then it is difficult to disagree with Lord Kerr's view that 'it is surely equally objectionable to be complicit in facilitating that result by providing material which has the same result'.[98]

It is also pertinent to observe briefly the practice of international criminal courts and tribunals. Because international criminal courts and tribunals lack enforcement mechanisms, the enforcement of warrants issued by them is solely dependent on cooperation by the enforcement agencies of the States which are party to the relevant treaty. Perhaps in light of this difficulty, these courts and tribunals have generally been reluctant in releasing accused individuals even if there has been a violation of fundamental rights in obtaining them. In the *Nikolić* case[99] before the International Criminal Tribunal for the former Yugoslavia ('ICTY'), the accused was kidnapped from the Federal Republic of Yugoslavia by individuals acting in their personal capacity and brought to Bosnia and Herzegovina where he was handed over to the North Atlantic Treaty Organization ('NATO') Stabilisation

[91] *Elgizouli v Secretary of State for the Home Department* [2020] UKSC 10.

[92] Ibid, paras 169–87 (Lord Reed with whom Lady Black and Lord Lloyd-Jones agree), 188–206 (Lord Carnwath) and 231–34 (Lord Hodge).

[93] Ibid, para 26.

[94] Ibid, para 102.

[95] Ibid, para 141.

[96] Ibid, paras 107–24.

[97] Ibid, paras 125–34.

[98] Ibid, para 141.

[99] ICTY Appeals Chamber, *Prosecutor v Dragan Nikolić* (Decision on Interlocutory Appeal Concerning Legality of Arrest) (5 June 2003) Case No IT-94-2-AR73.

Force which delivered him into the custody of the ICTY. The accused raised two objections, namely, a breach of State sovereignty and breach of his fundamental human rights. With respect to the first objection, the ICTY rationalised that the charge of crimes against humanity permitted a limited intrusion into State sovereignty, especially in the absence of any objection raised by the concerned State.[100] With respect to the second objection, the ICTY reiterated that the violation of fundamental rights could impede the exercise of its jurisdiction. However, the ICTY held that such a denial was only applicable in cases of a flagrant violation of human rights, as otherwise the denial of jurisdiction would be disproportionate to the concerned breach.[101] In its still nascent jurisprudence, the International Criminal Court ('ICC') seems to have followed a similar principle, namely, that the remedy provided for a violation of human rights must be proportionate, and only egregious violations of human rights adversely affecting the fundamental right to a fair trial may require the denial of exercise of jurisdiction by the Court.[102]

The foregoing cases demonstrate that it is not the extrajudicial surrender by police per se that most courts and tribunals consider unacceptable, but rather the failure to respect the fundamental rights of the persons concerned in international police cooperation.

C. Extrajudicial Gathering of Evidence Abroad

The foregoing conclusion applies *mutatis mutandis* to the extrajudicial gathering of evidence abroad. The effectiveness of State sovereignty depends on the extent to which its infringement is sanctioned either through inter-State dispute settlement, exclusionary rules in the forum State, or through criminal or civil sanctions under the law of the State whose sovereignty is violated. One approach, not followed by the majority of countries, favours unilateral action, as evidenced by how the law of the forum regards international law or foreign law when determining the admissibility of evidence obtained abroad. The total absence of any consideration of the relevant principles and rules of international or foreign law is particularly revealing in *US v Bin Laden*,[103] a case decided by the US District Court for the Southern District of New York in 2000 and affirmed by the US Court of Appeals for the Second Circuit *In re Terrorist Bombings of US Embassies in East Africa*.[104]

[100] Ibid, para 26.

[101] Ibid, paras 28–31.

[102] See: Bailey, S, 'Article 21(3) of the Rome Statute: a plea for clarity' (2014) 14 *International Criminal Law Review* 513–50.

[103] *US v Bin Laden*, 126 F. Supp. 2d 264 (S.D.N.Y. 2000).

[104] *In re Terrorist Bombings of US Embassies in East Africa*, 552 F.3d 93 (2nd Cir, 2008): the Court held that 'the Fourth Amendment's Warrant Clause has no extraterritorial application and that foreign searches of U.S. citizens conducted by U.S. agents are subject only to the Fourth Amendment's requirement of reasonableness' (at 171). Certiorari was denied in January 2010.

In this case, the defendants were charged with numerous offences arising out of their alleged participation in an international terrorist organisation led by Osama Bin Laden and that organisation's alleged involvement in the bombings of the US embassies in Nairobi and Dar es Salaam. One of the defendants, Wadih El Hage, an American national, moved to suppress evidence seized by US intelligence agents from the search of his residence in Nairobi, Kenya and evidence obtained from electronic surveillance of four telephone lines in Nairobi. El Hage argued that the search and the electronic surveillance were unlawful because they were not conducted pursuant to a valid search warrant. In denying the motion the Court held that, inter alia, (1) the foreign intelligence exception applies to the warrant requirement for searches targeting foreign powers (or their agents) when conducted abroad, and (2) despite the fact that the electronic surveillance was unlawful, the exclusion of the evidence obtained would be inappropriate because it would not have the deterrent effect which the 'exclusionary rule' requires and the surveillance was undertaken in good faith.

To understand the ruling in *US v Bin Laden*, one must recall that residents of the US are protected against 'unreasonable searches and seizures' under the Fourth Amendment to the US Constitution. Search warrants are not to be issued for less than 'probable cause, supported by Oath or affirmation, and particularly describing the place to be searched, and the persons or things to be seized'. If a judge finds that a police officer or other law enforcement agent violates an individual's Fourth Amendment rights, then all evidence they collected during that illegal search will be excluded at trial. This is what is known as the 'exclusionary rule'. The exclusionary rule has its roots in *Boyd v US*, a case decided by the US Supreme Court in 1886.[105] It was not until 1961, in the case of *Mapp v Ohio*, that the US Supreme Court made it clear that the exclusionary rule applied to all federal and state law enforcement officials.[106] However, the application of the exclusionary rule to foreigners was challenged in *US v Verdugo-Urquidez*. Rene Martin Verdugo-Urquidez, a Mexican national reputed to be a drug-lord and alleged to have been involved in the torture and murder of DEA agent Enrique Camarena Salazar, was arrested and brought to the US. The DEA decided to search the defendant's home in Mexico, so they obtained authorisation from the Mexican Government to do so. The agents discovered documents believed to be the defendant's records of his marijuana shipments. When the US Government sought to introduce the documents as evidence in court, the defendant objected, asserting that they were obtained without a warrant and, therefore, could not be used at trial. The US District Court agreed and invoked the exclusionary rule to suppress the use of the documents as evidence. The US Government successfully appealed

[105] *Boyd v US*, 116 U.S. 616 (1886) 625–26.

[106] *Mapp v Ohio*, 367 U.S. 643 (1961). In this case, the US Supreme Court decided that evidence obtained in violation of the Fourth Amendment, which protects against 'unreasonable searches and seizures', may not be used in criminal prosecutions in state courts, as well as federal courts.

this ruling before the US Court of Appeals for the Ninth Circuit. It held that the Fourth Amendment could not be invoked by a suspect of Mexican nationality to challenge a search and seizure because the drafters of the Constitution had not contemplated non-resident aliens within 'the people' that it would protect.[107] In effect, the US District Court in *US v Bin Laden* adopted a similar view on the Fourth Amendment when it decided not to apply the exclusionary rule to searches and seizures of American nationals performed by US law enforcement and intelligence agents abroad.[108]

It is remarkable that no consideration was given to the principle of sovereignty or whether there existed a treaty on mutual legal assistance in criminal matters or any ad hoc special arrangement that could have served as the legal basis for such extraterritorial enforcement action. Nor was consideration given to the relevant human rights treaties which might dictate exclusion of the evidence, irrespective of the scope of the Fourth Amendment. This approach is, however, not completely surprising. One may recall the Opinion of the Office of Legal Counsel of the US Department of Justice issued in 1989 reaffirming the conclusion reached in its 1980 Opinion that an arrest departing from international law did not violate the Fourth Amendment, and further concluding that – contrary to the view it held in 1980 – an arrest in violation of foreign law does not violate the Fourth Amendment.[109]

It remains to be seen if the attitude displayed in cases such as *US v Bin Laden* will be influenced by Article 10 of the International Convention for the Suppression of Terrorist Bombing. Under that provision, States parties must:

> afford one another the greatest measure of assistance in connection with investigations of criminals and extradition proceedings brought in respect of the offence of terrorist bombing, including assistance in obtaining evidence at their disposal where necessary for the proceedings. States Parties shall carry out their obligations in conformity with any treaties or other arrangements on mutual legal assistance that may exist between them. In the absence of such treaties or arrangements, States Parties shall afford one another assistance in accordance with their domestic law.[110]

In those jurisdictions where courts approach issues of international law differently, a case such as *US v Bin Laden* may have had a different outcome. For instance, in Canada the exclusion of illegally or improperly obtained evidence

[107] *US v Verdugo-Urquidez*, 494 U.S. 259 (1990) 274–75.

[108] *US v Bin Laden*, 126 F. Supp. 2d 264 (S.D.N.Y. 2000). See also: Then, CM, 'Searches and Seizures of Americans Abroad: Re-Examining the Fourth Amendment warrant clause and foreign intelligence exception five years after *United States v Bin Laden*' (2006) 55 *Duke Law Journal* 1059.

[109] Office of Legal Counsel of the US Department of Justice, 'Authority of the Federal Bureau of Investigation to Override International Law in Extraterritorial Enforcement Activities', Memorandum Opinion for the Attorney General (21 June 1989).

[110] International Convention for the Suppression of Terrorist Bombing (adopted on 15 December 1997, entered into force for the US on 26 July 2002) 2149 UNTS 256, Art 10. This Convention entered into force after the search of the individual's home in *US v Bin Laden*.

is grounded in the ICCPR, which requires States to ensure that individuals have an effective remedy when their rights are violated. This obligation has been implemented through the Canadian Charter of Rights and Freedoms, specifically through section 24(2).[111] The Canadian Supreme Court has considered the question of the extraterritorial application of the Charter to evidence gathering abroad in a series of cases, beginning with *R v Harrer*[112] in 1995 and culminating with the case of *R v Hape*[113] in 2007. This jurisprudence reveals an approach more in line with international law, raising fewer concerns from the point of view of the principle of sovereignty and carrying less risk in terms of the effectiveness of police enforcement.

Of an entirely different nature is reliance on, and the admissibility of, evidence obtained abroad through cruel and inhuman treatment of witnesses. In a significant judgment, *A and others v Secretary of State for the Home Department*,[114] the House of Lords of the UK held that evidence obtained by employing torturous methods by officials of a foreign State is not admissible before the Special Immigration Appeals Commission ('SIAC'). This case arose under the Anti-terrorism, Crime and Security Act 2001 ('ATCSA'), which permitted the UK Secretary of State to issue a certificate in respect of a foreign national whom he reasonably believed to pose a risk to national security and reasonably suspected of being a terrorist. A person certified under the ATCSA could challenge this certification before the SIAC. The appellants, all foreign nationals who were certified and detained, challenged their certification before the SIAC, which dismissed the appeals. The Court of Appeal of England and Wales upheld the decision of the SIAC. It held 'that the fact that evidence had, or might have been, procured by torture inflicted by foreign officials without the complicity of the British authorities was relevant to the weight of the evidence but did not render it legally inadmissible'. In the House of Lords, the appellants submitted that the common law, the ECHR and the principles of public international law all forbade the admission of evidence obtained by the infliction of torture irrespective of where, by whom or on whose authority the torture was inflicted. The Secretary of State, who indicated that he did not intend to use the evidence possibly procured by means of torture by foreign officials, contended that he would refrain from using this evidence as a matter of policy but not as a matter of law. Lord Bingham, who delivered the main judgment, rejected the arguments of the Secretary of State, stating that:

> [t]he English common law has regarded torture and its fruits with abhorrence for over 500 years, and that abhorrence is now shared by over 140 countries which have acceded to the Torture Convention. I am startled, even a little dismayed, at the suggestion

[111] See: Skinnider, E, 'Improperly or Illegally Obtained Evidence: The Exclusion Evidence Rule in Canada', International Centre for Criminal Law Reform and Criminal Justice Policy (Vancouver, 2005).

[112] *R v Harrer* [1995] 3 SCR 562.

[113] *R v Hape* [2007] 2 SCR 292, 2007 SCC 26.

[114] *A and others v Secretary of State for the Home Department (No 2)* [2005] UKHL 71. See also the judgments of the ECtHR: *Gafgen v Germany* [2011] 52 EHRR 1 and *Othman v UK* [2012] 55 EHRR 1.

> (and the acceptance by the Court of Appeal majority) that this deeply-rooted tradition and an international obligation solemnly and explicitly undertaken can be overridden by a statute and a procedural rule which makes no mention of torture at all. … The issue is one of constitutional principle, whether evidence obtained by torturing another human being may lawfully be admitted against a party to proceedings in a British court, irrespective of where, or by whom, or on whose authority the torture was inflicted. To that question I would give a very clear negative answer.[115]

Lord Bingham concluded that the exclusion of 'third party torture evidence' was mandated by common law, as well as by the ECHR.[116]

In light of the foregoing cases, it is obvious that, in the context of extrajudicial gathering of evidence abroad, the concern is not with the form of cooperation per se but with the need to ensure that the rule of law is respected in the process. Thus, it is possible to conclude that extrajudicial international police cooperation is permissible under international law to the extent that it respects the fundamental rights of the individuals involved.

VIII. The Appropriateness of INTERPOL's Object

It follows from the foregoing that the promotion of extrajudicial international police cooperation can only be considered an appropriate object of an international organisation if respect for the rule of law and fundamental human rights is inherent in such an object. The drafters of the current INTERPOL Constitution, and subsequently its General Assembly, seem to have realised this, and they have made sure that it is recognised in various ways in the INTERPOL Constitution and the Organisation's secondary rules.[117]

The articulation of INTERPOL's objective of promoting extrajudicial international police cooperation has remained fairly consistent since the incipience of the Organisation. The 1923[118] and 1939[119] Constitutions speak of guaranteeing and enhancing the widest possible mutual assistance between the police authorities in accordance with the laws of different States as well as establishing and developing

[115] *A and others v Secretary of State for the Home Department (No 2)* [2005] UKHL 71, para 51.

[116] On the issue of burden of proof, the appellants contended that once challenged, evidence would have to be established as admissible by the party seeking to introduce it. The UK Government submitted that the party trying to challenge the evidence would have to 'make good factual grounds on which he bases his challenge'. The Court did not take a unanimous decision on what requirements would have to be met in order for the evidence to be excluded.

[117] See: Babovic, B, 'INTERPOL et les droit de l'homme' (1998) 469/471 *Revue Internationale de Police Criminelle* 256–62; El Zein, S, 'Le rôle d'INTERPOL dans la protection des droit de l'homme' (1999) 474/475 *Revue Internationale de Police Criminelle* 2–4.

[118] See: Art 1(a): '*la garantie et le perfectionement de la plus large assistance réciproque entre toutes les autorités de police selon les lois des divers états*'.

[119] See: Art 1(a): '*La Commission assume la garantie et le développement de l'assistance mutuelle la plus large entre toutes les Polices criminelles dans le cadre des lois qui régissent les divers Etats*'.

all institutions likely to contribute effectively to combating crime. The direct antecedent of the current articulation of INTERPOL's aims, which expressly incorporates the principle of the rule of law and prescribes political and ideological neutrality, is Article 1 of the 1946 Constitution. When the members met to re-establish INTERPOL after the Second World War, they felt that the previous versions of the Organisation's constituent instrument had, by their simplicity, facilitated the Nazi Party's control over the Organisation.[120] Thus, for the first time, the term 'ordinary law crimes' was introduced in Article 1 of the 1946 Constitution. Henceforth, the Organisation's mandate was limited to those crimes.[121] The 1946 Constitution also expressly stated that the Organisation shall be prohibited from interfering in any matter of a political, religious, or racial character. In 1956, the Organisation mandated that its interventions comply with the 'spirit' of the Universal Declaration of Human Rights.[122] As a result, the principle of the rule of law, respect for fundamental human rights, and political and ideological neutrality were firmly established in the framework of the Organisation.

This framework is evident in the current INTERPOL Constitution and INTERPOL's secondary rules. First, Article 2(1) of the INTERPOL Constitution states that the aim of the Organisation is to 'ensure and promote the widest possible mutual assistance between all criminal police authorities within the limits of the laws existing in the different countries and in the spirit of the "Universal Declaration of Human Rights"'. Second, Article 3 of the INTERPOL Constitution dictates that '[i]t is strictly forbidden for the Organization to undertake any intervention or activities of a political, military, religious or racial character'. Third, Article 31 of the INTERPOL Constitution provides that '[i]n order to further its aims, the Organization needs the constant and active co-operation of its Members, who should do all within their power, which is compatible with the legislation of their countries to participate diligently in its activities'.[123] Outside the INTERPOL Constitution, Article 5(3) of INTERPOL's Rules on the Processing of Data ('IRPD') requires members to:

> endeavour to exchange a maximum of information of interest for the purposes of international police cooperation, with due observance of the Organization's political neutrality, independence and mandate, and of their respective national legislations and international conventions to which they are a party.

[120] Fooner, M, *INTERPOL: Issues of World Crime and International Criminal Justice* (New York, Springer, 1989) 40. The control of INTERPOL by the Nazi Party and the various other measures adopted to prevent recurrence of a similar event are considered in more detail when discussing the structure of the Organisation in Chapter 7.

[121] In 1956, when the current Constitution was adopted, the Organisation's aims were split in two, and the term 'ordinary law crimes' was linked only to the second aim of the Organisation, to 'establish and develop all institutions likely to contribute effectively to the prevention and suppression of ordinary law crimes' (see: INTERPOL Constitution, Art 2).

[122] See: INTERPOL Constitution, Art 2(1).

[123] This replaces Article 10(1)(a)(5) of the INTERPOL Rules on the Processing of Information for the Purposes of International Police Co-operation.

Article 5(3) must be read alongside Article 11(1) of the IRPD, which provides that:

> [d]ata processing in the INTERPOL Information System should be authorized with due regard for the law applicable to the National Central Bureau, national entity or international entity and should respect the basic rights of the persons who are the subject of the cooperation, in accordance with Article 2 of the Organization's Constitution and the Universal Declaration of Human Rights to which the said Article refers.

Article 34 of the IRPD further obligates an NCB, national entity or international entity to ensure, prior to any recording of data in a police database, 'the data are in compliance with Article 2 of the Organization's Constitution, and also that it is authorized to record such data pursuant to applicable national laws and international conventions and to the fundamental human rights enshrined in the Universal Declaration of Human Rights'.[124]

The condition articulated in Article 2 and the restriction laid down by Article 3 apply both to the General Secretariat and to INTERPOL members. The former must refrain from providing assistance when either the condition of consistency with national laws and human rights is not met or when Article 3 forbids an intervention, while the members must undertake to comply with the Constitution when they join INTERPOL and make use of its tools. The Organisation, therefore, must check that requests from NCBs do not violate the provisions which INTERPOL is obligated to observe. This monitoring means that INTERPOL may refuse to process a request or decide to delete data on the basis of Articles 2 and 3 (as discussed in detail in Chapter 8).

However, some members of the International Criminal Police Commission ('ICPC') (the prior name of INTERPOL)[125] thought that the restriction in Article 3 (first introduced in 1946 in respect of matters of a political, religious, or racial character) impaired the ICPC's effectiveness in combatting many forms of crimes that are of eminent importance to the world community. Not surprisingly, the ICPC was almost immediately prompted by members to determine a framework for interpreting Article 3 of its Constitution to take account of certain developments in international law, particularly extradition proceedings in respect of politicians and those associated with them. In 1951, the predominance test was

[124] The INTERPOL Constitution and its data processing rules are clearly responsive to evolving international law which is increasingly concerned with the need for entities processing personal data to respect the data privacy of those concerned. As noted by the ILC, international binding and non-binding instruments, national legislation adopted by States and judicial decisions reveal a number of core principles. Although these principles are not yet developed to fully fledged positive international law, they are indicative of the public policy concerns which cannot be ignored ('Protection of Personal Data in Transborder Flow of Information' in *Yearbook of the International Law Commission* (2006) Vol II, Part Two, Annex IV, para 11). On those concerns, see: Cooper, D and Kuner, C, 'Data Protection Law and International Dispute Resolution' (2015) 382 *Recueil des Cours* 9–174.

[125] As discussed in Chapter 7, the ICPC was created in 1923. In 1956, it changed its name to 'The International Criminal Police Organization – INTERPOL' (INTERPOL Constitution, Art 1).

introduced, according to which the Organisation does not consider itself bound by the categorisation of an offence as an ordinary law crime by the requesting country, but instead examines requests on a case-by-case basis to assess the nature of the offence.[126] In 1984, the INTERPOL General Assembly developed the predominance test further and paved the way for the Organisation to process requests and compile information concerning terrorist cases under certain conditions.[127] Finally, in 1994, the INTERPOL General Assembly enabled the Organisation to process requests concerning violations of international humanitarian law under certain conditions, hence the Organisation's active cooperation with the ICTY and the International Criminal Tribunal for Rwanda.[128] We discuss the Organisation's interpretative practice in respect of Article 3 further in Chapter 8.

More broadly, these provisions and resolutions reflect the view that only if the rule of law, respect for human rights, and political and ideological neutrality is observed in the process of international police cooperation through INTERPOL's channels will the Organisation's interventions be considered legitimate from the perspective of international law and be accepted by the courts that decide cases built on such cooperation.[129] Arguably, it is at least partly due to the recognition of INTERPOL's aims that various conventions and other international instruments mention INTERPOL's role in the field of international police cooperation and information exchange. These include conventions and instruments adopted under the auspices of the Council of Europe, the UN, the EU, the Commonwealth of Nations, the Economic Community of West African States, and the Organization of American States.

INTERPOL is, with the exception of the UN, the only international organisation cited in the Rome Statute of the ICC. Article 87(1)(b) of the Rome Statute allows requests for cooperation between the ICC and States parties to the Rome Statute to be transmitted through INTERPOL. INTERPOL's international function was also underscored in the UN International Instrument to Enable States to

[126] Resolution No AGN/20/RES/11, 'Request for international inquiries', International Criminal Police Commission General Assembly, 20th session (Lisbon, 1951).

[127] Resolution AGN/53/RES/7, 'Application of Article 3 of the Constitution', INTERPOL General Assembly, 53rd session (Luxembourg, 1984).

[128] Resolution AGN/63/Res/9, 'Application of Article 3 of the Constitution in the context of serious violations of international humanitarian law', INTERPOL General Assembly, 63rd session (Rome, 1994).

[129] Recital 33 of Regulation (EU) 2016/794 of the European Parliament and of the Council of 11 May 2016 on the European Union Agency for Law Enforcement Cooperation (Europol) also recognises this in the context of Europol's relationship with INTERPOL: 'it is appropriate to strengthen cooperation between Europol and Interpol by promoting an efficient exchange of personal data whilst ensuring respect for fundamental rights and freedoms regarding the automatic processing of personal data'. Recital 41 also states that '[a]ny processing of personal data by Europol should be lawful and fair in relation to the data subjects concerned', and Recital 50 provides that '[i]ndependent, transparent, accountable and effective structures for supervision are essential for the protection of individuals with regard to the processing of personal data as required by Article 8(3) of the Charter of Fundamental Rights of the European Union'.

Identify and Trace, in a Timely and Reliable Manner, Illicit Small Arms and Light Weapons.[130]

Moreover, on 29 July 2005, the recognition of INTERPOL's international function took the form of a UN Security Council Resolution under Chapter VII of the UN Charter. UN Security Council Resolution 1617 (2005) called on the UN Secretary-General to work with INTERPOL to provide better tools to help the UN Sanctions Committee established pursuant to Resolution 1267 (1999) carry out its mandate regarding the freezing of assets, travel bans and arms embargoes aimed at individuals and entities associated or belonging to ISIL (Da'esh), Al-Qaida and the Taliban.[131] One year later, in Resolution 1699 (2006), the UN Security Council requested the UN Secretary-General to take the necessary steps to increase cooperation between the UN and INTERPOL to provide the other UN sanctions committees with better tools to fulfil their mandates more effectively.[132] In line with successive UN Security Council resolutions, INTERPOL has therefore expanded its cooperation to other UN sanctions committees, including those concerning the Democratic Republic of Congo, Somalia, Sudan, Guinea-Bissau, the Central African Republic, Yemen, South Sudan and Libya.

Some UN conventions state that requests for mutual legal assistance and any communication related thereto should be transmitted through diplomatic channels and, in urgent situations, through INTERPOL.[133] The situation is the same in the case of the EU conventions which envisage such a role for INTERPOL in

[130] See: UN General Assembly, 'Report of the Open-Ended Working Group to Negotiate an International Instrument to Enable States to Identify and Trace, in a Timely and Reliable Manner, Illicit Small Arms and Light Weapons', Annex, UN Doc A/60/88 (27 June 2005) paras 33–5.

[131] The UN Sanctions Committee established pursuant to Resolution 1267 (1999) on 15 October 1999 was known as the Al-Qaida and Taliban Sanctions Committee. The sanctions regime has been modified and strengthened by subsequent resolutions, including Resolutions 1333 (2000), 1390 (2002), 1455 (2003), 1526 (2004), 1617 (2005), 1735 (2006) and 1822 (2008). With Resolutions 1988 (2011) and 1989 (2011), the UN Security Council split the Sanctions Committee into two: the Al-Qaida Sanctions Committee was mandated to oversee implementation of the measures against individuals and entities associated with Al-Qaida, and a separate Committee was established to oversee implementation of the measures against individuals and entities associated with the Taliban in constituting a threat to the peace, stability and security of Afghanistan. In 2015, the UN Security Council adopted Resolution 2253 (2015) and expanded the listing criteria to include individuals and entities supporting the Islamic State in Iraq and the Levant (ISIL). In Resolution 2368 (2017), the UN Security Council added a number of individuals to the ISIL and Al-Qaida Sanctions List. These resolutions have all been adopted under Chapter VII of the UN Charter and require all States to take the following measures in connection with any individual or entity associated with ISIL, Al-Qaida, and/or the Taliban as designated by the Sanctions Committees: (1) freeze without delay the funds and other financial assets or economic resources of designated individuals and entities, (2) prevent the entry into or transit through their territories by designated individuals, and (3) prevent the direct or indirect supply, sale and transfer from their territories or by their nationals outside their territories, or using their flag vessels or aircraft, of arms and related material of all types, spare parts, and technical advice, assistance, or training related to military activities, to designated individuals and entities.

[132] UN Security Council Resolution 1699, 8 August 2006.

[133] Article 18(13) of the UNCTOC and Article 46(13) of the UNCAC provide that: '[t]his requirement shall be without prejudice to the rights of a State Party to require that such requests and communications be addressed to it through diplomatic channels and, in urgent circumstances, where the

the context of international cooperation. Article 24(3) of the European Convention on Laundering, Search, Seizure and Confiscation of the Proceeds from Crime, Article 27(9b) of the European Convention on Cybercrime, and Article 30(3) of the Criminal Law Convention on Corruption provide that '[a]ny request or communication … may be made through [INTERPOL]'. The articulation of these provisions as permissive norms seems odd against the background of the freedom of action of sovereign States promulgated in the *Lotus* case. Rather, it seems to follow from the *Lotus* principle that, unless there is a norm requiring countries to cooperate via a specified channel, no permissive norm is needed to enable them to cooperate via INTERPOL's channels. In addition, one would assume the same by virtue of the fact that, when a country participates in INTERPOL, it agrees to use INTERPOL's channels. It is different with those provisions which purport to make INTERPOL's channels the exclusive means for cooperation, such as Article 3 of the Co-operation Agreement on Police Matters between Benin, Ghana, Nigeria and Togo, which determines that '[t]he INTERPOL National Central Bureaus shall serve as a liaison organ between the different security services of the Contracting Parties'.[134]

In any case, all these provisions demonstrate that the Organisation may provide its facilities to enable effective police cooperation between its members. INTERPOL may participate in the communication of requests for mutual legal assistance and may serve as a communication centre between the respective national authorities working on police matters. With this, it can be concluded that INTERPOL's object is appropriate and it has been recognised as such in various conventions and instruments. As discussed in Chapter 8, a host of juridical consequences naturally follow from this conclusion, as the existence of an appropriate object is a logically anterior determinant of an international organisation's competences.

States Parties agree, through the International Criminal Police Organisation, if possible'. Article 7(8) of the UN Convention against Illicit Traffic in Narcotic Drugs and Psychotropic Substances (adopted on 20 December 1988, entered into force on 11 November 1990) 1582 UNTS 95 provides that: '[t]ransmission of requests for mutual legal assistance and any communication related thereto shall be effected between the authorities designated by the Parties; this requirement shall be without prejudice to the right of a Party to require that such requests and communications be addressed to it through the diplomatic channels and, in urgent circumstances, where the Parties agree, through channels of the International Criminal Police Organisation, if possible'.

[134] Cooperation Agreement on Police Matters between Benin, Ghana, Nigeria and Togo (Lagos, 1984).

3

A Meeting of Wills and Consent to be Bound

Having explained in Chapter 2 that the International Criminal Police Organization ('INTERPOL' or the 'Organisation') has an appropriate object, the next step in our analysis is twofold: first, to determine whether the meeting of wills reflected in the INTERPOL Constitution can be attributed to the countries of the participating police bodies, and second, to determine whether these countries can be deemed to have expressed their consent to be bound by the INTERPOL Constitution.

I. A Meeting of Wills[1]

Article 2(1)(a) of the 1969 Vienna Convention on the Law of Treaties ('VCLT') defines a treaty as an international agreement between States in written form and governed by international law, whether embodied in a single instrument or in two or more related instruments and whatever the particular designation may be. Article 3 of the VCLT states that the Convention shall only apply to the treaties so defined. In other words, all the treaties covered by the VCLT are necessarily international agreements, but not all international agreements governed by public international law are treaties within the meaning of the VCLT.[2] Indeed, while the VCLT and the 1986 Vienna Convention on the Law of Treaties between States and International Organizations or between International Organizations ('VCLT-IO') cover a great part of the law of treaties, they do not cover the entire area of international law governing international agreements.[3] The International

[1] On the notion of the will of States in international law, see: Kamto, M, 'La volonté de l'État en droit international' (2004) 310 *Recueil des Cours* 9–428.

[2] Jiménez de Aréchaga, E, 'International Law in the Past Third of a Century' (1978) 159 *Recueil des Cours* 1–344 at 35–6. For a discussion on the concept of international agreements, see: Separate Opinion of Judge Jessup, Joint Dissenting Opinion of Judge Spender and Judge Fitzmaurice and Separate Opinion of Judge Mbanefo in the *South West Africa Cases (Ethiopia v South Africa; Liberia v South Africa)* (Preliminary Objections) [1962] ICJ Rep 319.

[3] Klabbers, J, *The Concept of Treaty in International Law* (The Hague, Kluwer Law International, 1996) 37–65.

Court of Justice ('ICJ') has adopted a broad definition of international agreement. In *Qatar v Bahrain*, the ICJ found that, in order to ascertain whether an international agreement has been concluded, 'the Court must have regard above all to its actual terms and to the particular circumstances in which it was drawn up'.[4] The ICJ elaborated that 'international agreements may take a number of forms and be given a diversity of names'.[5] Reuter also considers that a broad definition of treaty is needed, namely, that '[a] treaty is an expression of concurring wills attributable to two or more subjects of international law and intended to have legal effects under the rules of international law'.[6]

If we adopt a broad definition of a treaty, the first question is whether the meeting of wills reflected in the INTERPOL Constitution is, in fact, a meeting of wills of subjects of international law. To answer this question, it is instructive, as a preliminary matter, to examine whether the conduct of the participating police bodies during the negotiation and adoption of the INTERPOL Constitution can be attributed to their respective countries.[7]

A. Attribution of Conduct in the Negotiation and Adoption of a Treaty

For reasons that will be elaborated in the following paragraphs, the present authors are satisfied that the negotiation and adoption of the INTERPOL Constitution that took place in 1956 was attributable to the countries of the police bodies in attendance. In light of the popular, albeit erroneous, view that (the governments of) countries were not involved in the creation of INTERPOL, it would seem useful to examine this question further in light of the doctrine of attribution of conduct under international law.[8]

[4] *Maritime Delimitation and Territorial Questions between Qatar and Bahrain (Qatar v Bahrain)* (Jurisdiction and Admissibility, Judgment) [1994] ICJ Rep 112, para 23, citing *Aegean Sea Continental Shelf (Greece v Turkey)* (Judgment) [1978] ICJ Rep 3, para 96. See also: *Legal Status of Eastern Greenland (Denmark v Norway)* (Judgment) [1933] PCIJ Series A/B No 53; Widdows, K, 'What is an Agreement in International Law?' (1979) 50 *British Yearbook of International Law* 117–49; Fitzmaurice, M, 'The Identification and Character of Treaties and Treaty Obligations Between States in International Law' (2003) 73 *British Yearbook of International Law* 141–85 at 152; Gold, J, 'On the Difficulties of Defining International Agreements: Some Illustrations from the Experience of the International Monetary Fund' in Simha, SLN (ed), *Economic and Social Development: Essays in Honour of Dr. C.D. Deshmukh* (Bombay, Vora, 1972) 25–44.

[5] *Maritime Delimitation and Territorial Questions between Qatar and Bahrain (Qatar v Bahrain)* (Jurisdiction and Admissibility, Judgment) [1994] ICJ Rep 112, para 23.

[6] Reuter, P, *Introduction to the Law of Treaties* (translated by Mico, J and Haggenmacher, P) (London, Pinter Publishers, 1989) 22–3.

[7] The question of whether these countries are subjects of international law is addressed in Chapter 4.

[8] On the attribution of votes in organs of international organisations to the governments of the voting representatives, see: Lagrange, E, *La représentation institutionnelle dans l'ordre internationale* (The Hague, Kluwer Law International, 2002) 309–15.

In this regard, it should be noted that, while the International Law Commission ('ILC') distinguished between the attribution of conduct to a State in the context of State responsibility vis-à-vis other areas of international law,[9] the ILC also observed that:

> the basic task is to establish when, according to international law, it is the State which must be regarded as acting: what actions … can in principle be considered as conduct of the State, and in what circumstances, such conduct must have been engaged in, if it is to be actually attributable to the State as a subject of international law.[10]

The ICJ, basing its observations on the ILC's Draft Articles on State Responsibility, has held that according to 'a well-established rule of international law, the conduct of any organ of the State must be regarded as an act of that State', and that this rule 'is of a customary character'.[11] Under the rules on attribution in the law of State responsibility, the term 'organ' is 'not limited to the organs of the central government, to officials at a high level or to persons with responsibility for the external relations of the State. It extends to organs of government of whatever kind or classification, exercising whatever functions, and at whatever level in the hierarchy'.[12] The term 'organ' also extends to 'certain institutions performing public functions and exercising public powers (e.g. the police) … even if those institutions are regarded in internal law as autonomous and independent of the executive government'.[13]

This leads us to the question of whether international law employs different rules for the attribution of conduct in the law of State responsibility and in the law of treaties. There have been limited contributions by commentators and courts

[9] Eg, 'Report of the International Law Commission on the work of its twenty-fifth session (7 May–13 July 1973)' in *Yearbook of the International Law Commission* (1973) Vol II, 189, para 5; 'Draft articles on Responsibility of States for Internationally Wrongful Acts, with commentaries' in *Yearbook of the International Law Commission* (2001) Vol II, Part Two, 39, para 5.

[10] 'Report of the International Law Commission on the work of its twenty-fifth session (7 May–13 July 1973)' in *Yearbook of the International Law Commission* (1973) Vol II, 189, para 3.

[11] *Difference Relating to the Immunity from Legal Process of a Special Rapporteur of the Commission on Human Rights* (Advisory Opinion) [1999] ICJ Rep 62, para 62. That the State is responsible for the conduct of its own organs, acting in that capacity, has long been recognised in international judicial decisions (eg, see: *Claims of Italian Nationals Resident in Peru* (Decision of 30 September 1901) XV RIAA 389, 399 (*Chiessa* claim), 401 (*Sessarego* claim), 404 (*Sanguinetti* claim), 407 (*Vercelli* claim), 408 (*Queirolo* claim), 409 (*Roggero* claim), 411 (*Miglia* claim); *Claim of Finnish shipowners against Great Britain in respect of the use of certain Finnish vessels during the war (Finland, Great Britain)* (Award of 9 May 1934) III RIAA 1479, 1501; *The Claims of Rosa Gelbtrunk and the 'Salvador Commercial Company', et al (El Salvador, United States)* (Award of 8 May 1902) XV RIAA 455, 477).

[12] 'Draft articles on Responsibility of States for Internationally Wrongful Acts, with commentaries' in *Yearbook of the International Law Commission* (2001) Vol II, Part Two, 40, Commentary to Art 4, para 6. Writing in 1953, Bin Cheng was of the view that the acts of an official are imputable to the State under international law if the official occupies a position in which he exercises authority, or a fraction of authority, possessed by the government as a whole (Cheng, B, *General Principles of Law as Applied by International Courts and Tribunals* (London, Stevens, 1953) 193).

[13] 'Draft articles on Responsibility of States for Internationally Wrongful Acts, with commentaries' in *Yearbook of the International Law Commission* (2001) Vol II, Part Two, 39, para 6.

on this question. Most authors writing on the law of treaties cite the concept of full powers (a relic of the era of absolute monarchs and slow communications) to explain how and when a government official is vested with the power to negotiate and sign a treaty.[14] The view seems to be that the actions performed by persons who do not have full powers are devoid of a constitutive element for international agreements. However, such a view would seem untenable in cases of informal international agreements or international agreements in a simplified form. The issue, therefore, must be approached from a broader perspective. Quadri is one of the few authors who appears to treat attribution of conduct as an autonomous doctrine that is concerned with establishing what acts constitute acts of State for the purposes of international law. It can be inferred from his treatment of the matter that the conduct of any organ of a State is considered an act of that State, provided the act involved is by its nature a governmental act.[15]

For quite some time, decisions by international courts and tribunals on the issue of who (other than heads of state, heads of government, ministers of foreign affairs, and ambassadors)[16] is deemed to represent the State for the purposes of its international commitments were almost non-existent. However, in the last few decades, the ICJ has had to consider whether agreements of an informal nature can be concluded by officials of a State not specifically authorised to represent the State in its international relations.[17] The *Gulf of Maine* case[18] contains some passages that provide an indication of how the ICJ might deal with the ability of specialised government departments to negotiate and adopt an international agreement on behalf of their State.[19] One of the questions that the ICJ Chamber

[14] See: Aust, A, *Modern Treaty Law and Practice*, 3rd edn (Cambridge, Cambridge University Press, 2013) 71–8; Crawford, J, *Brownlie's Principles of Public International Law*, 9th edn (Oxford, Oxford University Press, 2019) 357.

[15] Quadri, R, (ed), *Diritto Internazionale Pubblico* (Napoli, Liguori, 1989) 391–95. See also: Quadri, R, 'Cours général de droit international public' (1964) 113 *Recueil des Cours* 237–483 at 382–83.

[16] The ICJ has previously held that 'it is a well established rule of international law that the Head of State, the Head of Government and the Minister of Foreign Affairs are deemed to represent the State merely by virtue of exercising their functions, including for the performance, on behalf of the said State, of unilateral acts having the force of international commitments' (*Armed Activities on the Territory of the Congo (New Application: 2002) (Democratic Republic of the Congo v Rwanda)* (Judgment) [2006] ICJ Rep 6, para 46). See also: *Nuclear Tests (Australia v France)* (Judgment) [1974] ICJ Rep 253, paras 49–51; *Application of the Convention on the Prevention and Punishment of the Crime of Genocide (Bosnia and Herzegovina v Yugoslavia* (Preliminary Objections) [1996] ICJ Rep 595, para 44; *Arrest Warrant of 11 April 2000 (Democratic Republic of the Congo v Belgium)* (Judgment) [2002] ICJ Rep 3, para 53; *Legal Status of Eastern Greenland (Denmark v Norway)* (Judgment) [1933] PCIJ Rep Series A/B No 53, 71.

[17] For a discussion, see: Thirlway, H, 'The Law and Procedure of the International Court of Justice 1960–1989, Supplement, 2007: Parts Four, Five and Six' (2008) 78 *British Yearbook of International Law* 17–175 at 39–42.

[18] *Delimitation of the Maritime Boundary in the Gulf of Maine Area (Canada/United States of America)* (Judgment) [1984] ICJ Rep 246.

[19] See: Kamto, M, *La volonté de l'Etat en droit international* (Leiden, Martinus Nijhoff Publishers, 2007) 82–4.

needed to address in this case was whether the terms of a letter from the United States ('US') Bureau of Land Management – the so-called 'Hoffman letter' – could be invoked by Canada against the US in a matter concerning the delimitation of certain maritime zones between the two States. The US argued that the authors of the 1965 correspondence were mid-level government officials who had no authority to define international boundaries or to take a position on behalf of their governments for foreign claims in this field.[20] The US especially disputed the argument that the 'Hoffman letter' could be regarded as constituting acquiescence because, as Mr Hoffman himself explained in his letter, he had no authority to commit the US as to the position of a median line. The Chamber was of the view that Mr Hoffman, like his Canadian counterpart, had acted within the limits of his technical responsibilities in writing to his US counterpart, even though he was unaware of the broader ramifications of his correspondence.[21] In other words, the conduct of a mid-level government official acting within his technical functions was attributable to the US. However, the situation did not authorise Canada to rely on the contents of the Hoffman letter – ie, it did not bind the US – because the Hoffman letter could not be treated as though it were an official declaration of the US government on its international maritime boundaries.[22]

This case suggests that, in considering the issue of attribution of conduct in the context of the negotiation and adoption of a treaty, one must also consider if the official acted within his or her technical functions. To us, it seems plausible to suggest that when police bodies from different parts of the world come together to negotiate and adopt an agreement with the view to establishing an organisation with the aims of 'ensur[ing] and promot[ing] the widest possible mutual assistance between all criminal police authorities' and 'establish[ing] and develop[ing] all institutions likely to contribute effectively to the prevention and suppression of ordinary law crimes',[23] these police bodies are performing a task within their technical functions, and, as a consequence, the negotiation and adoption of such an agreement can be attributed to their respective countries.[24]

B. Attribution of Conduct of Police Bodies at INTERPOL

In light of the foregoing, it is reasonable to assume that the delegates who negotiated and adopted the 1956 iteration of the INTERPOL Constitution represented their respective countries, and, given that even the *procès-verbal* of an international

[20] *Delimitation of the Maritime Boundary in the Gulf of Maine Area (Canada/United States of America)* (Judgment) [1984] ICJ Rep 246, para 133.

[21] Ibid, para 139.

[22] Ibid.

[23] INTERPOL Constitution, Art 2.

[24] In the same vein, see: Ruzié, D, 'L'Organisation internationale de police criminelle' (1956) 2 *Annuaire francais de droit international* 673–79 at 674.

conference may form an adequate record of an informal agreement,[25] there should be no legal objection to considering the legal instrument adopted in the 1956 conference as reflecting a *consensus ad idem* between countries.

Nevertheless, one of the often heard observations about INTERPOL's legal status is that it is a private organisation of police officers.[26] For instance, according to Schermers, INTERPOL fulfils important governmental functions but remains a non-governmental organisation established by private citizens.[27] Likewise, at the US Senate committee hearing of 24 April 1975, some congressional researchers characterised INTERPOL as a 'private organisation … masquerading as a *bona fide* intergovernmental organisation and a world police'.[28] Similarly, in 1990, some members of the Parliamentary Assembly of the Council of Europe tried to pass a resolution to the effect that INTERPOL had been created as a private organisation by police officers who had never submitted the INTERPOL Constitution to their governments for approval.[29] This pervasive view, advanced by some of those who now accept INTERPOL's status as an international organisation, is succinctly articulated by Fooner as follows:

> [a]t first glance, Interpol appears as an organization with a multinational membership that is engaged in official business with many governments and that comports itself as an international police organization. Yet the organization, which has no basis in any international treaty nor in any convention or similar legal instrument, was founded upon a Constitution that was written by a random group of police officers who did not submit the draft to their governments for approval or authorization. No diplomatic signatures were ever placed on the draft, nor was there any submission of the constitution to governments for ratification.[30]

To a large extent, part of the blame for this view may be ascribed to INTERPOL itself which, in 1948, applied to the United Nations ('UN') for a consultative status in the category of non-governmental organisation.[31]

As late as the 1970s, the UN Secretariat was also of the view that the consensus of wills reflected in the INTERPOL Constitution was not a meeting of wills of (the governments of) countries. Under the heading of treaties and international

[25] McNair, A, *The Law of Treaties* (Oxford, Clarendon Press, 1961) 14–5.

[26] See a discussion in: Fooner, M, *INTERPOL: Issues of World Crime and International Criminal Justice* (New York, Springer, 1989) 45–7 and the sources cited therein. See also: Barnett, M and Coleman, L, 'Designing Police: Interpol and the Study of Change in International Organizations' (2005) 49 *International Studies Quarterly* 593–619 at 603.

[27] Schermers, HG, 'The International Organisations' in Bedjaoui, M (ed), *International Law: Achievements and Prospects* (Dordrecht, Martinus Nijhoff Publishers,1991) 67–100 at 68.

[28] US Congress, 'Senate Hearings Before the Committee on Appropriations: Subcommittee on Treasury, Postal Service and General Government Appropriations', Fiscal Year 1976, 94th Congress, First Session, Part 3 (Washington, GPO) 2187–88.

[29] Council of Europe, Parliamentary Assembly, 'Use of Personal Information by INTERPOL, Motion for Resolution by René Uytendaele' (Belgium EPP/CD) Doc 6179 (31 January 1990).

[30] Fooner, M, *INTERPOL: Issues of World Crime and International Criminal Justice* (New York, Springer, 1989) 45.

[31] Ibid, 51.

agreements not subject to registration under Article 102 of the UN Charter, the UN Secretariat expressed itself as follows on the topic of INTERPOL and its special arrangements for cooperation (as more fully discussed in Chapter 7):

> [t]he special arrangements for co-operation between the United Nations and the International Criminal Police Organisation (INTERPOL) approved by resolution 1579 (L) of the Economic and Social Council were not subjected to filing and recording. One of the reasons for this was that under the constitution of INTERPOL, the members of that organization, although designated by governments, are the police departments of the respective countries, which do not necessarily represent their governments as such. Another reason was that the constitution of INTERPOL did not appear to constitute a treaty. A further consideration was that the arrangements in question were not in the form of an agreement, consisting as they did of two juxtaposed resolutions, one adopted by the Economic and Social Council, the other by the General Assembly of INTERPOL.[32]

Although the UN Secretariat, in making the assertion above, was clearly dealing with the question of whether an agreement between the UN Economic and Social Council ('ECOSOC') and INTERPOL needed to be registered under Article 102 of the UN Charter, and not whether the INTERPOL Constitution qualifies as a treaty or international agreement, it did not dispose of the question on the basis of the terms of Article 102. Instead, the UN Secretariat chose to embark on observations and assertions that were, with respect, uninformed and unnecessary. During this same period, the UN Secretariat also did not register two agreements concluded between the government of a UN Member State and the International Committee of the Red Cross ('ICRC'). The UN Secretariat took the position that, since the ICRC is not an inter-governmental organisation, but rather the international chapter of private national organisations, the government's agreements with the ICRC were not international agreements for the purposes of Article 102 of the UN Charter.[33] Whereas this stance may be understandable insofar as the ICRC is concerned given its legal foundation in Swiss private law, it remains unclear how, at the same time, the UN Secretariat accounted for the fact that (unlike the ICRC) INTERPOL is not the product of any national legal order (as discussed in Chapter 6).

In 1982, the UN Secretariat adjusted its view. In that year, the UN Office of Legal Affairs carried out a detailed analysis regarding the status of INTERPOL to answer the question of whether it was legally correct for ECOSOC to designate INTERPOL as an intergovernmental organisation. The conclusion reads as follows:

> INTERPOL is considered to be an intergovernmental organization .... The change in status at the United Nations was consequential upon the amendment in 1956 of the constitution of INTERPOL which evidenced the intergovernmental character of the organization .... In the light of this possibility of an international organisation acquiring

[32] Repertory of Practice of UN Organs, 'Article 102', Supplement No 5 (1970–1978), Vol 5, para 11.
[33] Ibid, para 6.

> intergovernmental status through changes to its existing constitution (which, incidentally, may be considered an international agreement in simplified form), it may be considered that the present constitutional provisions of INTERPOL fully justify the decisions of [ECOSOC] to consider INTERPOL as an intergovernmental, rather than a non-governmental organisation.[34]

The argument by the UN Office of Legal Affairs that the 1956 INTERPOL Constitution was the turning point in determining the nature of the Organisation perhaps seeks to harmonise the conflicting approaches of the UN with respect to INTERPOL. However, it remains unconvincing for the following reasons.

As will be more fully explained in Chapter 7, INTERPOL's creation traces its roots to an invitation by the Austrian Government (through Vienna's chief of police) to police officials around the world. The police bodies of 20 countries were represented at the 1923 conference. It is clear from the text of the very first International Criminal Police Commission ('ICPC') Constitution, adopted in 1923, that national police authorities were acting on behalf of their respective countries when the ICPC (the prior name of INTERPOL) was created. Article 3 of the 1923 ICPC Constitution provided that the governments of States not present at the conference shall be invited to appoint their representatives (ie, '*[l]es gouvernements des états qui ne sont pas représentés à ce Congrès Internationale de Police seront invités à désigner leurs représentants*').[35] When the 1923 ICPC Constitution was revised in 1939, a distinction between effective members ('*des membres effectifs*') and extraordinary members ('*des members extraordinaires*') was introduced in Article 3: extraordinary members needed to be elected, whereas effective members were delegated by their governments (ie, '*qui seront délégués par leur gouvernement*').[36] The same system was maintained under the 1946 ICPC Constitution. More importantly, paragraph 4 of Article 3 provided that the founding members would remain members of the ICPC, provided their governments did not interfere (ie, '*[l]es membres fondateurs élus par le Congrès International de la Police Criminelle en 1923 demeurent membres de la Commission, pour autant que leur Gouvernement n'y mette pas obstacle*').[37] Moreover, according to paragraph 3 of Article 3, only one delegate from each country had the right to vote in the General Assembly (ie, the delegates voted on behalf of their country, as opposed to voting on their own behalf).[38] Indeed, INTERPOL's records confirm that the delegates to the ICPC General Assembly were duly delegated by their governments and voted on the

[34] 'Status of the International Criminal Police Organization (INTERPOL) with the United Nations' in *UN Juridical Yearbook* (1982), Part Two, Ch VI, 179–80.

[35] 'The governments of the states which are not represented at this International Police Congress will be invited to appoint their representatives' (authors' translation).

[36] '[W]ho will be delegated by their government' (authors' translation).

[37] 'The founding members elected by the International Criminal Police Congress in 1923 remain members of the Commission, as long as their Government does not obstruct it' (authors' translation).

[38] '*N'aura droit de vote qu'un seul délégué effectif par pays*'.

basis of the 'one country one vote principle', as they continue to do today at the INTERPOL General Assembly.

When the current INTERPOL Constitution was adopted in 1956, police bodies of 41 countries were present. Quite significantly, there was only one abstention originating from the delegation of Argentina due to lack of instructions from the government. No other delegation considered that it was precluded from voting on the proposed text because of lack of governmental instruction.[39] Similarly, in some other instances, countries formally clarified their position with regard to the 1956 INTERPOL Constitution. For instance, on 28 August 1958, President Eisenhower signed a Bill passed by the US Congress stating expressly 'that the Attorney General is authorized to accept and maintain, on behalf of the United States, membership in the International Police Organization'.[40]

In light of the foregoing, it is clear that (the governments of) the countries concerned considered that the police bodies involved in negotiating and adopting the 1956 INTERPOL Constitution were acting on behalf of their respective countries in the same way as plenipotentiaries at formally convened diplomatic conferences.

II. Consent to be Bound

For the purposes of the law of treaties, a *consensus ad idem* with respect to the negotiation and adoption of the INTERPOL Constitution does not suffice; countries must also have expressed their consent to be bound. In the context of the constituent instrument of an organisation, a consent to be bound amounts to a commitment to participate in the organisation. The importance of the expression of a consent to be bound is reflected in the jurisprudence of the ICJ, which has held that an agreement not approved by the competent authorities does not have the binding force of a convention.[41] In other words, unless it can be established that the countries that negotiated and adopted the INTERPOL Constitution actually expressed their consent to be bound by it (eg, through ratification, acceptance, approval or tacit acceptance/approval) then it cannot be regarded as an international agreement that establishes an international organisation.

[39] Resolution No AG/25/1956, Report of the Ad Hoc Sub-Committee, 'Proposed Reform of the ICPC Statutes', 25th session (Vienna, 1956) 9. The Government of Argentina subsequently ratified the INTERPOL Constitution by presidential decree of 12 January 1962 on account of Argentina's continued participation in INTERPOL since 1947.

[40] US Code §263a, 'International Criminal Police Organization'. This authorisation was solidified in 1983 by President Ronald Reagan when he signed Executive Order 12425 of 16 June 1983 designating INTERPOL as a public international organisation.

[41] *Frontier Dispute (Burkina Faso/Republic of Mali)* (Judgment) [1986] ICJ Rep 554, paras 146–47. See also: *Land, Island and Maritime Frontier Dispute (El Salvador/Honduras: Nicaragua intervening)* (Judgment) [1992] ICJ Rep 351, para 261.

As previously mentioned, it is often argued that the INTERPOL Constitution was never submitted for governmental approval or ratification.[42] This allegation is difficult to understand in light of the *Exposé des motifs* of the draft INTERPOL Constitution submitted to the 1955 session of the General Assembly, which expressly stated that '[t]his means that the Organization places itself on an "administrative" level, with, of course, authorization and agreement of the appropriate governmental authorities in each country'.[43] More importantly, the conduct of countries, both during the critical moments in INTERPOL's creation, as well as thereafter, constitutes evidence that the contracting parties to the INTERPOL Constitution expressed their consent to be bound by it.

A. Tacit Acceptance or Approval

Article 45 of the INTERPOL Constitution stipulates that '[a]ll bodies representing the countries mentioned in Appendix I shall be deemed to be Members of the Organization unless they declare through the appropriate governmental authority that they cannot accept this Constitution'. Such a declaration was to be made within six months from the date of the coming into force of the INTERPOL Constitution. According to the President of the ICPC at the 1955 session of the General Assembly, the function of Article 45 is to ensure recognition by countries that were already represented in the ICPC prior to the adoption of the 1956 INTERPOL Constitution.[44] The 'opting out' technique, or rather the 'non-objection' technique, employed in Article 45 of the INTERPOL Constitution to generate consent to be bound was not novel for its time and has been used regularly since.[45] Variations of the technique can be found in Article 22 of the Constitution of the World Health Organization,[46] Article 90 of the Chicago Convention on

[42] Eg, Savino, M, 'Global Administrative Law Meets "Soft" Powers: The Uncomfortable Case of Interpol Red Notices' (2011) 43 *New York University Journal of International Law and Politics*, 263–336 at 271–75.

[43] Resolution No AG/25/1956, Report of the Ad Hoc Sub-Committee, 'Proposed Reform of the ICPC Statutes', 25th session (Vienna, 1956).

[44] Ibid, 8. Ruzié observes, with regard to Article 45, that '*[l]e lien juridique résulte du vote de l'organisme représentatif, suivi du silence de la autorité compétente*' ('[t]he legal link results from the vote of the representative body, followed by the silence of the competent authority' (authors' translation)) (Ruzié, D, 'L'Organisation internationale de police criminelle' (1956) *Annuaire français de droit international* 673–76 at 675). See also: Möllmann, H, *Internationale Kriminalpolizei. Polizei des Völkerrechts: zur Problematik der Abgrenzung öffentlicher und privater internationaler Organisationen am Beispiel der Internationale Kriminalpolizeilichen Organisation (IKPO – INTERPOL)* (Würzburg, Gugel, 1969) 98–9.

[45] See: Lagrange, E, *La représentation institutionnelle dans l'ordre international* (The Hague, Kluwer Law International, 2002) 364–70; Fitzmaurice, M, 'Expression of Consent to be Bound by a Treaty as Developed in Certain Environmental Treaties' in Klabbers, J and Lefeber, R (eds), *Essays on the Law of Treaties: A Collection of Essays in Honour of Bert Vierdag* (The Hague, Martinus Nijhoff Publishers, 1998) 59–80 at 66–70; Bentz, J, 'Le silence comme manifestation de volonté en droit international public' (1963) 67 *Revue Générale de Droit International Public* 144–91.

[46] Constitution of the World Health Organization (adopted on 7 April 1948, entered into force on 7 April 1948) 14 UNTS 185.

International Civil Aviation,[47] Article XV(2) of the Convention on the Prevention of Maritime Pollution by Dumping of Wastes and Other Matter,[48] and Article XV of the Convention to Regulate International Trade in Endangered Species of Flora and Fauna.[49] The typical pattern followed under this technique is summarised in the phrase *qui tacet consentire videtur* and entails the following procedure. First, an international conference or international organisation adopts the text of the agreement by a majority vote. Second, a provision in the text normally stipulates that the contracting parties are deemed to be bound by the agreement unless they express their intention not to be bound within a specified period of time.[50] If a contracting party remains silent, it is deemed to have consented.[51]

A tacit expression of consent to be bound by an international agreement is not excluded under general international law: both customary law and the Vienna Conventions (ie, the VCLT and the VCLT-IO) leave it to the parties as to which procedure they want to follow.[52] Article 11 of the VCLT and the VCLT-IO provides that signature, exchange of instruments constituting a treaty, ratification, acceptance, approval or accession are not the only means by which consent to be bound to a treaty may be expressed on the international plane: consent to be bound by a treaty may also be expressed 'by any other means if so agreed'.[53] In the *Case concerning the Loan Agreement between Italy and Costa Rica*,[54] an international arbitral tribunal confirmed that Article 11 of the VCLT reflects modes of expression of consent to be bound by a treaty.[55] The general position adopted by the ICJ is that where the law prescribes no particular form, the parties are free to choose whatever form they please, provided their intentions are clear.[56] The Court has observed that, while a two-step procedure consisting of signature

[47] Chicago Convention on International Civil Aviation (adopted on 7 December 1944, entered into force on 4 April 1947) 15 UNTS 295.

[48] Convention on the Prevention of Marine Pollution by Dumping of Wastes and Other Matter (adopted on 29 December 1972, entered into force on 30 August 1975) 1046 UNTS 120.

[49] Convention to Regulate International Trade in Endangered Species of Flora and Fauna (adopted on 3 March 1973, entered into force on 1 July 1975) 993 UNTS 243.

[50] Sinclair, I, *The Vienna Convention on the Law of Treaties*, 2nd edn (Manchester, Manchester University Press, 1984) 36.

[51] Fitzmaurice, M, 'The Practical Working of Treaties' in Evans, MD (ed), *International Law*, 5th edn (Oxford, Oxford University Press, 2018) 138–73 at 147. See also: Giuliano, M, Scovazzi, T and Treves, T, *Diritto internazionale* (Milan, Giuffrè, 1991) 296.

[52] *Land and Maritime Boundary between Cameroon and Nigeria (Cameroon v Nigeria: Equatorial Guinea intervening)* (Judgment) [2002] ICJ Rep 303, para 264.

[53] See also: Aust, A, *Modern Treaty Law and Practice*, 3rd edn (Cambridge, Cambridge University Press, 2013) 104.

[54] *Case concerning the Loan Agreement between Italy and Costa Rica (dispute arising under a financing agreement)* (Decision of 26 June 1998) XXV RIAA 21, para 17.

[55] See also: Poiret, F, *Le traité, acte juridique international* (Leiden, Martinus Nijhoff Publishers, 2004) 41–9.

[56] *Case concerning the Temple of Preah Vihear (Cambodia v Thailand)* (Preliminary Objections) [1961] ICJ Rep 17, 31. See also: Brierly, JL, *The Law of Nations* (Oxford, Clarendon Press, reprint 1989) 319–24; McNair, AD, *The Law of Treaties* (Oxford, Clarendon Press, 1961) 150.

and ratification is frequently provided for in provisions regarding the entry into force of a treaty, there are also cases where the treaty enters into force immediately upon signature.[57] However, as pointed out by the ICJ in *Continental Shelf (Tunisia/Libyan Arab Jamahiriya)*, a tacit expression of consent cannot be inferred when either the circumstances of the law or manifested attitude of the parties exclude the possibility.[58] That being said, the caution expressed in *Continental Shelf (Tunisia/Libyan Arab Jamahiriya)* is irrelevant in the case of INTERPOL because, on 17 September 1956, the INTERPOL Secretary General addressed the following letter to all the heads of the National Central Bureaux ('NCBs') of the countries referred to in Article 45 of the INTERPOL Constitution:

> [t]he General Assembly, meeting at its 25th session, adopted a new Constitution of which article 45 is as follows:
>
> > All bodies representing the countries mentioned in Appendix I shall be deemed to be Members of the Organisation unless they declare through the appropriate governmental authority that they cannot accept this Constitution. Such a declaration should be made within six months of the date of the coming into force of the present Constitution.
>
> Appendix I includes the following countries:
>
> > Argentina, Australia, Austria, Belgium, Brazil, Burma, Cambodia, Canada, Ceylon, Chile, Colombia, Costa Rica, Cuba, Denmark, Dominican Republic, Egypt, Eire, Finland, France, Federal German Republic, Greece, Guatemala, India, Indonesia, Iran, Israel, Italy, Japan, Jordan, Lebanon, Liberia, Libya, Luxembourg, Mexico, Monaco, Netherlands, Netherlands Antilles, New Zealand, Norway, Pakistan, Philippines, Portugal, Saar, Saudi Arabia, Spain, Sudan, Surinam, Sweden, Switzerland, Syria, Thailand, Turkey, United Kingdom of Great Britain and Northern Ireland, United States of America, Uruguay, Venezuela, Yugoslavia.
>
> As the Constitution came into force on 13 June 1956, I should like to remind you that if your country wishes to decline to accept this Constitution, it should do so before 13 December next, through the appropriate governmental authority.
>
> I enclose two copies of this text.
>
> However, we naturally very much hope that no country will apply article 45.

Following this, in his activities' report to the 1957 session of the General Assembly, the INTERPOL Secretary General reported as follows: '*il m'est agréable de dire que le nouveau statut a reçu un accueil unanimement favorable; pratiquement, tous les pays l'ont accepté*'.[59] The foregoing clearly refutes the assertion that the INTERPOL

[57] *Land and Maritime Boundary between Cameroon and Nigeria (Cameroon v Nigeria: Equatorial Guinea intervening)* (Judgment) [2002] ICJ Rep 303, para 264.

[58] *Continental Shelf (Tunisia/Libyan Arab Jamahiriya)* (Judgment) [1982] ICJ Rep 18, paras 117–18.

[59] '[I]t is nice to say that the new statute has received a unanimously favorable reception; practically all countries have accepted it' (authors' translation) (INTERPOL, Report No. 1, 'Rapport d'activité pour la période du Ier Juin 1956 au Ier Juin 1957, et programme de travail', Doc AG/26/1957). See also: Barnett, M and Coleman, L, 'Designing Police: Interpol and the Study of Change in International Organizations' (2005) 49 *International Studies Quarterly* 593–619 at 607 and the sources cited therein.

Constitution was not submitted for governmental approval or ratification, at least insofar as the countries who participated in the 1956 reconstitution of the Organisation are concerned. Indeed, Valleix explicitly calls the INTERPOL Constitution a tacit agreement ('*accord tacite*').[60]

B. Accession[61]

Whereas Article 45 deals with the acceptance of the INTERPOL Constitution by the countries of those police bodies which were represented at the 1956 conference, Article 4 of the INTERPOL Constitution concerns the consent to be bound by countries who joined the Organisation after 1956.[62] In respect of Article 4, it is interesting to note that, of the three authoritative versions of the INTERPOL Constitution, the versions do not completely correlate.[63] According to the French version of paragraph 2 of Article 4 of the INTERPOL Constitution, '*la demande d'adhésion*' should be submitted by the competent government authority.[64] However, the English version speaks of a 'request for membership' by the appropriate government authority and the Spanish version employs the language '*la solicitud de admisión*'.[65] What all three versions have in common is that a request from the government of a country is a *condition sine qua non* for countries that were not previously represented (ie, the countries not contemplated by Appendix I to the INTERPOL Constitution) to join the Organisation.

The public records of the Organisation show that requests under Article 4 of the INTERPOL Constitution have indeed been made by government authorities acting on behalf of their countries. In several cases, the requesting authority has been either the head of State or head of government.[66] The ICJ has remarked

[60] Valleix, C, 'INTERPOL' (1984) 88 *Revue Générale de Droit International Public* 629–30. In the same sense, see: Eick, C and Tritel, A, 'Verfassungsrechtliche bedenken gegen deutsche mitarbeit bei INTERPOL' (1985) 4 *Europäische Grundrechte Zeitschrift* 81–4 at 82.

[61] 'Where a treaty is the constitutive instrument of an international organization, the admission of a new Member State (on such terms and conditions as the constitutive instrument may lay down) may be regarded as equivalent to accession' (Berman, F and Bentley, D, 'Ratification, Accession, Acceptance and Approval, Treaty Succession' in Roberts, I (ed), *Satow's Diplomatic Practice*, 7th edn (Oxford, Oxford University Press, 2017) 628–43 at 637).

[62] See: *Membership of INTERPOL*, available at: www.interpol.int/en/Who-we-are/Legal-framework/Membership-of-INTERPOL.

[63] Article 43 of the INTERPOL Constitution declares that the French, English and Spanish texts shall be authoritative.

[64] '*La demande d'adhésion doit être présenté au Secrétaire General par l'autorité gouvernement compétente*'.

[65] '*La petición de ingreso deberá presentarse al Secretario General por la autoridad gubernamental competente*'.

[66] Eg, Azerbaijan, Andorra, Antigua and Barbuda, Bahamas, Bahrain, Botswana, Brunei, Burkina Faso, Chad, Columbia, Congo, Fiji, Gabon, Guinea, Jamaica, Libya, Lichtenstein, Lithuania, Malta, Malawi, Mauritius, Mauritania, Nigeria, Saint Lucia, Saint Vincent and the Grenadines, Sierra Leone, Swaziland, Tanzania, Tonga, Ukraine, Yemen, Zambia.

that, '[a]ccording to international law, there is no doubt that every Head of State is presumed to be able to act on behalf of the State in its international relations'.[67] Moreover, statements and communications, whether oral or written, by a head of State or head of government acting in that capacity are acts of the State concerned for the purposes of international relations.[68] Requests for participation in INTERPOL have also been made by ministers of foreign affairs.[69] As mentioned above, a well-established rule of international law prescribes that, in addition to the head of State or the head of government, the minister of foreign affairs is deemed to represent the State by the sole virtue of the exercise of his/her functions, including in creating a legal relationship that binds the said State to an international organisation.[70] Furthermore, in *Armed Activities on the Territory of the Congo*, the ICJ rejected the proposition that a minister of justice could not bind a State in matters of international relations. In so doing, it noted that:

> with increasing frequency in modern international relations other persons representing a State in specific fields may be authorized by that State to bind it by their statements in respect of matters falling within their purview. This may be true, for example, of holders of technical ministerial portfolios exercising powers in their field of competence in the area of foreign relations, and even of certain officials.[71]

This was confirmed by the ICJ in *Maritime Delimitation in the Indian Ocean (Somalia v Kenya)*. The Court observed that, under international law, other officials may be authorised to adopt, on behalf of a State, the text of a treaty or to express the consent of the State to be bound by a treaty.[72] In the context of Article 4 of the INTERPOL Constitution, many of the requests for membership have been made by different ministers, including ministers of justice and ministers of interior, in addition to various other officials whose responsibilities include

[67] *Application of the Convention on the Prevention and Punishment of the Crime of Genocide (Bosnia and Herzegovina v Yugoslavia)* (Preliminary Objections) [1996] ICJ Rep 595, para 44.

[68] *Nuclear Tests (New Zealand v France)* (Judgment) [1974] ICJ Rep 457, para 51.

[69] Eg, Algeria, Bangladesh, Barbados, Belize, Brazil (on its original admission in 1953), Bulgaria (on its readmission in 1989), Cambodia, Cameroon, Croatia, Czech Republic, Dominica, Dominican Republic, El Salvador, Equatorial Guinea, Georgia, Grenada, Guyana, Honduras, Iceland, Israel, Kenya, Kuwait, Laos, Lesotho, Liberia, Madagascar, Maldives, Monaco, Mozambique, Nauru, Nepal, New Zealand, Panama, Papua New Guinea, Paraguay, Qatar, Romania (on its readmission in 1973), Rwanda, Senegal, Seychelles, Slovenia, Somalia, South Africa (on its original admission in 1948), Sudan, Sri Lanka, Tajikistan, Vatican City State, Vietnam (on its original admission in 1970), Zimbabwe.

[70] *Armed Activities on the Territory of the Congo (New Application: 2002) (Democratic Republic of the Congo v Rwanda)* (Jurisdiction and Admissibility) [2006] ICJ Rep 6, para 46. See also: 'Guiding principles applicable to unilateral declarations of States capable of creating legal obligations' in *Yearbook of the International Law Commission* (2006) Vol II, Part Two, 161.

[71] *Armed Activities on the Territory of the Congo (New Application: 2002) (Democratic Republic of the Congo v Rwanda)* (Jurisdiction and Admissibility) [2006] ICJ Rep 6, para 47.

[72] *Maritime Delimitation in the Indian Ocean (Somalia v Kenya) (Preliminary Objections)* [2017] ICJ Rep 3, para 43.

international police enforcement cooperation.[73] Such requests for membership should be understood as expressions of consent to be bound by the INTERPOL Constitution.[74]

C. Conduct

The conduct of a country after the negotiation and adoption of an international agreement can be viewed as a reflection of 'treaty behaviour'.[75] That is, party behaviour after negotiations and the ceremonies associated with adoption can reflect the sustained implementation (or not) of an international agreement.[76] In applying this to INTERPOL, it can be said that the INTERPOL Constitution has enjoyed consistent adherence by the original, as well as subsequent, members. For instance, the INTERPOL Constitution provides that both the original members and the subsequent members should (1) appoint NCBs pursuant to Article 32, (2) appoint delegations to the INTERPOL General Assembly under Article 7, and (3) pay financial contributions (also known as subscriptions) pursuant to Article 38(a). In this context, the behaviour of members with respect to their financial contributions has proved to be very revealing. Article 39 of the INTERPOL Constitution states that the General Assembly shall establish the basis of members' subscriptions and determine the maximum annual expenditure based on an estimate provided by the INTERPOL Secretary General. Pursuant to Article 51 of the INTERPOL General Regulations,[77] the determination of statutory contributions and payment conditions shall be set out in the INTERPOL Financial Regulations.[78] Regulation 3(2)

[73] Eg, Albania, Angola, Argentina, Armenia, Aruba, Australia, Austria (on its readmission in 1948), Belarus, Bolivia, Bosnia and Herzegovina, Brazil (on its readmission in 1986), Burundi, Canada, Cape Verde, Central African Republic, China (on its readmission in 1984), Comoros, Democratic Republic of the Congo, Costa Rica, Cyprus, Djibouti, Ecuador, Eritrea, Estonia, Ethiopia, Spain, Estonia, Former Yugoslav Republic of Macedonia, Gambia, Germany (on its readmission in 1952), Ghana, Guatemala, Guinea-Bissau, Haiti, Hungary (on its readmission in 1981), India, Indonesia, Iran, Iraq, Ireland, Italy (on its readmission in 1947), Japan, Jordan, Kazakhstan, Kyrgyzstan, Latvia, Lebanon, Mali, Malaysia, Marshall Islands, Morocco, Mauritius, Mexico, Moldova, Mongolia, Montenegro, Morocco, Mozambique, Myanmar, Namibia, Netherlands Antilles, Nicaragua, Niger, Oman, Pakistan, Peru, Philippines, Poland (on its readmission in 1990), Republic of Korea, Russia, Saint Kitts and Nevis, Sao Tome and Principe, Saudi Arabia, Serbia and Montenegro, Singapore, Slovakia, South Africa (on its readmission in 1993), Spain, Suriname, Thailand, Togo, Trinidad and Tobago, Tunisia, Uganda, United Arab Emirates.

[74] Pezard, A, 'L'organisation internationale de police criminelle et son accord de siège' (1983) 29 *Annuaire français de droit international* 567.

[75] Johnston, DM, *Consent and Commitment in the World Community* (New York, Transnational Publishers, 1997) 143–63. See also: Poirat, F, *Le traité, acte juridique international* (Leiden, Martinus Nijhoff Publishers, 2004) 33, referring to Cot, J-P, 'La conduite subséquente des parties à un traité' (1966) 70 *Revue Générale de Droit International Public* 632–66.

[76] Johnston, DM, *Consent and Commitment in the World Community* (New York, Transnational Publishers, 1997) 143–63.

[77] INTERPOL General Regulations [I/GREG/GA/1956(2019)] ('General Regulations').

[78] INTERPOL Financial Regulations [II.C/FREG/GA/1985/1985(2019)] [II.C/FRUL/EC/2005(2014)] ('Financial Regulations').

of the Financial Regulations stipulates that statutory contributions are due annually and are compulsory. Statutory contributions are distributed among members on the basis of their ability to pay, while the procedures and scales used to determine the distribution of contributions are adopted by the INTERPOL General Assembly. In practice, members give full powers to their delegations to enable them to participate in the voting. Members that might have voted against the assessment or that were not represented at the session of the INTERPOL General Assembly are obligated to accept the assessment and pay their dues. Moreover, members that, for whatever reason, are unable to pay, are also obligated to acknowledge their financial obligations and enter into debt rescheduling agreements with the Organisation[79] or accept the sanctions on arrears enshrined in Article 52 of the General Regulations, which include suspension of voting rights, non-eligibility of its delegates for membership in the Executive Committee and the loss of the right to propose candidates for elected offices. The parties' continued compliance with these provisions represents a manifestation of their consent to be bound by the INTERPOL Constitution.

In light of the foregoing, it is clear that Reuter was right to observe that it is hardly imaginable how and on what ground any of the countries involved would be able to deny their consent to be bound by the INTERPOL Constitution.[80]

[79] Eg, 'Antigua and Barbuda Minister signs debt-rescheduling agreement with INTERPOL', INTERPOL press release (5 September 2007).

[80] Reuter, P, 'Problèmes juridiques relatifs au statut de l'OIPC-Interpol' in *INTERPOL–Les textes fondamentaux de l'Organisation internationale de police criminelle* (Paris, Presses Universitaires de France, 2001) 45–67 at 49–50.

4

Contracting Parties and Members

We now turn our attention to the topic of the capacity of the contracting parties to the Constitution of the International Criminal Police Organization ('INTERPOL' or the 'Organisation'). The question to be addressed in this chapter is whether the concurrence of wills reflected in the INTERPOL Constitution is attributable to two or more subjects of international law. As is shown by the case of the International Monetary Fund ('IMF'), whenever the constituent instrument of an international organisation employs a term other than 'State', legal discussions arise with respect to the nature of the organisation and its constituent instrument.[1] The INTERPOL Constitution employs the terms 'States', 'countries' and 'official police bod[ies]'.[2]

To understand who are the contracting parties to the INTERPOL Constitution, there are at least three approaches: (1) regard the INTERPOL Constitution as a special type of agreement under international law, (2) distinguish the issue of membership in INTERPOL from that of being a party to the INTERPOL Constitution, or (3) interpret the INTERPOL Constitution such that the parties to the INTERPOL Constitution are the members of the Organisation. As will become apparent, the third approach best reflects the practice of INTERPOL. However, for the sake of completeness, the two other approaches will be briefly discussed before analysing the third approach.

With respect to the first approach, namely, that which considers the INTERPOL Constitution as a special type of agreement under international law, the United Nations ('UN') Office of Legal Affairs considered the phenomenon of public authorities coming together and agreeing on institutionalised cooperation in 1971 in the context of the establishment of a clearing union by central banks and monetary authorities.[3] It observed:

> the principle that an international legal person can be created by virtue of a treaty is, after all, nothing more than a rule of customary international law, and it may well be

[1] See: Obeyesekere, SC, 'The Distinction between "Inter-Governmental" and "Inter-State" Treaties and Organizations: The International Monetary Fund Agreement' (1982) 22 *Indian Journal of International Law* 439–47; Gold, J, 'The Distinction between "Inter-Governmental" and "Inter-State" Treaties and Organizations: The International Monetary Fund Agreement: A Note on Obeyesekere's Note' in Gold, J, *Legal and Institutional Aspects of the International Monetary System: Selected Essays*, Vol II (Washington DC, International Monetary Fund, 1984) 879–89.

[2] See, eg: INTERPOL Constitution, Arts 4 and 45 and App 1.

[3] 'Fundamental legal issues raised by the draft of an Asian Clearing Union Agreement to be concluded between the "central banks and monetary authorities" of various countries – Question of the

> that a new customary rule of international law is emerging under which such a legal person could also be created by an agreement concluded solely by autonomous public entities, such an agreement being governed by international law pursuant to another new customary rule.[4]

For such a customary rule to have evolved, the practice of such public entities must constitute acts of States, ie, conduct attributable to States,[5] – a necessary element for the formation of custom under international law. If this is what the UN Office of Legal Affairs had in mind, it is safe to say that agreements concluded by these public entities qualify as treaties under international law.[6] Indeed, as pointed out by Klabbers, if inter-institutional agreements with foreign governmental agencies or international organisations are governed by international law, the responsibility of the State is involved.[7] It would appear that this approach inspired Morgenstern's assertion that INTERPOL's constituent instrument is a so-called inter-departmental agreement under international law.[8] Similarly, the foregoing theory supports Randelzhofer's conclusion that the INTERPOL Constitution is '*eines völkerrechtlichen Verwaltungsabkommens*'.[9]

The second approach distinguishes the issue of membership in INTERPOL from that of being a party to the INTERPOL Constitution. To appreciate this approach, one must acknowledge the difference between '(1) the constituent instrument of the organization which is subject to the *lex generalis* on the coming to birth of treaties, and (2) the constitution which sets up the *lex specialis* or rules to govern the life and functioning of the organization'.[10] Questions concerning membership and related rights and obligations pertain to the latter category, whereas questions concerning the characterisation of the constituent instrument

law governing such an agreement – Question whether the Clearing Union thus established would be endowed with legal personality and could claim privileges and immunities – Determination of the entitles eligible to become parties to the Agreement' in *United Nations Juridical Yearbook* (1971) Part Two, Chapter VI, 215–18. On such clearing unions, see: Edwards, R, *International Monetary Collaboration* (Dobbs Ferry, New York, Transnational Publishers, 1985) 303–10.

[4] 'Fundamental legal issues raised by the draft of an Asian Clearing Union Agreement to be concluded between the "central banks and monetary authorities" of various countries – Question of the law governing such an agreement – Question whether the Clearing Union thus established would be endowed with legal personality and could claim privileges and immunities – Determination of the entitles eligible to become parties to the Agreement' in *United Nations Juridical Yearbook* (1971) Part Two, Chapter VI, 218.

[5] Villiger, ME, *Customary International Law and Treaties*, 2nd edn (The Hague, Kluwer Law International, 1997) 16–7.

[6] But see: van den Brandhoff, JCE, 'Administratieve overeenkomsten in het internationaal publiekrecht' (1986) 40 *Nederlandse Juristenblad* 1277–82.

[7] Klabbers, J, *The Concept of Treaty in International Law* (The Hague, Kluwer Law International, 1996) 104.

[8] Morgenstern, F, *Legal Problems of International Organizations* (Cambridge, Grotius, 1986) 21–2.

[9] '[A]n international administrative agreement' (authors' translation) (Randelzhofer, A, 'Rechtsschutz gegen Maßnahmen von INTERPOL vor deutschen Gerichten?' in *Festschrift für Hans-Jürgen Schlochauer* (Berlin, Walter de Gruyter, 1981) 542).

[10] *Appeal Relating to the Jurisdiction of the ICAO Council* (Judgment) [1972] ICJ Rep 46, 129–30 (Separate Opinion of Judge de Castro).

as an agreement governed by international law belong to the former.[11] From the perspective of the law of treaties, the contracting parties to a constituent instrument of an international organisation need not be members of that organisation. This was recognised in 2002 by an ad hoc international arbitral tribunal in the *BIS Share Repurchase* case.[12] The arbitral tribunal observed that the Bank for International Settlements ('BIS') was established under international law in conformity with a treaty between the governments of Belgium, France, Germany, Italy, Japan and the United Kingdom ('UK'); however, the original members of the BIS were central banks.[13] Similarly, Article IV A of the Agreement for the establishment of the Joint Vienna Institute makes a distinction between the parties to the agreement and certain categories of members.[14] The Constitution of the World Health Organization ('WHO') also allows States to become members of the WHO without becoming a party to the constituent instrument, provided their application for membership has been approved by a simple majority vote of the World Health Assembly.[15] It could be argued that certain aspects of this approach are reflected in the Polish Government's study, as carried out by an expert group set up by the INTERPOL General Assembly to amend the INTERPOL Constitution. The study first answers the question whether the INTERPOL Constitution comprises an agreement under international law, and thereafter concludes that police bodies are the formal members of INTERPOL and not the countries or States themselves (although the Polish Government disapproves of this phenomenon as out of date).[16]

Finally, a third approach is suggested by Reuter, whose view is shared by Valleix,[17] in a 1980 legal opinion to INTERPOL.[18] This approach suggests that the parties to the INTERPOL Constitution are also the members of the Organisation

[11] Rosenne, S, *Developments in the Law of Treaties 1945–1986* (Cambridge, Cambridge University Press, 1989) 256–58.

[12] *Partial Award on the lawfulness of the recall of the privately held shares on 8 January 2001 and the applicable standards for valuation of those shares* (Partial Award of 22 November 2002) XXIII RIAA 183, paras 108 and 147.

[13] As at 1 April 2020, 62 central banks and monetary authorities are members of the BIS and have rights of voting and representation at General Meetings. On the legal status of the BIS, see: Bederman, D, 'The Unique Legal Status of the Bank for International Settlements Comes into Focus' (2003) 16 *Leiden Journal of International Law* 787–94. See also: Bermejo, R, 'La banque des recèlements internationaux: approche juridique' (1989) 2 *Hague Yearbook of International Law* 94–130 at 100–01. For an early discussion of BIS' legal character, see: Williams, JF, 'The Legal Character of the Bank for International Settlements' (October 1930) 24 *American Journal of International Law* 665–73.

[14] Agreement for the establishment of the Joint Vienna Institute (entered into force on 19 August 1994) 2029 UNTS 391.

[15] Constitution of the World Health Organization (adopted on 15 February 1946, entered into force on 7 April 1948) 14 UNTS 185, Art 6.

[16] 'Study by Poland on the legal nature of ICPO-INTERPOL', Doc AGN/63/RAP. No. 11, 63rd session (Rome, 1994).

[17] Valleix, C, 'INTERPOL' (1984) 88 *Revue Générale de Droit International Public* 631–33.

[18] Reuter, P, 'Problèmes juridiques relatifs au statut de l'OIPC-Interpol' in *INTERPOL–Les textes fondamentaux de l'Organisation internationale de police criminelle* (Paris, Presses Universitaires de France, 2001) 45–67.

and, in each case, are countries (or States, on which see below). The following sections are dedicated to this approach.

I. Countries as Parties to the INTERPOL Constitution and as Members

In Chapter 3, it was established that countries negotiated and adopted the INTERPOL Constitution and expressed their consent to be bound by it. In his legal opinion, Reuter equates parties to the INTERPOL Constitution with members of the Organisation. Reuter is of the view that when a country becomes a member of the Organisation through the procedure prescribed in Article 4 of the INTERPOL Constitution, then that country accedes to the INTERPOL Constitution.[19] Reuter's view that the parties to the INTERPOL Constitution and the members of the Organisation are countries is borne out by the practice of INTEROL. Consideration of three areas of INTERPOL's practice will suffice.

First, INTERPOL itself has expressly stated that it no longer regards police bodies as members of the Organisation. In 2007, the then INTERPOL Secretary General, Ronald K Noble, stated that:

> [b]ack in 1923, and back in the first half of Interpol's existence, countries did not join the organization, police organizations joined …
>
> Over time, as Interpol established itself more and more and without any express decision being taken to do so, countries eventually replaced the individual police organisations as its members. We became the world's largest police organisation of member countries.[20]

This may explain why, in speeches made during the sessions of the INTERPOL General Assembly and in the documents of the Organisation, as well as in some secondary rules, the terms 'Member State' and 'Member country' are used despite the fact that the INTERPOL Constitution does not use either of these terms. It is possible to regard these as non-prescriptive terms from which no defined legal consequences necessarily accrue;[21] however, the fact that the terms are used in some secondary rules adopted by the INTERPOL General Assembly confirms a 'self-understanding' on the part of the Organisation.

[19] Reuter, P, 'Problèmes juridiques relatifs au statut de l'OIPC-Interpol' in *INTERPOL–Les textes fondamentaux de l'Organisation internationale de police criminelle* (Paris, Presses Universitaires de France, 2001) 45–67 at 47–8. Article 4 provides that '[a]ny country may delegate as a Member to the Organisation any official police body whose functions come within the framework of the Organisation'.

[20] Noble, RK, Secretary General of INTERPOL, 'Preventing the Emergence of the Next Generation of Terrorists' (Speech at the International Terrorism Conference, Lyon, 3–5 April 2007).

[21] For a comparable discrepancy between the formal vocabulary and common language in another international organisation, see: de Vries, MG, *The International Monetary Fund 1972–1978* (Washington DC, International Monetary Fund, 1985) 661. And for the endless debate about the legal nature of IMF's stand-by arrangements, see: Gold, J, 'The Legal Character of the Fund's Stand-by Arrangements and Why it Matters' (Washington DC, IMF Pamphlet Series No 35, 1980).

Second, and relatedly, the practice of the INTERPOL General Assembly since 1956, as per Article 4 of the INTERPOL Constitution, has been to approve the membership applications of States or countries, rather than that of police bodies.[22]

Third, the practice followed by the Organisation in cases involving State continuity and State succession indicates that, in such cases, it is States (and not police bodies) which remain, or apply to be, members. Like other international organisations based on *inter potestas* agreements, INTERPOL has followed the rules and practices (to the extent settled rules and practices have emerged) with regard to State continuity and State succession as concerns membership in international organisations, even though the INTERPOL Constitution is silent on the matter. In most cases, the new State was required to apply for membership while the surviving State continued the membership. For instance, on the dissolution of the Union of Soviet Socialist Republics ('USSR'), the Russian Federation continued the membership of the USSR in the Organisation, while the other former Soviet republics were required to apply for new membership. The implications of the dissolution of the Socialist Federal Republic of Yugoslavia ('Yugoslavia') were not as straightforward. In the wake of the disintegration of Yugoslavia, the Federal Republic of Yugoslavia declared that it was the sole successor of Yugoslavia. Bosnia and Herzegovina, the Republic of Croatia, the Republic of Slovenia and the former Yugoslav Republic of Macedonia (now the Republic of North Macedonia) each submitted requests for membership to INTERPOL, which were approved by the INTERPOL General Assembly at its 61st session in Dakar in 1992. At this session, the UK delegation argued that the matter of the continuity of membership of Yugoslavia should also be given serious consideration, but the President was of the view that the matter should be discussed outside the General Assembly. At the request of the Belgian delegation, the issue of continuity of membership of Yugoslavia was considered at the 62nd session of the General Assembly. The INTERPOL General Assembly was of the view that continuity of membership would not be in conformity with the views of the international community. It referred to Resolution 47/1 of the UN General Assembly, which stated that the Federal Republic of Yugoslavia was not the legal continuation of Yugoslavia, a view primarily based on the opinion of the Badinter Arbitration Committee, which concluded that the Federal Republic of Yugoslavia is a new State and not the continuation of Yugoslavia.[23] Consequently, through Resolution AGN/62/RES/1,

[22] Eg, Resolution No AG-2004-RES-01, 'Application for membership by Tajikistan', INTERPOL General Assembly, 73rd session (Cancún, 2004); Resolution No AG-2005-RES-01, 'Application for membership from the Kingdom of Bhutan', INTERPOL General Assembly, 74th session (Berlin, 2005); Resolution No AG-2005-RES-02, 'Application for membership by the Republic of Turkmenistan', INTERPOL General Assembly, 74th session (Berlin, 2005).

[23] Ragazzi, M, 'Conference on Yugoslavia Arbitration Commission: Opinions on Questions Arising from the Dissolution of Yugoslavia' (1992), 31 *International Legal Materials* 1488. The International Court of Justice ('ICJ') confirmed this view in its judgment of 15 December 2004 in *Legality of Use of Force (Serbia and Montenegro v Belgium)* (Preliminary Objections) [2004] ICJ Rep 279.

the INTERPOL General Assembly decided that the Federal Republic of Yugoslavia could not continue the membership of Yugoslavia and that it should apply for a new membership.[24] The Federal Republic of Yugoslavia subsequently applied and was admitted as a member of INTERPOL by the General Assembly during its 70th session in Budapest in 2001.[25]

The Organisation's practice in cases involving State continuity and State succession should not, however, suggest that the INTERPOL General Assembly is subservient to the international community as regards membership. For example, South Africa was a member of the International Criminal Police Commission ('ICPC') (the prior name of INTERPOL) from 1948 to 1955. On 29 September 1993, South Africa applied for membership in INTERPOL. The INTERPOL Executive Committee considered its application at its 105th session. The members of the Executive Committee noted that South Africa's membership would be beneficial for INTERPOL. The INTERPOL Secretary General likewise agreed and observed that some countries in the region had already started cooperating with South Africa's police forces. Nevertheless, one of the concerns expressed by members from African countries and the INTERPOL President was related to South Africa's position in the UN. The elimination of apartheid had been on the agenda of the UN since its inception: the UN had imposed sanctions on South Africa for three decades, adopted General Assembly Resolution A/RES/S-16/1 ('Declaration on *Apartheid* and its Destructive Consequences in Southern Africa') in 1989, and established a UN Observation Mission in South Africa to report on the transition from apartheid in 1992. The INTERPOL Secretary General cautioned that INTERPOL should decide whether or not to admit South Africa as a member independently of its status within the UN, in light of what is best for the Organisation. The Executive Committee unanimously decided to submit South Africa's application for membership to the INTERPOL General Assembly. It was approved and South Africa became a member of INTERPOL on 29 September 1993.[26]

[24] Resolution No AGN/62/RES/1, 'Status of the Federal Republic of Yugoslavia', INTERPOL General Assembly, 62nd session (Aruba, 1993).

[25] Resolution No AG-2006-RES-01, 'Membership of the Republic of Montenegro', INTERPOL General Assembly, 75th session (Rio de Janeiro, 2006). After the adoption and promulgation of the Constitutional Charter of Serbia and Montenegro on 4 February 2003, the Federal Republic of Yugoslavia adopted the name Serbia and Montenegro. In May 2006, Montenegro voted for independence, and the Parliament of Montenegro adopted the Declaration of Independence on 3 June 2006. Serbia claimed continuity of membership of Serbia and Montenegro in INTERPOL, and Montenegro submitted a new request for membership. This approach was in line with the view of the international community whereby Serbia was the legal successor of Serbia and Montenegro, and Montenegro was a newly independent State. In this instance, Serbia's claim of continuity was not contested by Montenegro or any other INTERPOL member. The INTERPOL General Assembly, therefore, approved Montenegro's application as a new member of INTERPOL.

[26] For a discussion of South Africa's membership in INTERPOL, see: INTERPOL Membership – Historical Perspective, 11–2.

II. Are Countries Subjects of International Law?

As noted above, Reuter delivered a legal opinion to INTERPOL in 1980. Although his approach was correct (ie, the parties to the INTERPOL Constitution and the members of the Organisation are the same), his view that INTERPOL's members are States does not entirely explain INTERPOL's situation.[27] Reuter's approach needs to take better account of the reality of the Organisation. Specifically, his use of the term 'States' is not recommended for the purposes of determining who are the parties to the INTERPOL Constitution and whether they are subjects of international law.

The original proposal for the INTERPOL Constitution submitted to the 1955 session of the ICPC General Assembly provided in draft Article 3 that any 'State' has the right to become a member.[28] Draft Article 5 contemplated the 'associate' membership of territories or group of territories not responsible for the conduct of their international foreign relations. During the plenary session of 5 September 1955, these proposals encountered significant opposition. The Indian delegate was the first to oppose this approach in favour of a functional approach towards membership.[29] He voiced the view that any country, whether autonomous or not, should be able to join in its own right and that no distinction should be made between countries which, whatever their political status, had to solve the same problems in the field of crime. India was partly supported by the Dutch delegate who pointed to the position of Suriname and the Netherlands Antilles, which were already represented in the ICPC in their own right. Faced with many questions, proposed amendments and opposition related to several aspects of the proposed text, the ICPC General Assembly unanimously adopted a resolution to refer the matter back to the sub-committee responsible for drafting the INTERPOL Constitution. The resolution stated that '[t]he term "member states" should be replaced with some expression that the sub-committee – which was to continue its work until the next meeting of the Assembly – was attempting to find'.[30] When the draft was resubmitted to the 1956 session of the ICPC General Assembly, it no longer contained the proposal for membership of States, or the distinction between members and associate members.[31] Instead, the INTERPOL Constitution employed (and continues to employ) the terms 'countries', 'States' and 'official police body'. Article 45 of the INTERPOL Constitution states that '[a]ll

[27] Reuter, P, 'Problèmes juridiques relatifs au statut de l'OIPC-Interpol' in *INTERPOL–Les textes fondamentaux de l'Organisation internationale de police criminelle* (Paris, Presses Universitaires de France, 2001) 45–67 at 48.

[28] Resolution No AG/24/1955, Report No 3.

[29] On the concept of functional membership, see: Fawcett, JES, 'The Place of Law in an International Organization' (1960) 36 *British Yearbook of International Law* 321–42 at 341.

[30] Resolution No AG/24/1955, 4.

[31] Resolution No AG/25/1956, Report of the Ad Hoc Sub-Committee, 'Proposed Reform of the ICPC Statutes', ICPC General Assembly, 25th session (Vienna, 1956).

bodies representing the countries mentioned in Appendix I[32] shall be deemed to be Members of the Organization unless they declare through the appropriate governmental authority that they cannot accept this Constitution', and Article 4 provides that '[a]ny country may delegate as a Member to the Organization any official police body whose functions come within the framework of activities of the Organization', although membership is 'subject to approval by a two-thirds majority of the General Assembly'.

In 1986, the issue of membership came to the fore once again in a proposal from the INTERPOL Executive Committee to amend the INTERPOL Constitution to institute the membership of States.[33] The discussion in the Commission on the Revision of the INTERPOL Constitution revealed that there was no sympathy for the proposal.[34] The issue of who should be members of INTERPOL was revisited again during the 61st session of the INTERPOL General Assembly in 1992.[35] The discussions held on this occasion revealed that no majority solution would surface. The INTERPOL General Assembly therefore requested that an expert group study the possibility of amending the INTERPOL Constitution. Throughout 1993/94, no agreement could be reached, so the INTERPOL General Assembly resolved at its 63rd session in 1994 that the work of the expert group should be discontinued until such time as an amendment to the INTERPOL Constitution was imperative.[36] In June 2011, the INTERPOL General Secretariat presented the Executive Committee with a report titled 'INTERPOL's Policy Regarding Membership'.[37] The General Secretariat suggested that it was an appropriate time for INTERPOL to affirm that it interprets the term 'country' in Article 4 of the INTERPOL Constitution to mean 'sovereign State', and it attached a draft resolution to that effect. However, some Executive Committee members urged caution, so this suggestion was not placed on the agenda of the INTERPOL General Assembly.

In 2016, in light of requests for membership by the Republic of Kosovo ('Kosovo'), Palestine and the Solomon Islands, the INTERPOL General Assembly appointed Hans Corell as an Adviser to the Organisation to conduct a study and make recommendations on the process for membership of INTERPOL. He submitted a report to the 86th session of the INTERPOL General Assembly ('Report').

[32] Unhelpfully, Appendix 1 is titled 'list of States to which the provisions of Article 45 of the Constitution shall apply' (emphasis added) but includes a number of non-State entities in the list.

[33] Resolution No AGN/55, Report No 12, INTERPOL General Assembly, 55th session (Belgrade, 1956).

[34] AGN/55/COM/STAT.

[35] Resolution No AGN/61/RES/5, 'Expert Group on the amendment of INTERPOL's Constitution', INTERPOL General Assembly, 61st session (Dakar, 1992).

[36] Resolution No AGN/63/RES/8, 'Amendment of the Constitution', INTERPOL General Assembly, 63rd session (Rome, 1994).

[37] Report CE-2011-2-DOC-16, referred to in INTERPOL Membership – Historical Perspective, 19.

In reliance on the Report, the INTERPOL General Assembly resolved to interpret the term 'country' in Article 4 as 'State' and to restrict INTERPOL membership in the future to 'States'. It also adopted 'Guidelines for requests for membership of INTERPOL' and 'Procedures for joining INTERPOL'.[38]

There are three substantial difficulties that arise in equating 'country' with 'State'. First, equating the terms 'country' and 'State' is at odds with the original intention of the drafters of the INTERPOL Constitution, as well as its evolutive interpretation. Second, it further politicises INTERPOL membership. Finally, it is against the functional scope of the Organisation. Each of these issues is discussed in turn below.

First, as discussed above, the draft of the INTERPOL Constitution presented to the 24th session of the ICPC General Assembly in 1956 included the term 'State' in draft Article 3. However, some members feared that this language would detract from the technical character of the Organisation, thus reducing its independence and efficiency, and interfere with the ability of an autonomous police force to join the Organisation, regardless of its legal status.[39] Members, therefore, deliberately chose to adopt the term 'country' in the text of the INTERPOL Constitution to distinguish it from 'State' and to allow for the possibility of expanding the scope of the Organisation beyond the limiting markers of statehood. Further, although the practice of INTERPOL, with a few notable exceptions, has been to admit States as members, this is an insufficient indicator of evolving interpretation of the term 'country'. Membership patterns of INTERPOL are not per se reflective of a concerted practice disallowing membership to entities other than States. On the contrary, a development in law relating to membership would be manifest if INTERPOL had consistently rejected membership of entities that are not States.[40] Evolutive interpretation would, in fact, favour expanding the scope of membership to enhance the functional efficiency and effectiveness[41] of the technical organisation.[42]

Second, equating the terms 'country' and 'State' increases the likelihood of intensifying membership disputes at INTERPOL. A State is properly in existence

[38] Resolution No GA-2017-86-RES-01, 'The process for membership of INTERPOL', INTERPOL General Assembly, 86th session (Beijing, 2017), Annex 1 and 2.

[39] INTERPOL Membership – Historical Perspective, 15.

[40] For example, since 1956, INTERPOL has approved membership requests from non-State entities such as Aruba, Curaçao and Sint Maarten.

[41] Brölmann, C, 'Specialized Rules of Treaty Interpretation: International Organizations' in Hollis, DB (ed), *The Oxford Guide to Treaties*, 1st edn (Oxford, Oxford University Press, 2012) 507–24 at 513–14; *Interpretation of the Agreement of 25 March 1951 between the WHO and Egypt* (Advisory Opinion) [1980] ICJ Rep 73, 96.

[42] Bühler, KG, *State Succession and Membership in International Organisations* (The Hague, Kluwer Law International, 2001) 310–11.

when its people are settled in a defined territory under its own sovereign government and it has the capacity to enter into relations with other States.[43] Whereas reliance on these criteria of statehood ostensibly provides a non-political solution to the issue of membership, statehood is also dependent on recognition by other States.[44] Such dependency allows for the creeping in of politically-influenced deliberations at the stage of membership, whereby membership of disputed States with limited recognition, such as Kosovo,[45] can be denied.[46] For instance, Kosovo submitted an application for membership in INTERPOL in 2017, but it unilaterally withdrew its application before the 86th session of the INTERPOL General Assembly, at which the Report was adopted.[47] As opposed to 'State', the term 'country' allows for greater flexibility with regards to membership of politically contentious entities by precluding implications of recognition of statehood and, therefore, any potential or perceived compromise of the interests of other States.

Finally, it should be noted that political ramifications arising from membership are not unique to INTERPOL but common to membership of international

[43] Discussed in: Jennings, R and Watts, A (eds), *Oppenheim's International Law*, 9th edn, Vol I (Harlow, Longman, 1992) 120–26.

[44] See generally: Crawford, J, *The Creation of States in International Law*, 2nd edn (Oxford, Clarendon Press, 1979) 19–28.

[45] Perhaps the better way to have handled Kosovo's application would have been to apply the functional test. Indeed, as long as UN Security Council Resolution 1244 (1999) on the situation relating to Kosovo and the Memorandum of Understanding between INTERPOL and the UN Interim Administration Mission in Kosovo ('UNMIK') on Co-operation in Crime Prevention and Criminal Justice remains in force, Kosovo cannot be deemed to be in control of the mechanisms for international police cooperation which are indispensable for meaningful participation in INTERPOL. UN Security Council Resolution 1244 (1999) provides a framework for the resolution of the conflict in Kosovo by authorising the deployment of an international civilian and military presence to provide an international transitional administration and security presence to oversee the return of refugees and the withdrawal of military forces from Kosovo. The resolution also states that the international civilian presence will facilitate a political process to determine the future status of Kosovo. Hence, the question should not be whether Kosovo is a sovereign State or not, but whether it possesses the authority over its police affairs that is necessary for INTERPOL membership. On the governance of Kosovo, see: de Wet, E, 'The Governance of Kosovo: Security Council Resolution 1244 and the Establishment and Functioning of Eulex' (2009) 103 *American Journal of International Law* 83–96.

[46] See: Crawford, J, *Brownlie's Principles of Public International Law*, 9th edn (Oxford, Oxford University Press, 2019) 137–41; Brownlie, I, 'Recognition in Theory and Practice' (1982) 53 *British Yearbook of International Law* 197–211 at 198–200.

[47] In 2018, Kosovo applied for membership in INTERPOL and its application was considered at the 87th session of the INTERPOL General Assembly. The application was rejected: 68 members voted in favour, 51 voted against and 16 abstained (which meant Kosovo did not reach the required two-thirds majority for membership in INTERPOL). Serbia and Russia were vocal opponents of Kosovo's membership. In 2019, Kosovo submitted another application for membership, but it withdrew the application a few hours before the opening of the 88th session of the INTERPOL General Assembly and requested the application be postponed to 2020.

organisations in general.[48] This brings us to the third problem: the present interpretation adopted by INTERPOL is contrary to the functional objectives of the Organisation. Members of INTERPOL consciously adopted the functional approach to membership, similar to one adopted by other technical organisations,[49] rather than one dependent on politically divisive terminology such as 'State'. The membership of territories such as the Netherlands Antilles (an original contracting party to the 1956 INTERPOL Constitution)[50] and Aruba (an INTERPOL member since 1987) exemplifies that a functionalist approach opens membership to all territorial units with an independent police body capable of cooperating at the international level.[51] INTERPOL's approach to the Republic of China (Taiwan) ('Taiwan'), by contrast, exemplifies why its present interpretation is inherently political. Taiwan was a member of INTERPOL between 1961 and 1984. On 17 May 1984, the People's Republic of China ('PRC') applied for membership in INTERPOL. The PRC's membership application was subject to conditions, including that INTERPOL recognise the PRC as the sole representative of all the territory constituting the Chinese State.[52] The application was considered at the 53rd General Assembly. It initially failed to reach the two-thirds majority required pursuant to Article 4 of the INTERPOL Constitution;[53] however, on the second vote (which must be taken when the required two-thirds majority is not obtained in the first vote),[54] the application was accepted.[55] The PRC was therefore declared a member of INTERPOL,[56] and, pursuant to the terms of the application, the PRC was to be the sole representative of China.[57] Taiwan has since been systematically excluded from the Organisation, despite the express desire of Taiwan and a number of its members for INTERPOL to cooperate with Taiwan. For instance, various

[48] Bühler, KG, *State Succession and Membership in International Organisations* (The Hague, Kluwer Law International, 2001) 307–09; Crawford, J, *The Creation of States in International Law*, 2nd edn (Oxford, Clarendon Press, 1979) 179–82.

[49] Bühler, KG, *State Succession and Membership in International Organisations* (The Hague, Kluwer Law International, 2001) 310–11; Fawcett, JES 'The Place of Law in an International Organization' (1960) 36 *British Yearbook of International Law* 321–42 at 341.

[50] Following the dissolution of the Netherlands Antilles in 2010, Curaçao and Sint Maarten (which had each been part of the Netherlands Antilles) submitted requests for membership, which were accepted at the 80th session of the INTERPOL General Assembly in 2011.

[51] Fawcett, JES, 'The Place of Law in an International Organization' (1960) 36 *British Yearbook of International Law* 321–42 at 341.

[52] United States Congressional Record – Senate, 'The Status of the Republic of China as a Member of [INTERPOL]', Vol 131, Part 4 (14 March 1985) 5160.

[53] Minutes of the 53rd General Assembly, 53/AGN/PV/2 (4 September 1984) 13.

[54] Article 21 of the General Regulations of INTERPOL provides that '[v]oting shall be done by single ballot, except where a two-thirds majority is required. In the latter case, if the required majority is not obtained the first time, a second vote shall be taken'.

[55] Minutes of the 53rd General Assembly, 53/AGN/PV/3 (5 September 1984) 2.

[56] Ibid.

[57] INTERPOL Membership – Historical Perspective, 14.

members were prevented from speaking about Taiwan at the 87th INTERPOL General Assembly meeting. To deny INTERPOL members any cooperation with Taiwan – an area with a population of over 23 million people[58] and through which 66 million passengers travelled in 2017 alone – is clearly not in the Organisation's interest. The decision to do so is a political one that is contrary to the functional objectives of the Organisation and its Article 2 aims: it gives rise to major gaps in the global security network and compromises worldwide efforts of crime prevention, thereby leaving 'a huge void in the global crime-fighting efforts'.[59]

With the foregoing in mind, it is clear that the term 'country' in the INTERPOL Constitution should not be interpreted as referring to a 'State'. That being said, the term 'country' triggers problems of its own. Whereas statehood is a rather precise notion in contemporary international law,[60] 'country' has never found an internationally shared legal definition. Thus, the term 'country' must be interpreted in good faith, in accordance with the ordinary meaning to be given to this term, and in light of the context and the object and purpose of the instrument at hand.[61] As illustrated in *Burnet v Chicago Portrait Co*[62] and *Reel v Holder and another*,[63] the ordinary meaning of the term 'country' generally denotes two realities, namely, that of (1) a sovereign State and (2) a part of a sovereign State which enjoys autonomy in a specific area relevant to the purpose of an arrangement. For instance, Article 299(3) and Part Four of the Treaty Establishing the European Union employ the language 'countries and territories' to refer to the non-independent overseas territories that are subject to a special association regime in relation to the European Union.[64] It is also interesting to note the analogy with economic governance in this regard. For instance, for the purposes of balance of payments statistics, a vital tool for the IMF, it has long been accepted that:

> the term 'country' does not in all cases refer to a territorial entity that is a state as understood by international law and practice. As used here, the term also covers some territorial entities that are not states. Dependent territories of member countries are listed alphabetically followed by a description of the constitutional relationships with their member countries.[65]

[58] Central Intelligence Agency, The World Factbook (estimate as of July 2018).

[59] Public Law 114-139, United States Congress, 'Taiwan INTERPOL Observer Status', 8 March 2016, s 1(a)(7).

[60] See extensively: Crawford, J, *The Creation of States in International Law*, 2nd edn (Oxford, Clarendon Press, 1979) 37–95.

[61] Vienna Convention on the Law of Treaties (adopted on 23 May 1969, entered into force on 27 January 1980), 1155 UNTS 331, Art 31(1).

[62] *Burnet v Chicago Portrait Co*, 285 U.S. 1 (1932).

[63] *Reel v Holder and Another* [1981] 1 WLR 1226 (CA).

[64] Treaty Establishing the European Union, Official Journal C 325 (24 December 2002) 33–184.

[65] See the proviso included in each annual 'Balance of Payments Statistics Yearbook' and in the IMF's 'Annual Report on Exchange Arrangements and Exchange Restrictions'. See also: IMF Country Information, available at: www.imf.org/external/country/; Martha, RSJ, 'Effects of Self-Government and Supra-Nationalism in the International Monetary Fund' (2005) 2 *Manchester Journal of International Economic Law* 2–30 at 5–8.

It would, therefore, appear that the term 'country', unlike 'State', is inherently functional. The question is, however, whether a 'country' can be considered a subject of international law.[66] This question becomes particularly pertinent when one considers the fact that the parties that accepted the 1956 INTERPOL Constitution included the three component countries of the Kingdom of the Netherlands at that time (ie, the Netherlands, the Netherlands Antilles and Suriname)[67] and Saar (a short-lived protectorate administered by France after World War Two). According to Seidl-Hohenveldern, the component parts of a State which are unable to conclude treaties are also unable to establish international organisations.[68] However, the situation described above as regards the Kingdom of the Netherlands and Saar is not unique to INTERPOL, and a number of examples indicate that subjects of international law other than States may participate in treaties which create international organisations.[69] Even the UN Charter and the Articles of Agreement of the IMF included four British dominions and the Philippines, none of which were independent States at the time.[70]

[66] There are those who go as far as denying any meaningful use of the concept 'subject of international law' on account of the fact that States, international organisations, other entities and individuals are all, under certain circumstances, entitled to have rights and obligations under international law. See: Erades, L, *Interactions between International and Municipal Law* (The Hague, TMC Asser Instituut, 1993) 546–47; Kooijmans, PH, *International Publiekrecht in Vogelvlucht*, 9th edn (Deventer, Kluwer, 2002) 39.

[67] In the specific case of the Kingdom of the Netherlands, each of the three constituent countries constituted a separate legal order, each with its own police and criminal law. There existed neither a federal police body nor a federal criminal code or federal code of criminal procedure. On this structure, see: Hofstee, E and Schalken, TM, *Strafrecht Binnen het Koninkrijk* (Arnhem, Gouda Quint, 1991) 5–24; Reintjes, JM, *Het interregionale strafrecht van het Koninkrijk der Nederlanden*, 2nd edn (The Hague, Boom Juridische Uitgevers, 2015) 1–36. Given the decidedly functional nature of INTERPOL, it is understandable that these countries participated separately in INTERPOL (see: Hillebrink, S, *The Right to Self-Determination and Post-Colonial Governance – The Case of the Netherlands Antilles and Aruba* (The Hague, Asser Press, 2008) 143–82). The Kingdom of the Netherlands now consists of four countries: Aruba, Curaçao, Sint Maarten and the Netherlands. Aruba seceded from the Netherlands Antilles in January 1986, at which time it became a country within the Kingdom of the Netherlands in its own right. It became a member of INTERPOL on 23 November 1987. Following the dissolution of the Netherlands Antilles in 2010, Curaçao and Sint Maarten (which had each been part of the Netherlands Antilles) became countries within the Kingdom of the Netherlands. In 2010, Curaçao and Sint Maarten each submitted applications for independent membership in INTERPOL. The Kingdom of the Netherlands supported their applications. Both countries have independent police forces under the authority of their respective Ministries of Justice. They proposed that Curaçao maintain the existing National Central Bureau ('NCB') at Willemstad, and that Sint Maarten establish its own NCB within the police force of Sint Maarten. Their memberships were accepted at the 80th session of the INTERPOL General Assembly (Hanoi, 2011).

[68] Seidl-Hohenveldern, I, *Corporations in and under International Law* (Cambridge, Grotius Publishers, 1987) 110.

[69] Barberis, JA, 'Nouvelles questions concernant la personnalité juridique internationale' (1983–I) 179 *Recueil des Cours* 217–19.

[70] Gold, J, *Membership and Non-membership in the International Monetary Fund* (Washington DC, International Monetary Fund, 1974) 45–9; Klabbers, J, *An Introduction to International Institutional Law*, 2nd edn (Cambridge, Cambridge University Press, 2002) 94.

A similar situation exists with regard to the World Trade Organization ('WTO') which includes the Hong Kong Special Administrative Region among its original parties.[71] Moreover, the Memorandum of Understanding of the Caribbean Financial Action Task Force ('CFATF'), which established the CFATF as a fully-fledged independent international organisation, is an international agreement which was subscribed to by a number of British overseas territories in the Caribbean, the Netherlands Antilles and Aruba.[72] The same is also true for the Memorandum of Understanding establishing the Caribbean Customs Law Enforcement Council ('CCLEC').[73] Other examples include the participation of Montserrat as a party to the 1973 Treaty of Chaguaramas establishing the Caribbean Community ('CARICOM'),[74] the 1981 Treaty Establishing the Organisation of Eastern Caribbean States ('OECS'),[75] the 1983 Agreement Establishing the Eastern Caribbean Central Bank ('ECCB'),[76] and the 2001 Eastern Caribbean Securities Regulatory Commission ('ECSRC') Agreement.[77]

More broadly, in *Reparation for Injuries*, the ICJ observed that the subjects of law in any legal system are not necessarily identical in terms of their nature or the extent of their rights:[78] in other words, the contemporary global system has more than one type of subject of international law.[79] It is also accepted that it is not necessary for subjects of international law to bear all the indicia of international legal personality.[80] Although the predominant legal person in international law remains the State itself, a non-State entity with legal personality of a restricted kind (eg, a country) can be a subject of international law. Its status as a subject of international law depends on the agreement or acquiescence of States.[81] The question then becomes one of recognising the legal capacity of the non-State entity to perform the act of concluding the agreement comprising the constituent

[71] Eg, Qureshi, A, *The World Trade Organization* (Manchester, Manchester University Press, 1996) 8.

[72] A list of the original 21 members of the CFATF is set out in the CFATF 1996–1997 Annual Report, 4.

[73] See: CCLEC, 'CCLEC Organization', available at: www.cclec.org/about-us/cclec-organization/.

[74] See: CARICOM, 'Member States and Associate Members', available at: https://caricom.org/about-caricom/who-we-are/our-governance/members-and-associate-members/.

[75] See: OECS, 'Member States', available at: www.oecs.org/en/homepage/member-states.

[76] See: ECCB, 'Member Countries', available at: www.eccb-centralbank.org/p/member-countries.

[77] See: ECSRC, 'History', available at: www.ecsrc.com/cms/Cmspages/details/5/category.

[78] *Reparation for Injuries Suffered in the Service of the United Nations* (Advisory Opinion) [1949] ICJ Rep 174, 178.

[79] Seidl-Hohenveldern speaks of 'the widening of the notion of subjects of international law' (Seidl-Hohenveldern, I, *International Economic Law*, 2nd edn (Dordrecht, Martinus Nijhoff Publishers, 1992) 10–3). See also: Cassese, A, *International Law*, 2nd edn (Oxford, Oxford University Press, 2005) 134–35.

[80] Ie, the capacity to make treaties, the capacity to present international claims, liability for the consequence of breaches of international law, and privileges and immunities in relation to the national jurisdictions of States (Brownlie, I, *The Rule of Law in International Affairs* (The Hague, Martinus Nijhoff Publishers, 1998) 36).

[81] Brownlie, I, *The Rule of Law in International Affairs* (The Hague, Martinus Nijhoff Publishers, 1998) 35.

instrument of an international organisation,[82] or rather, of recognising an indication of willingness on the part of other entities to enter into the agreement with the non-State entity in question.[83] In Johnston's taxonomy, constituent instruments to which 'sub-States' are a party qualify as 'atypical instruments' on the basis that the 'sub-States' were granted external recognition by some or all States as having a degree of treaty-making capacity at the international level.[84] Against this background, and considering the willingness of over 40 States to enter into the INTERPOL Constitution in 1956 with a number of 'sub-States', it is justified to conclude that the sovereign States and countries which negotiated and adopted the INTERPOL Constitution and gave their consent to be bound by it acted in the capacity of subjects of international law.

[82] Article XXVI, paragraph 5(a) of the General Agreement on Tariffs and Trade, which contemplated the status of 'Contracting Party' for governments which had less than complete sovereignty, is a case in point. See: Jackson, JH, *World Trade and the Law of the GATT* (Charlottesville, Lexis Law Publishers, 1969) 89.

[83] Talmon, S, *Recognition of Governments in International Law* (Oxford, Oxford University Press, 1998) 23–33.

[84] Johnston, DM, *Consent and Commitment in the World Community* (New York, Transnational Publishers, 1997) 24–35.

5

Form and Formalities

I. The Distinction between Formal and Informal Agreements

It cannot be denied that the evolution of the Constitution of the International Criminal Police Organization ('INTERPOL' or the 'Organisation') is characterised by a certain level of informality.[1] Even so, the question that surfaces is whether its qualification as an informal international agreement matters under the law of treaties? This question receives a negative response,[2] as pointed out by McNair in his classic study, where he writes that the 'form of a particular instrument is not decisive of the question whether or not it constitutes an international engagement'.[3] In fact, because '[t]he very word "treaty" may conjure up some of the apparent fearsome formalities of diplomacy',[4] very often parties will intentionally draft informal instruments to disguise a valid international agreement.[5] As early as 1899, an international arbitral tribunal in *Lamu Island Arbitration (Germany/UK)* held that

[1] Benvenisti has written on the recent proliferation of informal intergovernmental networks and public-private partnerships (as opposed to informal international agreements). He argues that this proliferation challenges the vision of international law as a coherent legal system. In his view, the timeworn assumption that States cannot contract out (ie, opt out) of international law seems increasingly in tension with political, social and economic realities. The turn to informal international law, he argues, could reduce the opportunities for adjudicators to rely on a systematic approach as a means to reduce the disparities between strong and weak States, and between governments and individuals. In other words, the turn to informal international law diminishes the opportunities for judges to equalise power (see: Benvenisti, E, 'The Conception of International Law as a Legal System' (2007) 50 *German Yearbook of International Law* 393–406 at 403–04). See also: Benvenisti, E, '"Coalitions of the Willing" and the Evolution of Informal International Law' in Calliess, C et al (eds), *Coalitions of the Willing: Avantgarde of Threat?* (Köln, Carl Heymanns Verlag, 2007) 1–25; Benvenisti, E, *The Law of Global Governance* (The Hague, Brill, 2014) ch 2.

[2] See: Cassese, A, *International Law*, 2nd edn (Oxford, Oxford University Press, 2005) 172–73. See also: Nollkaemper, A, *Kern van het International Publiekrecht* (The Hague, Boom Juridische Uitgevers, 2004) 84; Dinh, NQ, Dailler, P and Pellet, A, *Droit International Public*, 7th edn (Paris, LGDJ, 2002) 143.

[3] McNair, A, *The Law of Treaties* (Oxford, Clarendon Press, 1961) 12.

[4] Aust, A, *Modern Treaty Law and Practice*, 3rd edn (Cambridge, Cambridge University Press, 2013) 29.

[5] See: Gottlieb, G, 'Global Bargaining: The Legal and Diplomatic Framework' in Onuf, NG (ed), *Law-making in the Global Community* (Durham, Carolina Academic Press, 1982) 109–72 at 121; Hillgenberg, H, 'Soft Law and the Legal Adviser' in United Nations (ed), *Collection of Essays by Legal Advisers of States, Legal Advisers of International Organizations and Practitioners in the Field of International Law* (New York, United Nations, 1999) 121–44. See also: Klabbers, J, 'Institutional Ambivalence by Design: Soft Organisations in International Law' (2001) 70 *Nordic Journal of International Law* 403–21 at 421; Kerwer, D and Hülsse, R, *How International Organizations*

there is no rule that prescribes any particular form of agreement between States.[6] In 1961, this was confirmed as good law in *Temple of Preah Vihear (Cambodia v Thailand)* by the International Court of Justice ('ICJ'), which noted that:

> [a]s regards the question of forms and formalities, as distinct from intentions, the Court considers that, to cite examples drawn from the field from private law, there are cases where, for the protection of the interested parties, or for reasons of public policy, or on other grounds, the law prescribes as mandatory certain formalities which, hence, become essential for the validity of certain transactions, such as for instance testamentary dispositions; and another example, amongst many possible ones, would be that of a marriage ceremony. But the position in the cases just mentioned (wills, marriage, etc.) arises because of the existence in those cases of mandatory requirements of law as to forms and formalities. Where, on the other hand, as is generally the case in international law, which places the principal emphasis on the intention of the parties, the law prescribes no particular form, parties are free to choose what form they please provided their intention clearly results from it.[7]

Similarly, in the *South West Africa Cases*,[8] the ICJ was adamant that, in international law, neither form nor terminology is a determinant factor in relation to the character of an international agreement or undertaking.[9] In the *Nuclear Tests* case,[10] whilst recognising that unilateral declarations can create binding obligations under international law, the ICJ reiterated that:

> [w]ith regard to the question of form, it should be observed that this is not a domain in which international law imposes any special or strict requirements. Whether a statement is made orally or in writing makes no essential difference, for such statements made in particular circumstances may create commitments in international law, which does not require that they should be couched in written form. Thus the question of form is not decisive.[11]

The commentary of the International Law Commission ('ILC') on the Draft Articles on the Law of Treaties also clearly states that the definition of treaty includes those international agreements which are drafted in a less formal manner.[12]

Rule the World: The Case of the Financial Action Task Force on Money Laundering (Berlin, United Nations Studies Association, 2011).

[6] '*Attendu que, si aucune loi ne prescrit une forme spéciale pour les conventions entre États indépendants* …' ('Whereas, if no law prescribes a special form for conventions between independent States') (authors' translation) (*Arbitration between Germany and the United Kingdom relating to Lamu Island* (Award of 17 August 1889) XXVIII RIAA 237–48 at 243).

[7] *Case concerning the Temple of Preah Vihear (Cambodia v Thailand)* (Preliminary Objections) [1961] ICJ Rep 17, 31. See also: *Case concerning the Northern Cameroons (Cameroon v UK)* (Preliminary Objections) [1963] ICJ Rep 15, 27–8.

[8] *South West Africa Cases (Ethiopia v South Africa; Liberia v South Africa)* (Preliminary Objections) [1962] ICJ Rep 319.

[9] Ibid, 331–32.

[10] *Nuclear Tests (New Zealand v France)* (Judgment) [1974] ICJ Rep 457.

[11] Ibid, para 48.

[12] 'Draft articles on the law of treaties with commentaries' in *Yearbook of the International Law Commission* (1966) Vol II, 188, Commentary to Art 2, para 2.

For instance, the conclusions of an international conference may comprise an informal international agreement.[13] Thus, whilst the distinction between formal and informal agreements might be relevant from the point of view of the constitutional law of certain countries,[14] it lacks any particular legal relevance on the international plane.[15] The ILC aptly observed, 'the juridical differences, in so far as they really exist at all, between formal treaties and treaties in simplified form lie almost exclusively in the method of conclusion and entry into force'.[16]

It follows that the requirement that an international organisation be established by treaty does not necessarily mean establishment by formal treaty.[17] As discussed in Chapter 1, many commentators have made it clear that the founding instrument of an international organisation does not need to be a formal treaty. For instance, after studying various examples, Barberis concludes:

> *[t]outefois, dans tous les exemples cites, bien qu'il n'y ait pas de traite formelle ou que celui-ci n'ait pas existe lors de la création de l'organisation internationale, il a eu sans aucun doute possible accord de volontés entre les États qui sont à l'origine de la constitution de l'organisation.*[18]

[13] Johnson, DHN, 'The Conclusions of International Conferences' (1959) 35 *British Yearbook of International Law* 1–33; McNair, A, *The Law of Treaties* (Oxford, Clarendon Press, 1961) 14–5.

[14] See: Bastid, S, *Les Traités dans la vie internationale: conclusion et effets* (Paris, Economica, 1985) 46–50.

[15] See: Hamzeh, FS, 'Agreements in Simplified Form: Modern Perspective' (1968–69) 43 *British Yearbook of International Law* 179–89 at 183–86. See also: Rosenne, S, *Developments in the Law of Treaties 1945–1986* (Cambridge, Cambridge University Press, 1989) 184; Jennings, R and Watts, A (eds), *Oppenheim's International Law*, 9th edn, Vol I (Harlow, Longman, 1992) 1200–01.

[16] 'Draft articles on the law of treaties with commentaries' in *Yearbook of the International Law Commission* (1966) Vol II, 188, Commentary to Art 2, para 3. As an aside, it is arguable that the approach of the European Union ('EU') to eliciting international commitments is also achieved by informal international agreement. With a view to ensuring the financial autonomy of the EU, the 'own resources' requirement set out in Article 311 of the Treaty on the Functioning of the EU is implemented through a special legislative procedure. The Council adopts a decision containing the basic provisions for financing the EU budget, which are implemented through a series of regulations. The Council decision is decided by unanimity, after consulting the European Parliament. EU Member States must then approve this decision, in accordance with their respective constitutional requirements, before it can enter into force. Once this is achieved, the Council decision establishes a legal entitlement of the EU to certain revenues which accrue to the EU budget (which is not conditional on the decisions of Member States' national authorities). That being said, a debate exists as to whether the Council decisions constitute international agreements or are merely decisions of an international organisation (see: Elphicke, C and Howe, M 'The withdrawal of the UK from the European Union: Analysis […] of potential financial liabilities and of jurisdiction to enforce them', *The Conservative European Research Group and Lawyers for Britain* (September 2017); Wordsworth, S and Aughey, S, 'Written evidence to the House of Lords sub-committee on EU financial affairs', FOB0002).

[17] Schermers, HG and Blokker, NM, *International Institutional Law: Unity within Diversity*, 6th revised edn (Leiden, Brill Nijhoff Publishers, 2018) 41. See also: Bekker, PH, *The Legal Position of Intergovernmental Organisations: A Functional Necessity Analysis of their Legal Status and Immunities* (Dordrecht, Martinus Nijhoff Publishers, 1994) 39.

[18] 'However, in all the examples cited, although there was no formal treaty or it did not exist during the creation of the international organisation, there was without any doubt a concurrence of wills between the States at the origin of the constitution of the organisation' (authors' translation) (Barberis, JA, 'Nouvelles questions concernant la personnalité juridique internationale' (1983–I) 179 *Recueil des Cours* 145, 217). See also: Seyersted, F, *Common Law of International Organizations* (Leiden, Martinus Nijhoff Publishers, 2008) 46–52.

Similarly, Amerasinghe speaks of 'establishment by some kind of international agreement'.[19] Klabbers distinctly states that, whether the organisation is created by treaty or some other legal act, '[t]he importance of this characteristic … is above all to indicate that the creation of an international organisation is an intentional act'.[20] The ILC has also endorsed the view that international organisations do not require establishment through a formal treaty but may be set up by an informal or even implicit agreement governed by international law. The ILC expressly acknowledged that 'forms of international cooperation are sometimes established without a treaty', such as the Organization for Security and Co-operation in Europe or the Pan American Institute of Geography and History.[21] It is for this reason that the ILC Draft Articles on the Responsibility of International Organizations define an international organisation as including those organisations established by any 'other instrument governed by international law'.[22]

In fact, the creation of international organisations by means of informal agreements is not unusual.[23] The most celebrated case is the General Agreement on Tariffs and Trade ('GATT'), which existed as an international organisation based on an informal provisional agreement until it was replaced by the World Trade Organization ('WTO') in 1994.[24] Similarly, the Council for Mutual Economic Assistance existed for 11 years on the basis of an informal agreement, reflected in a *communiqué*, until a formal charter was adopted in June 1962.[25]

The foregoing demonstrates that the concern regarding the informal nature of the INTERPOL Constitution is not warranted – an international organisation can be created by either a formal or an informal international agreement.[26] In

[19] Amerasinghe, CF, *Principles of the Institutional Law of International Organisations*, 2nd edn (Cambridge, Cambridge University Press, 2005) 10.

[20] Klabbers, J, *An Introduction to International Institutional Law*, 2nd edn (Cambridge, Cambridge University Press, 2012) 10.

[21] 'Draft articles on the responsibility of international organizations, with commentaries' in *Yearbook of the International Law Commission* (2011) Vol II, Part Two, 49, Commentary to Art 2, para 4.

[22] 'Draft articles on the responsibility of international organizations, with commentaries' in *Yearbook of the International Law Commission* (2011) Vol II, Part Two, 49, Art 2(a).

[23] See: Barberis, J-A, 'Nouvelles questions concernant la personnalité juridique internationale' (1983-I) 179 *Recueil des Cours* 145–304 at 217.

[24] See: Jackson, JH, 'The Puzzle of GATT: Legal Aspects of a Surprising Institution' in Jackson, JH, *The Jurisprudence of GATT and the WTO: Insights on Treaty Law and Economic* (Cambridge, Cambridge University Press, 2000) 17–33; Long, O, *Law and its Limitations in the GATT Multilateral Trade System* (Dordrecht, Martinus Nijhoff Publishers, 1985) 43–64; Weiss, F, 'From Havana to Marrakesh: Treaty Making for Trade' in Klabbers, J and Lefeber, R (eds), *Essays on the Law of Treaties – A Collection of Essays in Honour of Bert Vierdag* (The Hague, Martinus Nijhoff Publishers, 1998) 155–70; Matsushita, M, Shoenbaum, TJ and Mavroidis, PC, *The World Trade Organization* (Oxford, Oxford University Press, 2003) 2–3.

[25] See: Van Meerhaeghe, MAG, *A Handbook of International Economic Institutions* (The Hague, Martinus Nijhoff Publishers, 1980) 234–53; Voitovich, SA, *International Economic Organization in the International Legal Process* (Dordrecht, Martinus Nijhoff Publishers, 1995) 22.

[26] Yasseen, K, 'Création et personnalité des organisations internationales in Dupuy, RJ (ed), *Manuel sur les organisations internationales* (1988) 44 *Recueil des Cours* 33–55 at 33–4 and the sources cited therein.

view of the above, in his 1980 legal opinion to INTERPOL, Reuter qualifies the INTERPOL Constitution as an informal international agreement:

> *[i]l est vrai que presque toutes les organisations sont créées par les traités en forme solennelle. … Mais pour le moment … il faut rappeler que le droit international connaît des accords multilatéraux en forme non solennelle et que ces accords sont, du point de vue de droit international, des traités; aucune règle de droit international n'exige qu'une organisation internationale intergouvernementale soit établie par voie d'un traité en forme solennelle. Il est clair que le Statut actuel de l'O.I.P.C. est un accord international interétatique conclu entre les États membres et il est parfaitement valable* sur le plan international.[27]

The view that the INTERPOL Constitution could qualify as an informal international agreement is subscribed to by many in various contexts, including in a report prepared by the Polish Government,[28] a statement made by the Chinese Government,[29] and a study conducted by the United Nations ('UN') Office of Legal Affairs.[30] Given that the INTERPOL Constitution was adopted at the 1956 International Criminal Police Commission ('ICPC') General Assembly and opened for acceptance under Article 45 of the INTERPOL Constitution, it is difficult to understand why the INTERPOL Constitution should not be regarded as an international agreement. Thus, not surprisingly, Schermers and Blokker observe in their classic work on international institutional law that:

> [f]ormally, INTERPOL is not based on an agreement between States. However, such agreement may in fact be deduced from a number of factors. Although any official police bodies whose functions come within the framework of activities of the organisation may be members of INTERPOL (Article 4), these members are instructed by their governments. Furthermore, requests for membership have to be submitted 'by the appropriate governmental authority' (Article 4). Finally, the financial contributions from members come from the national budgets.[31]

[27] 'It is true that nearly all organisations were set up by formal treaties. … However, at the moment …, it must be remembered that international law recognises informal multilateral agreements and that such agreements are treaties from an international law perspective; no rule of international law stipulates that an intergovernmental organisation has to be founded on the basis of a formal treaty. It is obvious that the current INTERPOL Constitution is an international inter-State agreement concluded between member States and it is perfectly valid at the international level' (authors' translation) (Reuter, P, 'Problèmes juridiques relatifs au statut de l'OIPC-Interpol' in *INTERPOL: Les textes fondamentaux de l'Organisation internationale de police criminelle* (Paris, Presses Universitaires de France, 2001) 45–67 at 48).

[28] 'Study by Poland on the legal nature of ICPO-INTERPOL', Doc AGN/63/RAP. No. 11, 63rd session (Rome, 1994).

[29] See: Resolution No AGN/61/RES/5, 'Expert Group on the amendment of INTERPOL's Constitution', INTERPOL General Assembly, 61st session (Dakar, 1992). The Expert Group's discussions were the subject of 'Amendment of Interpol's Constitution', Report AGN/63/RAP/11 (1994).

[30] 'Status of the International Criminal Police Organization (INTERPOL) with the United Nations' in *United Nations Juridical Yearbook* (1982) Part Two, Chapter VI, 179–80.

[31] Schermers, HG and Blokker, NM, *International Institutional Law: Unity within Diversity*, 6th revised edn (Leiden, Brill Nijhoff Publishers, 2018) 40.

Accordingly, the qualification of the INTERPOL Constitution as an informal international agreement may, at most, say something about the way it came into being. Such qualification does not, however, impact the legal validity of the INTERPOL Constitution as a fully-fledged legal instrument under international law.

II. Registration and Publication

Article 102 of the UN Charter (like its predecessor, Article 18 of the Covenant of the League of Nations) provides that treaties and other international agreements to which a Member State of the UN becomes a party must be registered (in all their languages and with all their ancillary documents) with the UN Secretariat. Registered treaties are subsequently published by the UN Secretariat, both on the internet and on paper in the UN Treaty Series. The intention of Article 102 is to discourage secret treaties.[32] In accordance with Article 102(2), no UN Member State may invoke an unregistered treaty before the ICJ or any other organ of the UN. Regulations were adopted by the UN General Assembly on 14 December 1946 to give effect to Article 102, which were modified several times thereafter.[33] Article 80 of the 1969 Vienna Convention on the Law of Treaties and Article 81 of the 1986 Vienna Convention on the Law of Treaties between States and International Organizations or between International Organizations also direct the submission of treaties to the UN Secretariat for publication.

Neither of the two Constitutions of the ICPC (the prior name of INTERPOL) adopted before 1946 was registered with the League of Nations in accordance with Article 18 of the Covenant of the League of Nations, and neither the ICPC Constitution of 1946 nor the INTERPOL Constitution of 1956 was registered in conformity with Article 102 of the UN Charter. In addition, the INTERPOL Constitution was not published in the official journals of the countries participating in INTERPOL. Accordingly, for a very long period of time, INTERPOL's constituent instrument was not accessible to the public at large (which may help to explain the misunderstanding held about its legal character). Since the introduction of the Organisation's public website, the issue of the accessibility of the INTERPOL Constitution has somewhat diminished. That being said, practitioners

[32] Martens, E, 'Miscellaneous Provisions, Article 102' in Simma, B, et al (eds), *The Charter of the United Nations: A Commentary*, Vol II, 3rd edn (Oxford, Oxford University Press, 2012) 2089–2110 at 2091–92.

[33] UN General Assembly, 'Registration and Publication of Treaties and International Agreements: Regulations to give effect to Article 102 of the Charter of the United Nations', UN Doc A/RES/97(1) (14 December 1946). This regulation was modified by (1) UN General Assembly, 'Registration and publication of treaties and international agreements', UN Doc A/RES/364(IV) (1 December 1949), (2) UN General Assembly, 'Registration and publication of treaties and international agreements', UN Doc A/RES/482(V) (12 December 1950), and (3) UN General Assembly, 'Registration and publication of treaties and international agreements pursuant to Article 102 of the Charter of the UN', UN Doc A/RES/33/141 (19 December 1978).

(eg, prosecutors, judges and policy advisors in governmental ministries) normally rely on official sources, such as the UN Treaty Series or national publications of treaties and other international agreements. However, when they consult these sources, they will not find the INTERPOL Constitution because it has still not been registered by the UN Secretariat and, with limited exceptions, it has not been published in national official gazettes.

The fact that the INTERPOL Constitution has not been registered with the UN Secretariat begs the question as to whether this provides an indication that INTERPOL's constituent instrument is not considered to be an international agreement. This question is all the more relevant because, in the 1970s, the UN Secretariat had expressed the view that the INTERPOL Constitution 'did not appear to constitute a treaty'.[34] It was only in 1982 that the UN Secretariat retreated from this position when it recognised the INTERPOL Constitution as 'an international agreement in simplified form' and accepted INTERPOL's characterisation as an intergovernmental organisation.[35]

The question must be answered in the negative: registration under Article 102 of the UN Charter does not imply a judgment by the UN Secretariat on the nature of the instrument, the status of a party or the legal status of the instrument.[36] For that reason, registration with the UN Secretariat does not confer the status of 'treaty' or 'international agreement' on an instrument if it does not already possess that status. Conversely, the non-registration of an instrument does not necessarily imply that it lacks the status of a 'treaty' or 'international agreement' for the purposes of international law. It is, therefore, clear that Article 102 of the UN Charter is not concerned with the validity of an international instrument. Article 102 is, more simply, intended to assist the UN with internal recognition amongst its organs[37] (ie, non-registration entails 'relative invalidation' within the UN).[38]

The distinction between registration and the legal character of an instrument under international law can be traced back to the arbitration concerning the *Execution of German-Portuguese Arbitral Award of June 30th, 1930 (Germany/Portugal)*.[39] In this case, Portugal invoked the non-registration of the Hague Agreement of 20 January 1930 with the League of Nations as a means to avoid its

[34] Repertory of Practice of UN Organs, 'Article 102', Supplement No 5 (1970–1978), Vol 5, para 11.

[35] 'Status of the International Criminal Police Organization (INTERPOL) with the United Nations' in *United Nations Juridical Yearbook* (1982) Part Two, Ch VI, 179–80 at 180.

[36] Martens, E, 'Miscellaneous Provisions, Article 102' in Simma, B, et al (eds), *The Charter of the United Nations: A Commentary*, Vol II, 3rd edn (Oxford, Oxford University Press, 2012) 2089–2110 at 2093.

[37] However, it remains unlikely that INTERPOL, in the absence of registration, would not be recognised by UN organs considering that several specialised agencies of the UN, including the International Telecommunication Union, have cooperation agreements in place with INTERPOL.

[38] Martens, E, 'Miscellaneous Provisions, Article 102' in Simma, B, et al (eds), *The Charter of the United Nations: A Commentary*, Vol II, 3rd edn (Oxford, Oxford University Press, 2012) 2089–2110 at 2105; Kelsen, H, *The Law of the United Nations: A Critical Analysis of Its Fundamental Problems* (New York, Frederick A Praeger, 1954) 722.

[39] *Execution of German-Portuguese Arbitral Award of June 30th, 1930 (Germany/Portugal)* (Award of 16 February 1933) III RIAA 1371–86.

obligations thereunder. In dismissing this argument, the tribunal attached relevance to the manifest intention of the parties to be bound by the Hague Agreement and the fact that the registration was not a pre-requisite for the effectiveness of the agreement. In 1994, the ICJ seized the opportunity to add its view regarding the issue of the registration or non-registration of treaties and other international agreements in *Qatar v Bahrain*. In this case, a difference of opinion emerged between Bahrain and Qatar as to whether an agreement was concluded by virtue of the minutes of a 1990 meeting between the Foreign Ministers of Qatar and Bahrain, dubbed the 'Doha Minutes'. One of the points of contention was whether the registration of the Doha Minutes with the UN Secretariat by Qatar was sufficient proof of its status as an international agreement. The Doha Minutes refer to consultations between the two Foreign Ministers, in the presence of the Foreign Minister of Saudi Arabia, and include text as to what had been 'agreed' between the parties. Bahrain maintained that the subsequent conduct of the parties – namely, that Qatar waited until June 1991 before it applied to the UN Secretariat to register the Doha Minutes under Article 102 of the UN Charter and that Bahrain objected to such registration – showed that the parties never considered the Doha Minutes to be an agreement akin to a treaty and that both parties had originally subscribed to this position. Bahrain also argued that Qatar did not file the Doha Minutes with the General Secretariat of the League of Arab States, as required by Article 17 of the Pact of the League of Arab States. Bahrain, therefore, submitted that Qatar's conduct showed that it, much like Bahrain, never considered the Doha Minutes to be an international agreement. The ICJ rejected these arguments in the following terms:

> [t]he Court would observe that an international agreement or treaty that has not been registered with the Secretariat of the United Nations may not, according to the provisions of Article 102 of the Charter, be invoked by the parties before any organ of the United Nations. Non-registration or late registration, on the other hand, does not have any consequence for the actual validity of the agreement, which remains no less binding upon the parties. The Court therefore cannot infer from the fact that Qatar did not apply for registration of the 1990 Minutes until six months after they were signed that Qatar considered, in December 1990, that those Minutes did not constitute an international agreement. The same conclusion follows as regards the non-registration of the text with the General Secretariat of the Arab League. … Accordingly Bahrain's argument on these points also cannot be accepted.[40]

In this way, the ICJ made it clear that the non-registration of a treaty or other international agreement does not have any consequence on the actual validity of the agreement. Therefore, one can safely conclude that the fact that the INTERPOL Constitution has not (yet) been registered with the UN Secretariat does not hamper the assertion that the INTERPOL Constitution nevertheless constitutes an international agreement.

[40] *Maritime Delimitation and Territorial Questions between Qatar and Bahrain* (Jurisdiction and Admissibility) [1994] ICJ Rep 112, para 29.

In 2008, INTERPOL requested the UN Secretariat to express a view on whether the INTERPOL Constitution qualifies for registration and publication under Article 102 of the UN Charter. The UN Secretariat explained that it will only examine each instrument to satisfy itself that, prima facie, the agreement imposes on the parties legal obligations binding under international law.[41] Whether the INTERPOL Constitution is a treaty imposing legal obligations on INTERPOL's members binding under international law can only be determined by those members. Thereafter, in 2011, the INTERPOL General Assembly adopted Resolution No AG-2011-RES-15:

> RECALLING that the International Criminal Police Commission (ICPC) was created in 1923, and that its constituent instrument was revised in 1939 and 1946,
>
> RECALLING FURTHER that the new Constitution of the International Criminal Police Organization (ICPO-INTERPOL) was adopted at the 25th session of the ICPC General Assembly, held in Vienna from 7 to 13 June 1956,
>
> BEARING IN MIND that the 1956 Constitution defines INTERPOL as an international organization with a clear mandate, its own bodies, possessing an international legal personality and an existence separate from its member countries,
>
> UNDERLINING that the Organization is recognized as an international, independent legal entity by governments, courts and tribunals, as well as by other intergovernmental organizations, particularly the United Nations,
>
> CONSIDERING Resolution AG-2006-RES-04 (Statement to Reaffirm the Independence and Political Neutrality of INTERPOL), by which the General Assembly confirmed the principles of neutrality and independence enshrined in INTERPOL's Constitution,
>
> CONSIDERING ALSO Recommendation ERC-2010-REC-02 of the European Regional Conference on the registration of INTERPOL's Constitution with the United Nations, according to which the Conference recommended that the Constitution be submitted for registration and publication by the United Nations,
>
> NOTING the past studies conducted by working groups established by the General Assembly, by the Executive Committee, and by the General Secretariat,
>
> CONCLUDES, in light of the above, that INTERPOL's Constitution is to be considered as the international agreement establishing the International Criminal Police Organization – INTERPOL,
>
> CONSIDERS that registration and publication of INTERPOL's Constitution with the United Nations will clarify the nature of INTERPOL's Constitution and facilitate collaboration by the Organization with its member countries and with other international entities, without creating additional obligations on member countries,
>
> DECIDES that INTERPOL's Constitution should be submitted for registration and publication by the United Nations,

[41] Stalcup, M, 'Interpol and the Emergence of Global Policing' in Garriott, W (ed), *Policing and Contemporary Governance: The Anthropology of Police in Practice* (New York, Palgrave MacMillan, 2013) 231–61 at 237, referring to Michel, N, 'Letter of the United Nations' Under-Secretary General for Legal Affairs Dated May 6, 2008'.

> TASKS the General Secretariat to take all necessary steps for the purpose of submitting the Constitution to the Secretariat of the United Nations to be registered and published in accordance with Article 102 of the United Nations Charter.[42]

However, despite these proactive steps, certain countries have threatened to file an objection with the UN Secretary General if the INTERPOL Constitution is registered. Former INTERPOL Secretary General, Ronald K Noble, attempted to negotiate an agreement, but he was ultimately unsuccessful.

[42] Resolution No AG-2011-RES-15, 'Registration of INTERPOL's Constitution under Article 102 of the United Nations Charter', INTERPOL General Assembly, 80th session (Hanoi, 2011) (emphasis added).

6

Governing Law

The relevance of the question of the governing law of the Constitution of the International Criminal Police Organization ('INTERPOL' or the 'Organisation') derives from the fact that, as discussed in Chapter 1, an international organisation must be established by an agreement governed by international law. This is reflected in Article 2(1)(a) of the 1969 Vienna Convention on the Law of Treaties ('VCLT') and Article 2(1)(a) of the 1986 Vienna Convention on the Law of Treaties between States and International Organizations or between International Organizations ('VCLT-IO'), each of which defines a treaty as 'governed by international law'.[1] The International Law Commission ('ILC') commented that this phrase serves to distinguish between agreements regulated by public international law and those which, although concluded between subjects of international law, are regulated by the national law of one of the parties (or by some other national law system chosen by the parties).[2] The ILC also remarked that the phrase 'governed by international law' embraces the element of an 'intention to create obligations under international law'.[3] The ILC did not, however, include an element of intention in the VCLT because some members considered that its inclusion might imply that a subject of international law had the option to choose between international law and national law as the law to govern a treaty, and others considered that the very nature of subjects of international law made an agreement between them subject to international law, at any rate, in the first instance.[4]

Reuter, in his definition of a treaty, also states that the parties must have intended the agreement to 'have legal effects under the rules of public international law'.[5] Reuter acknowledges that subjects of international law are free to conclude agreements under a given domestic law, instead of international law,[6]

[1] VCLT (adopted on 23 May 1969, entered into force on 27 January 1980) 1155 UNTS 331; VCLT-IO (adopted on 21 March 1986, not yet in force). See also: Schermers, H and Blokker, N, *International Institution Law: Unity within Diversity*, 6th revised edn (Leiden, Brill Nijhoff Publishers, 2018) 50.

[2] '*Draft articles on the law of treaties with commentaries*' in *Yearbook of the International Law Commission* (1966) Vol II, 189, Commentary to Article 2, para 6.

[3] Ibid.

[4] Ibid.

[5] Reuter, P, *Introduction to the Law of Treaties* (translated by Mico, J and Haggenmacher, P) (London, Pinter Publishers, 1989) 26–7.

[6] Ibid, 26.

but the application of domestic law in respect of agreements between international persons cannot be presumed. In *Diverted Cargoes*, it was confirmed that, unless expressly agreed otherwise, transactions between subjects of international law are governed by international law.[7] It is, therefore, theoretically possible that, even if the INTERPOL Constitution is an expression of concurring wills attributable to two or more subjects of international law, it may not qualify as an international agreement if it is governed by national law.

I. Presumptive Exclusion of National Law

This section considers four examples which elucidate the distinction between organisations established under the national law of a country and those established by an agreement governed by international law.

The International Telecommunications Satellite Organization ('INTELSAT') was initially established by an agreement governed by international law but subsequently privatised and regulated by domestic law. On 20 August 1964, a number of States entered into interim arrangements for a global commercial communications satellite system.[8] This led to the establishment of INTELSAT on 12 February 1973. The purpose of INTELSAT was commercial – ie, 'to continue and carry forward on a definitive basis the design, development, construction, establishment, operation and maintenance of the space segment of the global commercial telecommunications satellite system'.[9] The contracting parties decided to establish INTELSAT by an agreement governed by international law because, at the time of INTELSAT's creation, it was believed that only an international organisation would be capable of constructing and operating a global satellite system. Its member States held ownership interests of varying degrees, assisted with the operation and management of the INTELSAT system, and distributed INTELSAT's services within their jurisdictions. For a host of reasons, including privileges and immunities and *de facto* and *de jure* barriers to entry, INTELSAT and its members held an advantage over privately-owned satellite systems in the marketplace, with the result

[7] *The Diverted Cargoes Case (Greece, United Kingdom of Great Britain and Northern Ireland)* (Award of 10 June 1955) XII RIAA 53 at 70. See also: *Russian Claim for Interest on Indemnities (Damages Claimed by Russia for Delay in Payment of Compensation Owed to Russians Injured During the War of 1877–1878 (Russia v Turkey))* (Award of 11 November 1912) XI RIAA 421 at 436; *Norwegian shipowners' claims (Norway v USA)* (Award of 13 October 1922) I RIAA 307 at 331. For a discussion of the presumption of applicability of international law, see: Martha, RSJ, *The Financial Obligation in International Law* (Oxford, Oxford University Press, 2015) 23–9; Mann, FA, 'Reflections on the Commercial Law of Nations' (1957) 33 *British Yearbook of International Law* 20–51 at 41–8.

[8] Agreement establishing interim arrangements for a Global Commercial Communications Satellite System (signed and entered into force on 20 August 1964) 541 UNTS 25.

[9] Agreement relating to the International Telecommunications Satellite Organization 'INTELSAT' (concluded on 20 August 1971, entered into force on 12 February 1973) 1220 UNTS 21, Art II.

that full competition was not possible. For these reasons, Seidl-Hohenveldern was critical of the fact that INTELSAT (and other inter-State commercial enterprises) enjoyed the status of an international organisation.[10] In 2001, in light of its monopoly, INTELSAT member States agreed to restructure INTELSAT. This restructuring led to the creation of a private company, known today as Intelsat Corporation, which is currently incorporated in Delaware and headquartered in Virginia.[11]

The second example concerns the Arab Organization for Industrialization ('AOI'). The AOI was established on 29 April 1975 by an agreement between the United Arab Emirates, Saudi Arabia, Qatar and the Arab Republic of Egypt ('Egypt'). The object of the AOI was the development of an arms industry for the benefit of its members (ie, the four States). To direct the AOI, the agreement created a Higher Committee, composed of ministers of its members. The Higher Committee drafted the internal rules of the AOI which were subsequently approved by the four States.[12] On 4 January 1978, the Higher Committee signed a Memorandum of Understanding with the Government of the United Kingdom ('UK'), guaranteeing the performance by the four States of any commitments which the AOI, or any companies controlled by it, might make towards UK companies. On 27 February 1978, the AOI and Westland Helicopters Ltd ('Westland'), a UK company, concluded a shareholders' agreement ('Shareholders' Agreement'), the aim of which was the creation of a joint stock company in which AOI was to have 70% and Westland 30% of the shares. The joint stock company was later known as the Arab British Helicopter Company ('ABHCO'). ABHCO was to serve as a legal base for the manufacture and marketing of the Lynx helicopter developed by Westland.[13]

Following the conclusion of a Treaty of Peace between Egypt and Israel, the United Arab Emirates, Saudi Arabia and Qatar announced, on 14 May 1979, that they were putting an end to the existence of the AOI with effect from 1 July 1979 and establishing a Liquidation Committee. Egypt responded by promulgating Decree Law No 30 of 1979, which provided that the AOI, having its place of business in Cairo, remained in existence as a legal person.[14] Westland subsequently filed a request for arbitration with the Court of Arbitration of the International Chamber of Commerce, in accordance with the Shareholders' Agreement, citing the AOI, the United Arab Emirates, Saudi Arabia, Qatar, Egypt and ABHCO as respondents. In the request, Westland claimed £126 million from the first five

[10] Seidl-Hohenveldern, I, *Corporations in and under International Law* (Cambridge, Grotius Publishers, 1987) 2–3 and 109–22.

[11] The International Telecommunications Satellite Organization is tasked with monitoring the performance of Intelsat Corporation's public service obligations.

[12] *Westland Helicopters Ltd and Arab Organization for Industrialization, United Arab Emirates, Kingdom of Saudi Arabia, State of Qatar, Arab Republic of Egypt and Arab British Helicopter Company* (5 March 1984) 80 ILR 600 at 602.

[13] Ibid, 602–03.

[14] Ibid, 603.

defendants and declarations that it was under no liability to, and was entitled to retain any payments received from, ABH.[15]

In the arbitration, the arbitral tribunal was required to determine the '"legal nature" and the status of the AOI'. It approached its task in the following way:

> [i]t is necessary to establish what are the legal rules governing this entity, what was the intention on foundation, in this respect, of the four States which created it, and what is the effect that they intended to achieve by their founding steps.
>
> In order to examine this problem reference must firstly be made to the founding documents, that is to say to the constitutional laws creating the AOI: the Treaty, the Basic Statute and the Resolution of the High Committee of the AOI signed on 17 August 1975 and approving the Basic Statute. ... From these it is clear that the four States, in drawing them up, intended to define in an exhaustive and exclusive manner all legal aspects pertaining to the AOI, and above all that they wished to exclude the application of any national law. This is what they sought to do in stating as follows: 'The Organization ... is not subject to the laws and regulations in effect in the participating countries ...' (Treaty Article 1 ss. 2, and in the same vein Article 8) and 'The Organization is not subject to the laws and internal systems in effect in the participating States, including the laws and systems concerning taxes and customs ...' (see also in this vein Basic Statute Article 9). This intention is normal and natural: the four States wanted to maintain equality between them within the context of the AOI and could not therefore select the domestic law of one or other of them as the legal basis for the AOI, in the same way that they could not in the nature of things select the domestic law of a third country. The reference to the 'Arab' character of the AOI, which is found in the very name of the organization as well as in the preamble to the Treaty, corresponds to the consciously intended supranational character of the AOI. As a result the law of no State can be applied to AOI and this entity is wholly governed by the founding documents mentioned above.[16]

More than 20 years after the decision of the arbitral tribunal in *Westland Helicopters*, the status of the International Federation of Red Cross and Red Crescent Societies ('IFRC') was considered by the Administrative Tribunal of the International Labour Organization ('ILOAT') in Judgment 2450 (2005). The complainants in this case were two staff members of the IFRC residing in France who, while not subject to taxation in Switzerland in accordance with the headquarters agreement signed by the IFRC and the Swiss Federal Council, were considered by the French tax authorities as liable to income tax on their salary since 1998 when the double taxation treaty between France and Switzerland was amended. The complainants, and a third staff member who had not filed a complaint but who had submitted an application to intervene, had filed a 'settlement demand', calling on the IFRC to refund the taxes they had to pay on their salaries since 1998. When that was rejected, the three staff members lodged an appeal with the Secretary General of the IFRC. The Secretary General recommended that they transmit a

[15] Ibid, 604.
[16] Ibid, 610–11.

formal request of reimbursement to the Head of Human Resources. This was the impugned decision. The complainants argued before the ILOAT that the exemption from taxation is a 'fundamental feature of employment as an international civil servant'.[17] However, the ILOAT noted that the IFRC is an association under Swiss law and is, therefore, not an international organisation:

> [t]he complainants believe that as international civil servants they are entitled to certain fundamental conditions of employment, among which the Tribunal has included 'exemption from national taxes' in Judgment 2032 delivered on 31 January 2001. However, the Federation is an association under Swiss law whose international legal personality has been recognised by Switzerland and which is not an intergovernmental organisation. That is why the Statute of the Tribunal was amended at the 86th Session of the International Labour Conference in June 1998 in order to extend the Tribunal's jurisdiction to the staff members of the Federation. At any event, States which are not bound by a Headquarters Agreement providing for tax immunity are not under any obligation arising either from international custom or from international treaties. …
>
> The plea whereby the organisation may be enriching itself unjustly at the expense of the staff members concerned also fails. The complainants refer in this respect to Judgment 2256 delivered on 16 July 2003, in which the Tribunal in accordance with constant precedent (see for example Judgment 2032) recalled that international organisations have a duty to protect their staff against the claims of the authorities of a member State and cannot evade this obligation on the grounds of the member State's reluctance. In this case, the Federation is not made up of member States and, as was pointed out above, case law concerning intergovernmental organisations cannot be purely and simply transposed to the Federation. The application of rules that are in force cannot in any case give rise to unjust enrichment.[18]

The approach adopted by the ILOAT in Judgment 2450 (2005) with regard to the IFRC conforms with the approach of the European Union ('EU'). In the European Convention on the Recognition of the Legal Personality of International Non-Governmental Organisations, Article 1 defines international non-governmental organisations ('NGOs') as:

> associations, foundations and other private institutions … which satisfy the following conditions:
>
> (a) have a non-profit-making aim of international utility;
> (b) have been established by an instrument governed by the internal law of a Party;
> (c) carry on their activities with effect in at least two States; and
> (d) have their statutory office in the territory of a Party and the central management and control in the territory of that Party or of another Party.[19]

[17] *NM and PRG v International Federation of Red Cross and Red Crescent Societies*, ILOAT, Judgment No 2450 (2005) 2.

[18] Ibid.

[19] European Convention on the Recognition of the Legal Personality of International Non-Governmental Organisations (opened for signature on 24 April 1986, entered into force on 1 January 1991) ETS No 124, Art 1 (emphasis added).

Conversely, organisations and institutions set up by treaties or other instruments governed by public international law are excluded. In the Explanatory Report on the Convention, it was explained that this exclusion is 'justified by the fact that such entities are subject to public international law and not to the domestic law of a contracting state, so that the problem of recognition by other states does not arise'.[20]

The Bank for International Settlements ('BIS') is another interesting example as it was established in a 'rather complicated manner' in 1930.[21] In the *BIS Share Repurchase* case, an arbitral tribunal considered, as a preliminary issue, the legal character and status of the BIS. It recalled that some of the parties to the treaty establishing the BIS had doubts as to whether a treaty could establish, under public international law, a company limited by shares and whether such company could be so recognised. For these reasons, the parties to the treaty chose to adopt a model whereby, pursuant to an obligation in the treaty, Switzerland undertook to grant the BIS a constituent charter and thereby create the BIS as a company. At the same time, however, the parties made it clear that, even though the charter (provided as an annex to the treaty) was issued under Swiss law, the BIS did not as a consequence become subject to Swiss law. The tribunal held that:

> [t]he Constituent Instruments confirm that the Bank was established under international law in conformity with a treaty between the Governments of Germany, Belgium, France, the United Kingdom, Italy, Japan and Switzerland, which was concluded on 20 January 1930. Under Article 1 of the Convention, Switzerland undertook 'to grant to the Bank for International Settlements, without delay, the following Constituent Charter having force of law …'. By approving the Convention, the Swiss Parliament gave the Swiss Government the competence to ratify this treaty and to grant the Constituent Charter, which is an integral part of the Convention. Article 1 of the Charter stated '[t]he Bank for International Settlements … is hereby incorporated'. Article 2 of the said Charter added that the constitution, the operations and the activities of the Bank were 'defined and governed by the annexed Statutes'. The Statutes of the Bank and its Constituent Charter were thus determined by an intergovernmental agreement and were annexed to the Convention. The granting of the Charter by Switzerland did not thereby subordinate the Bank to Swiss law. Paragraph 5 of the Charter provided that '[t]he said Statutes and any amendments which may be made thereto in accordance with Paragraphs 3 or 4 hereof respectively shall be valid and operative notwithstanding any inconsistency therewith in the provisions of any present or future Swiss law'.
>
> Thus, the sequence of steps by which the Bank was established demonstrates its international treaty origin. The Bank was created by Governments, through an international instrument, which instrument obligated Switzerland to provide a venue and local status,

[20] Union of International Associations (eds), *International Associations Statutes Series*, Vol 1 (1988) Appendix 4.11.

[21] *Partial Award on the lawfulness of the recall of the privately held shares on 8 January 2001 and the applicable standards for valuation of those shares* (Partial Award of 22 November 2002) XXIII RIAA 183, para 105.

> as well as prescribed immunities. The Bank is chartered as a company limited by shares under Swiss law, while it is registered as an 'Internationale Organisation mit eigenem Rechtsstatus' in the 'Handelsregister des Kantons Basel-Stadt Hauptregister'.[22]

A separate question (which should not be confused with the issue at hand) is the manner in which an international organisation is recognised in domestic law. The technique employed depends on the relationship between international law and the national law of the State concerned.[23] In States which adopt a monist system, the domestic legal personality of an organisation is often considered to flow directly from the relevant treaty. In dualist systems, the domestic legal personality of an organisation is conferred either through domestic legislation which gives effect to the State's treaty obligations or, where the State is not a party to the relevant treaty, through the application of private international law.[24] For instance, in 1990, in *Arab Monetary Fund v Hashim (No. 3)*,[25] the House of Lords of the UK considered whether the Arab Monetary Fund ('A.M.F.'), which was unquestionably established by a formal treaty (ie, the Articles of Agreement of the A.M.F.), could bring a claim in the English courts, notwithstanding the fact that the UK was neither a party to that treaty nor had that treaty been otherwise incorporated into UK law.[26] The House of Lords accepted that the A.M.F. was established with an 'independent juridical personality' but emphasised that, under English law, it was required to 'ignore the treaty and regard the A.M.F. as constituted under Abu Dhabi law as a domestic entity under ordinary conflict rules'.[27]

[22] '*International organisation with its own legal status in the Commercial register of the Canton of Basel-Stadt*' (authors' translation) (*Partial Award on the lawfulness of the recall of the privately held shares on 8 January 2001 and the applicable standards for valuation of those shares* (Partial Award of 22 November 2002) XXIII RIAA 183, para 108 (footnotes and references omitted)).

[23] See a discussion of the various approaches in: Higgins, R et al (eds), *Oppenheim's International Law: United Nations*, Vol I (Oxford, Oxford University Press, 2017) 396–97.

[24] In general, two main normative models are adopted under private international law, ie, the 'real seat' model and the 'incorporation' model. Under the 'real seat' model, the law applicable to a company is the law of the State where it has its effective central administration, whereas the 'incorporation' model refers to the law of the State of incorporation. Common law countries tend to apply the latter, but the majority of civil law countries adopt the former. For a discussion of these two models, see: Collins, L et al, *Dicey, Morris & Collins on the Conflict of Laws*, 15th edn, Vol 2 (Sweet & Maxwell, London, 2012) 1527–95; Rogerson, P, *Collier's Conflict of Laws*, 2nd edn (Cambridge, Cambridge University Press, 2014) 37–8.

[25] *Arab Monetary Fund v Hashim (No 3)* [1991] 2 WLR 729 (HL). See also: Staker, C, 'Decisions of British Courts During 1991 Involving Questions of Public or Private International Law' (1991) 62 *British Yearbook of International Law* 433–47.

[26] Mann, FA, 'International Organisations as National Corporations' in Mann, FA, *Notes and Comments on Cases in International Law, Commercial Law, and Arbitration* (Oxford, Clarendon Press, 1992) 269–73.

[27] *Arab Monetary Fund v Hashim (No 3)* [1991] 2 WLR 729 (HL) at 739 (Lord Templeton). But see: *Westland Helicopters Ltd v Arab Organisation for Industrialisation* [1995] QB 282 where the High Court clarified that, although the English courts will generally apply the law of the place of incorporation as the governing law, where a friendly foreign State has clothed an international organisation with legal personality and has thereby created a foreign corporation, that body is no ordinary domestic entity but an international body created by treaty and questions as to the meaning, effect and operation of its constitution, at least so far as they arise between the parties to the treaty, can only be determined by reference to the treaty and the principles of public international law and not by any body of domestic law.

The Munich District Court adopted a similar approach in *Scientology Kirche Deutschland v INTERPOL* (discussed at length in Chapter 7) with respect to INTERPOL. In considering the legal capacity of INTERPOL to be sued in the German courts, the District Court was of the view that INTERPOL's legal status in international law existed, but was 'of no interest to this case'.[28] It was concerned with INTERPOL's legal capacity 'in general German private law' which stipulated that 'the municipal legal status of international organisations is governed by the laws of the countries where their headquarters are located' (eg, France, in respect of INTERPOL).[29] The Court therefore concluded that INTERPOL had legal capacity in French private law.

The problem with the approach of the House of Lords of the UK and the Munich District Court is that, taken to its logical conclusion, the law governing the status and capabilities of an international organisation would be foreign domestic law.

It is also possible for a private organisation established under the domestic law of a State to be recognised by another State as an international organisation for the purposes of the application of certain domestic laws. However, such recognition by a national court does not equate to a proclamation that the organisation is a creature of international law. For instance, the International Air Transport Association ('IATA') was formed in April 1945 in Havana as the successor to the International Air Traffic Association, which had been founded in The Hague in 1919 (the year that marked the world's first international scheduled services). IATA is an international industry trade association composed of airlines which is headquartered in Montreal with an executive office in Geneva. The main objective of IATA is to assist airline companies in achieving lawful competition and uniformity in prices. IATA was not established by international agreement: as stated in Article II(1) of IATA's Articles of Association, the act of incorporation of IATA is a legal act under the Statutes of Canada, 1945, Chapter 51 (assented to on 18 December 1945, as amended from time to time). The members of IATA are commercial airlines. Moreover, IATA does not purport to perform a public (ie, governmental) function. The Swiss Federal Court considered the status of IATA in *Jenni and others v Conseil d'État of Geneva*.[30] 287 employees of IATA were based in Geneva, of whom only 48 were of Swiss nationality. In a draft agreement between the Swiss federal authorities and IATA, the Swiss federal authorities recognised IATA as an international organisation under Swiss law for the purposes of providing IATA's employees stationed in Geneva exemption from taxation at the cantonal level. This was approved by the Council of State of the Canton of Geneva. Jenni and others challenged this decision. One of the questions raised was whether the federal authorities had arbitrarily recognised

[28] *Scientology Kirche Deutschland et al v INTERPOL*, District Court of Munich, Az: 120 10 512/76 (5 January 1978) para 1.4

[29] Ibid.

[30] *Jenni and Others v Conseil d'État of Geneva*, Swiss Federal Tribunal (Public Law Chamber) (4 October 1978) 75 ILR 99.

IATA as an international organisation, thereby unduly impairing the tax base of the Canton of Geneva. The tribunal found that, taking into account the functions performed by IATA and the important role it plays in a significant sphere of inter-State relations, in addition to the opinions of 'certain authors' that IATA is a 'quasi-governmental organization', it was not 'untenable' that IATA constitutes a public international organisation within the meaning of the relevant public tax law. It therefore held that the decision of the Council of State was not arbitrary.[31] Conspicuously, the tribunal's decision was not based on the nature of the constituent instrument of IATA.

II. The Governing Law of the INTERPOL Constitution

INTERPOL's situation is arguably less complicated than that of INTELSAT, the IFRC or the BIS. INTERPOL was created by an agreement between subjects of international law (ie, countries) and this agreement cannot be presumed to be governed by the national law of any country. Commentators such as Daum suggest that INTERPOL is a private organisation.[32] However, Daum fails to meaningfully explain in what respect he considers INTERPOL to be a private organisation. Specifically, Daum does not identify any national law under which the Organisation might have been established, as is necessary to overcome the presumptive application of international law to agreements between subjects of international law.

Moreover, it is clear that the parties to the INTERPOL Constitution (and its previous iterations) intended for the INTERPOL Constitution to create legal effects under international law. The adoption of the 1923 Constitution of the International Criminal Police Commission ('ICPC') (the prior name of INTERPOL) was not made contingent on the completion of any formal process under the law of any country, nor did the 1923 ICPC Constitution give a supplementary role to the domestic law of any country. The same is true for the 1939 and the 1946 ICPC Constitutions, as well as for the 1956 INTERPOL Constitution. In the 1956 INTERPOL Constitution, INTERPOL and/or its organs are referred to as an 'international centre' of an 'international character' with an 'international task'.[33] The manifest intent of the contracting parties was to create a constituent instrument governed by international law, within the meaning of the law of treaties. In other words, INTERPOL was not established by an instrument governed by the domestic law of any country, the INTERPOL Constitution is governed by

[31] *Jenni and Others v Conseil d'État of Geneva*, Swiss Federal Tribunal (Public Law Chamber) (4 October 1978) 75 ILR 99 at 105.

[32] Daum, U, 'INTERPOL – öffentliche Gewalt ohne Kontrolle' (1980) 35 *JuristenZeitung* 798–801.

[33] INTERPOL Constitution, Arts 26(b), 30 and 41.

international law.[34] While not articulated in such terms, this fact informed the outcome in Judgment 1080 (1991), where the ILOAT dismissed the argument that INTERPOL employees should receive higher termination payments on the basis that employees of other international organisations (including some with headquarters in France) would fare better on termination. The ILOAT held that there was no basis on which to compare INTERPOL, an independent international organisation, with any other international organisation. The tribunal also observed that French law would only have applied if INTERPOL had agreed to apply French law and subscribed to the collective agreement the complainants sought to rely on.

The foregoing raises the question: can one international organisation enact legislation that binds another international organisation, without the latter having agreed to be subject to it? This question is relevant to INTERPOL (and other international organisations headquartered or operating in the territories of EU Member States) following the entry into force of the EU General Data Protection Regulation ('GDPR')[35] and Directive 2016/680, which is specifically applicable to personal data processed for law enforcement purposes.[36] It is suggested that, in the context of the EU, this question ought to be answered negatively because INTERPOL is not within the organic jurisdiction of the EU. Indeed, in the view of the European Commission 'Interpol as a legal personality is not subject to EC law'.[37] It is, therefore, no surprise that the European Data Protection Supervisor ('EDPS') is of the view that it does not have supervisory competence over other international organisations, only institutions, bodies and agencies of the EU.[38] It follows that the GDPR does not bind INTERPOL, nor do the national laws which give effect to Directive 2016/680.

The foregoing conclusion notwithstanding, the GDPR and Directive 2016/680 may nevertheless affect INTERPOL insofar as they condition the ability of law enforcement authorities of EU Member States to either populate the INTERPOL

[34] Amerasinghe, CF, *Principles of the Institutional Law of International Organisations*, 2nd edn (Cambridge, Cambridge University Press, 2005) 13–4.

[35] Regulation (EU) 2016/679 of the European Parliament and of the Council of 27 April 2016 on the protection of natural persons with regard to the processing of personal data and on the free movement of such data, and repealing Directive 95/46/EC (General Data Protection Regulation), Official Journal L119/1 (4 May 2016) 1–88. On this subject, see: Kuner, C, 'International Organizations and the EU General Data Protection Regulation: Exploring the Interaction between EU Law and International Law' (2019) 16 *International Organizations Law Review* 158–91.

[36] Directive (EU) 2016/680 of the European Parliament and of the Council of 27 April 2016 on the protection of natural persons with regard to the processing of personal data by competent authorities for the purposes of the prevention, investigation, detection or prosecution of criminal offences or the execution of criminal penalties, and on the free movement of such data, and repealing Council Framework Decision 2008/977/JHA, Official Journal L119/89 (4 May 2016) 89–131.

[37] Parliamentary questions, 'Answer given by Ms Malmström on behalf of the Commission', Official Journal C 229 E-011707/2013 (17 July 2014).

[38] EDPS, 'International Organisations', available at: https://edps.europa.eu/data-protection/notre-rôle-en-tant-que-contrôleur/international-organisations_en.

databases or use information obtained therefrom. Thus, it is necessary to consider whether data processors within the EU must observe the GDPR and the national laws which give effect to Directive 2016/680 when exchanging personal data with international organisations. This question is answered by the rules concerning the sharing of data with non-EU authorities. Under Article 45(1) of the GDPR, the transfer of data to a third country or an international organisation may be carried out if the European Commission determines that the third country or international organisation ensures an 'adequate' level of data protection. Article 35(1)(d) of Directive 2016/680 is more nuanced in respect of such transfers, but it nevertheless requires that either (1) the Commission has determined that the international organisation has an adequate level of protection, (2) specific safeguards are complied with, or (3) derogations for specific situations are applicable.

The question whether INTERPOL's data protection regime is deemed adequate for the purposes of Directive 2016/680 was raised by the Administrative Court of Wiesbaden in a request for a preliminary ruling to the Court of Justice of the EU ('CJEU') dated 3 July 2019.[39] The underlying case concerned an individual ('WS') in the Federal Republic of Germany ('Germany') who was the subject of a red notice at the request of the National Central Bureau in Washington, DC. Germany refused to extradite the individual on the basis of, inter alia, the prohibition on double jeopardy in Article 50 of the EU Charter of Fundamental Rights. INTERPOL, however, refused to delete the red notice. The individual therefore brought an action against Germany on the basis that he could not exercise his right to free movement within the EU and the Schengen area. The Administrative Court of Wiesbaden referred a number of questions to the CJEU. As of 1 January 2020, the CJEU was still considering the request, but the Administrative Court of Wiesbaden expressed grave doubts in its request as to whether INTERPOL has an adequate level of data protection within the meaning of Directive 2016/680:

> [i]f Interpol, despite the prohibition of double jeopardy, does not refrain from transmitting the data of the red notice to all the Member States and does not ensure that the data is erased without delay, the referring court has considerable doubts regarding the reliability under data protection law of the International Organisation 'Interpol'. This unreliability ultimately leads to the question of whether, due to the lack of appropriate safeguards at Interpol, the Member States should not refrain entirely in this respect from cooperating with Interpol, as this is the only way of safeguarding freedom of movement within the context of European Union. … As there is quite clearly no coordination of red notices within the EU and in the absence of a uniform regulatory framework, the freedom of the citizens of the Member States can only be ensured through withdrawal from Interpol.[40]

[39] *WS v Federal Republic of Germany*, Case C-505/19, 'Request for a preliminary ruling' (3 July 2019). It queried, inter alia, '[d]oes an international organisation such as the International Criminal Police Organisation – Interpol – have an adequate data protection level if there is no adequacy decision under Article 36 of Directive (EU) 2016/680 and/or there are no appropriate safeguards under Article 37 of Directive (EU) 2016/680?'.

[40] Ibid, para 27.

This line of enquiry begs the question whether compliance with INTERPOL requests that violate EU fundamental rights should be processed by EU Member States at all (on which, see Chapter 8). If the CJEU answers the questions of the Wiesbaden court in such a manner that suggests INTERPOL does not have an adequate level of data protection, this might lead some EU Member States to refuse to cooperate with the Organisation. If this occurred, then it would, almost certainly, trigger a dialogue between the European Commission and INTERPOL to remedy any inadequacy so as to avoid a disruption of the architecture for international police cooperation.

7

Organisation and Operations

Having concluded that the Constitution of the International Criminal Police Organization ('INTERPOL' or the 'Organisation') is an agreement between subjects of international law governed by international law, this final chapter in Part I considers whether the INTERPOL Constitution purports to create, and has actually created, a new subject of law with a distinct will (*volonté distincte*) that bears rights and duties derived from international law. As will be recalled, domestic law treats legal subjects as capable of bearing rights and duties through various fictions and abstractions: the law personifies an object (the *corpus*) and then confers upon it a fictitious personality (the *animus*). International law subscribes to the same pattern. This is apparent from the assertion of the International Court of Justice ('ICJ') that, once established, an international organisation 'acquires a life of its own, independent of the elements which have given birth to it'.[1] It is an entity 'having … its own purposes and functions, and thus a certain legal personality'.[2] It follows that the constituent instruments of international organisations are treaties of a particular type: 'their object is to create new subjects of law endowed with a certain autonomy, to which the parties entrust the task of realizing common goals'.[3] Therefore, an essential requirement of what constitutes an international agreement establishing an international organisation is that the instrument should purport to, and actually, create a new subject of

[1] *Admission of a State to the United Nations* (Advisory Opinion) [1948] ICJ Rep 57, 68 (Individual Opinion of Judge Alvarez). See also: Sands, P and Klein, P, *Bowett's Law of International Institutions*, 6th edn (London, Sweet & Maxwell, 2009) 15–6. On the problematic issues triggered by the notion of distinctive personality of international organisations, see: Blokker, N, 'International Organizations and their Members' (2004) 1 *International Organisations Law Review* 139–61.

[2] *Appeal Relating to the Jurisdiction of the ICAO Council* (Judgment) [1972] ICJ Rep 46, 130 (Separate Opinion of Judge de Castro).

[3] *Legality of the Use by a State of Nuclear Weapons in Armed Conflict* (Advisory Opinion) [1996] ICJ Rep 66, para 19. Unlike most other international agreements, the constituent instrument of an international organisation does not necessarily have to include significant obligations on the parties: it is an incorporating agreement ('*traité de société*' or '*traité d'association*'). Cogan speaks in this context of a difference between 'constitutive' and 'prescriptive' international agreements (Cogan, JK, 'Representation and Power in International Organizations: The Operational Constitution and Its Critics' (2009) 103 *American Journal of International Law* 209 at 213–14). See also: Seyersted, F, *Common Law of International Organizations* (Leiden, Martinus Nijhoff Publishers, 2008) 49–50; Rapisardi-Mirabelli, A, 'La Théorie Générale des Unions Internationales' (1925) 7 *Recueil des Cours* 340–93.

law with a distinct will (*volonté distincte*) capable of bearing rights and duties derived from international law.

A number of constitutions of international organisations expressly provide for the possession of international legal personality.[4] In other cases, it must be deduced by other means. For the purposes of this exercise, it is worth recalling that, in the eyes of the ICJ, the essential test is whether the constituent instrument gives the organisation 'such a position that it possesses, in regard to its Members, rights which it is entitled to ask them to respect'.[5] There are two basic schools of thought regarding the means by which personality should be deduced: the 'objective approach' and the 'will theory'.[6] The former, of which Seyersted is the main proponent, asserts that international legal personality exists so long as certain objective criteria are satisfied:

> [i]nternational organs (*i.e.* organs established by two or more sovereign States) which (1) are not all subject to the authority of any one State or other organized community … (2) perform 'sovereign' and/or international acts in their own name and (3) are not authorized by all their acts to assume obligations (merely) on behalf of the several participating States.[7]

The latter school of thought asserts that the personality of an international organisation must be derived from the will of its members to confer such personality, which is to be inferred from the capacities, powers, rights and duties bestowed on the organisation.[8] However, neither approach is entirely consonant with the approach of the ICJ in *Reparation for Injuries*. As Akande observes, '[w]hat the Court seemed to be saying was that the intention of the members to ascribe certain rights, functions and characteristics to the UN could only be given effect if the organization possessed its own legal personality'.[9] In other words, the possession of characteristics which satisfied the criteria for conferring international personality arose out of the will of its members. The ICJ simply searched to see if the characteristics necessary for international personality (which are predetermined by international law) had been conferred on the United Nations ('UN') by its members.

The primary task in this chapter is to embark on a similar exercise as that in *Reparation for Injuries* in respect of INTERPOL: ie, did the contracting parties to

[4] Eg, Agreement establishing the African Development Bank (signed on 4 August 1963, entered into force on 10 September 1964) 510 UNTS 3, Art 50.

[5] *Reparation for Injuries Suffered in the Service of the United Nations* (Advisory Opinion) [1949] ICJ Rep 174, 178.

[6] See: Akande, D, 'International Organizations' in Evans, MD (ed), *International* Law, 5th edn (Oxford, Oxford University Press, 2018) 227–58 at 231.

[7] Seyersted, F, *Common Law of International Organizations* (Leiden, Martinus Nijhoff Publishers, 2008) 43–4 (footnotes omitted).

[8] Schermers, HG and Blokker, NM, *International Institutional Law: Unity within Diversity*, 6th revised edn (Leiden, Brill Nijhoff Publishers, 2018) 1565.

[9] Akande, D, 'International Organizations' in Evans, MD (ed), *International Law*, 5th edn (Oxford, Oxford University Press, 2018) 272–58 at 232.

the INTERPOL Constitution ascribe characteristics to INTERPOL which confer legal personality on it? In order to make this assessment, this chapter focuses on the organisation and operations of INTERPOL.[10] It considers (1) the structure of the Organisation, (2) the functions ascribed to it, (3) the delegation of powers amongst INTERPOL's organs, (4) the privileges and immunities of the Organisation and its staff, and (5) the recognition of its legal personality. The chapter then briefly addresses the Organisation's consequential capacity to enter into international agreements with other international organisations and States.[11]

If international legal personality is not established, then the individual members of the Organisation remain responsible for the actions of the Organisation.[12] This was made clear by the ICJ in *Certain Phosphate Lands in Nauru*[13] where the question placed before the Court was whether the actions involved were acts of an international organisation or only acts of three States (ie, Australia, New Zealand, and the United Kingdom ('UK')) which together constituted the Administering Authority for the Trust Territory of Nauru ('Authority'). On analysis, it concluded that the 'Authority did not have an international legal personality distinct from those of the States thus designated';[14] therefore, the States remained responsible for the actions of the Authority.

However, before embarking on a discussion of the characteristics which confer international legal personality, this chapter considers the origins of the Organisation. This is important because, in so doing, it will become clear that the drafters of the INTERPOL Constitution not only clearly manifested their intention to create an international legal person, but also took great care to ensure that INTERPOL could never be controlled by a single country, as happened when the National Socialist German Workers Party ('Nazi Party') effectively assumed control of the Organisation during its first embodiment as the International Criminal

[10] The case of the International Trade Organization ('ITO') demonstrates that, absent actual organisation and operations, the new legal subject cannot come into existence. As agreed at the Bretton Woods Conference of 1944, the ITO was conceived in the Havana Charter for an International Trade Organization ('Havana Charter') as the institution responsible for the global governance of international trade. The Havana Charter was signed by 56 countries on 24 March 1948. Although the Havana Charter purported to create a new legal subject, that new subject was never actually created, in part, because the United States ('US') government announced that it would not submit the treaty to the Senate for ratification (therefore, no other country ratified the treaty). See: Diebold, W, 'From the ITO to GATT – and Back?' in Kirshner, O (ed), *The Bretton Woods-GATT System: Retrospect and Prospect After Fifty Years* (New York, Routledge, 2015) 152–73.

[11] *Reparation for Injuries Suffered in the Service of the United Nations* (Advisory Opinion) [1949] ICJ Rep 174, 178.

[12] Higgins, R, *Problems and Process: International Law and How We Use It* (Oxford, Clarendon Press, 1994) 47. See also: Alvarez, JE, *International Organisations as Law-Makers* (Oxford, Oxford University Press, 2005) 129–30.

[13] *Certain Phosphate Lands in Nauru (Nauru v Australia)* (Preliminary Objections) [1992] ICJ Rep 240.

[14] Ibid, para 47. See also: Sarooshi, D, *International Organisations and their Exercise of Sovereign Powers* (Oxford, Oxford University Press, 2005) 34.

Police Commission ('ICPC').[15] The following remarks of the former INTERPOL Secretary General stress this point:

> I am always amazed when I think about INTERPOL's origins. We were created back in 1923, when police chiefs and police representatives from 19 countries met in Vienna, Austria, to look for practical solutions for the growing problem of transnational crime. They did not begin their dream for a better way to cooperate by devising legal or international instruments to facilitate their cooperation. Instead, they were searching for practical ways for police to share information and to cooperate on a day-to-day basis internationally like they did nationally. The formal legal instruments that the Organization had at its disposal were minimal. In 1926, the principle of national contact points – forerunners to our National Central Bureaus – was introduced, but, generally speaking, the Organization's focus remained practically-oriented. However, world events caught up with us and in 1938, it became painfully clear that a global police organization, using state-of-the-art technology (at that time, its international radio network) needed to have clear and formal rules in place to safeguard the integrity of its work and its independence. These safeguards were not in place: when the Nazi Party invaded Austria in March 1938, they had to simply remove and arrest the Head of the Austrian Police, who under the statutes of the Organization at the time was automatically the President of the Organization. Heinrich Himmler, who controlled both the SS and the Gestapo, personally appointed an ex-convict and member of the Austrian Nazi Party as the Head of the Austrian police and, consequently, as the President of INTERPOL. At that point, the Organization ceased to exist as an independent and professional international police organization and – even worse – its know-how, technology, records on wanted persons, patiently developed over more than a decade, fell into the hands of a totalitarian regime, whose destructive ideology was at odds with everything INTERPOL stood for: professional policing in the service of citizens. Fortunately, immediately after the Second World War, the notion of an international police organization was revived. And at the very first meeting in 1946, INTERPOL began adopting more democratic processes for electing its President and Executive Committee. We had learned as an organization that we needed a Constitution; we learned that we needed formal rules and regulations; we learned that we needed external oversight; and we learned that we needed to do all in our power to ensure that the Organization's work was of the highest quality possible. And ten years later, in 1956, the Organization adopted its current Constitution, which for over 50 years has guided us well.[16]

I. Origins

INTERPOL's history began in April 1914 when legal experts and police officers from 24 different countries met in Monaco at the first International Criminal

[15] On the control of INTERPOL by the Nazi Party, see: Deflem, M, 'The Logic of Nazification: The Case of the International Criminal Police Commission ("Interpol")' (2002) 43 *International Journal of Comparative Sociology* 21–44.

[16] Noble, RK, Secretary General of INTERPOL, 'International Police Co-operation in the context of Public International Law' (Opening Speech at the INTERPOL Symposium, Lyon, 31 January – 1 February 2008).

Police Congress to discuss setting up an international criminal records office and harmonising extradition procedures. Despite the suggestion implied by the name of the Congress, the meeting focused on criminal law enforcement duties, a development that had been anticipated since the late nineteenth century.[17] However, the Congress failed to institute an international police organisation, largely because the meeting was not organised by police officials but by politicians and legal officials.[18] Proposals that concerned police measures were only discussed at an abstract legal and normative level, resulting in a summary of 12 'wishes'.[19]

After the outbreak of the First World War, there was no further progress in creating an international police organisation until 1923 when the second Congress was held in Vienna at the invitation of the Austrian Government to police officials around the world.[20] The 1923 International Criminal Police Congress was not a classic diplomatic conference. Although not convoked for the purpose of establishing the ICPC, the Congress produced the Constitution of the ICPC in five days. The minutes of the 1923 Congress do not mention any formality for the conclusion and ratification of the ICPC Constitution.

The ICPC's headquarters was established in Vienna, and the head of the Vienna police, Johannes Schober, became its first President. The ICPC flourished until 1938, when Nazi Germany annexed Austria, and the ICPC was subsequently relocated to Berlin. The outbreak of the Second World War effectively ended the ICPC's activities. After the war, the ICPC accepted an offer from the French Government to establish a headquarters in Paris together with staff consisting of French police officials in the General Secretariat. The ICPC was thus revived, although the loss or destruction of all its pre-war records required that it be completely reorganised.

When the ICPC was reconstituted in 1946 in the post-war era, the world had become familiar with a wide range of international organisations based on formally celebrated treaties. The challenge, then, was to increase the profile of the ICPC without sacrificing its autonomy. Reportedly, at the 1946 meeting, the delegates decided to make only minor modifications to the 1939 ICPC Constitution out of

[17] Since 1898, European diplomats had been engaged in discussions about a framework for international police cooperation (see: Masters, A 'INTERPOL: From Vienna to Canberra – The evolution of Australia's relationship with INTERPOL (1923–1975)' (June 2001) *Australian Police Journal* 58–67 at 58–9.

[18] Deflem, M, 'History of International Police Cooperation' in Wright, RA and Miller, JM (eds), *The Encyclopedia of Criminology*, Vol 2: H-P (New York, Routledge, 2005) 795 at 797.

[19] 'Summary of the Wishes Expressed at the Sessions or Assemblies', International Criminal Police Congress, 1st session (Monaco, 1914).

[20] For an account, see: Möllmann, H, *Internationale Kriminalpolizei Polizei des Völkerrechts?: zur Problematik der Abgrenzung öffentlicher und privater internationaler Organisationen am Beispiel der Internationale Kriminalpolizeilichen Organisation (IKPO – INTERPOL)* (Würzburg, Gugel, 1969) 37–59. See also: Babovic, B, 'Dates d'adhésion à INTERPOL' (1998) 469/471 *Revue Internationale de Police Criminelle* 247–51; Marabuto, P (a representative of the ICPC at the 5th session of the Commission on Narcotic Drugs), 'The International Criminal Police Commission and the Illicit Traffic of Narcotics' (1951) 3-002 *UNODC Bulletin on Narcotics*.

a desire to retain the atmosphere of a 'policeman's club'.[21] According to Barnett and Coleman, the ICPC staff adopted the tactic of 'ceremonial conformity': they believed that the secret to success was to remake the design of the ICPC so that it had the appearance of a respectable and modern international organisation, whilst simultaneously avoiding any loss of autonomy that might compromise its ability to do its work and define its goals as it saw fit.[22] In 1949, the ICPC was granted consultative status by the UN. From 1946 to 1955 its membership grew from 19 countries to 55. In 1956, the ICPC ratified a new Constitution, under which it was renamed the 'International Criminal Police Organization – INTERPOL'.

In its early years of the ICPC, it was mainly a European organisation, drawing only limited support from non-European countries (eg, the United States ('US') did not become a participant in the ICPC until 1938). Under the leadership of former Secretary General Jean Népote (1963–78), INTERPOL became increasingly effective. By the mid-1980s, the number of members had risen to more than 125, representing all of the world's inhabited continents; by the early twenty-first century, membership had surpassed 190, reaching 194 in 2018. The Organisation moved its headquarters to Lyon in 1989.[23]

The Organisation underwent substantial change following the '9/11' attacks on the US. The INTERPOL General Secretariat was reorganised and a new post of Executive Director for Police Services was created to oversee the operational functioning of the Organisation, including coordinating and supervising all law enforcement activities performed at the General Secretariat and in the regional bureaux and National Central Bureaux ('NCBs'). In 2003, the Organisation's approach to technology as a means to support international police communications radically changed with the creation of the I-24/7 Global Police Communications System (with Canada being the first country to connect). The system connects the INTERPOL General Secretariat and NCBs, creating a global network for the exchange of police information and providing law enforcement authorities in each country with instant access to the Organisation's databases and other services. The specific software and databases now utilised by INTERPOL are explored in section III below.

II. Structure

INTERPOL's internal structure comprises the General Assembly, the Executive Committee, the General Secretariat, NCBs, Advisers, and the Commission for the Control of INTERPOL's Files ('CCF' or 'Commission').[24]

[21] Barnett, M and Coleman, L, 'Designing Police: Interpol and the Study of Change in International Organizations' (2005) 49 *International Studies Quarterly* 593–619 at 601.

[22] Ibid. The 1956 INTERPOL Constitution contains several features that lend support to this analysis.

[23] 'INTERPOL celebrates 30 years in Lyon as the Organization's centenary approaches', INTERPOL press release (Lyon, 27 November 2019).

[24] INTERPOL Constitution, Art 5. See also: Valleix, C, 'INTERPOL' (1984) 88 *Revue Générale de Droit International Public* 646–51; Pezard, A, 'L'organisation internationale de police criminelle et son

A. The INTERPOL General Assembly

The General Assembly is the main plenary body of INTERPOL. Each country's delegation to the General Assembly is made up of one or more delegates, with a head of delegation appointed by the competent governmental authority of that country.[25] Consistent with the institutional autonomy that characterises the police in all countries,[26] Article 7 of the INTERPOL Constitution provides that, because of the technical nature of the Organisation, members should attempt to include in their delegations senior police officials, national officials whose normal duties are connected with the activities of the Organisation, and specialists in the subjects on the agenda for the relevant session.[27] In practice, countries primarily choose high-ranking police officials as delegates to the General Assembly. However, it is not uncommon for countries to include diplomats in their delegations (often the ambassador accredited to the country where the General Assembly session is held). In recent years, it has become common for countries that are involved in a dispute over the issuance of INTERPOL notices to be represented by ambassadors, lawyers and, in one case, a former member of the International Law Commission. In addition, police bodies from countries which are not members of the Organisation and international organisations can be invited to attend General Assembly sessions as observers.[28]

The General Assembly meets in an ordinary session every year at a location determined by the Assembly itself. Any member country may invite the General Assembly to meet on its territory, and the Assembly chooses, from among the invitations received, where it will meet. The exact date is fixed in conjunction with the host country and the President of the Organisation, after consulting with the Secretary General. The General Assembly may also meet in an extraordinary session to discuss a specific matter at the request of the Executive Committee or at the request of a majority of the members. In principle, that session is held at the Organisation's headquarters.[29]

accord de siège' (1983) 29 *Annuaire français de Droit International* 564–75 at 572–75; El Zein, S, 'Nature juridique de la Commission de contrôle des fichiers de l'OIPC-INTERPOL' (2000) 480 *Revue Internationale de Police Criminelle* 2–10.

[25] Article 8(2) of the Rules of Procedure of the ICPO-INTERPOL General Assembly [II.A/RPGA/GA/1996(2019)] ('Rules of Procedure') prescribes that '[b]efore the beginning of the session, the head of each delegation or a member of the delegation appointed by him to act on his behalf, shall give the Credentials Bureau the credentials he has received from the appropriate government authority. Under the terms of Article 7(1) of the Constitution and in conformity with the procedures applying in the country concerned, the credentials allowing him to represent his country at the General Assembly session must have been issued by the country's head of State, head of government, Minister of Foreign Affairs or minister in charge of the INTERPOL National Central Bureau, or by any plenipotentiary.'

[26] See: Deflem, M, 'Bureaucratization and Social Control: Historical Foundations of International Police Cooperation' (2000) 34 *Law and Society Review* 739–78.

[27] See: Babovic, B, 'A propos de l'article 7 du statut de l'OIPC-INTERPOL' (1995) 542/543 *Revue Internationale de Police Criminelle* 5–6.

[28] General Regulations [I/GREG/GA/1956(2019)] ('General Regulations'), Art 8.

[29] Ibid, Arts 14 and 15.

The responsibility of drawing up a provisional agenda for the General Assembly is bestowed on the INTERPOL Executive Committee.[30] The provisional agenda will include (1) the report of the Secretary General on the work of the Organisation, (2) the Secretary General's financial report and the draft budget, (3) the general programme of activities proposed by the Secretary General for the coming year, (4) items whose inclusion have been ordered at the previous session of the Assembly, (5) items proposed by members, and (6) items inserted by the Executive Committee or the Secretary General.[31] Up to 30 days before the opening of the session, any member may request that an item be added to the agenda. Any such request should be accompanied by an explanation, a draft resolution referring to the item (if appropriate) and possibly a report. If inclusion of the item on the final agenda is approved, these documents should be drafted in one of the Organisation's working languages and distributed to delegates at the General Assembly session,[32] together with any other item proposed by the General Secretariat or added by the Executive Committee as a supplement to the agenda. Before the opening of the General Assembly session, the Executive Committee must combine the provisional agenda and the supplement to the agenda into a final agenda.[33] The General Assembly may also decide to add to its agenda any item which is both urgent and important.[34]

The General Assembly sessions are chaired by the President of the Organisation who conducts discussions in accordance with the rules on conduct of business laid down in Articles 26–32 of the General Regulations and in accordance with the Rules of Procedure. The President is elected for four years[35] and acts in a representative capacity of the Organisation, not as a representative of any country.[36]

i. *Subsidiary Bodies and Regional Conferences*

The General Assembly may form any committees it deems necessary and allocate work relating to the various items on the agenda to these committees.[37] Article 54 of the Rules of Procedure stipulates that, subject to the General Assembly's power to set up or abolish committees, and depending on the agenda prepared by the Executive Committee, the following committees or other groups shall, as a rule, hold meetings: heads of NCBs, delegates from each continent, a Finance Committee, and a Computerisation and Telecommunications Committee. Each committee elects its own chairman and each committee member has the right to

[30] Ibid, Art 9; Rules of Procedure, Art 10(1).
[31] General Regulations, Art 10; Rules of Procedure, Art 11(1).
[32] General Regulations, Art 11; Rules of Procedure, Art 12.
[33] General Regulations, Art 12; Rules of Procedure, Art 13(1).
[34] Rules of Procedure, Art 13(2).
[35] INTERPOL Constitution, Art 17.
[36] Ibid, Art 21.
[37] Ibid, Art 11(1). See also: General Regulations, Arts 35–38; Rules of Procedure, Art 55.

vote at meetings.[38] Meetings of committees are subject to the same rules as the plenary sessions of the General Assembly. Committees report verbally on their work to the General Assembly in plenary session, either through their chairman or through reporters appointed by them. Committees may be consulted between sessions, unless the General Assembly decides otherwise. The President, after consulting the Secretary General, may allow a committee to meet between sessions, provided that any resulting financial implications are approved beforehand by the Executive Committee.[39]

Moreover, at the beginning of each session, the General Assembly elects at least three heads of delegations who will form the Election Committee.[40] The members of this committee act as scrutineers. The Election Committee examines all nominations, which must be given to them, to determine whether they are valid before submitting them to the General Assembly.[41] In addition, whenever a decision to be taken by the General Assembly involves amendment of the INTERPOL Constitution or General Regulations or appendices thereto, an ad hoc committee must be set up to study the project and provide its opinion. The ad hoc committee is composed of three delegates elected by the General Assembly and two persons appointed by the Executive Committee.[42]

Like other international organisations with universal membership, INTERPOL conducts some of its activities on a regional basis. To that end, INTERPOL has developed an internal system of regionalisation. It is possible to identify two forms of regionalisation within INTERPOL's internal law and practice: operational regionalisation and statutory regionalisation. The two categories were developed separately, for different purposes, and are not necessarily synchronised. Regionalisation for operational purposes is based on the Secretary General's powers to 'ensure the efficient administration of the Organisation'[43] and to 'organise and direct the permanent departments' of the Organisation.[44] Based on that power, the General Secretariat created the European Sub-Directorate, and the Middle East and North Africa Sub-Directorate, among others. Statutory regionalisation, on the other hand, is of significant consequence for INTERPOL members because it not only determines the regional positions on the Executive Committee for which potential candidates may stand,[45] but also gives their NCBs full member status at the relevant regional conference.

Regional conferences bring together NCBs in each of INTERPOL's four statutory regions to discuss global and regional policing issues. Habitually, the

[38] General Regulations, Art 36(1); Rules of Procedure, Art 55(1).
[39] General Regulations, Arts 35–38; Rules of Procedure, Arts 53–57.
[40] General Regulations, Art 40.
[41] Ibid, Art 40.
[42] Ibid, Art 56.
[43] INTERPOL Constitution, Art 26(d).
[44] Ibid, Art 29.
[45] The regional aspects of the Executive Committee will be discussed below.

European Regional Conference is held once a year and the conferences in Africa, the Americas and Asia (which Australia and New Zealand attend) are held once every two years. The members of each conference are the NCBs of the member countries in that region. NCB representatives from countries outside the region and those from regional law enforcement or other organisations may attend as observers. The regional conferences are technically committees of the General Assembly, and, therefore, subsidiary bodies of the General Assembly. However, regional conferences have not always enjoyed the status of subsidiary bodies. It was only with the introduction of Article 11(2) to the INTERPOL Constitution[46] and Article 35(2) to the General Regulations[47] at the 66th session of the General Assembly in 1997 that regional conferences were elevated to this status.[48]

Despite amending the INTERPOL Constitution in 1997, the General Assembly did not define the objectives, authorities or duties of the regional conferences. Recognising the need for some direction, the General Assembly adopted the Terms of Reference for the Regional Conferences in 2004. Article 3 defines the objectives of the regional conferences as, inter alia, identifying 'real, specific problems of criminality that transcend national boundaries, that are found within all or part of their regions, that are either of an operational or of a strategic or policy nature, and that are amenable to action or solutions on an institutional level that could not otherwise be achieved through action by individual NCBs'. From this objective alone, it is clear that the regional conferences were established, inter alia, as a tool to promote INTERPOL's general aim of ensuring and promoting 'the widest possible mutual assistance between all criminal police authorities'.[49]

Since the regional conferences are non-plenary committees of the General Assembly, the General Assembly is the only organ competent to determine their composition. However, a question arises as to whether the INTERPOL Constitution or the General Regulations imposes any criteria or restrictions that could bar the General Assembly from honouring a country's request to move from one region to another, a question that INTERPOL faced when Israel asked, for functional reasons, to be included in the European Regional Conference rather than in the Asian Regional Conference.[50] In support of its request, Israel argued that, as regional conferences are created by the General Assembly pursuant to Article 35 of the General Regulations (the same Article which governs the power of the General

[46] Article 11(2) of the INTERPOL Constitution provides that the General Assembly 'may also decide to hold regional conferences between two General Assembly sessions.'

[47] Article 35(2) of the General Regulations provides that '[w]hen it decides to create a regional conference, the General Assembly shall delegate to the latter the power to fix the date, place and conditions of its meetings, taking into account the proposals of member countries. If the regional conference does not take the appropriate decisions, the General Assembly shall take them.'

[48] Resolution No AGN/66/RES/2, 'Regional Conferences', INTERPOL General Assembly, 66th session (New Delhi, 1997).

[49] INTERPOL Constitution, Art 2(1).

[50] See: UN Secretariat, 'Letter to the Acting Chief Counsel, O.I.P.C., Interpol' in *United Nations Juridical Yearbook* (2003), Part Two, Chapter VI, 528–29.

Assembly to form other committees) and in the absence of any specific provision to the contrary, the same procedure which governs the formation and composition of INTERPOL committees should govern the formation and composition of regional conferences. It is clear that the relevant texts contain no manifest limitation on the composition of regional conferences. Moreover, none of INTERPOL's legal instruments explicitly address the manner in which regional conferences should be composed. Israel's request to move from the Asian Regional Conference to the European Regional Conference, therefore, triggered the question whether the General Assembly can reasonably use a non-geographical consideration criterion when deciding on the composition of regional conferences.

Other international organisations have dealt with similar questions, such as the International Labour Organization ('ILO'). Like the INTERPOL Constitution, the ILO Constitution also contains a provision (Article 38) concerning the convening of regional conferences. Also, like Article 11(2) of the INTERPOL Constitution, Article 38 was introduced in the ILO Constitution to reflect and reinforce the ILO's long-standing practice regarding regional activities. In the ILO, four regions have been delineated for the purposes of regional conferences (Africa, the Americas, Asia and the Pacific, and Europe and Central Asia). The ILO traditionally decided the composition of these regions on the basis of the geographical location of the members concerned. However, when the Union of Soviet Socialist Republics was dissolved, some former Soviet republics were allowed to choose the regional conference to which they wanted to belong. Moreover, in the case of countries having territories in more than one continent (eg, France and the UK), they are allowed to attend more than one regional conference.

A comparable pattern can be discerned in INTERPOL. Since the first regional conference in 1962 (in Africa), countries with territories in more than one continent have been allowed to participate in more than one of the regional conferences.[51] This practice continued after the regional conferences were formally given the status of committees of the General Assembly in 1997. Indeed, it is desirable that INTERPOL should maintain some flexibility in designating the composition of regional conferences, as pointed out by INTERPOL's Secretary General at the 32nd European Regional Conference held at Noordwijk in 2003:

> INTERPOL's conferences tend to be structured based on regions and geography. To some extent the prevailing thinking is that we need to be organised on the basis of geographic regions because we tend to co-operate more frequently with our neighbours. But, this is not true with all of our member countries. Israel, Japan and the

[51] Several of INTERPOL's members have sovereignty over territories located on different continents. For example, the UK has sovereignty over Anguilla, Bermuda, Cayman Islands, British Virgin Islands and Montserrat (geographically located in the Americas); France has sovereignty over territories such as French Polynesia and New Caledonia (geographically located in Asia), Réunion and Mayotte (geographically located in Africa), and Saint Pierre and Miquelon, Guyana and Guadeloupe (geographically located in the Americas); and the US has sovereignty over Guam, Wake Island and Northern Mariana Island (geographically located in Asia).

> U.S. regularly attend European Regional Conferences because so much of their police work is done with their European partners. INTERPOL's flexibility permits countries outside the region to attend other regions' conferences. We also have a rich array of observers … in recognition of the fact that Europe's crime concerns are also the world's crime concerns.
>
> Geography is used by the police in other ways to help understand criminal activity. For example, we tend to identify many criminal organisations based on the country of origin of their major participants. Yet, in each of these cases we are not only talking about one group for each country. In fact, organized crime groups contain several different crime organisations of varying sizes operating in different regions. And, when we speak of organized crime groups in terms of one country's citizens, the citizens of those countries are disturbed because they feel tainted.[52]

This view finds support in Article 3 of the Terms of Reference for the Regional Conferences, as cited above. Thus, at the 75th session of the General Assembly, the General Assembly acceded to Israel's request. In so doing, the General Assembly appears to have confirmed the functional approach[53] followed by certain other international organisations that were confronted with a similar request from Israel, such as the ILO, the UN Educational, Scientific and Cultural Organization ('UNESCO') and the World Meteorological Organization.

ii. Decision-Making Procedure

One of the lessons from the period during which the Nazi Party controlled the ICPC is that a decision-making process needs to be put in place that cannot be abused. Following the death of ICPC President Otto Steinhäusl in June 1940, ICPC Secretary General Oskar Dressler sent a report to all ICPC members stating that he and other police, including Nazi Party officials Arthur Nebe and Karl Zindel, had decided to request the Chief of Security Police in Germany to accept the presidency of the ICPC. It is reported that 27 police officials representing 15 countries consented to the suggestion. This was less than two-thirds of the total ICPC membership, which meant that the countries that could not be contacted were not counted and those that had abstained were considered as not voting against the motion. On the basis of this vote, Reinhard Heydrich declared, in a letter dated 24 August 1940, that his candidacy as ICPC President had 'passed unanimously'. Heydrich continued that he would 'lead the Commission into a new and successful future' and that the ICPC headquarters would, instead of being located in Vienna, 'from now on be located in Berlin'.[54]

[52] Noble, RK, Secretary General of INTERPOL (Speech at the 32nd INTERPOL European Regional Conference, Noordwijk, The Netherlands, 2003).

[53] See: Saban, I, 'Israel Police admitted into INTERPOL', *Ynetnews.com* (25 September 2006).

[54] Deflem, M, 'The Logic of Nazification: The Case of the International Criminal Police Commission ("Interpol")' (2002) 43 *International Journal of Comparative Sociology* 21–44 at 26.

Under the current INTERPOL Constitution, this situation cannot repeat itself. It provides that the General Assembly may only take decisions in plenary session. By their nature, except in rare cases of supranational organisations, decisions of various organs of international organisations have as their object and effect the functioning of the organisation and the delivery of the services for which the organisation was created. In addition, international organisations can adopt decisions in which they either recommend or call for certain actions of their members, without such decisions being binding. Decisions of the INTERPOL General Assembly take the form of (1) resolutions, in accordance with Article 17 of the General Regulations, or (2) the outcome of the voting recorded in the summary record of the General Assembly session, in accordance with Article 34 of the Rules of Procedure. The latter is the case for the election of officials, decisions about the accession of new members (according to the practice followed until 2003), adoption of the programme of activities for the following year and the choice of venue for General Assembly sessions. Generally speaking, the former includes two types of resolutions: (1) decisional resolutions relating to the functioning of the Organisation (eg, budget, structure, adoption and amendment of statutory and regulatory texts, establishment of subsidiary organs and adoption of agreements between INTERPOL and individual governments or international organisations), and (2) hortatory resolutions dealing with different aspects of international law enforcement (eg, declarations of principle expressing determination to combat a given type of crime, incitement to take particular action, encouragement to pass laws, recommendations on regulations or working methods covering a particular subject, and invitations to send certain types of information or establish forms). All decisions of the INTERPOL General Assembly, whether in the form of a resolution or not, relating to the functioning of the Organisation or to law enforcement, and which are addressed to the General Secretariat, the Executive Committee or subsidiary organs, are binding. Article 9 of the INTERPOL Constitution provides that members shall do all within their power, insofar as is compatible with their own obligations, to carry out the decisions of the General Assembly.

The ability to take decisions by majority is an important marker of the *volonté distincte* of an international organisation. In principle, the General Assembly takes decisions by a 'simple majority'.[55] However, proposed amendments to the INTERPOL Constitution require a 'two-thirds majority of the Members of the Organisation',[56] and certain decisions, such as the accession of new members, the election of the President, and the adoption and amendment of the General Regulations and the appendices thereto (eg, the Financial Regulations), require a 'two-thirds majority of the Members present and voting'.[57] Each member has

[55] INTERPOL Constitution, Art 14; General Regulations, Art 19; Rules of Procedure, Art 37(1).
[56] INTERPOL Constitution, Art 42; Rules of Procedure, Art 38(1).
[57] INTERPOL Constitution, Arts 4, 16 and 44; Rules of Procedure, Art 38(2).

one vote,[58] which is expressed by the head of its delegation, unless the country has been deprived of its voting rights on account of arrears to the Organisation.[59]

There are divergent views on the phrase 'simple majority' in writings about international organisations. It certainly cannot be said that the phrase has only one ordinary meaning. One view holds that 'simple majority' means more than half of the voters who actually voted, disregarding abstentions.[60] According to another view, 'simple majority' means the majority of those who actually voted[61] (including abstentions). Yet another view regards 'simple majority' and 'relative majority' as synonyms and defines these phrases to mean more votes than anyone else ('*plus de voix que n'en a obtenues un autre concurrent*').[62]

In the context of INTERPOL, one must have regard to the INTERPOL Constitution, the General Regulations and the Rules of Procedure to understand the meaning of 'simple majority' and 'two-thirds majority'. As noted above, there exist two variations of the latter, namely, 'two-thirds majority of the Members of the Organisation'[63] and 'two-thirds majority of the Members present and voting'.[64] Remarkably, neither the INTERPOL Constitution nor the General Regulations contains a provision requiring the presence of a certain minimum number of members of the Organisation, ie, a quorum, for a valid session of the General Assembly.

While the relevant provisions of the INTERPOL Constitution, the General Regulations and the Rules of Procedure are far from clear, it would appear, as a matter of construction, that: (1) where a 'simple majority' or 'two-thirds majority of the Members present and voting' is required, the outcome is calculated on the basis of those present and casting an affirmative or a negative vote (with those abstaining not considered to have voted),[65] and (2) where 'two-thirds majority of the Members of the Organisation' is required, the outcome is calculated on the basis of the total number of the members of the Organisation, whether or not they are represented at the session of the Assembly.[66]

iii. Dispute Settlement Function

Disputes about the consistency of a particular activity or action with the prescribed rules are bound to arise in any international organisation. Since the Second World

[58] INTERPOL Constitution, Arts 7 and 13; General Regulations, Art 18; Rules of Procedure, Art 35(1).

[59] General Regulations, Art 52(1); Rules of Procedure, Art 36(1). Such voting restrictions do not apply when amendments to the INTERPOL Constitution are the subject of the vote.

[60] Schermers, HG and Blokker, NM, *International Institutional Law: Unity within Diversity*, 6th revised edn (Leiden, Brill Nijhoff Publishers, 2018) 589–91.

[61] Garner, BA (ed), *Black's Law Dictionary*, 7th edn (St Paul, Minn, West Group, 1999) 966.

[62] '[M]ore votes than any other competitor' (authors' translation) (Guillen, R and Vincent, J, *Lexique des termes juridiques*, 2nd edn (Paris, Dalloz, 1972)).

[63] INTERPOL Constitution, Art 42; Rules of Procedure, Art 38(1).

[64] INTERPOL Constitution, Arts 4, 16 and 44; Rules of Procedure, Art 38(2).

[65] General Regulations, Arts 19 and 20; Rules of Procedure, Art 37(1).

[66] General Regulations, Art 20; Rules of Procedure, Art 37(2).

War, disputes amongst INTERPOL members often relate to the Organisation's professed political and ideological neutrality. The General Assembly's role in resolving such disputes is discussed in Chapter 10.

B. The INTERPOL Executive Committee

The design of the Executive Committee is perhaps the most elaborate attempt of the architects of INTERPOL in the post-war period to ensure regional balance, avoid predominance by any country or region, and provide guarantees against the hijacking of the Organisation by any group of countries, let alone a single country as occurred during the Second World War.

The Executive Committee has 13 members: the President of the Organisation, three Vice-Presidents and nine delegates.[67] According to Article 22 of the INTERPOL Constitution, the Executive Committee shall (1) supervise the execution of the decisions of the General Assembly, (2) prepare the agenda for sessions of the General Assembly, (3) submit to the General Assembly any programme of work or project which it considers useful, (4) supervise the administration and work of the Secretary General, and (5) exercise all the powers delegated to it by the General Assembly. In addition, the Executive Committee must propose a candidate to the General Assembly for the position of Secretary General and, in exceptional circumstances, propose at a meeting of the General Assembly that the Secretary General be removed from office. According to Article 47 of the Rules of Procedure, only members of General Assembly delegations may stand for election to the Executive Committee. Delegates from a country which has not fulfilled its financial obligations vis-à-vis the Organisation are not eligible for election to the Executive Committee.[68]

The term of office of the members of the Executive Committee is also designed to minimise the possibility that any one country or person can dominate the Organisation. The term of the President is four years and the term of the Vice-Presidents is three years.[69] Neither the President nor the Vice-Presidents are immediately eligible for re-election either to the same posts or as delegates on the Executive Committee.[70] Delegates are elected for a term of three years.[71] They also are not immediately eligible for re-election to the same post.[72] Executive Committee members must remain in office until the end of the session of the General Assembly held in the year in which their term of office expires.[73] However, no

[67] INTERPOL Constitution, Art 15.
[68] General Regulations, Art 39.
[69] INTERPOL Constitution, Art 17.
[70] Ibid.
[71] Ibid, Art 19.
[72] Ibid.
[73] Ibid, Art 24.

member of the Executive Committee may remain in office should he or she cease to be a delegate to the Organisation.[74] In cases of resignation or death of any of the members of the Executive Committee, the General Assembly must elect another member of the General Assembly to replace him or her, whose term of office must end on the same date as his or her predecessor's.[75]

With a view to preserving geographical diversity, and thus excluding the possibility of regional dominance, three peremptory principles apply to the composition of the Executive Committee. First, Executive Committee members must belong to different countries.[76] According to the established practice of the Organisation, the candidacy for membership to the Executive Committee of any person belonging to the same country of a current member of the Executive Committee should not be included in the ballot. The nationality criterion has been applied very strictly to date, and in the history of the Organisation there have never been two members of the same country holding a post in the Executive Committee at the same time. This assertion is not refuted by the fact that a delegate from Aruba and a delegate from the Netherlands were members of the Executive Committee at the same time. Although the delegates were from the same State for the purposes of international law and shared the same nationality, they were delegates from two distinct members which were represented in INTERPOL in their own right. Second, the INTERPOL Constitution requires that 'due weight' be 'given to geographical distribution' in the composition of the Executive Committee.[77] In the 1964 General Assembly session held in Caracas, the geographical distribution was defined as follows: four delegates from Europe and three from each of Africa, Asia and America. This geographical distribution was part of a particularly difficult compromise made whilst amending the composition of the Executive Committee. It has not been amended since; on the contrary, it was confirmed in the minutes of the 1977 General Assembly session during which Article 17 of the INTERPOL Constitution was modified. The geographical distribution has suffered no exception since its introduction. Third, the INTERPOL Constitution requires that the President and the Vice-Presidents must be from four different continents.[78] The foregoing peremptory principles aim at ensuring that members of the Executive Committee conduct themselves as representatives of the Organisation (and not as representatives of their respective countries),[79] and that an international approach

[74] Ibid, Art 23; Rules of Procedure, Art 47(1). A special tribunal set up by UNESCO had the opportunity to clarify the meaning of a comparable condition in Article V(1) of the UNESCO Constitution. The tribunal held that to be eligible the candidate must be a member of his or her country's delegation at the General Conference session at which the election takes place (*UNESCO (Constitution) Case*, Special Arbitral Tribunal (19 September 1949) 16 ILR 331).

[75] INTERPOL Constitution, Art 23.

[76] Ibid, Art 15.

[77] Ibid.

[78] Ibid, Art 16.

[79] Ibid, Art 21. Article 21 has been consistently construed as requiring members of the Executive Committee to act in the interests of all members of the Organisation and exercise their mandate independently from their national administrations.

to police cooperation is adopted rather than a regional one. Whether enshrined or not in the constitutional texts of other international organisations, some or all of these peremptory principles are commonly found in the composition of the organs of other international organisations.

Notwithstanding the care invested in the design of the Executive Committee, problems do arise on occasion. For instance, on 10 April 2006, the General Affairs and External Relations Council of the European Union ('EU') concluded that the elections in Belarus on 19 March 2006 were severely flawed, and it started discussions on restrictive measures against those responsible.[80] On 4 May 2006, INTERPOL received a letter from the Chairman of the Permanent Representatives Committee of the EU inviting INTERPOL to rearrange the 35th European Regional Conference, which was to be held in Minsk later that year. The Organisation would not rearrange, so members of INTERPOL who were also members of the EU decided not to send their delegations to the conference.[81] This included all members of the Executive Committee from Europe (among them, the Vice-President for Europe who was the statutory chairman of the Regional Conference). Arguably, this was at odds with the obligation on members of the Executive Committee to conduct themselves as representatives of the Organisation (and not as representatives of their respective countries).

C. The INTERPOL General Secretariat

The history of the predecessor of the INTERPOL General Secretariat, the Central International Bureau,[82] exemplifies why secretariats of international organisations must be independent from their members to ensure the international character of the organisation. With respect to the ICPC, it was agreed in 1923 that its headquarters would be in Vienna, and the President of the ICPC would be from within the Viennese criminal police. According to Deflem, this was acceptable to the ICPC members because the Austrian police had extensive experience in the fight against international criminals, particularly in developing systems of information exchange.[83] The view seems to have been that the acquired expertise, means and technical prowess of Austrian police and their long-standing involvement in international police cooperation could now be put to good use. It is said that the technically dominant position of the Viennese

[80] '2719th Council Meeting', Council of the EU General Affairs and External Relations press release, 7035/09 (20 March 2006).

[81] Zagaris, B, 'EU Imposes Visa Ban and Asset Freezes against Belarus, but Interpol will hold Regional Conference as planned' (2006) 22 *International Enforcement Law Reporter* 278–80.

[82] See: 1946 ICPC Constitution, Art 2.

[83] Deflem, M, *'Bureaucratization and Social Control: Historical Foundations of International Police Cooperation'* (2000) 34 *Law & Society Review* 739–78 at 756.

police in the ICPC was also accepted because police from the smaller European countries lacked the necessary resources to maintain an international office, and police from Germany and France, though both participants in the ICPC, were unacceptable in any leadership position given their antagonistic positions during and after the First World War.[84]

At that time, this arrangement was certainly not out of step with other international organisations. With the notable and trend-setting exceptions of the small secretarial services of the International Telegraphic Union (1865) and the Universal Postal Union (1874), permanent secretariats of international organisations had been practically non-existent. In the nineteenth century, the secretarial functions of international organisations were normally entrusted to the so-called *état directeur*, ie, one of the member countries.[85] The true predecessor of the modern independent international secretariat and civil service was the staff of the International Institute of Agriculture, established in Rome in 1905.[86] However, it is Sir Eric Drummond, the first Secretary-General of the League of Nations, who is generally regarded as responsible for building a truly international secretariat.[87] Thereafter, secretariats of international organisations composed of international officials expanded as an unavoidable consequence of the growth of international organisations. The extension of their activities and their role in dealing with an interminable array of international problems, all of which gave rise to the principle of international loyalty, rendered the practice of *état directeur* no longer tenable.[88]

Thus, the arrangement with Austria to provide the secretariat of the ICPC was not an odd decision at that time. It was, however, the combination of this arrangement with a decision adopted in 1934 for the presidency of the ICPC to reside permanently with Austria that proved devastating for the international and neutral character of the ICPC during the Second World War,[89] unwittingly paving the way for the Nazi Party to control the ICPC.[90] During this time, Austrian police officials who were not loyal to the Nazi Party were dismissed.[91]

[84] Deflem, M, '*Bureaucratization and Social Control: Historical Foundations of International Police Cooperation*' (2000) 34 *Law & Society Review* 739–78 at 757.

[85] Akehurst, MB, 'Unilateral Amendment of Conditions of Employment in International Organisations' (1964) 40 *British Yearbook of International Law* 286–335 at 286.

[86] José Gascon y Marin, M, 'Les transformations du droit administratif international' (1930) 34 *Recueil des Cours* 1–73 at 53.

[87] Hammarskjöld, D, 'The International Civil Servant in Law and in Fact' (Lecture at Oxford University, 30 May 1961).

[88] See: Clapham, A (ed), *Brierly's Law of Nations: An Introduction to the Role of International Law in International Relations*, 7th edn, (Oxford, Oxford University Press, 2012) 111–19.

[89] Deflem, M, 'The Logic of Nazification: The Case of the International Criminal Police Commission ("Interpol")' (2002) 43 *International Journal of Comparative Sociology* 21–44.

[90] Deflem suggests that this was a strategic move in which the two Axis-powers cooperated (Deflem, M, 'The Logic of Nazification: The Case of the International Criminal Police Commission ("Interpol")' (2002) 43 *International Journal of Comparative Sociology* 21–44 at 29–30).

[91] See: Fooner, M, *INTERPOL: Issues of World Crime and International Criminal Justice* (New York, Springer, 1989) 49.

Those who sympathised with the Nazi Party, such as Oskar Dressler, the first Secretary General of the ICPC from 1923 to 1946, were allowed to remain.[92] The Nazi Party's control of the ICPC culminated in the appointment of Heydrich as President and the placement of the headquarters in the Reichskriminalpolizeiamt offices in Berlin, as discussed above. When Heydrich died, he was provisionally replaced by Nebe, who was succeeded in 1943 by Ernst Kaltenbrunner, the leader of the Austrian SS.[93]

It was not until the reconstitution of the ICPC in 1946 that it was able to start the process of establishing the international character of its secretariat. Article 1(1) of the 1946 ICPC Constitution created a permanent Central International Bureau, the direct predecessor of the current General Secretariat. However, the 1946 Constitution remained silent on the issue of the international character of the staff, their appointment and their conditions of employment. A *de facto* situation of *état directeur* thus prevailed, only now with France in that role. In fact, of the 11 factors impacting the decision of the US Federal Bureau of Investigation ('FBI') to withdraw from the ICPC in 1950,[94] the following figured prominently:

> [s]ince its reorganization, the ICPC has been dominated by the French Government. It is not, in reality an international organization since its Secretariat General is supported by the French Ministry of the Interior. The ICPC headquarters are in the Interior Ministry Building and no less than twenty permanent full time employees of the Sûreté Nationale are assigned to the ICPC in various capacities. The bulk of the equipment used by the ICPC is donated by the Interior Ministry. It is to be expected, therefore, [that] the French Government will make sure that ICPC policies are not at variance with the interests of the French authorities.[95]

This defect was remedied in the 1956 INTERPOL Constitution, which broke away from the idea of *état directeur* almost completely. One notable remnant of that idea was previously found in Article 43 of the General Regulations, which stated that the Secretary General should preferably be a national of the country in which the seat of the Organisation is situated (ie, a French national). This preference was followed until 1989 (and it can be said that, until then, the idea of *état directeur* survived, as the majority of the staff were also French).[96] However, at the 82nd

[92] Dressler cooperated with the ICPC President appointed by the Nazi Party and was editor of the ICPC periodical, which contributed to the growing prominence of Nazi Party views (Deflem, M, 'The Logic of Nazification of Interpol: The Case of the International Criminal Police Commission' (2002) 43 *International Journal of Comparative Sociology* 21–44 at 29).

[93] It will be recalled that Kaltenbrunner was the highest-ranking member of the SS to face trial at the first Nuremberg trials, where he was found guilty of war crimes and crimes against humanity. His involvement with the ICPC is painfully remembered in INTERPOL's General Secretariat (Riding, A, 'Interpol Regrets Shady Past, Vows Better Future', *The New York Times* (22 February 1990)).

[94] Further information on the withdrawal of the US from the ICPC in 1950 can be found in Chapter 10.

[95] Administrative records regarding the relationship between the FBI and the International Criminal Police Commission (Interpol) from 1935 to 1958, Part 6a, 64.

[96] Fooner, M, *INTERPOL: Issues of World Crime and International Criminal Justice* (New York, Springer, 1989) 91.

General Assembly, Article 43 of the General Regulations was amended, so that it only requires the Secretary General to 'be or have been a police official', thereby removing any nationality preference.

Today, the General Secretariat, which is constituted by the permanent departments of the Organisation,[97] consists of the Secretary General and a technical and administrative staff entrusted with the work of the Organisation.[98] The General Secretariat has a global presence. It comprises the headquarters in Lyon, the 'Global Complex for Innovation' in Singapore, seven regional bureaux (in Buenos Aires, Yaoundé, Abidjan, San Salvador, Nairobi, Bangkok and Harare), three special representative offices (in Addis Ababa, Brussels and New York), and a liaison office at the UN Office on Drugs and Crime in Vienna.

The Secretary General is proposed by the Executive Committee and approved by the General Assembly for a period of five years.[99] The Secretary General must be chosen from among persons highly competent in police matters.[100] Previously, the Secretary General was eligible for re-appointment for any number of terms, provided he/she left office on reaching the age of 65 (although he/she may have been allowed to complete the term of office on reaching this age). However, the INTERPOL Constitution was amended at the 86th session of the General Assembly in 2017, and the Secretary General may now be reappointed only once, for a further period of five years.[101] In exceptional circumstances, the Executive Committee may propose at a meeting of the General Assembly that the Secretary General be removed from office.[102]

Article 30 of the INTERPOL Constitution, which was central to the move away from *état directeur*, provides that '[i]n the exercise of their duties, the Secretary General and the staff shall neither solicit nor accept instructions from any government or authority outside the Organization. They shall abstain from any action which might be prejudicial to their international task.' It further provides that '[e]ach member of the Organization shall undertake to respect the exclusively international character of the duties of the Secretary General and the staff, and abstain from influencing them in the discharge of their official duties.' Article 30 further states that '[a]ll Members of the Organization shall do their best to assist the Secretary General and the staff in the discharge of their functions'. Article 30 consecrates the Secretary General and the staff of INTERPOL as international civil servants. This type of provision is common in the constituent instruments of international organisations or staff regulations adopted by international organisations.[103]

[97] INTERPOL Constitution, Art 25.
[98] Ibid, Art 27.
[99] Ibid, Art 28; General Regulations, Art 42.
[100] INTERPOL Constitution, Art 28.
[101] Ibid.
[102] Ibid.
[103] Eg, the Administrative Tribunal of the International Labour Organization ('ILOAT') held that it 'is inadmissible that a staff member should involve government officials in questioning the Organization's internal workings' (*Mrs Bel Ghazi v World Health Organisation*, ILOAT, Judgment

In respect of the UN, the ICJ has held that obligations entered into by States to enable agents of the UN to perform their duties are undertaken not in the interest of the agents, but in the interest of the UN.[104] The ICJ has also emphasised that the independence of international civil servants must be respected by all countries, including the country of nationality and the country of residence of the international civil servant.[105]

Indeed, one of the most distinguishing features of employment with an international organisation is the putative independence from any national authority,[106] whether legislative, executive or judicial, 'for unless this independence exists the Organisation itself will not be independent'.[107] As stated in *Bustani v Organisation for the Prohibition of Chemical Weapons*:

> [i]n accordance with the established case law of all international administrative tribunals, the Tribunal reaffirms that the independence of international civil servants is an essential guarantee, not only for the civil servants themselves, but also for the proper functioning of international organisations.[108]

An implication of this independence from any national authority is the obligation of allegiance to the international organisation. In INTERPOL's case, the essence of the obligation of allegiance is set out in Regulation 1.2 of the Staff Manual.[109] It provides that:

> (1) The officials of the Organization are international officials and, as such, their responsibilities are not national but exclusively international. By accepting appointment, they pledge themselves to discharge their functions and to regulate their conduct with the interests of the Organization alone in view.
> (2) In the performance of their functions within the Organization, officials of the Organization shall not seek or accept any instructions from any government or from any authority external to the Organization. They may not represent a government or a national administration.

Regulation 1.3(4) of the Staff Manual further provides that '[o]fficials of the Organization shall not hold any other post or engage in any paid outside activity without the prior authorization of the Secretary General'.

No 1475 (1996) para 17). See also: Gascon y Marin, J, 'Les transformations du droit administratif international', (1930) 34 *Recueil des Cours* 1–73 at 53–7; Negulesco, P, 'Principes du droit international administrative' (1935) 51 *Recueil des Cours* 583–690 at 650.

[104] *Reparation for Injuries Suffered in the Service of the United Nations* (Advisory Opinion) [1949] ICJ Rep 174, 184.

[105] *Applicability of Article VI, Section 22, of the Convention on the Privileges and Immunities of the United Nations* (Advisory Opinion) [1989] ICJ Rep 177, para 51.

[106] Quadri, R, *Diritto Internazionale Pubblico*, 5th edn (Napoli, Liguori, 1989) 559.

[107] Fitzmaurice, G, *The Law and Procedure of the International Court of Justice*, Vol 1 (Cambridge, Cambridge University Press, 1993) 81.

[108] *Mr J.M.B. v Organisation for the Prohibition of Chemical Weapons*, ILOAT, Judgment No 2232 (2003) para 16. See also: *Difference Relating to Immunity from Legal Process of a Special Rapporteur of the Commission on Human Rights* (Advisory Opinion) [1999] ICJ Rep 62, 96 (Separate Opinion of Vice-President Weeramantry).

[109] Staff Manual [II.C/SREG/GA/1987(2006)] [II.C/SRUL/EC/1988(2019)].

With respect to the General Secretariat's functions, Article 26 of the INTERPOL Constitution demarcates the specific tasks of the General Secretariat and, in so doing, confirms its institutional autonomy. The General Secretariat must (1) put into application the decisions of the General Assembly and the Executive Committee, (2) serve as an international centre in the fight against ordinary crime, (3) serve as a technical and information centre, (4) ensure the efficient administration of the Organisation, (5) maintain contact with national and international authorities, (6) produce any publications which may be considered useful, (7) organise and perform secretarial work at the sessions of the General Assembly, the Executive Committee and any other body of the Organisation, (8) draw up a draft programme of work for the following year for the consideration and approval of the General Assembly and the Executive Committee, and (9) maintain as far as is possible direct and constant contact with the President of the Organisation.

In 2003, the General Assembly charged the General Secretariat with specific duties regarding the I-24/7 Global Police Communications System.[110] In 2011, the General Assembly adopted INTERPOL's Rules on the Processing of Data ('IRPD'),[111] abrogating the RPI,[112] and, in so doing, expanded the duties of the General Secretariat. Under the IRPD, and as fully explained in Chapter 9, the General Secretariat is responsible for the general administration of the INTERPOL Information System.[113] In addition to this responsibility, the General Secretariat is responsible for the transparency of INTERPOL's data processing operations and the functioning of the Organisation's databases,[114] the confidentiality of data processed in the INTERPOL Information System,[115] and the security of data in the INTERPOL Information System.[116]

The General Secretariat is also empowered to take certain steps which may contribute effectively to combating international ordinary-law crime. For that purpose, it may, inter alia, request information or conclude cooperation agreements. For instance, according to Article 102(1) of the IRPD, the General Secretariat is authorised to request information from sources for cooperation purposes if (1) the request is made in the context of either a specific project or an event with specific interest for the purposes of international police cooperation or

[110] Rules on the Processing of Information for the Purposes of International Police Co-operation ('RPI'), Art 4.1. The RPI was adopted at the 72nd session of the General Assembly (Resolution No AG-2003-RES-04, 'Draft Rules on the Processing of Information for the Purposes of International Police Co-operation', INTERPOL General Assembly, 72nd session (Benidorm, 2003)) and entered into force on 1 January 2004.

[111] IRPD [III/IRPD/GA/2011(2019)].

[112] See: Resolution No AG-2011-RES-07, 'INTERPOL's Rules on the Processing of Data', INTERPOL General Assembly, 80th session (Hanoi, 2011).

[113] IRPD, Art 22(1).

[114] Ibid, Art 13(2).

[115] Ibid, Art 14(3) and (4).

[116] Ibid, Art 15(2), (3), (4) and (6).

(2) it has reasons to believe that such a request is necessary to achieve the objectives of the Organisation and is in keeping with the aims pursued.[117]

The foregoing provisions place the General Secretariat in a strong position to serve as a truly international executive organ that exercises its own powers, thereby avoiding dominance and control by any one country.

D. The National Central Bureaux

i. The Concept

Article 31 of the INTERPOL Constitution requires that, in order to further its aims, INTERPOL 'needs the constant and active cooperation of its members, who should do all within their power which is compatible with the legislations of their countries to participate diligently in its activities'. In order to ensure this cooperation, Article 32 provides that each country shall appoint a body which shall serve as its NCB. The NCB shall ensure liaison with (1) the various departments in the country, (2) those bodies in other countries serving as NCBs, and (3) the Organisation's General Secretariat.[118] Together with the General Secretariat, the NCBs constitute the cornerstone of INTERPOL's operational strength. The INTERPOL Constitution is not the only international instrument that prescribes a centralised national channel for cooperation. For instance, Article V, Section 1 of the Articles of Agreement of the International Monetary Fund ('IMF') states that '[e]ach member shall deal with the Fund only through its Treasury, central bank, stabilisation fund, or other similar fiscal agency, and the Fund shall deal only with or through the same agencies'.[119]

Articles 5 and 31–33 of the INTERPOL Constitution codify a concept of NCBs that can be traced back to the 1923 International Criminal Police Congress, where police emphasised the need to centralise national law enforcement to combat certain types of offences. The concept of an NCB evolved through four resolutions adopted by the ICPC between 1927 and 1954. In particular, at its 1927 conference, the ICPC adopted a resolution which suggested that each of its members create a bureau of national and international criminal records for the rapid exchange of

[117] The General Secretariat may not request such information from a national entity without having first obtained prior authorisation from the NCB of the country concerned. Authorisation will be deemed to have been granted if the NCB does not reply to the General Secretariat within 30 days of the request for authorisation. However, 'it is understood that the [NCB] retains the right to oppose this request for information from one of its national entities at any moment' (IRPD, Art 102(2)).

[118] INTERPOL Constitution, Art 32(a)–(c).

[119] This provision, however, is not as far-reaching as Article 32 of the INTERPOL Constitution because it does not dictate relations between bodies within the country. More importantly, unlike NCBs, the fiscal agencies in Article V, Section 1 of the Articles of Agreement of the IMF are not described as part of the structure of the Fund. By contrast, Articles 5 and 31–33 of the INTERPOL Constitution suggest NCBs are an organ of INTERPOL.

information on international criminals with the bureaux of other countries. In 1947, having studied a report by the ICPC Vice President, Dr Drtina, on the 'principle of centralisation in international relations', the ICPC adopted a resolution which recommended the creation of NCBs to:

> centralize and coordinate the documentation in connection with national and international criminals; they will assure all relations with the foreign police departments in criminal matters, as also with the International Bureau of the [ICPC] in Paris [i.e., the predecessor of the General Secretariat].
>
> In accordance with the circumstances most suitable for each Country, they will determine, in agreement with their respective authorities, the limits within which they will authorize direct international relations between police and police, but with the reservation that these relations take place under their control and on condition that the National Central Bureau of the Country in which the help of police authorities has been called upon, is also informed. In every case, the International Bureau will be informed.[120]

At the 1948 session, there was further discussion on 'National Central Offices', and another resolution was adopted which recommended that each member country set up a National Central Office. The resolution also included three significant additions:

> that they keep in close contact with the other national authorities and departments likely to help the National Offices;
>
> that, in all cases, they act making use of the legal possibilities in force in each Country, thus fostering a true spirit of international solidarity and co-operation; and
>
> that they adopt, in so far as practicable, the 'INTERPOL' denomination.[121]

In 1954, the ICPC adopted yet another resolution. It recalled that '[m]ember States should ensure their permanent participation in the various activities of the I.C.P.C. through a single office having the backing of the highest possible authority and responsible for all liaison at national and international level (Central National Bureau)'.[122] The resolution further reminded 'the Heads of National Bureaux … that they should reply with as little delay as possible', and stressed the fact that, in cases of requests for information, it is important to keep strictly to cases of a judicial nature, providing a precise indication of the reasons for the request and legal references if necessary.[123]

In 1956, the INTERPOL Constitution expressly prescribed the functions of NCBs within the structure of the Organisation in Articles 5 and 31–33. Article 33 of the INTERPOL Constitution, when read with Article 32, contemplates a scenario

[120] 'The National Bureaux', ICPC General Assembly, 16th session (Paris, 1947) 19.

[121] 'The National Central Offices', ICPC General Assembly, 17th session (Prague, 1948) 21. The change in terminology from NCB to National Central Office is not explained.

[122] 'Central National Bureaux', ICPC General Assembly, 23rd session (Rome, 1954) 322.

[123] Ibid.

where it is impossible or impracticable for an NCB to liaise with various national police departments, other NCBs or the General Secretariat. In such cases, Article 33 obligates the General Secretariat to decide, with the country concerned, the most suitable alternative means of co-operation. Based on this provision, the notion of a sub-bureau has been developed.[124] INTERPOL has established sub-bureaux in British overseas territories (Bermuda, Gibraltar, Cayman Islands, Anguilla, Montserrat, British Virgin Islands, and Turks and Caicos Islands), in unincorporated territories of the US (American Samoa and Puerto Rico) and in Asia (Hong Kong and Macau). It is also feasible that Article 33 could be relied upon by the General Secretariat to broker an agreement in circumstances where it is impossible or impractical for an NCB to liaise with a police department in a region that has declared itself independent.

ii. NCB Quality Standards

In 1965, the 34th session of the INTERPOL General Assembly adopted the document 'The National Central Bureaus: Policy' as an appendix to the General Regulations.[125] This document served as the policy for NCBs without amendment until 1994. Changes were considered in 1993 by the 22nd European Regional Conference, which considered a report on the 'minimum requirements for the effective operation of a European National Central Bureau'. This report served as the basis for a document titled 'INTERPOL – Service Standards', which was adopted in 1994 by the 23rd European Regional Conference in Sinaia, Romania. This initiative was endorsed by the Organisation, and, in October 1994, the General Assembly approved and adopted 'The National Central Bureaus of the ICPO-Interpol: Policy' as a set of policy guidelines.[126] The 1994 policy not only revised the 1965 policy document, but also incorporated service standards for NCBs ('NCB Service Standards'). The NCB Service Standards were minimum standards that the Organisation suggested all NCBs should strive to attain to meet the needs of international police cooperation as contemplated by the INTERPOL Constitution. In other words, they set out best practices for NCBs. The NCB Service Standards suggested that NCBs should, inter alia, (1) provide 24-hour communication 365 days a year in the working languages of the Organisation (ie, English, French, Spanish and Arabic), (2) classify messages transmitted on behalf of national police agencies according to the degree of urgency/importance and broadcast those messages through INTERPOL's channels within

[124] Fooner, M, *INTERPOL: Issues of World Crime and International Criminal Justice* (New York, Springer, 1989) 124–25.

[125] Resolution No AGN/34/RES/5, 'The National Central Bureaus: Policy', INTERPOL General Assembly, 34th session (Rio de Janeiro, 1965).

[126] Resolution No AGN/63/RES/14, 'The National Central Bureaus of the ICPO-INTERPOL', INTERPOL General Assembly, 63rd session (Rome, 1994). In so doing, INTERPOL deleted the 1965 policy as an appendix to the General Regulations.

precise maximum timescales,[127] (3) require national police agencies to respond to enquiries from the NCB within agreed maximum timescales,[128] (4) respond to requests for information from other NCBs in categories of maximum response times,[129] (5) implement a system to monitor the progress of late or outstanding messages or enquiries, (6) create a registry system to allow immediate and accurate retrieval of requested case files, (7) check the accuracy and content of outgoing messages, and (8) nominate emergency contact officers.

In light of the substantial increase in transnational crime throughout the 1990s and early 2000s, and the consequent developments in international police cooperation and technology, the General Assembly decided to revise the NCB Service Standards in 2004, increasing the number of standards to 24.[130] A significant feature of the revised NCB Service Standards was a mechanism of peer evaluation to measure compliance with the standards under the 'Exchange of Good Practice programme'.[131] Under this programme, the NCB to be evaluated completed a questionnaire in advance of a site visit by staff members from the General Secretariat and officials from another NCB in the region. Subject to the agreement of the NCB, the team was empowered to meet with any relevant persons at the NCB. The team then compiled and sent to the NCB a report identifying good practices and highlighting suggested areas for improvement. The NCB also received recommendations, which, when implemented, would lead to full compliance with the NCB Service Standards. In some instances, the visits persuaded national governments to increase staff and resources for NCBs and prompted the NCB concerned to exchange more messages with the General Secretariat.[132]

In 2016, the General Assembly approved recommendations made by the General Secretariat to establish 'quality standards' for NCBs.[133] A global consultation process was then launched and a questionnaire was circulated to all members to assess the value of the NCB Service Standards and the challenges faced by members in achieving full compliance with those standards. Following this process, in 2018, the General Assembly abrogated the NCB Service Standards and approved the NCB Quality Standards. The new NCB Quality Standards

[127] 'Urgent': immediate; 'normal': two hours; 'non-urgent': 24 hours.

[128] 'Urgent': respond within 24 hours; 'normal': as soon as possible and within ten days; 'non-urgent': as soon as possible and within one month.

[129] In respect of (1) wanted persons, missing persons, stolen motor vehicles, other stolen property (within 2 hours), (2) convicted persons, criminal records, fingerprints, photographed criminals, serving prisoners, telephone subscribers, vehicle owners/registration (within 24 hours), and (3) passport applications/photos, company registers, driving licences, censor/voters registers, tax registers (within seven days to allow for copies of documentation to be obtained). The NCB Service Standards also recommended creating a fast-track system for progressing urgent messages.

[130] Resolution No AG-2004-RES-13, 'Revised Interpol NCB Service Standards', INTERPOL General Assembly, 73rd session (Cancún, 2004).

[131] INTERPOL 2005 Annual Report, 25.

[132] INTERPOL 2006 Annual Report, 17.

[133] Resolution No AG-2016-RES-02, 'Endorsement of the INTERPOL 2020 Consolidated Recommendations', INTERPOL General Assembly, 85th session (Bali, 2016).

provide for, inter alia, an online self-certification process and visits to NCBs by the General Secretariat 'to assist those NCBs which are facing challenges in complying with the NCB Quality Standards or to share the best practices of high performing NCBs'.[134] In approving the NCB Quality Standards, the General Assembly reaffirmed that NCBs 'occupy an important and strategic position within INTERPOL's structure … and that INTERPOL's collective success relies upon having efficient and effective NCBs'.[135]

iii. Legal Status of NCBs

The legal status of NCBs is the subject of debate. Articles 5 and 31–33 of the INTERPOL Constitution suggest that they are to be considered organs of the Organisation, and the General Assembly is empowered to exercise a certain degree of organic jurisdiction over the NCBs.[136] Reuter, however, does not agree. He considers that an NCB, despite the fact that it is a 'cornerstone' of the Organisation, is not an organ of the Organisation proper, but of the 'system' represented by INTERPOL.[137] Similarly, some national courts have adopted a rather radical position by stating in absolute terms that an NCB is neither an 'agent' of the Organisation nor able to act on behalf of INTERPOL.[138] However, such a view is contrary to the General Assembly's own understanding of NCBs, particularly in light of Article 5 of the INTERPOL Constitution. This was clear as early as 1965. As mentioned above, in 1965, the General Assembly adopted 'The National Central Bureaus: Policy', which it elevated to the status of an appendix to the General Regulations.[139] According to the preamble of the 1965 resolution, the General Assembly was motivated to do so by the 'essential importance of the National Central Bureaus as the footholds of the Organization and the absence of any text concerning their structure and their functions'.[140] According to Article 44

[134] Resolution No GA-2018-87-RES-07, 'National Central Bureau Quality Standards', INTERPOL General Assembly, 87th session (Dubai, 2018).

[135] Ibid.

[136] On the concept of organic jurisdiction of international organisations, see: Seyersted, F, *Common Law of International Organizations*, (Leiden, Martinus Nijhoff Publishers, 2008) 107–82.

[137] Reuter, P, 'Problèmes juridiques relatifs au statut de l'OIPC–Interpol' in *INTERPOL: Les textes fondamentaux de l'Organisation internationale de police criminelle* (Paris, Presses Universitaires de France, 2001) 45–67 at 60–1.

[138] See, eg: *Founding Church of Scientology of Washington, DC, Inc v Donald T Regan, Secretary of the Treasury et al*, 670 F.2d 1158 (D.C. Cir. 1981); *Mohammad Sami v United States of America et al*, 617 F.2d 755 (D.C. Cir. 1979); *Scientology Kirche Deutschland et al v INTERPOL*, District Court of Munich, Az: 120 10 512/76 (5 January 1978); *X and Y v INTERPOL*, District Court of Jerusalem (27 March 2009) para 10. These courts were considering whether an NCB was operating as an agent, or on behalf, of INTERPOL in the context of a specific factual matrix and applying their relevant national law. Each of these cases is discussed in detail below.

[139] Resolution No AGN/34/RES/5, 'The National Central Bureaus: Policy', INTERPOL General Assembly, 34th session (Rio de Janeiro, 1965).

[140] Ibid.

of the INTERPOL Constitution, the application of the INTERPOL Constitution is determined by the General Assembly through the General Regulations and Appendices. Thus, by appending the NCB policy to the General Regulations, the General Assembly was seeking to give the document the utmost authority and incorporate it as part of INTERPOL's internal law.[141] It is also notable that the General Assembly explicitly sought to enforce the NCB policy: '[t]he ICPO-Interpol General Assembly … BINDS all countries affiliated in the Organization to apply the policy concepts which it contains'. In the 2018 resolution approving the NCB Quality Standards, the General Assembly reaffirmed that NCBs 'occupy an important and strategic position within INTERPOL's structure'.[142]

The fact that the NCB Quality Standards are not an appendix to the General Regulations should not be regarded as a retreat of the General Assembly from its ostensible view that it has competence to regulate the NCBs. In addition to the resolutions discussed above, the IRPD contains several provisions which reveal the pivotal place of NCBs within the structure of the Organisation. Article 5(4) provides that, '[a]t the national level, the National Central Bureaus shall play a central role concerning the processing of data in the INTERPOL Information System'. Article 19 provides that NCBs are responsible for (1) coordinating at the national level the processing of data in the INTERPOL Information System provided by their countries and (2) providing the institutions in their countries with data processed in the INTERPOL Information System. NCBs are also responsible for coordinating at the national level the processing of requests for cooperation and of international alerts sent to them by means of INTERPOL notices, diffusions and messages.[143] NCBs alone are entitled to authorise institutions in their countries to access the INTERPOL Information System and determine the extent of their access and processing rights,[144] and NCBs remain responsible for the processing of data by the national entities they authorise to access the INTERPOL Information System.[145]

Similarly, NCBs are responsible for ensuring that the minimum recording conditions in the IRPD are met when recording data in a police database.[146] The NCB that recorded data must update that data 'regularly' to ensure that the conditions for recording the data continue to be met.[147] NCBs are also responsible for the quality of the data they record and transmit in the INTERPOL Information System.[148] Any NCB about to use data in the INTERPOL Information System must

[141] Ibid.

[142] Resolution No GA-2018-87-RES-07, 'National Central Bureau Quality Standards', INTERPOL General Assembly, 87th session (Dubai, 2018) (emphasis added).

[143] IRPD, Art 20(2).

[144] Ibid, Art 21(1).

[145] Ibid, Art 21(7).

[146] Ibid, Art 37(4).

[147] Ibid, Art 46(1) and (3). See also: Article 50 of the IRPD on periodic assessments.

[148] Ibid, Art 12(1). See also: Article 76(2)(a) of the IRPD in respect of requests for the publication of notices and Article 80(2)(a) in respect of the implementation of notices.

ensure that the data is still accurate and relevant before doing so.[149] Furthermore, pursuant to Articles 7 and 58 of the IRPD, NCBs are free to restrict the access to, or the use of, their data in the Organisation's databases. This right can be exercised at any time and access restrictions may not be lifted by the General Secretariat except in urgent situations or when the data has become public.[150]

At its 77th session in St Petersburg in 2008, the General Assembly was very clear about its understanding of Article 5 of the INTERPOL Constitution when it adopted a resolution to amend the INTERPOL Constitution in order to provide the CCF with a legal basis in the INTERPOL Constitution.[151] In that process, the General Assembly expressly approved:

> the conclusions contained in Report AG-2008-RAP-09, 'Strengthening the legal status of the Commission for the Control of INTERPOL's Files: Amendment of the Constitution', concerning the need to integrate the Commission for the Control of Files in the Organization's internal legal structure and to establish it as a body of the Organization in the same way as the General Assembly, Executive Committee, General Secretariat, National Central Bureaus and Advisers, in conformity with Article 5 of INTERPOL's Constitution.[152]

There seems to be no doubt in the General Assembly's mind that the NCBs are a part of the structure of the Organisation as determined by Article 5 of the INTERPOL Constitution.

However, this is not the same as saying that NCBs are exclusively organs of the Organisation. NCBs should be understood in light of the theory of *dédoublement fonctionnel* in international law.[153] As pointed out by Kelsen[154] and Scelle,[155] the notion that entities can fulfil functions both as national organs as well as international organs is not alien to either the theory or practice of international law.[156] The conclusion that the NCBs are organs of INTERPOL does not mean that all their actions are attributable to the Organisation or that they are the representatives

[149] IRPD, Arts 12(4) and 63(1).

[150] Ibid, Art 58(1) and (7).

[151] Resolution No AG-2008-77-RES-03, 'Draft amendments to the Constitution aimed at incorporating the Commission for the Control of INTERPOL's Files – Article 5 and Articles 34 to 37', INTERPOL General Assembly, 77th session (St Petersburg, 2008).

[152] Ibid.

[153] See: 'Responsibility of International Organizations: Comments and observations received from Governments and international organizations' in *Yearbook of the International Law Commission* (2005) Vol II, Part One, 36–9.

[154] Kelsen, H, *The General Theory of Law and State* (Cambridge, Harvard University Press, 1945) 351–54.

[155] Scelle, G, *Manuel de Droit International Public* (Paris, Domat-Montchrestien, 1948) 21.

[156] See further on the notion of *dédoublement fonctionnel*: Kopelmanas, L, 'La Théorie du dédoublement fonctionnel et son utilisation pour la solution du problème édit des conflits de loi' in Scelle, G, *La technique et les principes du droit public: Études en l'honneur de Georges Scelle*, Vol II (Paris, Librairie générale de droit et de jurisprudence, 1950) 753 et seq; Gross, L, 'States as Organs of International Law and the Problem of Auto-interpretation' in Gross, L (ed), *Selected Essays on International Law and Organization* (Dordrecht, Martinus Nijhoff Publishers, 1993) 367–97.

of the Organisation for all purposes. This follows from Articles 31 and 32 of the INTERPOL Constitution, which make clear that the functions of the NCB are only those stated expressly. By virtue of those provisions, the liaison function of NCBs is limited to the realm of furthering the Organisation's aims as set out in Article 2 of the INTERPOL Constitution. For example, as an organ of INTERPOL, an NCB must liaise with various departments in its country when, for instance, a national court wishes to obtain police information from INTERPOL's databases. By contrast, it is beyond the function and competence of an NCB to appear before a domestic court in a civil case against INTERPOL as an agent or representative of the Organisation.

The application of the theory of *dédoublement fonctionnel* is aptly illustrated when service of process is attempted at NCBs in relation to a challenge to the actions of INTERPOL in domestic courts.[157] It is not uncommon for national legislation to provide that service of process to a registered or authorised agent can substitute for personal service on the principal party to be served. In respect of INTERPOL, domestic courts have considered whether service of process to either the NCB in the relevant country or to a member of the Executive Committee can be regarded as service of process to an agent of the Organisation. The US Court of Appeals for the District of Columbia ('DC') Circuit was asked to consider this question in *Sami v United States*.[158] In this case, Sami brought a claim against INTERPOL, the US Government, and two officials at NCB Washington for, inter alia, false arrest and imprisonment, libel and slander. Sami had been arrested in Germany on the basis of messages from NCB Washington in relation to a child custody dispute. Sami attempted to obtain jurisdiction over INTERPOL by serving (1) a Vice-President of INTERPOL, who at that time was also the Director of the US Secret Services, and (2) the Chief of NCB Washington, on the basis that the Organisation was a corporation doing business in Washington, DC and that the individuals served were its agents. The District Court concluded that INTERPOL was not doing business in Washington, DC and dismissed the action against the Organisation. On appeal, the Court of Appeals confirmed this decision. The Court of Appeals also found that the plaintiff had failed to establish that the Court had personal jurisdiction over INTERPOL (addressed in this section below), regardless of the method by which process was served.

A few years later, the US Court of Appeals for the DC Circuit was confronted with this issue again in *Steinberg v International Criminal Police Organisation*.[159] In this case, Steinberg commenced a defamation claim against INTERPOL and its Secretary General. Steinberg alleged that INTERPOL published a document in the US and 125 other countries erroneously describing him as a wanted international

[157] See also: Slomanson, WR, 'Civil Actions against Interpol: A Field Compass' (1984) 57 *Temple Law Quarterly* 553–99.

[158] *Mohammad Sami v United States of America et al*, 617 F.2d 755 (D.C. Cir. 1979).

[159] *Leon Steinberg v International Criminal Police Organisation et al*, 672 F.2d 927 (D.C. Cir. 1981).

criminal. Steinberg attempted service of process to officials at NCB Washington and to the INTERPOL Secretary General at his residence in France. INTERPOL and the Secretary General did not acknowledge service and did not appear in court. In the Court of Appeals, the US, as *amicus curiae*, successfully moved to quash service on NCB Washington on the ground that it is not an agent of INTERPOL for service of process.[160]

The question of the propriety of service of process to an NCB was also the subject of the decision of the District Court of Jerusalem in *X and Y v INTERPOL*.[161] In this case, the plaintiffs sought a prohibitive order and a mandatory injunction against the Organisation to prevent the transfer of their information (ie, names, photographs and an arrest warrant in respect of them issued in Belarus) to the public and to NCBs. The plaintiffs also petitioned the District Court to instruct the NCBs in every country to erase and remove any information transferred by INTERPOL concerning them. The statement of claim was served on NCB Jerusalem at the National Headquarters of the Israeli Police, and the District Court was asked to consider this as service of process to the Organisation. To accept this as service to INTERPOL, the District Court had to be satisfied, pursuant to the relevant civil procedure regulations, that INTERPOL was a 'business' and that NCB Jerusalem was 'authorized in management of business' to receive service of process. First, the District Court noted that INTERPOL is 'an international police organization established out of the power of international law. The Organization's location of residence and the General Secretariat Offices are located in France, and therefore, the subject is a foreign Defendant'.[162] Second, the Court found it 'difficult' to assert that an international police organisation is a 'business' within the meaning of the relevant civil procedure regulations.[163] Third, the District Court underlined that the question of whether the NCB was 'authorized in management of business', should be determined by considering the intensiveness of the relationship that exists between INTERPOL and NCB Jerusalem:

> the case law precedents determine that this question should be decided by the measure of intensiveness of the relationship that exist between the Defendant and the Authorized. So, insomuch as it will be possible to extract more signs of business cooperation between the Defendant and the body managing its businesses, so will grow the tendency to view the same body as an Authorized. … The Intensiveness Examination was designated for the determination whether from a normative point

[160] Ibid, fn 10. However, as discussed below, the Court was of the view that no assertion had been made that INTERPOL (ie, operating from its headquarters in France) lacked notice of this litigation. The Court observed that any objection to the sufficiency of process or of the service of process made in France may be interposed by INTERPOL, but notice-related objections did not go to the root question of whether the nexus between INTERPOL, the forum and the claim was sufficient to justify maintenance of the action in the US. It, therefore, reversed the judgment of the District Court and remanded the case.

[161] *X and Y v INTERPOL*, District Court of Jerusalem (27 March 2009).

[162] Ibid, para 9.

[163] Ibid, para 11.

> of view it is to be expected that the Authorized will transfer the Processes of Court to the hands of the Defendant, even if in practice the Authorized updated the Defendant regarding the existence of proceedings against it. … The subject is a situation in which the Authorized appeared to be the Defendant's long hand, in a manner that service to its hands is regarded as service to the body of the Defendant. This determination is decided in each case in accordance with its circumstances.[164]

The District Court held that, although the NCB has 'a tight connection and cooperation' with INTERPOL, it does not act on behalf of INTERPOL.[165] Moreover, an intensive relationship between INTERPOL and the NCB was not sufficient; the context in which the intensive relationship existed also had to be examined. It held that NCB Jerusalem is an Israeli body established on behalf of Israel for the purposes of liaison between Israel and the Organisation. It was of the view that the NCB cannot be viewed as the Organisation's 'long arm' because (1) NCB Jerusalem is subject to the Israeli Police and operates under its instructions, (2) NCB Jerusalem staff are workers of the Israeli Police, which is their sole superior in terms of management and employment, (3) the Organisation does not have full control over the NCB, the manner of its work and its conduct in Israel, and (4) the Organisation does not manage the NCB. Rather, NCB Jerusalem is 'two bodies having no common hierarchy but a relationship of cooperation and transfer of information'.[166] The District Court, therefore, held that the conditions required under the relevant civil procedure regulations were not satisfied and service of process to NCB Jerusalem on behalf of the Organisation was not possible.[167]

In *Scientology Kirche Deutschland v INTERPOL*, the Church of Scientology in Germany alleged that INTERPOL had infringed its 'personal rights' because the Federal Criminal Police Office (*Bundeskriminalamt*) ('BKA'), which fulfils the function of NCB in Germany, had drafted and circulated an 'offensive and false report'. The Court concluded that the BKA, in its capacity as an NCB, was not an organ of the Organisation according to the terms of the relevant German civil code.[168] However (and perhaps aware of the weakness in its reasoning)[169] the

[164] Ibid, para 12.
[165] Ibid, para 13.
[166] Ibid, para 13.
[167] Ibid, para 14.
[168] *Scientology Kirche Deutschland et al v INTERPOL*, District Court of Munich, Az: 120 10 512/76 (5 January 1978).
[169] The Court reasoned as follows: '[w]hen the plaintiff states that the defendant has infringed [its] personal rights …, the reference is essentially to the Bundeskriminalamt report … in which there appeared all other items of information mentioned, received from Scotland Yard, the F.B.I., etc. In this connection, the plaintiff considers the BKA – in its capacity as Interpol NCB – is also an INTERPOL organ and that, according to the terms of Articles 30, 31 and 89 of the Civil Code, responsibility for this offensive and false report is attributable to the defendant; in this connection, the plaintiff invokes Articles 5 and 4 of the Interpol Constitution. The Court cannot accept this argument. The above-mentioned Article 5 of the Interpol Constitution is introductory and encompasses the entire Organization, not just its organs. This Article also mentions "Advisors" whose duties with regard to the Organization are outlined in greater detail in Articles 34 to 37 of the Constitution. There can be no

Munich District Court considered the alternative position (ie, if BKA, in its capacity as an NCB, was an organ of INTERPOL). It held that, in this circumstance, INTERPOL still would not be made to pay compensation since the BKA was not acting in its capacity as an NCB when it drafted and circulated the report, but as a police authority of the Federal Republic of Germany which was carrying out a specific order received from its hierarchical superior, the Federal Ministry of the Interior.[170]

The authors' view that NCBs are not to be regarded as part of INTERPOL other than for the purposes defined in the INTERPOL Constitution may also serve to explain why the presence of an NCB does not assist a domestic court in establishing personal jurisdiction over INTERPOL in civil suits. By virtue of its territorial sovereignty, a State can exercise jurisdiction over persons within its territory. Conversely, a State typically cannot exercise jurisdiction over persons outside its territory without leave of the court, and leave often depends on an assessment of the existence and strength of a territorial nexus to the subject matter of the cause of action.[171] The circumstances in which domestic courts might exercise jurisdiction over international organisations are complex in light of the nature of an international organisation. In this regard, Judge Ago observed:

> [a]n international organization is like a State, a subject of international law, but it is one which enjoys limited international legal capacity, and in particular, unlike a State, it is a subject of law which lacks all territorial basis. Its 'establishment' in the territory of a given State is therefore a *conditio sine qua non* of its actually functioning as an organization, carrying on its activities and fulfilling its object and purpose.[172]

And whilst an international organisation is 'established' in the territory of a given State, it operates on an international basis, by definition. As such, in circumstances where a domestic court is seeking to establish personal jurisdiction over INTERPOL, it might consider whether INTERPOL's worldwide exchange of information and provision of databases and/or the presence of an NCB in its

argument over the fact that the Advisers are not "organs" of the ICPO-Interpol. However, on the other hand, the General Assembly, the Executive Committee, and the General Secretariat with the Secretary General in charge of it, are undoubtedly the defendant's organs – or rather, representatives 'organically linked' with the Organization. … The position of the NCBs is totally different; it is outlined in Articles 5 and 31 to 33, account being taken of Articles 1 to 4 of the Constitution. The defendant is justified in pointing out that the NCBs can in no way be considered to be representatives "organically linked" to the Organization. … They were created to act as services ensuring liaison with the various departments in their respective countries, with those bodies in other countries serving as National Central Bureaus, and with the Organization's General Secretariat' (ibid, para 2.1).

[170] Ibid, para 2.1.2. The Court held that the same argument applied to the information supplied and circulated via INTERPOL's channels by the FBI and Scotland Yard (at para 2.1.3).

[171] Crawford, J, *Brownlie's Principles of Public International Law*, 9th edn (Oxford, Oxford University Press, 2019) 456.

[172] *Interpretation of the Agreement of 25 March 1951 between the WHO and Egypt* (Advisory Opinion) [1980] ICJ Rep 73, 155 (Separate Opinion of Judge Ago). See also: Morgenstern, F, *Legal Problems of International Organizations* (Cambridge, Grotius, 1986) 5; Higgins, R, *Problems and Process–International Law and How We Use It* (Oxford, Clarendon Press, 1994) 90.

territory is sufficient to exercise jurisdiction. This issue was considered by the District Court of Stockholm in 1977 in *Steinberg v International Criminal Police Organization*. The District Court was of the view that, since neither the plaintiff nor INTERPOL was domiciled in Sweden and no other reason existed that the case should be tried by the District Court, the claim should be dismissed.[173] By contrast, in 1978, in *Scientology Kirche Deutschland v INTERPOL*, the Munich District Court was satisfied that there was a sufficient territorial nexus in light of the fact that the police report in question originated in Wiesbaden and was revealed in Munich during a civil action brought by the plaintiffs, whereupon it became known to the wider public.[174] From this, the Court inferred personal jurisdiction on the basis of the place where the alleged tort was committed (*lex loci delicti commissi*) and the place where the moral injury was felt (*pretium doloris*). In *Sami v United States*, the Court of Appeals applied *International Shoe Co v Washington*[175] when considering whether the performance of liaison functions by NCB Washington constituted 'minimum contacts' to establish personal jurisdiction.[176] It held that neither the contacts which INTERPOL had with the forum through NCB Washington nor the communications received in the forum from abroad from INTERPOL could suffice to warrant the exercise of personal jurisdiction.[177] Moreover, it was not proved that the INTERPOL Vice-President performed any of his duties in Washington, DC.[178] It further observed that, even if there were proof of such contacts, they would probably not have evinced the kind of 'substantial' contacts required by *International Shoe Co v Washington*.

By contrast, in the US case of *Steinberg v International Criminal Police Organization*,[179] the plaintiff did not seek to assimilate NCB Washington with INTERPOL to establish personal jurisdiction. To the contrary, the plaintiff emphasised the distinct personality of INTERPOL and used the liaison tie with NCB Washington to substantiate his claim that INTERPOL was a non-resident acting within the US. To this end, he relied on the DC Long Arm Statute, which authorises the courts in DC to exercise jurisdiction where, inter alia, a non-resident engages in a 'persistent course of conduct' in DC and causes tortious injury there. On this basis, the Court of Appeals held:

> [i]t is undisputed that the United States, pursuant to statutory authorization, 22 U.S.C. § 263a, participates in Interpol, that USNCB, situated in the District, acts as this

[173] *Steinberg et al v International Criminal Police Organization*, District Court of Stockholm, Final Decision (7 July 1977).

[174] *Scientology Kirche Deutschland et al v INTERPOL*, District Court of Munich, Az: 120 10 512/76 (5 January 1978) para 1.3.

[175] *International Shoe Co v State of Washington* 326 U.S. 310 (1945). In *Daimler AG v Bauman*, the US Supreme Court curtailed the test in *International Shoe Co v State of Washington*; the Court held that it would only exercise 'general' personal jurisdiction over claims arising outside the US against foreign corporations that are incorporated in the US or have their principal place of business there (134 S Ct 746, 761 (2014)).

[176] *Mohammad Sami v United States of America et al*, 617 F.2d 755 (D.C. Cir. 1979).

[177] Ibid, 759–60.

[178] Ibid, 760, fn 6.

[179] *Leon Steinberg v International Criminal Police Organisation et al*, 672 F.2d 927 (D.C. Cir. 1981).

> country's Interpol liaison, and that USNCB regularly sends information to and receives information from Interpol. Even without the further Interpol-Washington, D. C., links indicated in discovery pursued in this action (e.g., dealings between Interpol and United States agencies other than USNCB; meetings here attended by Interpol officers), the subsection (a)(4) 'persistent course of conduct' proviso is met. Interpol has constant liaison with the nation's capital. Its longstanding ties to this forum, while they do not add up to 'doing business' here, suffice to supply the 'something more' subsection (a)(4) requires.[180]

It might be said that the decision in *Founding Church of Scientology v Regan, Secretary of the Treasury* best captures the dual role of the NCB. In this case, the US District Court for the DC Circuit had ordered NCB Washington, pursuant to the Freedom of Information Act, to (1) disclose documentary materials received from foreign police agencies through INTERPOL concerning the Church of Scientology and (2) retrieve and index similar documents formerly in the possession of NCB Washington from INTERPOL's files at its headquarters in France. It came to this conclusion on the basis that, inter alia, NCB Washington was 'essentially a field facility of Interpol', ie, an 'affiliate office'.[181] The US Court of Appeals for the DC Circuit did not agree:

> Interpol has established a world wide (sic) communications network, but all actual investigative and enforcement functions are performed by domestic police authorities of participating governments. Each member country designates a national law enforcement agency – the United States has appointed USNCB – referred to as its 'national central bureau', to serve as a message and information exchange between that country and Interpol. Official inquiries emanating from law enforcement entities within a member country are channeled through its national central bureau to Interpol, and the route is reversed for responses. The national central bureaus thus serve as transmitters between domestic law enforcers and Interpol, which, in turn, is the conduit of communication among the national central bureaus of different nations.[182] …

It concluded that '[a]lthough a member of the organization, the USNCB is not Interpol'.[183] On this basis, the Court of Appeals reversed the orders of the District Court.

[180] Ibid, para 16 (footnotes omitted). INTERPOL, which had originally failed to appear as a party to the case before the US District Court or US Court of Appeals, filed a petition for rehearing. The US Court of Appeals denied INTERPOL's petition. The Court of Appeals was not swayed by INTERPOL's complaint that the Court had accepted as true Steinberg's factual allegations relating to jurisdictional contacts. It held that the Organisation bore full responsibility because it could have utilised the mechanisms provided by the US Federal Rules of Civil Procedure, which would have enabled INTERPOL's participation in the case without jeopardising its arguments that personal jurisdiction was lacking.

[181] *Founding Church of Scientology of Washington, DC, Inc v Donald T Regan, Secretary of the Treasury et al*, 670 F.2d 1158 (D.C. Cir. 1981).

[182] Ibid.

[183] Ibid (footnotes omitted).

The foregoing examples concerning service of process and jurisdiction support the view that NCBs are not to be regarded as part of INTERPOL other than for the purposes defined in the INTERPOL Constitution.

E. The Advisers

The INTERPOL Constitution provides that the Organisation may consult 'Advisers'.[184] The role of Advisers is 'purely advisory'.[185] They are appointed for a term of three years by the Executive Committee, and their appointment is definite 'only after notification by the General Assembly'. Advisers are chosen from among those who have a 'world-wide reputation in some field of interest to the Organization'. An Adviser may be removed from office by decision of the General Assembly.[186]

Advisers may be individually or collectively consulted on the initiative of the General Assembly, the Executive Committee, the President or the Secretary General. They may make suggestions of a 'scientific' nature to the General Secretariat or the Executive Committee (the term 'scientific' should be understood to mean technical, rather than relating to the field of science).[187] At the request of the General Assembly, the Executive Committee or the Secretary General, Advisers may submit reports or papers to the General Assembly.[188] Advisers may be present at meetings of the General Assembly as observers and, on the invitation of the President, may take part in the discussions.[189] Advisers may be nationals of the same country,[190] and may meet when convened by the President of the Organisation.[191] A recent example of the invocation of Articles 34 and 35 of the INTERPOL Constitution can be seen in the appointment of former UN Under-Secretary-General for Legal Affairs, Hans Corell, to conduct a study and make recommendations on the process for membership of INTERPOL.[192]

Advisers should not be confused with consultants and other professionals that the General Secretariat may engage in the process of efficient administration of the Organisation, nor with panels that might be established to serve as an advisory board for the General Secretariat. For instance, in 2005, the Executive

[184] INTERPOL Constitution, Art 34.
[185] Ibid.
[186] Ibid, Art 35.
[187] Ibid, Art 46.
[188] Ibid, Art 47.
[189] Ibid, Art 48.
[190] Ibid, Art 49.
[191] Ibid, Art 50.
[192] Resolution No AG-2016-RES-01, 'Study on the process for the membership of INTERPOL', INTERPOL General Assembly, 85th session (Bali, 2016).

Committee and the Secretary General established the INTERPOL Strategic Advisory Panel ('ISAP') to assist in understanding the needs and roles of police authorities and INTERPOL in an increasingly complex, interconnected world. The aim of the ISAP was to provide the Executive Committee, the Secretary General and the Organisation with strategic advice on emerging issues relevant to international police cooperation. The ISAP was created in the belief that, by convening such a panel and by having the Secretary General consult with its members as required, it could enhance the role and importance of NCBs and the General Secretariat, as well as promote the paramount importance of international police cooperation to combat serious transnational crime.[193]

F. The Commission for the Control of INTERPOL's Files

Long before the introduction of the much-heralded World Bank Inspection Panel in 1993,[194] INTERPOL recognised that, if the actions of an international organisation directly affect individuals, it should establish a forum in which individuals may bring claims on their own behalf. The establishment of the CCF[195] was INTERPOL's response to the need for international organisations to provide appropriate modes of dispute settlement.[196] The history of the CCF is discussed in Chapter 8 and a detailed discussion on how an individual or entity might bring proceedings before the CCF is set out in Chapter 9. This section focuses solely on the CCF as it pertains to the structure of the Organisation.

The CCF (also known as the Commission) is empowered to ensure that the processing of personal information by the Organisation is compliant with INTERPOL's rules.[197] The Commission also provides the Organisation with advice on any project, operation, set of rules or other matter involving the processing of personal information.[198] It is an independent body.[199] The CCF consists of two Chambers:

[193] 'International experts brought together on INTERPOL Panel Strategic Advisory Group to enhance police co-operation', INTERPOL press release (9 June 2005).

[194] See: Bradlow, D and Schlemmer-Schulte, S, 'The World Bank New Inspection Panel' (1999) 45 *Recht der Internationales Wirschaft* 175–81 at 179; Suzuki, E and Nanwani, S, 'Responsibility of International Organizations: The Accountability Mechanisms of Multilateral Development Bank' (2005) 27 *Michigan Journal of International Law* 177–225.

[195] See: Valleix, C, 'INTERPOL' (1984) 88 *Revue Générale de Droit International Public* 572–75; El Zein, S, 'Nature juridique de la Commission de contrôle des fichiers de l'OIPC-INTERPOL' (2000) 480 *Revue Internationale de Police Criminelle* 2–10.

[196] See: Wellens, K, *Remedies Against International Organisations* (Cambridge, Cambridge University Press, 2002) 209–13. Many surveys on accountability mechanisms in international organisations fail to acknowledge, or engage, with the CCF. For example, see: De Wet, E, 'Holding International Institutions Accountable: The Complementary Role of Non-Judicial Oversight Mechanisms and Judicial Review' (2008) 9 *German Law Journal* 1987–2012.

[197] INTERPOL Constitution, Art 36.

[198] Ibid.

[199] Ibid. See also: Statute of the Commission for the Control of INTERPOL's Files [II.E/RCIA/GA/2016] ('CCF Statute'), Arts 4, 11 and 12.

(1) the Supervisory and Advisory Chamber and (2) the Requests Chamber.[200] In its supervisory capacity, the Supervisory and Advisory Chamber is empowered to 'carry out the necessary checks to ensure that the processing of personal data by the Organization is in compliance with INTERPOL's rules' and to 'take decisions binding on the Organization on the measures required to remedy any non-compliance with INTERPOL's rules as well as recommendations on how to improve the processing of personal data by the Organization'.[201] In its advisory capacity, the Supervisory and Advisory Chamber gives 'opinions on all matters referred to in the [IRPD] and on any other matter involving the processing of personal data, either on its own initiative or at the request of the General Secretariat.'[202] The Requests Chamber is empowered to 'decide on its competence to process requests submitted under the [CCF Statute]' and 'examine and decide on requests for access to, or correction and/or deletion of, data processed in the INTERPOL Information System'.[203]

CCF members are elected from among persons of high moral character, impartiality and integrity, who possess the qualifications required for appointment to senior positions in their field of expertise.[204] Two members are elected to the Supervisory and Advisory Chamber and five members to the Requests Chamber.[205] The Chairperson of the CCF is elected by all the members of the CCF from among the members of the Requests Chamber.[206] The Chairperson is also part of the Supervisory and Advisory Chamber.[207] Article 8(3) and (4) of the CCF Statute specify the composition and the required specialisations of members of the Supervisory and Advisory Chamber and the Requests Chamber. It is noteworthy that the Rules on the Control of Information and Access to INTERPOL's Files,[208] the predecessor to the CCF Statute, provided that the composition of the CCF must include a member of the Executive Committee. However, by way of Resolution AG-2009-RES-13 in 2009,[209] the General Assembly decided that a member of the Executive Committee should not be a member of the CCF. The CCF Statute reflects this conclusion. Members of the CCF are elected for a five-year term of office, renewable once for an additional term of three years.[210] The seven members of the Commission must

[200] CCF Statute, Art 6.
[201] Ibid, Art 26(1).
[202] Ibid, Art 26(2).
[203] Ibid, Art 28(1).
[204] Ibid, Art 8(1).
[205] Ibid, Art 8(3) and (4).
[206] Ibid, Art 7(2).
[207] Ibid, Art 8(3).
[208] The Rules on the Control of Information and Access to INTERPOL's Files were adopted in 2004 (Resolution No AG-2004-RES-08, 'Draft Rules relating to the Control of Information and Access to INTERPOL's Files', INTERPOL General Assembly, 73rd session (Cancún, 2004)).
[209] Resolution No AG-2009-RES-13, 'Composition of the Commission for the Control of INTERPOL's Files (the Commission) – Amendment to Article 2 of the Rules on the Control of Information and Access to INTERPOL's Files (RCI)', INTERPOL General Assembly, 78th session (Singapore, 2009).
[210] CCF Statute, Art 10(1).

be 'nationals of the Organization's Members, be of different nationalities, and be fluent at least in one of the working languages of the Organization.'[211] As far as possible, the members of the Requests Chamber should represent the principal legal systems of the world.[212]

III. Essential Functions

The Organisation provides four principal services, referred to as its core functions:[213] (1) secure global police communications services, (2) operational data services and databases, (3) operational police support services, and (4) capacity building and training.

A. Secure Global Police Communications Services

The prerequisite for effective international police cooperation is for police bodies to be able to communicate with each other securely throughout the world.[214] Therefore, one of INTERPOL's core functions is to enable the world's police to exchange information securely and rapidly. Facilitating international police communications was considered a core function of the Organisation from its inception. Soon after the ICPC became operational in its original headquarters in Vienna, it became obvious that reliance on public systems for international police communications could not ensure the rapid, secure and reliable system needed for international police cooperation.[215] Thus, in 1927, at the conference at which the International Radiotelegraph Convention was adopted, a number of radio frequencies were reserved for international police communications services. In 1929, five European countries set up police radio stations that linked together with a central station. This was the starting point for INTERPOL's international police radio network.

From a legal standpoint, it is noteworthy that, throughout its different incarnations, INTERPOL's global police communications services have always been accompanied by a regulatory framework. In 1949, the ICPC adopted the Regulations of International Police Radiocommunications. In keeping with the

[211] Ibid, Art 8(2).

[212] Ibid.

[213] See: Kersten, U, 'Enhancing International Law Enforcement Co-operation: A Global Overview by INTERPOL' in Aromaa, K and Viljanen, T (eds), *Enhancing International Law Enforcement Co-operation, including Extradition Measures* (Monsey, Criminal Justice Press, 2005) 40–50.

[214] Higdon, P, 'INTERPOL's Role in International Police Cooperation' in Koening, DJ and Das, DK (eds), *International Police Cooperation: A World Perspective* (Lanham, MD, Lexington Books, 2001) 29–42 at 29.

[215] Fooner, M, *INTERPOL: Issues of World Crime and International Criminal Justice* (New York, Springer, 1989) 147.

structure created in 1929, the Regulations enshrined a regional division for the purposes of police communication. Each regional network was to be adapted to the geographic zone that it served. As a general rule, regions were to be formed based on geographic or economic units, capitalising on their existing means of communication by land, air or sea. In 1979, the Regulations of International Police Radiocommunications were replaced with the International Police Telecommunications Regulations, which were subsequently replaced with the ICPO-Interpol Telecommunications Regulations in 1989.

In considering the operations of INTERPOL, it is appropriate to consider where the regional telecommunications stations were situated within the institutional structure of the Organisation: were they part of the Organisation, and, if so, were they subsidiary bodies of the General Assembly, or were they decentralised permanent departments of the General Secretariat? Despite the absence of any known agreements with host countries in respect of regional telecommunications stations which could have shed light on their status, there is evidence that, on the institutional level, INTERPOL considered the regional telecommunications stations part of the Organisation. First, regional stations were established by way of General Assembly resolutions.[216] Second, regional stations were specifically mentioned in the Telecommunications Regulations, and the Organisation was liable for the security of information sent to the regional stations and from the regional stations to the NCBs. Third, the Telecommunications Regulations provided that the role of the regional stations was to provide a platform for establishing secure global police communications services, one of the core functions of the Organisation. Fourth, the equipment at the regional telecommunications stations was provided and maintained by the Organisation, and the Organisation provided the necessary training that facilitated the operation of the stations. Finally, the regional stations were represented in the INTERPOL Standing Committee on Information Technology.

In 1990, a communication system was developed for the electronic exchange of messages between NCBs and the General Secretariat (ie, the X.400 network).[217] As a result, the Telecommunications Regulations were revised in 1992 and 1994 (however, the system of regionalisation was retained in Article 3(5) of the revised Telecommunications Regulations). By 2002, the X.400 network had become technically obsolete, so the Organisation launched the I-24/7 Global Police Communications System ('I-24/7 System'). With the implementation of the I-24/7 System and the adoption of the I-24/7 Security Charter in 2003, the Telecommunications Regulations were *de facto* overridden. The I-24/7 System connects

[216] Eg, Resolution No AGN/33/RES/5, 'Designation of the Buenos Aires radio station as regional station', INTERPOL General Assembly, 33rd session (Caracas, 1964); Resolution No AGN/59/RES/11, 'Regional Telecommunications Station for the South Pacific', INTERPOL General Assembly, 59th session (Ottawa, 1990).

[217] Suc, D, 'New Era for Police Telecommunications' (1994) 446 *International Criminal Police Review* 2–6.

police authorities in all member countries and provides them with the means to share sensitive and urgent police information with their counterparts across the globe. The I-24/7 System also allows users to search and cross-check data in a matter of seconds, providing direct access to INTERPOL's 18 databases (discussed in detail in section III.B below). Although the I-24/7 System is initially installed in NCBs, in the spirit of Article 32 of the INTERPOL Constitution, INTERPOL encourages NCBs to allow national law enforcement authorities, such as border police, and customs and immigration officials to connect to the I-24/7 System. By virtue of the IRPD, NCBs control the level of access to INTERPOL's services at the national level and are responsible for the processing of data by any entities that they authorise.[218] The I-24/7 Security Charter does not subscribe to a system of regionalisation. It sets out common principles to maintain a high degree of security amongst all 'connected entities' (ie, any NCB or authorised entity directly connected to the I-24/7 System).[219]

In light of the foregoing, it is clear that the creation of global police communications services, which is exclusively governed by the Organisation's own regulatory framework, was and continues to be a remarkable display of INTERPOL's institutional autonomy.

B. Operational Data Services and Databases

The origin of this core function can be traced back to Article 1(b) of the 1923 ICPC Constitution which provided that one of the aims of the ICPC was to establish and develop all institutions capable of effectively contributing to the prevention and suppression of crimes (an aim which has been elaborated upon in successive iterations of the Constitution). To this end, the ICPC published wanted persons notices in the *International Public Safety Journal*. In the 1939 ICPC Constitution, Article 1 established (1) an international central bureau to combat counterfeit currency and cheques, (2) the journal *Sûreté Publique Internationale* (which was replaced in 1946 with the *Revue Internationale de Police Criminelle*),[220] (3) a central criminal information service (ie, database) with information concerning, inter alia, international criminals, international wanted persons and persons generally deemed dangerous, (4) the means to transmit fingerprints and photographs of international criminals, and (5) an international central bureau to combat the falsification of passports.[221] In 1946, the ICPC initiated its colour-coded system of descriptive notices and issued the first red notices for wanted persons

[218] IRPD, Arts 19–21.

[219] I-24/7 Security Charter (App 1 to the addendum to Report AG-2003-RAP-04) adopted in Resolution No AG-2003-RES-05, 'Urgent action required for the effective implementation of Interpol's I-24/7 Global Communication System', INTERPOL General Assembly, 72nd session (Benidorm, 2003).

[220] 1946 ICPC Constitution, Art 1(2)(b).

[221] 1939 ICPC Constitution, Art 1(1)-(5).

The present authors, therefore, beg to differ with Fooner who asserts that, for more than 60 years, INTERPOL operated a central criminal records system without a formal grant of authority.[222] While it is true that the Rules on International Police Co-operation and on the Internal Control of INTERPOL's Archives ('RIPC')[223] is the first comprehensive set of rules concerning the processing of information by INTERPOL, it is clear that Article 1 of the 1939 ICPC Constitution provided an express legal basis for the development of databases by the ICPC. Moreover, under Article 1(2) of the 1946 ICPC Constitution, the Central International Bureau (the predecessor to the General Secretariat) was explicitly empowered, inter alia, to maintain the central criminal information service.

Since 1956, Article 26(b) of the INTERPOL Constitution has provided that the General Secretariat shall '[s]erve as an international centre in the fight against ordinary crime' and Article 26(c) of the INTERPOL Constitution has provided that the General Secretariat shall '[s]erve as a technical and information centre'. Against this background, the General Secretariat has developed and maintains a range of global databases, enabling the global law enforcement community to 'connect seemingly unrelated pieces of data, thereby facilitating investigations and enhancing international police cooperation'.[224]

There are currently 18 databases accessible through the I-24/7 System. Secretary General Jürgen Stock has described INTERPOL's databases as 'the heart of our services to countries'.[225] The databases contain over 91 million records. In 2018 alone, there were 5.4 billion searches on INTERPOL's databases (an increase of 17% from 2017).[226] The most well-known database is the INTERPOL Criminal Information System which contains INTERPOL's system of notices. The other 17 databases include the following (available as at the end of 2019):

(1) The nominal database contains personal data and the criminal history of people subject to requests for international police cooperation, oftentimes including their photographs, fingerprints, etc. The origin of this database is Article 1(3) and (4) of the 1939 ICPC Constitution.
(2) Information on travel documents reported lost or stolen by countries is stored in the stolen and lost travel documents ('SLTD') database. This database

[222] Fooner, M, *INTERPOL: Issues of World Crime and International Criminal Justice* (New York, Springer, 1989) 129, fn 5.

[223] The RIPC was adopted by the General Assembly at its 51st session in 1982 (Resolution No AGN/51/RES/1, 'Approval of a draft Headquarters Agreement and exchange of letters between the Government of the French Republic and the ICPO–INTERPOL; Adoption of Rules on International Police Co-operation and on the Internal Control of INTERPOL's Archives', INTERPOL General Assembly, 51st session (Torremolinos, 1982)). It came into force on 14 February 1984.

[224] Higdon, P, 'INTERPOL's Role in International Police Cooperation' in Koening, DJ and Das, DK (eds), *International Police Cooperation: A World Perspective* (Lanham, Lexington Books, 2001) 29–42 at 31–2.

[225] Stock, J, 'Secretary General's Forward', INTERPOL 2018 Annual Report, 3.

[226] INTERPOL 2018 Annual Report, 4.

enables NCBs and other law enforcement entities, such as immigration and border control officers in countries which have expanded access to front-line units, to ascertain the validity of a suspect's travel documents in seconds. This database can be traced back to Article 1(5) of the 1939 ICPC Constitution, which provided that there shall be an international bureau, whose function is to combat false passports. In 2018, the SLTD database was searched nearly 3 billion times, resulting in more than 289,000 positive matches.[227]

(3) The stolen administrative documents ('SAD') database contains records of stolen official documents, such as vehicle registration documents and clearance certificates for import/export, to help identify stolen items.

(4) The database on stolen motor vehicles provides extensive identification details on millions of vehicles reported stolen around the world.

(5) The works of art database contains descriptions and pictures of over 50,000 objects reported as stolen or missing by NCBs and international partners of INTERPOL, such as the International Council of Museums and UNESCO. It includes, for example, items looted during crisis periods in Afghanistan, Iraq and Syria.

(6) The DNA database contains more than 180,000 DNA profiles from offenders, crime scenes, missing persons and unidentified bodies. DNA profiles can be compared against other profiles in the database. It can also be used to identify victims of disasters, locate missing persons and pinpoint the origination of trafficked goods such as ivory or wood.

(7) INTERPOL's fingerprint database, known as the automated fingerprint identification system ('AFIS'), contains more than 220,000 fingerprint records and 17,000 crime scene marks. Users can view, submit and cross-check records by scanning or importing electronic files and latent prints collected from crime scenes.

(8) The international child sexual exploitation image and video database uses image and video recognition software to allow investigators to make connections between victims, abusers and places. In 2018, 15 children were identified every day through the database.[228]

(9) The facial recognition system database, launched in 2016, provides a platform to store and cross-check images for the purpose of identifying fugitives, missing persons and persons of interest. In 2018, 288 faces were identified using this system.[229]

(10) The digital INTERPOL alert library ('Dial-Doc') is a joint G8-INTERPOL initiative which allows countries to share alerts on newly detected forms of document counterfeiting.

(11) The electronic documentation and information system on investigation networks ('Edison') provides examples of genuine travel documents in order

[227] Ibid, 12.
[228] Ibid, 8.
[229] Ibid, 5.

to help identify fakes. It contains images, descriptions and security features of genuine travel and identity documents issued by countries and international organisations.

(12) The stolen vessels database serves as a centralised tool for tracing and tracking stolen vessels and engines.

(13) The INTERPOL firearms reference table is an interactive online tool that provides a standardised methodology to identify and describe firearms more accurately so they can then be traced in cross-border investigations.

(14) The INTERPOL illicit arms records and tracing management system ('iARMS'), a project funded by the EU, supports the transnational tracing of illicit, lost or stolen firearms. It improves information exchange and cooperation between law enforcement agencies on terrorism and other firearm-related crimes.

(15) The INTERPOL ballistic information network ('IBIN') is a ballistics data sharing network. It allows the storage and cross-comparison of ballistics data by capturing digital images of the microscopic markings that are found on fired bullets and cartridge cases. An electronic signature is extracted from each image and is compared against the database of previously entered images.

(16) The maritime piracy database stores intelligence related to cases of piracy and armed robbery at sea, including data on individuals, telephone numbers, email addresses, piracy incidents, locations, businesses and financial information.

(17) The Geiger database includes law enforcement data on incidents involving radiological or nuclear material. It is used for analysing patterns and trends, risks and threats, routes and methods, and weaknesses and vulnerabilities, and it provides member countries with information related to investigations of terrorist and criminal acts involving radiological and nuclear materials.

In the context of processing data for the purposes of international police cooperation, the principle of proportionality has been articulated in the following terms:

> [d]ata should be adequate, relevant and non excessive in relation to the purpose of their processing. Proportionality should be looked into case by case, covering the nature and the gravity of the offence. The request to access or transfer data should be justified and accompanied by an explanation of how less privacy invasive measures are unable to establish the facts. This kind of 'ultima ratio' rule requires sufficiently specific and targeted data requests (specific person, categories of data, specific computer). This means that when law enforcement authorities do have access to data from a service provider on a suspect's connection, only those connections associated with an enquiry into specific criminal activities can be processed by them. Data on surfing activities of the individual, but through lawful access, are for ex[ample] not relevant in a case on illegal access activities. Non-relevant data should, therefore, be deleted. The 'need to know' rule may not be confused with the 'you never know' mentality![230]

[230] De Schutter, B, President of the Institute for European Studies and a Member of the Belgian Data Protection Authority, 'The Processing of Data in the Police and Judicial Area and the Protection of Privacy' (Speech, 11 February 2003).

The Organisation's approach to the DNA database is exemplary in terms of the application of the principle of proportionality. DNA is, of course, unique to an individual, and DNA profiling can greatly assist in an investigation. However, this revolution in policing has been accompanied by an ethical debate over the full use of information derived from DNA. In light of this concern, there is sensitivity and unease when public entities store this information about individuals. In light of the importance of DNA profiling, the General Secretariat developed a DNA database (see above).[231] However, to address ethical concerns, INTERPOL adhered to internationally recognised standards. No nominal data is attached to a DNA profile in the DNA database. The profile also does not contain information about an individual's physical or psychological characteristics, diseases or predisposition for diseases. A DNA profile is submitted in the form of an alphanumerical code, and the database performs a search of DNA profiles already in the database. If there is a match because another country has previously submitted the DNA profile, then the search result is positive. In this case, INTERPOL informs both countries about the match and invites them to pursue the investigation once the two countries have verified the database hit. If the profile is entered into the database for the first time, it results in a negative search result. In this case, and with permission from the submitting NCB, the profile remains in the database for potential future matches.

In 2005, the Fixed INTERPOL Network Database ('FIND') and the Mobile INTERPOL Network Database ('MIND') were developed to provide front-line law enforcement officers, such as border guards, with direct access to certain INTERPOL databases. FIND allows real-time online access to databases, whereas MIND is an offline copy of the databases, which is downloaded and updated from time to time. FIND and MIND are tools to enable NCBs to fulfil their liaison function with regard to the various departments in the country. The range of entities and agencies that can utilise FIND/MIND corresponds to the position adopted by the General Assembly in 1965 with regard to the words 'various departments' in Article 32(a) of the INTERPOL Constitution:

> [t]he words 'different departments'[232] are to be taken broadly. They cover not only departments under the authority of the same administrative service but also all other departments in the country liable to be concerned in international police cooperation: local police branches in decentralised areas (states, provinces, towns, Customs and Immigration offices, the Treasury Department). … It should also be borne in mind that all branches of the police may possibly be concerned (not merely the criminal investigation department).[233]

[231] Resolution No AGN/67/RES/8, 'DNA Profiling', INTERPOL General Assembly, 67th session (Cairo, 1998).

[232] Although the words 'different departments' are used in the extract of this document, it is understood to be a reference to 'various departments' in Article 32(a) of the INTERPOL Constitution.

[233] The National Central Bureau Policy attached to Resolution No AGN/34/RES/5, 'The National Central Bureaus: Policy', INTERPOL General Assembly, 34th session (Rio de Janeiro, 1965).

The Organisation is continuing to broaden the scope of its operational data services and databases. In 2014, it developed I-Checkit – a screening service that allows certain entities in the private sector (eg, airlines and cruise lines) to conduct advance checks on identification documents in the SLTD database.

C. Operational Police Support Services

In light of INTERPOL's provision of secure global police communications services and operational data services and databases, the Organisation is well-placed to provide operational support to police throughout the world. In 1989, Fooner acknowledged that there is considerable potential for the Organisation to develop its role in the area of criminal intelligence, rather than simply operating as a clearing house for information.[234] The Organisation has capitalised on these opportunities, which is one of the main reasons it has been able to remain at the centre of the web of international police cooperation, and it has embraced operational police support services as its third core function. Admittedly, INTERPOL has had to revitalise its operational police support services regularly to keep pace with the evolving international landscape. For instance, in the aftermath of the '9/11' attacks, the Secretary General decided that the services of the Organisation should henceforth be delivered on a 24/7 basis to all members, including emergency support and operational activities centred on the Organisation's priority crime areas (ie, fugitives, public safety and terrorism, drugs and organised crime, trafficking in human beings, and financial and high-tech crime).[235]

To realise this goal, INTERPOL created a Command and Co-ordination Centre ('CCC') in 2003, which operates around the clock in INTERPOL's four working languages from Singapore, Lyon and Buenos Aires. The CCC serves as the first point of contact for any country requiring assistance from the General Secretariat or from another member. Its activities are varied: it acts upon police messages received through the I-24/7 System, replies to urgent queries from members, handles information from members of the public and monitors and analyses open sources. It also assumes a crisis management role in the wake of terrorist attacks or natural disasters. In such scenarios, the CCC can deploy specialised response teams: the INTERPOL Incident Response Team ('IRT') or the INTERPOL Major Event Support Team ('IMEST'), each of which is composed of officers from the General Secretariat and experts in the relevant field. An IRT can be dispatched to the scene of an incident within 12 to 24 hours. It provides

[234] Fooner, M, *INTERPOL: Issues of World Crime and International Criminal Justice* (New York, Springer, 1989) 128.

[235] The Organisation has now narrowed its focus to three main crime programmes, namely, counter-terrorism, organised and emerging crime, and cybercrime (INTERPOL, 'What is INTERPOL?', available at: www.interpol.int/en/Who-we-are/What-is-INTERPOL).

investigative and analytical support. The first IRT was deployed in October 2002 to Indonesia following a terrorist attack in Bali. As of January 2020, 117 IRTs had been deployed. An IMEST assists members in the preparation and implementation of security arrangements for major international events. The first IMEST was deployed in 2002 to the US for the Winter Olympic Games. As of January 2020, 127 IMESTs had been deployed. The CCC can also assume a coordination role if an attack or disaster involves several member countries.

INTERPOL also has a team of criminal intelligence analysts who provide analytical support from an operational (ie, to achieve a specific law enforcement outcome) and strategic (ie, to inform higher-level decision makers) perspective to crime-related projects, investigations and operations. In light of the millions of records that INTERPOL stores, this was a logical step for the Organisation. For instance, INTERPOL criminal intelligence analysts can manage and manipulate the data provided from law enforcement entities in INTERPOL's databases. They have generated reports on issues including drug trafficking, illicit markets, Eurasian organised crime, foreign terrorist fighters, and bomb-making and improvised explosive devices. The analysts can also provide member countries with threat or risk assessments and consultancy services, or deploy in the field to directly assist police with ongoing investigations.

Perhaps the most important police support service, as discussed in section III.B above, is the notices system.[236] In 2018, the General Secretariat issued 21,025 new notices, and 92,395 notices were valid at the end of 2018.[237] Generally, notices contain identity particulars and judicial data. Identity particulars comprise a name, sex, date of birth, identifier (such as a physical description, DNA profile, fingerprints or data contained in identity documents), photograph and other relevant information particular to the type of notice. Judicial data can include the offence with which the person is charged, references to the laws under which the offence is made or conviction was obtained, the maximum penalty which has been or can be imposed and, in the case of the red notice, reference to the arrest warrant or judicial decision having the same effect. Based on requests from NCBs or international organisations with which INTERPOL has special agreements, the notices are published by the General Secretariat in all of the Organisation's working languages. The General Secretariat can also publish notices at its own initiative to issue an alert or to request information.[238]

The IRPD determines the general legal framework governing notices. A 'notice' is defined as 'any request for international cooperation or any international alert published by the Organization at the request of [an NCB] or an international entity, or at the initiative of the General Secretariat, and sent to all

[236] IRPD, Art 73.
[237] INTERPOL 2018 Annual Report, 5.
[238] IRPD, Arts 25(4) and 103.

the Organization's members.'[239] The publication of notices are thus acts of the Organisation itself. Any notice containing a request for action triggers the application of Article 31 of the INTERPOL Constitution, which calls on 'the constant and active co-operation of the [Organisation's] members, who should do all within their power which is compatible with the legislations of their countries to participate diligently in its activities.' By contrast, a 'diffusion' is defined as 'any request for international cooperation or any international alert from [an NCB] or an international entity, sent directly to one or several [NCBs] or to one or several international entities, and simultaneously recorded in a police database of the Organization'.[240] As such, members only rely on a general expectation to cooperate with each other when a diffusion is circulated. Publication of a notice, therefore, entails a higher degree of responsibility for the General Secretariat than the circulation of diffusions.

The *Arrest Warrant* case concerned the circulation of an arrest warrant through INTERPOL's channels. In this case, a Belgian examining judge had issued an arrest warrant against the acting Congolese Minister for Foreign Affairs, Mr Abdoulaye Yerodia Ndombasi, on 11 April 2000, which NCB Brussels then circulated (it would appear, via a diffusion) through INTERPOL's channels. In his Dissenting Opinion, Judge Oda commented as follows on the arrest warrant:

> [w]ithout more … the warrant is not directly binding on foreign authorities, who are not part of the law enforcement mechanism of the issuing State. The individual may be arrested abroad (that is, outside the issuing State) only by the authorities of the State where he or she is present, since jurisdiction over that territory lies exclusively with that State. Those authorities will arrest the individual being sought by the issuing State only if the requested State is committed to do so pursuant to international arrangements with the issuing State. Interpol is merely an organization which transmits the arrest request from one State to another; it has no enforcement powers of its own.
>
> It bears stressing that the issuance of an arrest warrant by one State and the international circulation of the warrant through Interpol have no legal impact unless the arrest request is validated by the receiving State. The Congo appears to have failed to grasp that the mere issuance and international circulation of an arrest warrant have little significance. There is even some doubt whether the Court itself properly understood this, particularly as regards a warrant's legal effect. The crucial point in this regard is not the issuance or international circulation of an arrest warrant but the response of the State receiving it.[241]

Whilst this may be the position in respect of an arrest warrant circulated by means of a diffusion, this is a more difficult position to adopt where a red notice is utilised to give extra-territorial effect to an arrest warrant. In the latter

[239] Ibid, Art 1(13) (emphasis added).
[240] Ibid, Art 1(14) (emphasis added).
[241] *Arrest Warrant of 11 April 2000 (Democratic Republic of the Congo v Belgium)* (Judgment) [2002] ICJ Rep 3, 46, para 13 (Dissenting Opinion of Judge Oda).

scenario, not only is there an expectation of good faith cooperation with the Organisation,[242] but there is a legal impact under the IRPD.[243]

Of the nine notices, the red notice stands out. It serves to seek the location of a wanted person and his/her detention, arrest or restriction of movement for the purposes of extradition, surrender, or similar lawful action.[244] The red notice is a prototypical operational police response to match the rapid move of wanted persons across borders in light of the much slower process of mutual legal assistance and extradition. As Marabuto explained to the 5th session of the UN Commission on Narcotic Drugs in 1951 on behalf of the ICPC,[245] the practice of extradition was considered to have two inconveniences from an operational police perspective. First, before the procedure could be started, it was necessary to know the place of refuge of the criminal. Second, once the place was known, the procedure was often very long and the international malefactor, aware of the action concerning him, could change his domicile to hinder the action. It was therefore thought that many extradition treaties were not suitable for the necessities of the period. INTERPOL endeavoured to remedy these inconveniences; it was of the view that the police departments of its members should be able to contact each other to seek the location of the international malefactor, before starting the normal procedure of extradition. INTERPOL therefore developed a procedure to assist in the provisional arrest of wanted persons (which is provided for in the majority of extradition treaties as an urgent method to allow police bodies to take precautionary measures with regard to the wanted person and the evidence which might be in his possession).[246]

The steps to be taken following the location of a wanted person who is the subject of a red notice are set out in Article 87(a) of the IRPD. It provides that:

> [t]he country where the person has been located shall: (i) immediately inform the requesting [NCB] and the General Secretariat of the fact that the person has been located … [and] (ii) take all other measures permitted under national law and applicable international treaties, such as provisionally arresting the wanted person or monitoring or restricting his/her movement.

Once the requesting NCB has been informed that the person subject to the red notice has been located, it is required to 'act immediately'.[247] In particular, it must ensure 'the swift transmission … of data and supporting documents requested by

[242] INTERPOL Constitution, Art 31.

[243] See: IRPD, Art 87(a) (set out below).

[244] Ibid, Art 82.

[245] Marabuto, P, 'The International Criminal Police: Commission and the Illicit Traffic of Narcotics' (1951) Issue 3-002 *UNODC Bulletin on Narcotics*.

[246] Fooner, M, *INTERPOL: Issues of World Crime and International Criminal Justice* (New York, Springer, 1989) 142–43.

[247] IRPD, Art 87(b).

the country where the person was located or by the General Secretariat'.[248] Then, a further period elapses during which the normal procedure of extradition takes place. It is in this period that the matter is examined by the country where the wanted person was located, after which the decision to extradite or not to extradite is taken. Thus, through extrajudicial cooperation, the police accomplish their task by putting the wanted individual at the disposal of the judicial authorities.

By virtue of Article 31 of the INTERPOL Constitution, the red notice is effectively a request *erga omnes* for the provisional detention, arrest or restriction of movement of an individual, pending extradition, surrender or similar lawful action.[249] The foundational legal condition for a red notice is an arrest warrant or judicial decision having the same effect.[250] Many of INTERPOL's members have passed legislation or adopted measures with equivalent effect to acknowledge a red notice as a valid request for provisional arrest. Furthermore, INTERPOL is recognised as an official channel for transmitting requests for provisional arrest in a number of bilateral and multilateral extradition treaties, including the European Convention on Extradition[251] and the Economic Community of West African States ('ECOWAS') Convention on Extradition.[252] However, this is not to suggest that non-members of INTERPOL are the addressees of a red notice. This is evident in a letter of 14 July 2005 from the UN to the Chairperson of the Commission on Human Rights concerning the accreditation and participation of representatives of non-governmental organisations who are the subject of INTERPOL red notices in the work of the Commission of Human Rights:

> [w]ith respect to your second question, we wish to advise that there is no general prohibition as such to prevent individuals subject to Interpol 'red notices' from being accredited to any meeting of the United Nations. Although certain Member States may have obligations to act upon Interpol 'red notices', the United Nations is not obliged to act with respect to notices issued by Interpol. However, it may, if it chooses. Indeed, in our view, it is clear that the [United Nations], having the duty to protect its officials, visitors and assets, can deny access to its premises to any individual on the grounds of security concerns. We wish to note that, in each location where the United Nations has a presence, there is a 'Designated Official' responsible for security. The Designated Official for security in Geneva is the Director-General at the United Nations Office at Geneva. It is therefore for the good judgment of the Designated Official to assess the risks in any given situation and take the appropriate measures. Although, as indicated

[248] Ibid.

[249] See: General Secretariat, 'Les notices rouges d'INTERPOL' (1999) 468 *Revue Internationale de Police Criminelle* 8–14.

[250] IRPD, Art 83(2)(b)(v). The General Secretariat has been empowered by the General Assembly to refuse to publish a red notice when it is not satisfied that the notice contains all the information needed to formulate a valid request for provisional arrest.

[251] European Convention on Extradition (opened for signature on 13 December 1957, entered into force on 18 April 1960), Art 16(3).

[252] Convention A/P1/8/94 on Extradition (signed on 6 August 1994, entered into force on 8 December 2005), Art 22(3).

> above, the Organization is not legally bound to take any action in respect of Interpol 'red notices', they may be a key element to be considered when assessing security risks. Finally, it should be noted that we consider the decision of the Commission at its fifty ninth session to deny NGO representatives subject to Interpol notices access to meetings, to be procedural in nature, and as such, not binding on the Commission at its subsequent sessions. The fact that the Commission renewed this decision, explicitly or implicitly, at its sixtieth and sixty-first sessions does not alter this position. The Commission, therefore, should consider itself free to deal with similar requests differently at its sixty-second session.[253]

The Organisation also publishes blue, green, yellow, purple, orange and black notices, as well as stolen work of art notices and INTERPOL–UN Security Council Special Notices. The purpose of a blue notice is to obtain information, locate and/or identify a person of interest in a criminal investigation.[254] Green notices provide warnings about a person's criminal activities.[255] Yellow notices are published to locate missing persons or to identify persons who are unable to identify themselves.[256] Purple notices are published to 'warn about modi operandi, objects, devices or concealment methods used by offenders' and/or 'request information on offences to resolve them or assist in their investigation'.[257] Orange notices are published to 'notify about an event, a person, an object, a process or a modus operandi representing an imminent threat to public safety and likely to cause serious damage to property or injury to persons'.[258] Stolen work of art notices are published to locate works of art or items of cultural value which have been stolen, or to identify such objects discovered in suspicious circumstances.[259]

Black notices are published to identify dead bodies.[260] Disaster victim identification ('DVI'), normally the responsibility of the police, is a difficult and demanding exercise that can only be brought to a successful conclusion if properly planned and that, of necessity, must involve the active participation of many other agencies. Further to the rationale underlying the black notice, INTERPOL has for many years sponsored a programme of activities relating to the identification of disaster victims in order to encourage members to adopt a common policy in this field.[261] At the 49th session of the General Assembly in 1980, the General Assembly set up a working party to take account of procedures and techniques

[253] UN Secretariat, 'Letter to the Chairperson of the Commission on Human Rights concerning the accreditation and participation of non-governmental organization representatives who are subject to requests for arrest or detention by Interpol in the work of the Commission on Human Rights' in *United Nations Juridical Yearbook* (2005), Part Two, Chapter VI, 455–57.

[254] IRPD, Art 88(1).

[255] Ibid, Art 89(1).

[256] Ibid, Art 90(1).

[257] Ibid, Art 92(1).

[258] Ibid, Art 93(1).

[259] Ibid, Art 94(1).

[260] Ibid, Art 91(1).

[261] For instance, following the tsunami in December 2004, INTERPOL coordinated the international effort to identify victims of the disaster. Rotating teams of INTERPOL officials, Thai authorities and international DVI teams staffed the Thai Tsunami Victim Identification Information Management

currently used in the identification of disaster victims.[262] This effort resulted in the publication of the first INTERPOL Disaster Victim Identification Guide ('Guide') in 1984. The Guide is updated by the INTERPOL DVI Standing Committee and the INTERPOL DVI Working Group every five years (most recently, in 2018). The Guide is the only globally accepted standard for DVI protocols. The guidelines contained therein are not mandatory but are presented as baseline standards and recommendations. The implementation of the guidelines depends on the will and desire of members of the Organisation. However, the recommendations are of fundamental value in that they expressly recognise the basic right of individuals to be identified after death, consistent with the spirit of the Universal Declaration of Human Rights, which conditions all of the Organisation's interventions and activities. Part A of the Guide includes a DVI command structure and responsibilities, a summary of DVI phases, methods of identification, primary considerations for DVI operations, guidance on occupational health and safety, and recommended training and equipment. Part B of the Guide consists of a series of annexes on a range of specific topics.[263] In addition, INTERPOL provides a variety of forms and guidelines relevant to DVI.

The INTERPOL–UN Security Council Special Notice stands in a league of its own. It serves to inform INTERPOL members that an individual or entity is subject to UN Security Council sanctions.[264] The INTERPOL–UN Security Council Special Notice was created in 2005 in response to UN Security Council Resolution 1617 (2005). As noted in Chapter 2, UN Security Council Resolution 1617 (2005) called on the UN Secretary-General to work with INTERPOL to provide better tools to help the UN Sanctions Committee established pursuant to Resolution 1267 (1999) carry out its mandate regarding the freezing of assets, travel bans and arms embargoes aimed at individuals and entities associated or belonging to the Islamic State in Iraq and the Levant ('ISIL'), Al-Qaida and the Taliban.[265] In welcoming UN Security Council Resolution 1617 (2005) and

Centre, where approximately 5,000 victims were identified. In total, more than 2,000 personnel from 31 countries were involved in the victim identification process in Thailand alone, collecting DNA samples, conducting forensic analysis, logging data and helping with the repatriation of remains.

[262] Resolution No AGN/49/RES/2, 'Identification of Disaster Victims', INTERPOL General Assembly, 49th session (Manila, 1980). This resolution was abrogated by Resolution No AGN/65/RES/13, 'Disaster victim identification', INTERPOL General Assembly, 65th session (Antalya, 1996).

[263] As of January 2020, there were 17 Annexures.

[264] IRPD, Art 95(1).

[265] As noted in Chapter 2, the UN Sanctions Committee established pursuant to Resolution 1267 (1999) on 15 October 1999 was known as the Al-Qaida and Taliban Sanctions Committee. The sanctions regime has been modified and strengthened by subsequent resolutions, including Resolutions 1333 (2000), 1390 (2002), 1455 (2003), 1526 (2004), 1617 (2005), 1735 (2006) and 1822 (2008). With Resolutions 1988 (2011) and 1989 (2011), the UN Security Council split the Sanctions Committee into two: the Al-Qaida Sanctions Committee was mandated to oversee implementation of the measures against individuals and entities associated with Al-Qaida, and a separate Committee was established to oversee implementation of the measures against individuals and entities associated with the Taliban in constituting a threat to the peace, stability and security of Afghanistan. In 2015, the UN Security Council adopted Resolution 2253 (2015) and expanded the listing criteria to include individuals and

establishing the INTERPOL–UN Security Council Special Notice, the INTERPOL General Assembly had regard to the fact that 'INTERPOL's notices system, combined with the Organization's global secured police communication system, and the various databases, is the only global system available that could be used in order to ensure that police and other law enforcement authorities are alerted and that they can act when it becomes necessary'.[266] In line with successive UN Security Council resolutions, INTERPOL has expanded its cooperation to other UN sanctions committees, including those concerning the Democratic Republic of Congo, Somalia, Sudan, Guinea-Bissau, the Central African Republic, Yemen, South Sudan and Libya.

INTERPOL added another form of operational support to its arsenal in 2007 – public appeals – when it undertook Operation Vico.[267] For the first time in the Organisation's history, it published, on its own initiative, the photos of an unknown man who had been photographed sexually abusing young boys in images which had been posted to the Internet. These photos assisted in the individual's arrest 11 days later. At the time, some argued that INTERPOL did not have the authorisation to launch a public appeal because public appeals are not mentioned in the INTERPOL legal regime so there was no procedural requirement or guarantee for legal protection. According to the same view, such a public search initiated by the Organisation did not conform to basic requirements for criminal or administrative procedures affecting individual rights.[268] This view does not take account of the specific circumstances. INTERPOL had numerous images in which it could clearly be seen that the person in question was sexually abusing several children. INTERPOL considered that these were images of crime scenes and of crimes in progress, and the public appeal did not breach the perpetrator's right to privacy (a qualified right). Having been unable to identify the person committing those acts through other means, it was judged appropriate and proportionate to undertake a public search. This was the only means available since it had not been possible to identify the location of the crime, which made it impossible for the police of any individual country to launch the request on its own. Furthermore, police authorities throughout the world required assistance to identify

entities supporting ISIL. In Resolution 2368 (2017), the UN Security Council added a number of individuals to the ISIL and Al-Qaida Sanctions List. These resolutions have all been adopted under Chapter VII of the UN Charter and require all States to take certain measures in connection with any individual or entity associated with ISIL, Al-Qaida, and/or the Taliban as designated by the Sanctions Committees.

[266] Resolution No AG/2005/RES/05, 'The United Nations Security Council's request to Interpol to assist the UN's anti-terrorism fight', INTERPOL General Assembly, 74th session (Berlin, 2005).

[267] 'INTERPOL seeks public's help to identify man photographed sexually abusing children: Operation Vico', INTERPOL press release (8 October 2007).

[268] Schöndorf-Haubold, B, 'The Administration of Information in International Administrative Law' (2008) 9 *German Law Journal* 1719–52 at 1741–42.

the presumed child abuser in order to subject him to the process of criminal justice and to prevent him from continuing to victimise children. In endorsing the actions of the General Secretariat, the General Assembly elucidated the legal authority and conditions for the operation:

> MINDFUL of the need to ensure a proper balance between the rights of the perpetrators and the rights of the child victims,
>
> TAKING INTO CONSIDERATION the profound impact that digitalization and distributed networks, especially the use of public information systems such as the Worldwide Web, have had on police/public interaction,
>
> BEARING IN MIND that when such material is discovered the victims are often unidentified and will remain so in spite of intensive efforts by the international law enforcement community and that, as long as the perpetrators are free, many more children run the risk of being sexually abused,
>
> RECALLING that under Article 26(b), (c) and (e) of INTERPOL's Constitution, the General Secretariat shall serve as an international centre in the fight against ordinary crime and as a technical and information centre,
>
> ENDORSES the initiative to publish information on the INTERPOL website to enable the public to assist INTERPOL's member countries to identify the child sex abuse perpetrators, victims or crime scenes, in compliance with INTERPOL's rules on the processing of police information, and so long as the consent of the NCB that provided the information has been obtained and no facial images of the child victims are published,
>
> STRESSES that, each case must be treated individually, and that consideration may only be given to publishing information to the public if and when the NCB that provided the information establishes that all other avenues of investigation have been exhausted, including diffusion to all National Central Bureaus.[269]

It is clear from the foregoing that the General Assembly is of the view that public searches by the General Secretariat are authorised under Article 26(b), (c) and (e) of the INTERPOL Constitution and that such action can be undertaken if the source of the information consents and it is an *ultimum remedium*.[270] Since 2007, INTERPOL has made a number of public appeals. Most recently, in connection with World Environment Day 2019, INTERPOL made a public appeal to locate seven individuals subject to red notices relating to environmental crimes, such as the smuggling of protected species or illegal logging, on the INTERPOL public website.[271]

[269] Resolution No AG-2007-RES-01, 'Requesting Public Assistance in Solving Crime', INTERPOL General Assembly, 76th session (Marrakesh, 2007).

[270] 'INTERPOL General Assembly endorses use of public appeals to assist in child sex abuse investigations', INTERPOL press release (7 November 2007).

[271] 'INTERPOL makes public appeal to help track environmental fugitives', INTERPOL press release (4 June 2019).

Since the entry into force of the IRPD in 2012, the disclosure of data to the public is regulated specifically by Article 61 of the IRPD. Article 61(2) of the IRPD provides that data processed in the INTERPOL Information System may only be disclosed to the public if all the following conditions are met:

(a) The disclosure is for at least one of the following purposes:
  (i) to alert the public;
  (ii) to request help from the public;
  (iii) for any other purpose intended to promote international police cooperation;
(b) The source of the data has authorized the disclosure beforehand, including details of the type of data to be disclosed, the method of disclosure, and the potential recipients of the disclosure, and the source has indicated any specific conditions concerning the disclosure;
(c) The disclosure complies with the aims and activities of the Organization and respects the basic rights of the persons who are subjects of international police cooperation;
(d) The disclosure is not such that it might prejudice the Organization's image or interests, or those of its Members;
(e) The disclosure does not concern an offender or an alleged offender who, at the time of the offence in question, was considered to be a minor under the law applicable in the country of the National Central Bureau or of the international entity which entered the data in the system, unless that National Central Bureau or international entity and the General Secretariat consider that such disclosure is essential to international police cooperation, and if the disclosure in question complies with the applicable principles of the national laws and of international law.

Article 61 of the IRPD also regulates (in practice) the use of the INTERPOL public website to display extracts of red, yellow and INTERPOL-UN Security Council Special Notices. At the end of 2019, 7,175 of approximately 58,000 red notices were published on the public website. Yellow notices more easily satisfy the criteria in Article 61(2) of the IRPD as they concern missing persons. 7,371 of approximately 11,000 yellow notices were published on INTERPOL's public website in the same period. All INTERPOL-UN Security Council Special Notices – 614 as at 31 January 2020 – are disclosed on the INTERPOL public website.

The fact that not all red notices are published on INTERPOL's public website is often overlooked. For instance, in 2017, the President of Belarus, Alexander Lukashenko, stated that the blogger Alexander Lapshin had been detained in Belarus in accordance with an INTERPOL notice. A number of media outlets reported that this 'had nothing to do with reality' because Lapshin's notice could not be located on the INTERPOL public website.[272] The media outlets failed to appreciate that only a small proportion of red notices are made available to the public.

[272] 'Lapshin is Not on Interpol's Wanted List. Lukashenko Lied', *Fact Investigation Platform* (9 February 2017).

D. Capacity Building and Training

In 2007, following a sharp increase in demand, capacity building and training was recognised as the Organisation's fourth core function. It is said to play a key role in INTERPOL's overall mission to promote international police cooperation. The aim of capacity building and training is to help law enforcement officials in INTERPOL's member countries improve their operational effectiveness, enhance their skills and build their capacity to address the increasingly globalised and sophisticated nature of contemporary criminality.

By asserting its competence to engage in training and development, INTERPOL appears to have relied on the doctrine of implied powers, which is common to all international organisations. As discussed in Chapter 8, under the doctrine of implied powers, an international organisation is impliedly conferred with such powers as are essential to the performance of the organisation's duties or which are necessarily implied in the light of the purposes assigned to it by its members. In light of INTERPOL's aims of 'ensur[ing] and promot[ing] the widest possible mutual assistance between all criminal police authorities' and 'establish[ing] and develop[ing] all institutions likely to contribute effectively to the prevention and suppression of ordinary law crimes', it is difficult to argue that INTERPOL did not have the implied power to undertake the type of capacity building and training described below.

In 2006, the General Assembly decided to establish a global anti-corruption academy in Austria.[273] The International Anti-Corruption Academy was established in 2010 and registered with the UN as an international organisation in 2011. Since 2007, INTERPOL has also established a variety of training programmes. Certified INTERPOL instructors, who are guided by the INTERPOL Guide to Effective Training, coordinate and deliver (1) training for NCBs aimed at strengthening the skills of NCB staff in the use of INTERPOL policing capabilities, (2) donor-funded training programmes tailored to address regional needs and focus on specific crime areas, and (3) specialised crime training in support of the Organisation's three Global Programmes (ie, counter-terrorism, cybercrime, and organised and emerging crime). INTERPOL can also accredit law enforcement training programmes that meet its internal standards.

The INTERPOL Global Learning Centre provides access to online e-learning modules and documents, alongside more than 60 courses for law enforcement personnel. It can be accessed through the I-24/7 System, but other law enforcement organisations can also request access. INTERPOL also hosts the INTERPOL Police Training Symposium – a biannual event which brings together representatives

[273] Resolution No AG-2006-RES-03, 'Creation of an Interpol Anti-Corruption Academy', INTERPOL General Assembly, 75th session (Rio De Janeiro, 2006). See also: Resolution AG-2007-RES-11, 'Headquarters Agreement required for the establishment of an INTERPOL Anti-Corruption Academy in Austria', INTERPOL General Assembly, 76th session (Marrakesh, 2007).

from law enforcement agencies, academic institutions and international organisations to share their insights and experiences in international police training. INTERPOL has also announced its intention to establish the INTERPOL Global Academy – a network of regional law enforcement training institutions to enhance law enforcement training initiatives in its member countries.

IV. Delegation of Powers

Another characteristic of international personality is that the entity has a distinct legal order. For international organisations, this legal order must be independent from its members so as to preserve the organisation's independence from national pressures and to protect it from control by a member over its activities in a member's territory.[274] According to Amerasinghe, this principle is 'basic for the operation of international organisations'.[275]

The legal order of INTERPOL comprises the INTERPOL Constitution as the foundation and the secondary norms adopted under Article 44 of the INTERPOL Constitution.[276] These classes of norms constitute a hierarchy and are of paramount importance. Article 1 of the General Regulations provides that the General Regulations and Appendices are adopted in accordance with Article 44 of the INTERPOL Constitution, and if there is any difference between the two, the INTERPOL Constitution prevails.

Article 6 of the INTERPOL Constitution consecrates the General Assembly as the body of supreme authority in the Organisation. However, unlike some international organisations where all the powers of the organisation are vested in its general congress,[277] the INTERPOL Constitution follows the principle that, within the general competence of the Organisation, more specific competences are given to various bodies. Hence the delegation of powers is prominent in INTERPOL's legal order, as reflected in the way the INTERPOL Constitution distributes powers between the bodies of the Organisation.[278] The General Assembly exercises policy-making powers through normative, elective and

[274] *Mendaro v World Bank*, 717 F.2d 610 (D.C. Cir. 1983) 615. See also: Cahier, P, 'L'ordre interne des organisations internationales' in Dupuy, RJ (ed), *Manuel sur les organisations internationales* (Dordrecht, Martinus Nijhoff Publishers, 1988) 237–58.

[275] Amerasinghe, CF, *The Law of the International Civil Service*, Vol I (Oxford, Clarendon Press, 1988) 7. See also: Reinisch, A, *International Organisations before National Courts* (Cambridge, Cambridge University Press, 2000) 242–43.

[276] See: Schöndorf-Haubold, B, 'The Administration of Information in International Administrative Law', (2008) 9 *German Law Journal* 1719–52 at 1727–32.

[277] This is particularly the case in the universal financial institutions (eg, the World Bank, the IMF and the International Fund for Agricultural Development).

[278] On the distribution of powers within international organisations, see: Schifano, A, 'Distribution of Power within International Organizations' (2017) 14 *International Organizations Law Review* 346–401.

control functions which, in conformity with Article 8 of the INTERPOL Constitution, are to (1) carry out the duties laid down in the INTERPOL Constitution, which include taking decisions on fundamental matters such as the admission of new members[279] or approving amendments to the INTERPOL Constitution,[280] (2) determine principles and lay down the general measures suitable for attaining the aims of the Organisation in Article 2 of the INTERPOL Constitution, (3) examine and approve the general programme of activities prepared by the Secretary General for the coming year, (4) determine any other regulations deemed necessary,[281] (5) elect persons to perform the functions mentioned in the INTERPOL Constitution, (6) adopt resolutions and make recommendations to members on matters in which the Organisation is competent,[282] (7) determine the financial policy of the Organisation,[283] and (8) examine and approve any agreements to be made with other organisations.[284]

The Executive Committee is designed as a typical non-plenary governing body that is empowered to (1) exercise oversight, (2) function as the preparatory body for plenary deliberations and decision-making, and (3) exercise certain executive powers that are deemed to be of such an importance that they exceed the scope of powers of the Secretary General. In this spirit, the INTERPOL Constitution mandates the Executive Committee to (1) supervise the execution of the decisions of the General Assembly,[285] (2) prepare the agenda for sessions of the General Assembly,[286] (3) submit to the General Assembly any programme of work or project which it considers useful,[287] (4) supervise the administration and work of the Secretary General,[288] (5) accept or approve gifts, bequests, subsidies, grants and other resources to the Organisation,[289] (6) approve the draft budget,[290] and (7) take all the necessary steps according to the general outlines of the preceding budget where the General Assembly has not had the opportunity to approve the budget.[291]

[279] See also: INTERPOL Constitution, Art 4.
[280] Ibid, Art 42.
[281] Ibid, Art 44.
[282] See also: General Regulations, Art 17.
[283] See also: INTERPOL Constitution, Arts 39 and 40; Rules of Procedure, Art 1(h).
[284] See also: INTERPOL Constitution, Art 41. Particular regard should be had to Resolution No AGN/67/RES/4, 'Application of Article 41 of the Organization's Constitution', INTERPOL General Assembly, 67th session (Cairo, 1998), where the General Assembly considered it 'necessary to make the procedure for approving certain co-operation agreements with other international organizations more flexible' and decided to delegate to 'the Executive Committee the power to approve such co-operation agreements'.
[285] INTERPOL Constitution, Art 22(a).
[286] Ibid, Art 22(b).
[287] Ibid, Art 22(c).
[288] Ibid, Art 22(d).
[289] Ibid, Art 38(b).
[290] Ibid, Art 40.
[291] Ibid.

The tasks bestowed on the General Secretariat by Article 26 of the INTERPOL Constitution underscore the executive character of the General Secretariat. In the same vein, the executive nature of the Secretary General is highlighted in Article 29 of the INTERPOL Constitution, which states that the Secretary General shall engage and direct the staff, administer the budget, and organise and direct the permanent departments of the Organisation, according to the directives decided upon by the General Assembly or the Executive Committee. The Secretary General is also responsible for submitting any propositions or projects concerning the work of the Organisation. He or she is 'responsible to the Executive Committee and the General Assembly'.[292]

The delegation of financial powers within the Organisation best serves to illustrate the institutional balance created by the INTERPOL Constitution. The General Assembly determines the financial policy of the Organisation.[293] In so doing, it establishes the basis of members' subscriptions and the maximum annual expenditure according to estimates provided by the Secretary General.[294] The draft budget is then prepared by the Secretary General and submitted to the Executive Committee for approval. The General Assembly is ultimately responsible for accepting the final budget.[295]

V. Privileges and Immunities

Like any international organisation, and unlike States who have a choice in limiting their activities to their own territories, INTERPOL must operate in the territory of a State. This reality constitutes a *conditio sine qua non* for the normal functioning of international organisations, the execution of their activities and the fulfilment of their objectives and purposes.[296] As a consequence, to ensure that the resources (human, financial or other) of international organisations remain available for their operations, it becomes necessary to establish safeguards against the interference with these resources by any country. This was articulated in the following terms at the UN Conference on International Organization in 1945: 'if there is one certain principle it is that no member state may hinder in any way the working of the Organization or take any measures the effect of which

[292] Ibid, Art 29.
[293] Ibid, Art 8(g).
[294] Ibid, Art 39.
[295] Ibid, Art 40.
[296] *Interpretation of the Agreement of 25 March 1951 between the WHO and Egypt* (Advisory Opinion) [1980] ICJ Rep 73, 155 (Separate Opinion of Judge Ago). See also: Reinisch, A, *International Organisations before National Courts* (Cambridge, Cambridge University Press, 2000) 127.

might be to increase its burdens, financial or other'.[297] In *Cumaraswamy*, Judge Rezek observed that:

> [t]here is no obligation on sovereign States to found international organizations, or to remain members of them against their will. However, the fact of membership – even in the case of an organization whose objectives are less essential than those of the United Nations, and in fields less salient than that of human rights – requires that every State, in its relations with the organization and its agents, display an attitude at least as constructive as that which characterizes diplomatic relations between States.[298]

It can be argued that this principle of non-interference should be understood to harbour a negative norm and a positive norm. For instance, the EU (ie, an international organisation) has expressed the principle of loyalty in Article 4(3) of the Treaty on European Union as inclusive of a positive norm – 'Member States shall take any appropriate measure, general or particular, to ensure fulfilment of the obligations arising out of the Treaties or resulting from the acts of the institutions of the Union' – and a negative norm – 'Member States shall … refrain from any measure which could jeopardise the attainment of the Union's objectives'.[299] The principle of 'sincere cooperation', enshrined in Article 4(3) of the Treaty on European Union, is also framed as a positive norm: 'the Union and Member States shall, in full mutual respect, assist each other in carrying out tasks which flow from the Treaties'.

A similar approach is set out in Articles 30 and 31 of the INTERPOL Constitution. With regard to the staff members of the Organisation, Article 30 of the INTERPOL Constitution stipulates, inter alia, that:

> [e]ach Member of the Organisation shall undertake to respect the exclusively international character of the duties of the Secretary General and the staff, and abstain from influencing them in the discharge of their duties.
>
> All Members of the Organisation shall do their best to assist the Secretary General and the staff in the discharge of their functions.

Article 31 adds, more generally, that: '[i]n order to further its aims, the Organization needs the constant and active co-operation of its Members, who should do all within their power which is compatible with the legislations of their countries to participate diligently in its activities'.

While these provisions establish some safeguards against undue interference, they clearly require further elaboration to protect the Organisation adequately. In the absence of a formal conventional foundation which would contain a clause

[297] 'Report of the Rapporteur of Committee IV/2 to Commission IV' in *Documents of the United Nations Conference on International Organization*, Vol XIII (San Francisco, 1945) 683, 705. This principle finds a parallel in the principle *ne impediatur legatio*.

[298] *Difference Relating to Immunity from Legal Process of a Special Rapporteur of the Commission on Human Rights* (Advisory Opinion) [1999] ICJ Rep 62, 109–10 (Separate Opinion of Judge Rezek).

[299] Consolidated version of the Treaty on European Union [2016] Official Journal C 202, 13–388.

equivalent to Article 105 of the UN Charter detailing a general arrangement, INTERPOL is left to find bilateral solutions for the privileges and immunities needed for its operation. The solutions found so far cover several sets of privileges and immunities that can be found in the agreements concluded with host countries where the Organisation has (or plans to have) its offices (eg, France, Austria, Thailand, Argentina, Ivory Coast, Zimbabwe, Kenya, El Salvador, Cameroon, Singapore and Belgium)[300] and the ad hoc conference-hosting agreements that it regularly concludes with countries hosting the sessions of the General Assembly

[300] The Organisation has concluded the following headquarters agreements: (1) Agreement between the ICPO-INTERPOL and the Government of the French Republic regarding INTERPOL's Headquarters in France (in force on 1 September 2009), replacing the Headquarters Agreement concluded on 3 November 1982, as amended by Decree No 2016-326 of 17 March 2016 promulgating the additional protocol in the form of an exchange of letters between the Government of the French Republic and ICPO-INTERPOL on the interpretation and application of Article 24 of the Agreement of 14 and 24 April 2008 regarding INTERPOL's headquarters in France (signed in Paris on 9 February 2016 and in Lyon on 12 February 2016, entered into force on 16 February 2016), (2) Headquarters Agreement with Austria regarding the creation of an INTERPOL Anti-Corruption Academy (AG-2007-RAP-10) approved by Resolution No AG-2007-RES-11, 'Headquarters Agreement required for the establishment of an INTERPOL Anti-Corruption Academy in Austria', INTERPOL General Assembly, 76th session (Marrakesh, 2007), (3) Agreement between the ICPO-INTERPOL and the Government of the Kingdom of Thailand regarding the privileges and immunities of the INTERPOL Office for South-East Asia in Bangkok (AGN/55/RAP/22) (signed on 4 February 1987, entered into force on 22 February 1992), (4) Agreement between the ICPO-INTERPOL and the Government of the Argentine Republic regarding a Sub-Regional Bureau for South America and its immunities and privileges on Argentine territory (AGN/58/RAP/7) (signed on 22 May 1990, entered into force on 7 April 1993), as amended by an additional protocol approved by Resolution No AG-2014-RES-10, 'Protocol modifying the "Headquarters Agreement between the Government of the Argentine Republic and the International Criminal Police Organization – INTERPOL regarding a Sub-Regional Bureau for South America"', INTERPOL General Assembly, 83rd session (Monaco, 2014), (5) Agreement between the ICPO-INTERPOL and the Republic of Côte d'Ivoire regarding a Sub-Regional Bureau for West Africa and its privileges and immunities on Ivorian territory (AGN/61/RAP/11) (signed on 7 September 1994), (6) Agreement between the ICPO-INTERPOL and the Government of the Republic of Zimbabwe regarding a Sub-Regional Bureau in Harare and its privileges and immunities on Zimbabwean Territory (AGN/65/RAP/10) (signed on 3 February 1997), as amended by Resolution No AGN/65/RES/19, 'Amendments to the Agreement between the Government of Zimbabwe and the International Criminal Police Organization – Interpol regarding a Sub-Regional Bureau in Harare and its Privileges and Immunities on Zimbabwean Territory', INTERPOL General Assembly, 65th session (Antalya, 1996), (7) Agreement between the ICPO-INTERPOL and the Government of the Republic of Kenya regarding a Sub-Regional Bureau in Nairobi and its privileges and immunities on Kenyan territory (AGN/65/RAP/9) (signed on 11 September 1999), (8) Agreement between the ICPO-INTERPOL and the Government of the Republic of El Salvador regarding a Sub-Regional Bureau for Central America and its privileges and immunities on Salvadoran territory (AGN/68/RES/1) (signed on 25 June 2001), (9) Agreement with the Republic of Cameroon regarding the Sub-Regional Bureau in Yaoundé and Agreement on Privileges and Immunities and the Headquarters Agreement (signed on 26 March 2007), (10) Agreement between INTERPOL and the Government of the Republic of Singapore regarding the establishment of the INTERPOL Global Complex in Singapore (signed on 9 November 2010), and (11) Headquarters Agreement with Exchange of Letters between the International Criminal Police Organization – INTERPOL (ICPO-INTERPOL) and the Kingdom of Belgium (AG-2015-RAP-08), approved by Resolution No AG-2015-RES-10, 'Headquarters Agreement with Exchange of Letters between the International Criminal Police Organization – INTERPOL (ICPO-INTERPOL) and the Kingdom of Belgium', INTERPOL General Assembly, 84th session (Kigali, 2015).

and Regional Conferences. The privileges and immunities covered in these agreements are those that are (1) deemed necessary for the Organisation to exercise its mandate effectively and independently from national authorities, (2) granted to INTERPOL officials in the exercise of their official duties and not for their personal benefit, (3) extended to representatives of members, observers and their substitutes at meetings convened by INTERPOL, and (4) granted to experts serving on committees of, or performing missions for, the Organisation.

The first category of privileges and immunities, ie, those that pertain to the Organisation itself, include (1) immunity from jurisdiction for the Organisation, its property and its assets, (2) inviolability of the premises and archives of the Organisation, (3) immunity from financial controls, regulations or moratoria, (4) inviolability of official correspondence, and (5) exemption from direct taxes, customs duties and prohibitions or restrictions on the import and export of articles for official use.

The second category of privileges and immunities, ie, those that pertain to INTERPOL officials, vary according to the status of the official within the Organisation and the laws of the contracting States. As a minimum, these privileges and immunities include (1) immunity from jurisdiction in respect of acts performed in an official capacity, (2) immunity from immigration restrictions and alien registration, (3) exemption from national service obligations and from taxation in respect of salaries and emoluments received from INTERPOL, (4) the right to import free of duty furniture and effects upon first taking up a post, and (5) certain exchange and repatriation facilities.

The third category of privileges and immunities pertains to representatives of members, observers, and their substitutes at meetings convened by INTERPOL. These privileges and immunities include, among others, (1) immunity from personal arrest or detention, (2) immunity from seizure of personal baggage, (3) immunity from legal process of every kind in respect of words spoken or written and all acts performed in their official capacity, (4) inviolability of all papers and documents, (5) exemption from immigration restrictions, alien registration or national service obligations, and (6) some facilities in respect of currency exchange and personal baggage. Finally, experts serving on INTERPOL committees or performing missions for INTERPOL also enjoy a limited set of privileges and immunities necessary for the effective exercise of their functions.

The various arrangements reiterate that the privileges and immunities are granted in the interests of the Organisation and not for the personal benefit of the individuals themselves. Therefore, the Organisation has the right to waive the immunity of any official or expert in any case where, in its opinion, the application of immunity would impede the course of justice and where immunity can be waived without prejudice to the interests of the Organisation.

That being said, the Organisation recognises that its situation with respect to privileges and immunities is not ideal. The Statement to Reaffirm the Independence and Political Neutrality of INTERPOL ('Statement') adopted by the INTERPOL General Assembly at its 74th session in 2006 is an acknowledgment of the shortcomings of INTERPOL's current arrangements for privileges and immunities.[301] The Statement recalled that, in 1955, it was necessary to revise the constituent instrument of the ICPC in order to ensure and strengthen its position as an independent and neutral intergovernmental organisation, following which the current INTERPOL Constitution was adopted. The Statement also welcomed the fact that the Organisation's independence has been confirmed by courts, and that national tribunals have recognised that the Organisation has an existence separate from its members. On the other hand, the Statement noted that it has become increasingly necessary to take steps to preserve the independence and neutrality of the Organisation, such as the enactment of data protection rules, the creation of the CCF ('in order to avoid interference by national data protection bodies'), the enactment of staff regulations, and the acceptance of the jurisdiction of the ILOAT ('in order to avoid being subjected to national labour laws and labour courts'). The Statement then expressed concern about INTERPOL's continuous, ongoing challenges, such as measures affecting (1) member countries' freedom to compose delegations to statutory meetings of the Organisation, (2) the independence of staff members seconded to the General Secretariat, (3) the independence of members of the Executive Committee, and (4) the venue of sessions of statutory bodies. In light of the foregoing, the General Assembly, inter alia, called upon all member countries and intergovernmental organisations 'to respect the independence and neutrality of either the Organization itself, the Executive Committee, or the General Secretariat', and called upon the General Secretariat and member countries 'to consult with one another or with any intergovernmental institution contemplating to take measures which would interfere with the Organization's neutrality and independence'.[302]

In 2011, in light of the increasing number of IRTs and IMESTs deployed by the Organisation, the General Assembly explicitly called on its members to respect the privileges and immunities of its staff. It stated, inter alia:

> RECOGNIZING the need for the Organization's staff to enjoy privileges and immunities in order to be able to carry out their duties independently while deployed as members of IRTs or IMESTs on the territory of a member country,
>
> RECOGNIZING that diplomatic privileges and immunities are among the oldest international guarantees created and that their aim is mainly to maintain relations of mutual assistance and international exchanges in times of crisis,
>
> CONSIDERING that privileges and immunities are recognized by international law as the fundamental guarantee of the independence of international organizations in times of crisis,

[301] Resolution No AG-2006-RES-04, 'Statement to Reaffirm the Independence and Political Neutrality of Interpol', INTERPOL General Assembly, 75th session (Rio de Janeiro, 2006).

[302] Resolution No AG-2006-RES-04, 'Statement to Reaffirm the Independence and Political Neutrality of Interpol', INTERPOL General Assembly, 75th session (Rio de Janeiro, 2006), operative paras 3–4.

> RECALLING that privileges and immunities are accorded to the Organization and its staff by member countries with which the Organization has concluded Headquarters Agreements,
>
> ALSO RECALLING that privileges and immunities are granted by countries hosting the statutory meetings of the Organization,
>
> ASKS the National Central Bureaus of member countries requesting the deployment of an IRT or an IMEST to urge the competent national authorities to grant the Organization and its staff the privileges and immunities necessary for the proper conduct of the team's activities and the accomplishment of its mission in conformity with international public law.[303]

The concerns expressed in the Statement and Resolution No AG-2010-RES-11 confirm the challenges that the Organisation faces, particularly in those countries where no bilateral arrangements are in place.

That being said, courts in countries where no bilateral arrangements exist have generally found various ways to shield the Organisation, typically on the basis of immunity from jurisdiction (on which, see Chapter 12). However, the Organisation should remain cognisant that 'the rules governing the jurisdiction of national courts must be carefully distinguished from those governing jurisdictional immunities: jurisdiction does not imply absence of immunity, while absence of immunity does not imply jurisdiction.'[304] A State is entitled to exercise jurisdiction over all individuals and entities in its territory, except when the individual or entity in question enjoys immunity.[305] But, 'it is only where a State has jurisdiction under international law in relation to a particular matter that there can be any question of immunities in regard to the exercise of that jurisdiction.'[306] This view was echoed by Judge Guillaume in his Separate Opinion in the *Arrest Warrant* case: 'a court's jurisdiction is a question which it must decide before considering the immunity of those before it. In other words, there can only be immunity from jurisdiction where there is jurisdiction.'[307] Similarly, in their Joint Separate Opinion, Judges Higgins, Kooijmans and Buergenthal stated that '[i]f there is no jurisdiction *en principe*, then the question of an immunity from a jurisdiction which would otherwise exist simply does not arise.'[308]

[303] Resolution No AG-2010-RES-11, 'Privileges and immunities in the framework of IRT and IMEST deployments', INTERPOL General Assembly, 79th session (Doha, 2010).

[304] *Arrest Warrant of 11 April 2000 (Democratic Republic of the Congo v Belgium)* (Judgment) [2002] ICJ Rep 3, para 59.

[305] See: 'Draft Declaration on Rights and Duties of States' in *Yearbook of the International Law Commission* (1949), 287–88. Draft Article 2 states that '[e]very State has the right to exercise jurisdiction over its territory and over all persons and things therein, subject to the immunities recognised by international law'. The commentary to this draft article notes that 'the concluding phrase is a safeguard for protecting such immunities as those of diplomatic officers and officials of international organizations'.

[306] *Arrest Warrant of 11 April 2000 (Democratic Republic of the Congo v Belgium)* (Judgment) [2002] ICJ Rep 3, para 46.

[307] Ibid, 35, para 1 (Separate Opinion of President Guillaume).

[308] Ibid, 64, para 3 (Joint Separate Opinion of Judges Higgins, Kooijmans and Buergenthal). See also: *Jurisdictional Immunities of the State case (Germany v Italy: Greece intervening)* (Judgment) [2012]

This was the approach adopted by the US Court of Appeals for the DC Circuit in the *Steinberg* case (discussed in section II.D above). One of the arguments invoked by INTERPOL in its initial petition to the Court of Appeals was immunity from jurisdiction. In a separate concurring statement, Chief Judge Robinson III held that it was not the appropriate occasion to raise the issue of immunity:

> Interpol also vigorously argues various issues of immunity. As my colleagues have noted, this action has yet to proceed to the point where these may become relevant, and no question of official or sovereign immunity was tendered on appeal. We ruled simply on the question of personal jurisdiction, and it is generally accepted that immunity is not a facet of that issue.[309]

Similarly, in *Scientology Kirche Deutschland v INTERPOL* (discussed in section II.D above), the Munich District Court held that even if INTERPOL were to benefit from immunity in Germany, that did not pre-empt the court's jurisdiction.[310] In light of the above, it is clear that INTERPOL must at least consider the substance of the question of jurisdiction, rather than seeking to rely only on arguments of immunity.

VI. Recognition as an International Organisation

The foregoing discussion indicates that the members did intend to, and did in fact, ascribe certain characteristics to INTERPOL which confer international legal personality. Further to this exercise, there are many commentators who adopt the view that recognition[311] can also have important legal and political effects for international organisations,[312] as is the case for the creation of States.[313] Recognition can constitute evidence that the recognising body endorses the view that

ICJ Rep 99; Martha, RSJ, *The Jurisdiction to Tax in International Law: Theory and Practice of Legislative Fiscal Jurisdiction* (Deventer, Kluwer Law, 1989) 17–8.

[309] *Leon Steinberg v International Criminal Police Organisation et al*, 672 F.2d 927 (D.C. Cir. 1981) para 31.

[310] *Scientology Kirche Deutschland et al v INTERPOL*, District Court of Munich, Az: 120 10 512/76 (5 January 1978) para 1.664.

[311] In this sense, recognition has two meanings, which (in general) coincide. The term 'recognition' may mean a manifestation of an opinion on the legal status of the organisation in question. It may also mean an indication of willingness on the part of the recognising entity to establish or maintain official relations with the organisation in question (see: Talmon, S, *Recognition of Governments in International Law* (Oxford, Oxford University Press, 1998) 21–43).

[312] Seidl-Hohenveldern, I, *Collected Essays on International Investments and on International Organizations* (The Hague, Kluwer Law International, 1998) 12. See also: Czapliński, W, 'Recognition and International Legal Personality of Non-State Actors' (2016) 1 *Pécs Journal of International and European Law* 7–17; Worster, WT, 'Relative International Legal Personality of Non-State Actors' (2016) 42 *Brooklyn Journal of International Law* 207.

[313] Crawford, J, *The Creation of States in International Law*, 2nd edn (Oxford, Oxford University Press, 2006) 29.

the organisation possesses a legal identity as a subject of law in its own right. Indeed, in *Reparation for Injuries*,[314] the ICJ made a statement which rarely attracts attention but is nevertheless of importance:

> the Court must first enquire whether the Charter has given the Organization such a position that it possesses, in regard to its Members, rights which it is entitled to ask them to respect. In other words, does the Organization possess international personality? This is no doubt a doctrinal expression, which has sometimes given rise to controversy. But it will be used here to mean that if the Organization is recognized as having that personality, it is an entity capable of availing itself of obligations incumbent upon its Members.[315]

It follows that, if INTERPOL has been recognised as an international organisation, implicit in this is an acknowledgment that INTERPOL possesses legal personality.

In Judgment No 1080, the ILOAT stated that 'Interpol is an independent international organisation'.[316] Various domestic courts have also referred to the Organisation in a similar manner. The most unequivocal description was made by the District Court of Jerusalem, which stated that INTERPOL 'is an international police organization established out of the power of international law'.[317] The Munich District Court also expressly acknowledged INTERPOL's legal status under international law.[318] However, other courts have been less clear. In *Sami*, the US Court of Appeals for the DC Circuit simply referred to INTERPOL as 'an organization whose aims, according to its Constitution, are "… to ensure and promote the widest possible mutual assistance between all criminal police authorities"'.[319] Similarly, in *Founding Church of Scientology*, the same court spoke of INTERPOL as an 'international body organized "to ensure and promote the widest possible mutual assistance between all criminal police authorities"'.[320]

The recognition of INTERPOL as an international organisation by the UN was a slow process. Pursuant to UN Economic and Social Council ('ECOSOC') Resolution 1225 (XLII) of 6 June 1967, the Committee on Non-Governmental Organisations ('Committee') met in 1968 and 1969 to carry out ECOSOC's request to review the activities of non-governmental organisations already granted consultative status with ECOSOC, including INTERPOL. The debates on the issue of INTERPOL's status stemmed from Article 4 of the INTERPOL Constitution, which provides that '[a]ny country may delegate as a member to the Organization

[314] *Reparation for Injuries Suffered in the Service of the United Nations* (Advisory Opinion) [1949] ICJ Rep 174.

[315] *Reparation for Injuries Suffered in the Service of the United Nations* (Advisory Opinion) [1949] ICJ Rep 174, 178 (emphasis added).

[316] *Mr OB v the International Criminal Police Organization*, ILOAT, Judgment No 1080 (1991) para 12.

[317] *X and Y v INTERPOL*, District Court of Jerusalem (27 March 2009) para 9.

[318] *Scientology Kirche Deutschland, et al. v INTERPOL*, District Court of Munich, Az: 120 10 512/76 (5 January 1978).

[319] *Mohammad Sami v United States of America et al*, 617 F.2d 755 (D.C. Cir. 1979).

[320] *Founding Church of Scientology of Washington, DC, Inc v Donald T Regan, Secretary of the Treasury et al*, 670 F.2d 1158 (D.C. Cir. 1981) para 2.

any official police body whose functions come within the framework of activities of the Organization.' Some UN Member States considered the composition of INTERPOL's membership as grounds for qualifying the Organisation as an intergovernmental organisation within the meaning of Article 57 of the UN Charter, rather than a non-governmental organisation.[321] Others were of the view that INTERPOL was not strictly intergovernmental, yet it could not be classified as being completely non-governmental.[322]

To end the stalemate, several proposals concerning the matter were formulated. A three-part proposal garnered the majority of the Committee's votes. In the first part of the proposal, it was tentatively decided that INTERPOL would have a consultative status of category II (ie, non-governmental organisation). By virtue of the second part of the proposal, the Committee decided that the entire question regarding the examination of INTERPOL's application was a 'complicated one'. In the third part of the proposal, the Committee decided that a 'special arrangement' should be put in place with INTERPOL. Two delegations requested that reservations be included in the Committee's proposal. The first reservation stated that placing an intergovernmental organisation in category II status was 'both inadmissible and illegal'. The second reservation stated that the Committee had 'committed a most flagrant legal violation when considering INTERPOL, which is strictly an intergovernmental organisation'.[323] A third delegation countered that INTERPOL should be placed in category II because it had not been established by intergovernmental agreement. During ECOSOC's subsequent assessment of the Committee's three-part proposal, it decided on a compromise of sorts (by 23 votes to none with two abstentions): it agreed to

[321] Article 57 of the UN Charter provides that '(1) The specialized agencies, established by intergovernmental agreement and having wide international responsibilities, as defined in their basic instruments, in economic, social, cultural, educational, health, and related fields, shall be brought into relationship with the United Nations in accordance with the provisions of Article 63. (2) Such agencies thus brought into relationship with the United Nations are hereinafter referred to as specialized agencies.' With regard to other intergovernmental organisations not defined as specialised agencies (and despite the text of Article 57 which refers to specialised agencies), ECOSOC nevertheless possesses the discretion to bring such other intergovernmental organisations into relationship with it. In its report to the General Assembly, the Preparatory Commission observed that ECOSOC might, 'at its discretion, negotiate agreements with the competent authorities, bringing into relationship such other intergovernmental agencies, including those of a regional character, as are not considered as being within the definition of Article 57 but which it is considered desirable to bring into relationship' (Report of the Preparatory Commission of the UN, UN Doc PC/20 (22 December 1945) Chapter III, Section 5, para 2). See also: Documents of the UN Conference on International Organization (San Francisco, 1945) Vol X, 231, 272 wherein it was stated that Article 57 should not be regarded as precluding ECOSOC from 'negotiating at its discretion, subject to the approval of the General Assembly, agreements bringing other types of intergovernmental agencies into relationship with the Organisation'. The foregoing is in line with the intended purpose of the provisions in the UN Charter of providing for arrangements sufficiently flexible to enable satisfactory arrangements to be worked out on the basis of need and experience.

[322] Repertory of Practice of UN Organs, Supplement No 5 (1970–1978), Vol 3, Art 57, 108.

[323] ECOSOC Official Records, 46th session (12 May – 6 June 1969), Annexes, 'Agenda item 17: Non-governmental organisations', Document No E/4657, 4.

place INTERPOL in category II for the time being and requested the Committee to study a special arrangement with INTERPOL.[324]

In February 1970, during the subsequent meetings of the Committee, it was decided that the UN Secretariat, in consultation with INTERPOL, would submit to the Committee's 1971 session the draft of a special arrangement between INTERPOL and ECOSOC. Until such new arrangements were reached, INTERPOL would retain its category II status. ECOSOC endorsed this recommendation. INTERPOL and the UN Secretariat then held consultations to produce a draft arrangement, which was subsequently included in a memorandum to the Committee. During the 1971 session of the Committee, there was general satisfaction with the proposed draft arrangement, subject to one amendment.[325] The Committee then approved the draft arrangement and submitted it, together with a draft resolution, to ECOSOC. ECOSOC adopted the draft resolution on the arrangement for cooperation between the UN and INTERPOL as contained in ECOSOC Resolution E/RES/1971/1579(L) and its annex.[326] In 1971, INTERPOL and the UN concluded the 'special arrangement', which removed INTERPOL from its consultative status.[327] In 1975, and in accordance with Rule 79 of ECOSOC's rules of procedure and by virtue of Council Decision 109 (LIX) of 23 July 1975 ('Participation of intergovernmental organizations in the work of the Council'), ECOSOC designated INTERPOL an intergovernmental organisation so it could participate in the work of ECOSOC on a continuing basis. In 1996, the UN General Assembly conferred observer status on INTERPOL.[328] As the conferral of observer status in the UN is generally reserved for non-Member States and international organisations other than the specialised agencies, this decision also indicated the UN's recognition of INTERPOL as an international organisation.

The recognition of INTERPOL as an international organisation by other international organisations (or organs thereof) was not as arduous. The first such act of recognition came as early as 1929 at the conference adopting the 1929 International Convention for the Suppression of Counterfeiting Currency ('1929 Convention').[329] The contracting parties to the 1929 Convention designated the ICPC to perform

[324] Repertory of Practice of UN Organs, Supplement No 5 (1970–1978), Vol 3, Art 57, 109.

[325] One representative emphasised that section 4, concerning representation by observers, 'should not be understood to imply legal commitment on the part of any United Nations body other than the Economic and Social Council and its subsidiary organs'.

[326] The arrangement covered matters that concern INTERPOL, namely, questions regarding the exchange of information and documentation, consultations and technical cooperation, representation by observers at meetings, exchange of written statements and the proposal of agenda items (ECOSOC Resolution E/RES/1971/1579(L), 'Special arrangement for co-operation between the United Nations and the International Criminal Police Organization (INTERPOL)' (20 May 1971)).

[327] Repertory of Practice of UN Organs, Supplement No 5 (1970–1978) Vol 3, Art 71, 240.

[328] UN General Assembly Resolution A/RES/51/1, 'Observer status for the International Criminal Police Organization (Interpol) in the General Assembly' (22 October 1996).

[329] International Convention for the Suppression of Counterfeiting Currency (signed on 20 April 1929, entered into force on 22 February 1931) 1112 League of Nations Treaty Series 371.

the functions of an 'international bureau' within the meaning of Article 15 of the 1929 Convention, a role which the General Secretariat continues to fulfil today as the International Central Office for the Suppression of Counterfeit Currency. Some cooperation agreements concluded between INTERPOL and other international organisations (or organs thereof) recognise INTERPOL's status in explicit terms. The agreement between the General Secretariat of INTERPOL and the General Secretariat of the Organization of American States expressly designates INTERPOL as 'a public international organization'.[330] The cooperation agreement between INTERPOL and the Office of the Prosecutor of the International Criminal Court ('ICC') clearly refers to INTERPOL as an 'intergovernmental organization'.[331] This is of particular importance because the Office of the Prosecutor of the ICC has the power to enter into international agreements, as conferred by the 1998 Rome Statute,[332] which envisages cooperation with 'intergovernmental organisations'.[333] Similarly, in 2004, INTERPOL concluded a cooperation agreement with the European Central Bank ('ECB'),[334] and the preamble specifically refers to INTERPOL as an 'international organisation having its seat [in Lyon]'. In 2014, INTERPOL concluded a cooperation agreement with the International Organization for Migration which recognises 'that INTERPOL is an independent intergovernmental organization'.[335]

Various EU legal instruments have acknowledged INTERPOL's status as an international organisation, although this was a gradual process. In the 1990s, some EU acts referred to INTERPOL simply as a 'body'. For instance, in Council Act of 26 July 1995 drawing up the Convention based on Article K.3 of the

[330] 'Recognizing that INTERPOL, represented by its General Secretariat in Lyon, France, is a public international organisation responsible for …' (General Co-operation Agreement between the General Secretariat of the International Criminal Police Organisation-INTERPOL and the General Secretariat of the Organization of the American States (signed on 2 May 2000), third preambular paragraph).

[331] Co-operation agreement between the Office of the Prosecutor of the International Criminal Court and the International Criminal Police Organisation-INTERPOL (signed on 22 December 2004, entered into force on 22 March 2005) ICC-OTP-20041222-85, fourth preambular paragraph.

[332] Article 54(3) of the Rome Statute (originally circulated as document A/CONF183/9 of 17 July 1998, entered into force on 1 July 2002) provides that '[t]he Prosecutor may: … (c) [s]eek the cooperation of any State or intergovernmental Organisation or arrangement in accordance with its respective competence and/or mandate; (d) [e]nter into such arrangements or agreements, not inconsistent with this Statute, as may be necessary to facilitate the cooperation of a State, intergovernmental Organisation or person; …'.

[333] 'Recalling that pursuant to Article 54(3) (c) and (d) of the Rome Statute, the Prosecutor may seek the co-operation of intergovernmental organisations in accordance with its respective competence and mandate, and may enter into such agreements as may be necessary to facilitate the co-operation of an intergovernmental organisation …' (Co-operation agreement between the Office of the Prosecutor of the International Criminal Court and the International Criminal Police Organisation-INTERPOL, fourth preambular paragraph).

[334] Cooperation Agreement between the European Central Bank–ECB and the International Criminal Police Organisation–INTERPOL (signed on 25 March 2004).

[335] Cooperation Agreement between the International Criminal Police Organization–INTERPOL and the International Organization for Migration (IOM) (signed on 5 March 2014).

Treaty on European Union, on the establishment of a European Police Office ('Europol Convention'), INTERPOL was referred to as a 'third body'.[336] The very same designation was also employed in Council Act of 12 March 1999 adopting the rules governing the transmission of personal data by Europol to third States and third bodies.[337] The Europol Convention and Council Act of 12 March 1999 were replaced by Council Decision 2009/371/JHA of 6 April 2009 establishing the European Police Office (Europol), which provided that '[i]n so far as it is necessary for the performance of its tasks, Europol may establish and maintain cooperative relations with … organisations such as … the International Criminal Police Organisation (Interpol)'.[338] Council Decision 2009/371/JHA was most recently replaced by Regulation (EU) of the European Parliament and of the Council of 11 May 2016 on the European Union Agency for Law Enforcement Cooperation (Europol). This provides in preambular paragraph 32 that 'Europol should therefore be able to exchange personal data with authorities of third countries and with international organisations such as the International Criminal Police Organisation – Interpol to the extent necessary for the accomplishment of its tasks'.[339] Similarly, Council Resolution of 25 June 2001 on the exchange of DNA analysis results expressly refers to INTERPOL as an international organisation.[340] Furthermore, in Council Resolution on the establishment of national systems for surveillance and control of the presence of radioactive materials in the recycling of metallic materials in the Member States, INTERPOL is referred to as an international organisation alongside a number of other international organisations including the International Atomic Energy Agency and the World Customs Organization.[341] Finally,

[336] Article 42(2) of the Europol Convention stated: '[i]n so far as is required for the performance of the tasks described in Article 3, Europol may also establish and maintain relations with third States and third bodies within the meaning of Article 10(4), points 4, 5, 6 and 7'. Article 10(4), point 7, lists INTERPOL as such a 'third body'.

[337] Council Act of 12 March 1999 adopting the rules governing the transmission of personal data by Europol to third States and third bodies, 1999/C 88/01, Official Journal C 88 (30 March 1999) 1, Art 1(b): '"third bodies" means the bodies referred to in Article 10(4)(1) to (3) and (5) to (7) of the Europol Convention'.

[338] Council Decision of 6 April 2009 establishing the European Police Office (Europol), 2009/371/JHA, Official Journal L 121/37 (15 May 2009), 37–66, Art 23.

[339] Regulation (EU) 2016/794 of the European Parliament and of the Council of 11 May 2016 on the European Union Agency for Law Enforcement Cooperation (Europol) and replacing and repealing Council Decisions 2009/371/JHA, 2009/934/JHA, 2009/935/JHA, 2009/936/JHA and 2009/968/JHA, Official Journal L 135/53 (24 May 2016), preambular para 32.

[340] Resolution of the Council of the European Union on the exchange of DNA analysis results, 2001/C 187/01 (25 June 2001) Official Journal C 187 (3 July 2001) 1–4. The resolution provides under Part III that '3. Member States are encouraged to use the form in Annex II, which is based on the standard already in use in other international organisations such as Interpol, for the exchange of results obtained through the ESS. Member States are urged to designate one contact point for this purpose'.

[341] Resolution of the Council of the European Union on the establishment of national systems for surveillance and control of the presence of radioactive materials in the recycling of metallic materials in the Member States, 2002/C 119/05, Official Journal C 119 (22 May 2002) 7–9. Preambular paragraph 11 provides that '[i]n recent years, and as a result of the radiological accidents that have occurred in the metallic materials recycling sector, various international organisations, among them the International Atomic Energy Agency (IAEA), the World Customs Organisation (WCO), the International Criminal

in a memorandum of understanding on cooperation between EUROJUST and INTERPOL, INTERPOL was recognised by the parties as 'an independent intergovernmental organisation'.[342] It can, therefore, confidently be said that the EU recognises INTERPOL as an international organisation.

VII. Recognition of Legal Capacity

A consequence of the possession of international legal personality by an international organisation is the capacity to conclude agreements which are subject to the law of treaties.[343] This is clear from *Reparation for Injuries*[344] and *Judgment No 2867 of the [ILOAT] upon a Complaint Filed against the International Fund for Agricultural Development*.[345] In the latter case, the ICJ held that the Global Mechanism of the UN Convention to Combat Desertification in Those Countries Experiencing Serious Drought and/or Desertification, Particularly in Africa ('Global Mechanism') was not an international organisation in the absence of evidence that it was empowered to enter into international agreements in its own capacity.[346] Doctrinal writings on the matter also suggest that, where an organisation has concluded a host State agreement, this is evidence of both its legal personality and its status as an international organisation.[347]

Police Organisation (ICPO-Interpol) and the Economic Commission of the United Nations for Europe (ECE), in collaboration with the Bureau of International Recycling (BIR), have adopted initiatives aimed at minimising radiological risk in this industrial sector'.

[342] Memorandum of Understanding on Cooperation between EUROJUST and the International Criminal Police Organisation (ICPO-INTERPOL) (signed on 15 July 2013, entered into force on 1 August 2013).

[343] See: Akande, D, 'International Organizations' in Evans, MD (ed), *International* Law, 5th edn (Oxford, Oxford University Press, 2018) 227–58 at 233.

[344] *Reparation for Injuries Suffered in the Service of the United Nations* (Advisory Opinion) [1949] ICJ Rep 174, 181.

[345] *Judgment No 2867 of the Administrative Tribunal of the International Labour Organization upon a Complaint Filed against the International Fund for Agricultural Development* (Advisory Opinion) [2012] ICJ Rep 10.

[346] *Judgment No 2867 of the Administrative Tribunal of the International Labour Organization upon a Complaint Filed against the International Fund for Agricultural Development* (Advisory Opinion) [2012] ICJ Rep 10, paras 57–58. It should be emphasised that the opinion of the ICJ was factually erroneous as the Global Mechanism had been entering into international agreements (as noted in the Written Comments of the International Fund for Agricultural Development (11 March 2011), para 44). Such agreements were not furnished before the ICJ as there was no request by the Court to consider these agreements and previous decisions of the Conference of the Parties acknowledged the capacity of the Global Mechanism to enter into such agreements (see: Martha, RSJ, 'Attribution of conduct after the Advisory Opinion on the Global Mechanism', in Ragazzi, M (ed), *Responsibility of International Organizations: Essays in Memory of Sir Ian Brownlie* (Leiden, Brill Nijhoff Publishers, 2013) 275–87 at 285).

[347] Eg, Müller, AS, *International Organizations and their Host States: Aspects of their Legal Relationship* (The Hague, Kluwer Law International, 1995) 268.

Three articles in the INTERPOL Constitution evidence that INTERPOL is empowered to enter into international agreements in its own capacity. First, Article 8(h) of the INTERPOL Constitution provides that one of the functions of the General Assembly shall be to examine and approve any agreement to be made with other organisations.[348] Second, Article 26(e) of the INTERPOL Constitution provides that the General Secretariat shall maintain contact with national and international authorities. Third, Article 41 of the INTERPOL Constitution provides:

> [w]henever it deems fit, having regard to the aims and objects provided in the Constitution, the Organization shall establish relations and collaborate with other intergovernmental or non-governmental international organizations.
>
> The general provisions concerning the relations with international, intergovernmental or non-governmental organizations will only be valid after their approval by the General Assembly. …
>
> With the approval of the General Assembly, the Executive Committee or, in urgent cases, the Secretary General may accept duties within the scope of its activities and competence either from other international institutions or organizations or in application of international conventions.

In reliance on these provisions, and in furtherance of its aims in Article 2 of the INTERPOL Constitution, INTERPOL has entered into numerous international agreements with States and international organisations, including host State agreements and numerous ad hoc conference-hosting agreements, as discussed in section V above. INTERPOL is also a contracting organisation to the 1986 Vienna Convention on the Law of Treaties between States and International Organizations and between International Organizations ('VCLT-IO').[349] Each of these agreements suggests that INTERPOL possesses the legal capacity to conclude agreements governed by public international law with other international legal persons. Indeed, it would be hard to conceive how these agreements could operate other than on the international plane and between parties possessing international personality.[350]

[348] See also: Rules of Procedure, Art 1(i).

[349] As of 31 January 2020, the VCLT-IO is not in force. The VCLT-IO will enter into force upon its ratification by 35 States.

[350] *Reparation for Injuries Suffered in the Service of the United* Nations (Advisory Opinion) [1949] ICJ Rep 174, 179.

PART II

8

Internal Law

In Part One, it was established that the International Criminal Police Organization ('INTERPOL' or the 'Organisation') is an organisation established by a treaty and possessing its own international legal personality. Part Two of the book considers INTERPOL's internal law and situates INTERPOL's assistance to its members in the legal regime of responsibility.

In general terms, the sources of INTERPOL's legal obligations can be divided into two broad categories: internal law and external law. The former includes 'the constituent instruments, decisions and resolutions adopted in accordance with them, and established practice of the organisation'.[1] The latter includes international agreements, customary international law of a universal (or almost universal) character, and general principles of law. To illustrate the importance of the distinction between internal law and external law when considering the Organisation's responsibility, it is helpful to recall the *BIS Share Repurchase* case,[2] where an arbitral tribunal had jurisdiction to consider whether the actions of the Bank for International Settlements ('BIS') (an international organisation) complied with both its Statutes and general international law. The impugned conduct in that case concerned the recall of privately held shares in the BIS. The arbitral tribunal observed that:

> [t]he legality of the repurchase has been contested principally under the Statutes of the Bank and secondarily under principles of international law regarding expropriation. In the first case, the question is whether the modification of the Statutes, assuming conformity with principles of international law, was carried out in accordance with Articles 57 and 58 of the Statutes … If that question is answered in the affirmative, the validity of the modification must still be examined under principles of international law.[3]

This chapter is concerned with the internal law of the Organisation, with a particular focus on the substantive provisions that regulate the processing of data by the Organisation. We consider how to challenge the processing or publication of

[1] Vienna Convention on the Law of Treaties between States and International Organizations or between International Organizations 1986 (adopted on 21 March 1986, not yet in force), Art 2(1)(j).

[2] *Partial Award on the lawfulness of the recall of the privately held shares on 8 January 2001 and the applicable standards for valuation of those shares* (Partial Award of 22 November 2002) XXIII RIAA 183.

[3] Ibid, para 142.

such data (eg notices) on the basis of a breach of these provisions. Finally, this chapter briefly considers the internal law of the Organisation which regulates employment relations between INTERPOL and its staff members.

I. Internal Legal Order

'As international organizations are creations of law, their normative structure needs to be consistent with the rule of law'.[4] The foundation of the Organisation's internal law is the INTERPOL Constitution. As an international agreement governed by international law, the INTERPOL Constitution is subject to the customary international law rules of interpretation reflected in Articles 31 and 32 of the 1969 Vienna Convention on the Law of Treaties[5] ('VCLT').[6] Pursuant to Article 44 of the INTERPOL Constitution, the application of the INTERPOL Constitution is determined by the General Assembly through the General Regulations and Appendices.

With respect to the processing of information, the INTERPOL General Assembly has stated that 'the processing of information by the General Secretariat … is not subject to any national laws':[7] 'it is the responsibility of the General Assembly … to determine the operating rules for the INTERPOL Information System regarding data processing'.[8] Thus, acting under Article 44 of the INTERPOL Constitution, the General Assembly has established an elaborate system of internal rules that have continued to evolve within INTERPOL.

The concept of an internal review in respect of data processing came into being when INTERPOL renegotiated its headquarters agreement with the French Government. France claimed that Act N°78-17 of 6 January 1978 on Information Technology, Data Files and Civil Liberties was applicable to the data stored in INTERPOL's premises. As a result, the French Government argued that individuals should have access to data relating to them, a right which could be exercised through the *Commission Nationale de l'Informatique et des Libertés*, an administrative authority set up to apply the aforementioned law. To accept the French view would have meant that the Organisation was not autonomous. INTERPOL argued that French law should not be applicable to the police information processed by

[4] Droesse, G, *Membership in International Organizations* (The Hague, T.M.C. Asser Press, 2020) 122.

[5] Vienna Convention on the Law of Treaties (adopted on 23 May 1969, entered into force on 27 January 1980) 1155 UNTS 331.

[6] See: *Legality of the Use by a State of Nuclear Weapons in Armed Conflict* (Advisory Opinion) [1996] ICJ Rep 66, para 19; Crawford, J, *Brownlie's Principles of Public International Law* (Oxford, Oxford University Press, 2019) 366; Sands, P and Klein, P, *Bowett's Law of International Institutions*, 6th edn (London, Sweet & Maxwell, 2009) 454–56.

[7] See: Rules on the Processing of Information for the Purposes of International Police Co-operation (entered into force on 1 January 2004), preamble, para 5.

[8] See: INTERPOL's Rules on the Processing of Data [III/IRPD/GA/2011(2019)], preamble.

the General Secretariat for two reasons. First, INTERPOL merely acts as a depository: information sent by members does not belong to the Organisation. Second, applying Act N°78-17 to INTERPOL's files in France could hamper international police cooperation since certain countries would prefer not to communicate police information which could be disclosed to French bodies. Although it acknowledged these arguments, France was nevertheless unwilling to strengthen INTERPOL's status on its territory without some kind of guarantee concerning the processing of personal data protected by the 1978 law.[9]

The conflicting aims of France and the Organisation were reconciled as a result of both parties' commitment to data protection, both in order to protect international police cooperation and to protect individual rights.[10] An agreement was made official on 3 November 1982 with the signing of a new headquarters agreement and an exchange of letters between France and INTERPOL. The agreement and exchange of letters came into force on 14 February 1984.[11] By entering into the headquarters agreement, France accepted the obvious, which is that the 1978 law cannot apply to data stored in INTERPOL's premises. Articles 7 and 9 of the 1982 headquarters agreement guaranteed the inviolability of INTERPOL's archives, documents and official correspondence, and Article 8 provided for the internal control of INTERPOL's archives. The exchange of letters between France and INTERPOL invited INTERPOL to set up a Supervisory Board to verify that personal information contained in INTERPOL's archives satisfied certain conditions, including whether it was obtained and processed in accordance with the INTERPOL Constitution. The exchange of letters also proposed that the Supervisory Board should carry out this verification exercise at the request of nationals or permanent residents of the Organisation's members. The Supervisory Board was formally established, in accordance with the exchange of letters, by the Rules on International Police Co-operation and on the Internal Control of INTERPOL's Archives ('RIPC') in 1982. The purpose of these rules, as stated in Article 1(2), was '... to protect police information processed and communicated within the ICPO-INTERPOL international police co-operation system against any misuse, especially in order to avoid any threat to individual rights'. The implication of these developments for domestic courts with respect to INTERPOL is alluded to in the 1993 decision of *Balkir v INTERPOL*. In that case, the Tribunal de Grande Instance de Lyon found that it lacked jurisdiction over INTERPOL's activities due to a combination of factors deriving from the headquarters agreement between

[9] Martha, RSJ, 'Remedies against INTERPOL: role and practice of defence lawyers' (Speech at the European Criminal Bar Association, Autumn Conference, Lyon, 6 October 2007).

[10] Article 2 of the INTERPOL Constitution states that the Organisation must act within the spirit of the Universal Declaration of Human Rights (proclaimed by UN General Assembly Resolution 217 A (10 December 1948)) ('UDHR').

[11] This agreement formed the basis of the system for the control of INTERPOL's files until 1 September 2009, when a new headquarters agreement with France entered into force.

France and INTERPOL, including INTERPOL's system of internal control of the processing of police information.[12]

In the 1990s and 2000s, INTERPOL was gradually influenced by developments in international human rights law, which increasingly suggested that the immunity from jurisdiction which international organisations enjoy should be counterbalanced by a concomitant international legal obligation to provide or arrange alternative modes and procedures for the settlement of disputes or claims.[13] The jurisprudence of the European Court of Human Rights ('ECtHR') has been of particular influence as it impacts the State where INTERPOL has its seat. In its decisions of 18 February 1999 in the parallel cases of *Waite and Kennedy v Germany*[14] and *Beer and Regan v Germany*,[15] the ECtHR considered how to resolve the conflict between the right of access to the courts, guaranteed by Article 6(1) of the European Convention on Human Rights ('ECHR')[16] and the immunity from jurisdiction enjoyed by the European Space Agency ('ESA') under the Convention for the Establishment of a European Space Agency of 30 May 1975 ('ESA Convention') and its Annex. In both cases, the applicants had performed services for ESA for several years but in the legal capacity of employees of firms with which ESA had contracted. The applicants instituted proceedings before the Darmstadt Labour Court in Germany, arguing that pursuant to German law they had acquired the status of employees of ESA. The Labour Court declared the applications inadmissible due to ESA's immunity from jurisdiction under the ESA Convention. The ECtHR, however, found that it must examine 'whether this degree of access limited to a preliminary issue was sufficient to secure the applicants' "right to a court", having regard to the rule of law in a democratic society'.[17] The ECtHR recognised that, on the one hand, Article 6(1) of the ECHR 'secures to everyone the right to have any claim relating to his civil rights and obligations brought before a court or tribunal'[18] and, on the other hand, that this right:

> may be subject to limitations; these are permitted by implication since the right of access by its very nature calls for regulation by the State. In this respect, the Contracting States enjoy a certain margin of appreciation, although the final decision as to the observance of the Convention's requirements rests with the Court.[19]

[12] *Balkir v INTERPOL*, High Court of Lyon, RG No 92/12077 (17 March 1993).

[13] See: Reinisch, A, 'The Immunity of International Organisations and the Jurisdiction of their Administrative Tribunals' (2008) 7 *Chinese Journal of International Law* 285 306.

[14] *Waite and Kennedy v Germany* [1999] ECHR 13.

[15] *Beer and Regan v Germany* [1999] ECHR 6.

[16] Convention for the Protection of Human Rights and Fundamental Freedoms (adopted on 4 November 1950, entered into force on 3 September 1953) 213 UNTS 221.

[17] *Waite and Kennedy v Germany* [1999] ECHR 13, para 58; *Beer and Regan v Germany* [1999] ECHR 6, para 48.

[18] *Waite and Kennedy v Germany* [1999] ECHR 13, para 50; *Beer and Regan v Germany* [1999] ECHR 6, para 40.

[19] *Waite and Kennedy v Germany* [1999] ECHR 13, para 59; *Beer and Regan v Germany* [1999] ECHR 6, para 49.

The ECtHR then set out criteria to be applied in making this determination, including that (1) the limitations are not so extensive 'that the very essence of the right is impaired', (2) the limitations 'pursue a legitimate aim', and (3) there is a 'reasonable relationship of proportionality between the means employed and the aim sought to be achieved'.[20] In considering proportionality, the ECtHR found that:

> where States establish international organisations in order to pursue or strengthen their cooperation in certain fields of activities, and where they attribute to these organisations certain competences and accord them immunities, there may be implications as to the protection of fundamental rights. It would be incompatible with the purpose and object of the Convention, however, if the Contracting States were thereby absolved from their responsibility under the Convention in relation to the field of activity covered by such attribution.[21]

The ECtHR then concluded that immunity from jurisdiction would only be permissible under the ECHR if the 'applicants had available to them reasonable alternative means to protect effectively their rights under the Convention'.[22]

With the aim of adequately responding to these developments, INTERPOL reviewed its procedures to ensure that they were consistent with the demands regarding effective remedies for individuals vis-à-vis international organisations. In 2003 and 2004, the INTERPOL General Assembly abrogated most provisions of the RIPC through the adoption of the Rules on the Processing of Information for the Purposes of International Police Co-operation ('RPI')[23] and the Rules on the Control of Information and Access to INTERPOL's Files ('RCI').[24] It was at this time that the Supervisory Board was renamed the Commission for the Control of INTERPOL's Files ('CCF' or 'Commission') – the name the body goes by today.

In 2005, international organisations based in France, including INTERPOL, were placed on higher alert due to the ruling of the French Court of Cassation in *Banque Africaine de Développement v MA Degboe*. In that case, it was decided that the right of access to justice is a matter of '*l'ordre public international*' and any organisation that does not provide such access forfeits its immunity.[25] In his

[20] Ibid.

[21] *Waite and Kennedy v Germany* [1999] ECHR 13, para 67; *Beer and Regan v Germany* [1999] ECHR 6, para 57.

[22] *Waite and Kennedy v Germany* [1999] ECHR 13, para 68; *Beer and Regan v Germany* [1999] ECHR 6, para 58.

[23] See: Resolution No AG-2003-RES-04, 'Draft Rules on the Processing of Information for the Purposes of International Police Co-operation', INTERPOL General Assembly, 72nd session (Benidorm, 2003).

[24] See: Resolution No AG-2004-RES-08, 'Draft Rules relating to the Control of Information and Access to Interpol's Files', INTERPOL General Assembly, 73rd session (Cancun, 2004). Pending amendment of the headquarters agreement with France, the provisions concerning the composition of the Supervisory Board remained in force.

[25] *Banque Africaine de Développement v MA Degboe*, French Court of Cassation (25 January 2005) 132 *Journal du droit international* (2005) 1142.

2006 annual address to the INTERPOL General Assembly, the chairman of the Commission acknowledged the potential ramifications for INTERPOL:

> there is a tendency to look more critically at international organisations, and to withdraw their immunity from national jurisdiction under international law, if they cannot demonstrate the existence of sufficient internal procedures and effective remedies.[26]

Thus, the CCF intensified its discussions with the General Secretariat about how to protect the interests of both INTERPOL and individuals concerned in light of these developments.[27] This resulted in the adoption of the first version of the CCF Operating Rules in October 2008 ('2008 Operating Rules'). The 2008 Operating Rules constituted a major step towards enhancing legal protection and due process for individuals.[28] The INTERPOL General Assembly also strengthened the status of the CCF by amending the INTERPOL Constitution to list the CCF as one of the bodies of the Organisation[29] and to include provisions dedicated to its composition and functions.[30] In 2011, the INTERPOL General Assembly adopted INTERPOL's Rules on the Processing of Data ('IRPD'), abrogating the RPI.[31]

Despite these developments in the structure and practice of the CCF, many practitioners and human rights organisations argued, throughout the 2010s, that the CCF was not an effective redress mechanism.[32] They (quite rightly) complained that 'its proceedings took years; its members had insufficient expertise; its decisions were insufficiently reasoned … and not formally binding on INTERPOL; and … the evidence put forward by countries seeking to justify maintaining their red notices was not disclosed to the individuals challenging them'.[33] As a result, a number of international bodies, such as the Parliamentary Assembly of the Council of Europe,[34] the Parliamentary Assembly of the Organization for Security

[26] Hustinx, P, Chairman of the CCF, 'Annual Report 2005 of the Commission for the Control of INTERPOL's Files' (Speech to the INTERPOL General Assembly, Rio de Janeiro, 21 September 2006).

[27] Ibid.

[28] Operating Rules of the Commission (adopted on 31 October 2008, entered into force on 1 November 2008).

[29] INTERPOL Constitution, Art 5.

[30] Ibid, Arts 36 and 37. See: Resolution No AG-2008-RES-03, 'Draft amendments to the Constitution aimed at incorporating the Commission for the Control of INTERPOL's Files – Article 5 and Articles 34 to 37', INTERPOL General Assembly, 77th session (St Petersburg, 2008). See also: Cheah, WL, 'Policing Interpol: The Commission for the Control of Interpol's Files and the Right to a Remedy' (2010) 7 *International Organizational Law Review* 375–404.

[31] See: Resolution No AG-2011-RES-07, 'INTERPOL's Rules on the Processing of Data', INTERPOL General Assembly, 80th session (Hanoi, 2011).

[32] Eg, Fair Trials International, 'Written Submission to INTERPOL's Working Group on the Processing of Information' (10 June 2015), which argues that the CCF fails to meet basic procedural standards and lacks transparency. See also: Tyler, T, Gottlieb, Y and Bentley, D, 'Policing INTERPOL', *Chatham House International Law Roundtable Summary* (5 December 2012).

[33] Tinsley, A, 'Echoes of Kadi: Reforms to Interpol Remedies at INTERPOL', *EJIL: Talk!* (20 January 2017).

[34] See: Parliamentary Assembly of the Council of Europe, Recommendation 2037 (2014), 'Accountability of international organisations for human rights violations' (31 January 2014 (9th Sitting)); Parliamentary Assembly of the Council of Europe, Resolution 2161 (2017), 'Abusive recourse to the Interpol system: the need for more stringent legal safeguards' (26 April 2017 (15th Sitting)).

and Co-operation in Europe ('OSCE')[35] and the European Parliament[36] took notice and called upon INTERPOL to provide an effective redress mechanism for those affected by its actions. In response, the INTERPOL General Assembly adopted the Statute of the Commission for the Control of INTERPOL's Files ('CCF Statute'), abrogating the RCI and amending the IRPD, in 2016.[37] The Commission also adopted new Operating Rules in March 2017, which it replaced with its most recent Operating Rules on 1 February 2019 ('2019 Operating Rules').[38] As such, the legal framework relevant to the Commission now includes (1) the INTERPOL Constitution, (2) the CCF Statute, (3) the IRPD (as amended in 2014, 2016 and 2019), and (4) the 2019 Operating Rules.

II. Challenges to the Processing of Data

This section will primarily detail the substantive bases on which to challenge the processing of data by the Organisation before the Commission. It is important to note that there are 135 provisions in the IRPD and dozens of grounds on which data in the INTERPOL Information System can be challenged. The following section focuses on three general standards of review applicable to all types of data processed in the INTERPOL Information System: (1) lawfulness, (2) quality and (3) neutrality. The section then considers specific rules applicable to red notices.

A. Lawfulness

i. INTERPOL's Aims

International organisations like INTERPOL possess legal personality in international law in a different manner than States.[39] States, by virtue of their mere

[35] See: OSCE Parliamentary Assembly, 'Baku Declaration and Resolutions' (adopted at the twenty-third annual session) (28 June – 2 July 2014) 14: '[u]rges all OSCE participating States to encourage the reform of INTERPOL to avoid the political use of Red Notices, which are currently being used in some countries to round up political opponents instead of for legitimate law enforcement purposes'.

[36] See: Lochbihler, B et al, 'Political abuse of INTERPOL's Systems' (Letter from six members of the European Parliament to the European Commission and associated individuals, 26 November 2013) 2: 'there is no effective remedy to those affected. The process for making requests and/or complaints relating to information on INTERPOL's files is plainly not compliant with basic standards identified by the Court of Justice and the European Court of Human Rights'.

[37] See: Resolution No AG-2016-RES-06, 'INTERPOL's supervisory mechanisms for the processing of data in the INTERPOL Information System', INTERPOL General Assembly, 85th session (Bali, 2016).

[38] CCF Operating Rules, CCF/107/d488 (1 February 2019).

[39] See generally: Gazzini, T, 'Personality of international organizations' in Klabbers, J and Wallendahl, Å (eds), *Research Handbook on the Law of International Organizations* (Cheltenham, Edward Elgar Publishing Limited, 2011) 33–55.

existence, enjoy an inherent and general competence to act,[40] limited only insofar as international law cares to dictate.[41] By contrast, as far as international organisations like INTERPOL are concerned, the aim of the organisation precedes and defines its competence. That is, under the principle of speciality,[42] an international organisation's competence to act is not general but conferred, and is necessarily delimited by the circumstances and conditions of such a conferral.[43] In the words of the International Court of Justice ('ICJ'):

> international organizations are subjects of international law which do not, unlike States, possess a general competence. International organizations are governed by the 'principle of speciality', that is to say, they are invested by the States which create them with powers, the limits of which are a function of the common interests whose promotion those States entrust to them.[44]

The principle of speciality operates in tandem with the doctrine of implied powers. The doctrine of implied powers holds that an international organisation, like INTERPOL, is impliedly conferred with such powers as are 'essential to the performance of its duties' or which are necessarily 'implied … in the light of the purposes assigned to it by its member States'.[45] Thus, in addressing whether or not the World Health Organization ('WHO') possessed the competence to seek an advisory opinion from the ICJ on the legality of nuclear warfare, the majority of the Court reasoned from the fact that the WHO Constitution could not be interpreted as conferring upon the WHO an implied power to address the legality of the use of nuclear weapons.[46] It is the speciality principle and the doctrine of implied powers that enable us conceptually to speak of international organisations

[40] *Reparation for Injuries Suffered in the Service of the United Nations* (Advisory Opinion) [1949] ICJ Rep 174, 180.

[41] *Case of the SS Lotus (France v Turkey)* (Judgment) [1927] PCIJ Rep Series A No 10.

[42] See: *Jurisdiction of the European Commission of the Danube Between Galatz and Braila* (Advisory Opinion) [1927] PCIJ Rep Series B No 14, 64, cited in *Legality of the Use by a State of Nuclear Weapons in Armed Conflict* (Advisory Opinion) [1996] ICJ Rep 66, para 25. See further: Schermers, HG and Blokker NM, *International Institutional Law: Unity within Diversity*, 6th revised edn (Leiden, Brill Nijhoff Publishers, 2018) 167–71.

[43] *Legality of the Use by a State of Nuclear Weapons in Armed Conflict* (Advisory Opinion) [1996] ICJ Rep 66, para 25. See further: Sarooshi, D, *International Organizations and their Exercise of Sovereign Powers* (Oxford, Oxford University Press, 2007), 18–27.

[44] *Legality of the Use by a State of Nuclear Weapons in Armed Conflict* (Advisory Opinion) [1996] ICJ Rep 66, para 25.

[45] Ibid. See further: Blokker, N, 'International Organizations or Institutions, Implied Powers' in Wolfrum, C (ed), *Max Planck Encyclopedia of Public International Law* (Oxford, Oxford University Press, 2009) para 17.

[46] *Legality of the Use by a State of Nuclear Weapons in Armed Conflict* (Advisory Opinion) [1996] ICJ Rep 66, paras 20 and 26. This decision has been broadly criticised for adopting a myopic view of the WHO's competence. See, for instance: Dissenting Opinion of Judge Shahabuddeen (at 98); Dissenting Opinion of Judge Weeramantry (at 129–34). See also: Akande, D, 'The Competence of International Organizations and the Advisory Jurisdiction of the International Court of Justice' (1998) 9 *European Journal of International Law* 437–67.

acting *ultra vires*.[47] An international organisation acts *ultra vires* when, in simple terms, it acts outside the scope of its competence.[48]

Typically, an international organisation's conferred competence is expressly prescribed by its constituent instrument,[49] as in the case of the European Union ('EU') and the World Trade Organization.[50] INTERPOL's case is, however, unusual. The INTERPOL Constitution does not expressly prescribe INTERPOL's competence but prescribes two aims in Article 2 and imposes an overarching restriction in Article 3. As such, the majority of its powers to act are implied. They must be derivatively identified, first, from its stipulated Article 2 aims, and, second, from the Article 3 prohibition restricting and invalidating that which might otherwise be impliedly permitted by Article 2. It is for this reason that an appreciation of the content of INTERPOL's aims must be had when one seeks to determine whether INTERPOL is acting lawfully. Only by identifying the content of the aims can we identify the content of its powers, and, consequently, where its limits lie.

Article 2(1) prescribes that INTERPOL's first aim is that of ensuring and promoting the 'widest possible mutual assistance between all criminal police authorities'. Two components of this aim should be considered: 'mutual assistance' and 'between all criminal police authorities'. 'Mutual assistance' comprises, in practice, INTERPOL's four core functions, to provide (1) secure global police communication services, (2) operational data services and databases, (3) operational police support services, and (4) capacity building and training.[51] Its functions exclude the power to take any form of coercive enforcement action because INTERPOL's aims clearly prescribe facilitation, not enforcement.[52] The aim of achieving 'mutual assistance' also signals the power possessed by INTERPOL, expressly enshrined in

[47] See: Cannizzaro, E and Palchetti, P, '*Ultra Vires* Acts of International Organizations' in Klabbers, J and Wallendahl, Å (eds), *Research Handbook on the Law of International Organizations* (Cheltenham, Edward Elgar Publishing Limited, 2011) 365–97; Ferstman, C, *International Organizations and the Fight for Accountability* (Oxford, Oxford University Press, 2017) 47; Second report on responsibility of international organizations by Special Rapporteur Giorgio Gaja, UN Doc A/CN.4/541 (2 April 2004) para 51.

[48] Cannizzaro, E and Palchetti, P, '*Ultra Vires* Acts of International Organizations' in Klabbers, J and Wallendahl, Å (eds), *Research Handbook on the Law of International Organizations* (Gloucester, Edward Elgar Publishing, 2011) 365–97 at 365–66; Morgenstern, F, 'Legality in International Organizations' (1976) 48 *British Yearbook of International Law* 241–57; Osieke, E, '*Ultra Vires* acts in International Organizations – the Experience of the International Labour Organization' (1976) 48 *British Yearbook of International Law* 259–80.

[49] See: Blokker, N, 'International Organizations or Institutions, Implied Powers' in Wolfrum, R (ed), *Max Planck Encyclopedia of Public International Law* (Oxford, Oxford University Press, 2009) Vol VI, 18–27, para 2.

[50] 'Consolidated version of the Treaty on the Functioning of the European Union', C 326 Official Journal (26 October 2012) 47-390, Arts 3, 4 and 6; Marrakesh Agreement establishing the World Trade Organization (concluded on 15 April 1994) 1867 UNTS 154, Art III.

[51] See: Chapter 7 for an in-depth discussion of each of these functions.

[52] See: Cheah, WL, 'Policing Interpol: The Commission for the Control of Interpol's Files and the Right to a Remedy' (2010) 7 *International Organizations Law Review* 375–404 at 381.

Article 41 of the INTERPOL Constitution, to enter into cooperation agreements with other international organisations.

Taken alone, the concept of 'widest possible mutual assistance' appears to be demonstrably broad and general, so as to enable INTERPOL to '... confront new challenges without the need to resort to amendments of [its] legal framework'.[53] It conveys the power to request the widest measure of mutual assistance in investigations, prosecutions and legal proceedings. Accordingly, members have established procedures by which to accommodate these requests.[54] That said, it remains an open question as to whether a member has complete discretion over whether or not to accede to a given request. The case of *Certain Questions of Mutual Assistance in Criminal Matters (Djibouti v France)*, which involved a comparable provision under the Convention on Mutual Assistance in Criminal Matters of 27 September 1986 between France and Djibouti, suggests that there exists some level of discretion on the part of a member to refuse a request, possibly moderated by the existence of a requirement of good faith on the part of the member.[55]

The fact that the aim of mutual assistance in Article 2(1) is contemplated to be had only 'between all criminal police authorities' imposes a qualification on INTERPOL's competence. First, the phrase suggests that INTERPOL does not have the competence to act in relation to matters which are of a non-criminal nature (ie, private, administrative, or civil matters or disputes). This is reinforced by Article 2(2) of the INTERPOL Constitution which prescribes a second but related aim for INTERPOL (discussed below) 'to establish and develop institutions likely to contribute effectively to the prevention and suppression of ordinary law crimes'. It is also reinforced by Article 35(1) of the IRPD which states that any data recorded in INTERPOL's files must be 'of interest for the purposes of international police cooperation'. As such, INTERPOL would act *ultra vires* if it were to undertake an intervention in relation to a non-criminal matter, such as issuing a red notice against an individual based on non-criminal conduct. Second, and relatedly, the phrase 'widest possible mutual assistance between all criminal police authorities' in Article 2(1) implies that INTERPOL lacks the competence to promote mutual assistance between police organisations that are not 'criminal police authorities', such as a given member's military or political police. This is corroborated by Article 3 of the INTERPOL Constitution, which imposes a strict prohibition against undertaking 'any intervention or activities of a political, military, religious, or racial character'.

[53] Gottlieb, Y, 'Article 3 of Interpol's Constitution: Balancing International Police Cooperation with the Prohibition on Engaging in Political, Military, Religious, or Racial Activities' (2011) 23 *Florida Journal of International Law* 135–86 at 139.

[54] Eg, Crime (International Co-operation) Act 2003, s 8(3)(a). See also: UK Home Office, 'Requests for Mutual Legal Assistance in Criminal Matters: Guidelines for Authorities Outside of the United Kingdom', 12th edn (2015).

[55] *Certain Questions of Mutual Assistance in Criminal Matters (Djibouti v France)* (Judgment) [2008] ICJ Rep 177.

Article 2(2) of the INTERPOL Constitution prescribes the second stipulated aim of INTERPOL: '[t]o establish and develop all institutions likely to contribute effectively to the prevention and suppression of ordinary law crimes'. Article 2(2) of the INTERPOL Constitution has a positive, as well as a circumscriptive aspect. Article 2(2)'s positive aspect lies in its aim to establish and develop institutions likely to contribute effectively to the prevention and suppression of ordinary law crimes. Concomitantly, Article 2(2)'s circumscriptive aspect consists in its mention of 'ordinary law crimes' as the object of this aim. The circumscriptive aspect complements INTERPOL's first aim of ensuring and promoting the 'widest possible mutual assistance between all criminal police authorities' in Article 2(1): both would make it such that INTERPOL lacks the competence to act in respect of data processing requests which are not criminal or do not involve 'ordinary law crimes'. Article 1(1) of the IRPD reinforces this by defining 'ordinary-law crime' as 'any criminal offences, with the exception of those that fall within the scope of application of Article 3 of the Constitution and those for which specific rules have been defined by the General Assembly'.

Thus, pursuant to Article 2(2), it is abundantly clear that INTERPOL is mandated only to establish and develop institutions likely to contribute to the prevention and suppression of 'ordinary law crimes' as opposed to non-criminal, civil law matters.[56] The idea is echoed and finds confirmation in Article 83(1)(a)(i) of the IRPD, which concerns red notices (discussed in detail in section II.D below), and Article 26(b) of the INTERPOL Constitution. The former provides:

> [r]ed notices may not be published for the following categories of offences … offences relating to family/private matters; … offences originating from a violation of laws or regulations of an administrative nature or deriving from private disputes, unless the criminal activity is aimed at facilitating a serious crime or is suspected of being connected to organised crime.[57]

The latter states that the General Secretariat, as the organ exclusively responsible for the publication of notices, is mandated only to serve as an 'international centre in the fight against ordinary crime'.[58] In that way, Article 2(2) illustrates how a provision prescribing an international organisation's aims informs the content of its implied powers. By stating that INTERPOL's mandate is restricted to that of acting in respect of 'ordinary law crimes', Article 2(2) has the effect of negating the implication of any powers to act or intervene in respect of crimes which are not 'ordinary law crimes'.

[56] For an objection based on this ground brought in practice, see, eg: Decision of the Commission, Decision No 2018-02 (January 2018) paras 22–32; Decision of the Commission, Decision No 2018-03 (January 2018) paras 25–31.

[57] See also: Decision of the Commission, Decision No 2017-08 (March 2017) para 26.

[58] INTERPOL Constitution, Art 26(b).

ii. Limits on INTERPOL's Aims: 'Within the Limits of the Laws Existing in the Different Countries'

The effect of the phrase 'within the limits of the laws existing in the different countries' in Article 2(1) of the INTERPOL Constitution is that all acts undertaken by INTERPOL in pursuance of its aims must be consistent with the laws in the jurisdiction(s) engaged by the act(s). In the context of data processing, this restriction is further supplemented by Article 11(1) of the IRPD which provides that data processing in the INTERPOL Information System[59] 'should be authorized with due regard for the law applicable to the National Central Bureau [('NCB')], national entity or international entity'. As regards red notices (discussed in section II.D below), Article 83(2)(b)(v) of the IRPD provides that a red notice cannot be published without reference to a 'valid arrest warrant or judicial decision having the same effect', whereas Article 84 of the IRPD demands that the requesting entity provides assurances that (1) the 'authority which issued the arrest warrant or handed down the judicial decision has the necessary power', (2) 'the red notice request has been coordinated with the relevant authorities responsible for extradition, and … that extradition will be sought upon arrest of the person, in conformity with national laws and/or the applicable bilateral and multilateral treaties', and (3) the laws … provide for a mechanism of appeal before a judicial authority where the arrest warrant has not been issued by a judicial authority.

For example, INTERPOL cannot issue a red notice which is premised on criminal charges which have no legal basis (whether in terms of substantive criminal law or procedure) in the jurisdiction concerned or which is based on a domestic criminal conviction procured by corruption. This was the issue in *AMIA I*, which concerned the publication of red notices by the INTERPOL General Secretariat at the request of NCB Buenos Aires in November 2003 against 12 Iranian nationals for allegedly participating in the bombing of the Asociación Mutual Israelita Argentina ('AMIA') building in 1994. In January 2004, NCB Tehran challenged the General Secretariat's publication of the red notices on the ground that they were issued in violation of the INTERPOL Constitution and INTERPOL's rules because of alleged irregularities concerning the Argentinean investigating judge, Judge Galeano (including the bribery of a main witness).[60] The dispute could not be resolved, so it was submitted to the Executive Committee.[61] In a unanimous decision, the Executive Committee ordered the General Secretariat to cancel the 12 red notices. NCB Buenos

[59] See the definition of 'INTERPOL Information System' in Article 1(4) of the IRPD.

[60] Following a finding of the Argentinean judiciary in September 2004 that Judge Galeano should be removed for judicial misconduct, the General Secretariat suspended (by way of a provisional measure) the red notices in October 2004.

[61] See Chapter 10 for a discussion of the applicable procedure for disputes referred to the Executive Committee and the General Assembly within the framework of the IRPD.

Aires appealed the decision of the Executive Committee, but it was subsequently endorsed by the General Assembly. The INTERPOL President at the time, Jackie Selebi, explained that INTERPOL deleted the red notices because it could not 'validate the arrest warrants signed by a judge removed by Argentine authorities for pervasive misconduct in this very case'.[62]

The Organisation also does not possess the competence to act in a way so as to require police authorities to act unlawfully. Equally, INTERPOL cannot act in a manner inconsistent with local data protection laws or conduct an investigation conjointly with a given police authority in a manner inconsistent with administrative laws in that authority's jurisdiction. Moreover, both as a textual and teleological matter, the restriction in Article 2(1) is not confined to laws of a domestic provenance *stricto sensu*, but also extends to international law standards applicable in a given member country, such as international human rights norms. Reference to the 'law applicable to the [NCB], national entity, or international entity' in Article 11(1) of the IRPD reflects the policy concern that INTERPOL's data processing activities should not involve or result in an NCB, national entity, or international entity violating the laws applicable to it, so as to render INTERPOL causative of, or complicit in, that entity's unlawful acts.

INTERPOL's practice confirms that the requirement to operate 'within the limits of the laws' is interpreted as set out above. In a case concerning Djamel Ktiti, a French national, it was successfully argued before the CCF that a red notice, based on evidence obtained by torture and that risked a given individual being extradited to be tortured, was contrary to INTERPOL's general obligation under Article 2 of the INTERPOL Constitution to refrain 'knowingly [from participating] in a potential violation of international law'.[63] What is noteworthy about this argument is that it alleges non-compliance with international law *tout court*, and is founded on the premise that the proviso 'within the limits of the laws existing in the different countries' in Article 2(1) obligates INTERPOL not to act in a way contrary to international law.[64] Similarly, the implication to be gleaned from the General Assembly's decision in *AMIA I* is that, as a matter of INTERPOL's internal law, the proviso 'within the limits of the laws existing in the different countries' in Article 2(1) of the INTERPOL Constitution obligates INTERPOL not to aid or assist members that act in violation of international human rights law.

[62] 'Argentinean Red Notices for Iranian officials cancelled', INTERPOL press release (27 September 2005).

[63] Ferstman, C and Russell, C, Letter from Redress and Fair Trials International to the CCF (26 January 2015) 2, 7.

[64] Ibid, 2: '[t]he publication of the red notice is contrary to Article 2 of INTERPOL's Constitution, as it leads INTERPOL knowingly to participate in a potential violation of international law' (emphasis added).

In recent years, the Commission has released a limited number of its decisions which help elucidate the Commission's interpretation of the INTERPOL Constitution and INTERPOL's rules. In Decision No 2018-04, an applicant was successful in arguing that the data processed in respect of him was not lawful on the basis of a national court decision which 'strongly denounce[d] major procedural flaws during the investigation phase and severely dismisse[d] the merits of the prosecution case'.[65] In particular, a court in Country A had discharged all of the accused in a criminal case, except the applicant and other defendants in Country B, whose cases had been severed. The applicant argued that, although his case was severed because Country A could not serve the summons to him in Country B, the decision of the court in Country A was fully and equally applicable to his case as it ruled on the quality of the evidence, the procedural flaws and the absence of criminal acts in the whole case. The applicant contended that the entire case on which the red notice against him was based had collapsed. The CCF was of the view that, 'being the latest judicial decision on the case, adopted by the same court who initially issued the arrest warrant which forms the basis of the red notice request, its informed findings bear a strong weight on the case', especially as the decision coincided with the applicant's submission to the Commission.[66] The CCF, therefore, decided that the red notice was not compliant with INTERPOL's rules.[67]

It is not only in respect of notices that INTERPOL must act 'within the limits of the laws existing in different countries'. In Decision No 2019-04, an applicant challenged the lawfulness of the entry of his passport as 'Revoked' in the INTERPOL Stolen and Lost Travel Documents ('SLTD') database. On the basis of this entry, the applicant's passport had been seized by border police at a national airport. The applicant filed a request for the deletion of his data from the SLTD database on the basis that, inter alia, his passport was revoked without lawful justification. The Commission consulted with the relevant NCB (as is required by the rules, on which, see Chapter 9) which informed the Commission that the competent authorities in its country had cancelled the applicant's passport and a red notice request in respect of the applicant would be sent to INTERPOL 'in due time'.[68] The Commission examined the national legal framework that the NCB provided in respect of the cancellation of the applicant's passport and found it was simply not applicable. It accordingly found that the NCB had not 'provided coherent information'.[69] It then (repeatedly) asked the NCB for a copy of the decision revoking the applicant's passport and a copy of the arrest warrant issued against the applicant. When the NCB did not provide

[65] Decision of the Commission, Decision No 2018-04 (January 2018) para 63.
[66] Ibid, para 62.
[67] Ibid, para 64.
[68] Decision of the Commission, Decision No 2019-04 (January-February 2019) para 16.
[69] Ibid, para 25.

the requested documents, the Commission found that the data in the SLTD database in respect of the applicant was not compliant with INTERPOL's rules and deleted it from the database.[70]

In sum, the effect of the provision 'within the limits of the laws existing in the different countries' in Article 2(1) of the INTERPOL Constitution (and Article 11(1) of the IRPD in the context of data processing) is that INTERPOL lacks the competence to act in a manner inconsistent with the laws, national or international, in the jurisdiction(s) engaged by INTERPOL's act(s).

iii. Limits on INTERPOL's Aims: '… In the Spirit of the "Universal Declaration of Human Rights"'

Article 2(1) contains a second important proviso which conditions INTERPOL's aim to facilitate 'mutual assistance between all criminal police authorities'. On its face, the proviso provides that INTERPOL must pursue its aim '… in the spirit of the "Universal Declaration of Human Rights"' ('the human rights proviso'). The requirement is further reflected in Articles 2 and 11(1) of the IRPD in respect of data processing. Article 2 of the IRPD requires that INTERPOL processes information 'with due respect for the basic rights of … persons … in conformity with Article 2 of the Organization's Constitution and the [UDHR]'. Correspondingly, Article 11(1) of the IRPD states that data processing in the INTERPOL Information System 'should respect the basic rights of the persons who are the subject of the cooperation, in accordance with Article 2 of the Organization's Constitution and the [UDHR]'.

In practice, the human rights proviso in Article 2(1) serves to qualify or condition INTERPOL's competence to the effect that it cannot act inconsistently with international human rights norms.[71] This means more than just saying that INTERPOL is bound by, and liable to comply with, international human rights law, as all States and international organisations, as international actors, are.[72] Generally speaking, an international organisation is capable of violating international human rights law in many ways when it acts in the sphere of its functional competences,[73] rendering unlawful under international human rights law that which is not *ultra vires* the organisation. In this regard, INTERPOL's situation differs from that of other international organisations because of the proviso in Article 2(1), which

[70] Ibid, para 28.

[71] Eg, Decision of the Commission, Decision No 2017-05 (March 2017) para 18; Decision of the Commission, Decision No 2018-02 (January 2018) para 13.

[72] *Interpretation of the Agreement of 25 March 1951 between the WHO and Egypt* (Advisory Opinion) [1980] ICJ Rep 73, para 37.

[73] See generally: Parliamentary Assembly of the Council of Europe, Recommendation 2037 (2014), 'Accountability of international organisations for human rights violations' (31 January 2014 (9th Sitting)); Parliamentary Assembly of the Council of Europe, Resolution 2161 (2017), 'Abusive recourse to the Interpol system: the need for more stringent legal safeguards' (26 April 2017 (15th Sitting)).

renders unlawful and necessarily *ultra vires* any act which is contrary to the 'spirit' of the UDHR. The inclusion of Article 2(1) in the INTERPOL Constitution means that, if INTERPOL acts contrary to international human rights law, it not only breaches its external law obligations (on which, see Chapter 11), but also would be acting *ultra vires*.

It is notable that the proviso in Article 2(1) refers to the 'spirit' of the UDHR, as opposed to merely its black-letter *corpus juris*. As such, the substantive content of the proviso appears to extend further than the content of the UDHR per se, notwithstanding that the CCF has spoken at times as if it were applying the substantive provisions of the UDHR.[74] The important question is, how much further than the content of the UDHR does Article 2(1) go? Technically speaking, the question is an interpretative one, turning on a construction of the phrase '… the spirit of the [UDHR]'. An argument could be made that the 'spirit' of the UDHR keeps apace with the times. Further, where the international human rights norm in question is of a *jus cogens* character, there is little doubt that INTERPOL would lack the competence as a matter of public international law to act in violation of the same, irrespective of whether the 'spirit' of the UDHR encompasses that norm. INTERPOL's own interpretation, as stated publicly in 2012, is (rather unhelpfully) that the requisite human rights norm must be 'well recognized on the international level'.[75] It was on this basis that INTERPOL stated that it was prohibited from publishing a red notice based upon a death sentence issued against a minor by virtue of the 'international agreed standard' in the United Nations ('UN') Convention on the Rights of the Child but that it could issue a red notice in respect of an adult in relation to a crime over which the maximum penalty is death because 'there is no internationally agreed standard on the matter of the death penalty'.[76]

That being said, more recent decisions of the Commission suggest that it might be broadening its view of what falls within the 'spirit' of the UDHR. For instance, in Decision No 2019-05, the Commission deleted a red notice due to 'issues related to the right to health and security in the event of sickness (Article 25 of the UDHR) and … the right to be prevented from degrading treatment (Article 5 of the UDHR)'.[77] What is particularly interesting is that it arrived at its interpretation of these provisions by endorsing the approach of the ECtHR in two progressive cases, *N v United Kingdom*[78] and *Paposhvili v Belgium*,[79] rather than on the basis of any 'well recognized' international norm.

A review of the Commission's decisions reveals that numerous challenges have been brought against INTERPOL's data processing activities on the grounds

[74] Eg, Decision of the Commission, Decision No 2018-03 (January 2018) para 49.

[75] Tyler, T, Gottlieb, Y and Bentley, D, 'Policing INTERPOL', Chatham House International Law Roundtable Summary (5 December 2012) 6.

[76] Ibid, 9.

[77] Decision of the Commission, Decision No 2019-05 (April 2019) para 27.

[78] *N v United Kingdom* [2008] ECHR 453.

[79] *Paposhvili v Belgium* [2016] ECHR 1113.

of inconsistency with the human rights proviso, many of which have succeeded before the CCF. The following sections discuss three of the most common rights that applicants seek to rely on in such challenges – the right to a fair trial, the right not to be subjected to torture or to cruel, inhuman or degrading treatment or punishment, and the right to asylum – and the most fruitful approach to arguing these challenges.

a. Right to a Fair Trial

Fair trial guarantees can be found in the UDHR,[80] and most universal[81] and regional[82] human rights treaties provide for the right to a fair trial. The Organisation cannot intervene in respect of an individual in any manner which would be incompatible with an individual's right to a fair trial. To do so would be contrary to Article 2(1) of the INTERPOL Constitution and Articles 2 and 11(1) of the IRPD (in addition to a breach of INTERPOL's external law obligations, as discussed in Chapter 11).

INTERPOL is hesitant to come to its own conclusion about whether the right to a fair trial has been infringed (or whether there is a real risk that the right to a fair trial would be infringed), preferring instead to defer to decisions of national courts or tribunals. For instance, in Decision No 2017-05, the Commission considered an application from a political opponent of the incumbent regime in Country B, who had been sentenced to life imprisonment following two trials *in absentia*.[83] The applicant claimed, inter alia, that 'the suits … lack due process'.[84] He alleged that the relevant country had 'utilized various means to manipulate the proceedings in an effort to gather evidence against him to fabricate a case from multiple layers of hearsay', and he claimed 'the existence of procedural errors during his trial in absentia' (ie, the court refused to summon requested defence witnesses and to allow cross-examination of the prosecution evidence).[85] Critically, there existed at least five other decisions by one or more unidentified tribunals which found that Country B's courts had failed to provide the applicant

[80] UDHR, Arts 10 and 11.

[81] See, eg: International Covenant on Civil and Political Rights (adopted on 16 December 1966, entered into force on 23 March 1976) 999 UNTS 171 and 1057 UNTS 407 ('ICCPR'), Art 14; Convention on the Rights of the Child (adopted on 20 November 1989, entered into force on 2 September 1990) 1577 UNTS 3, Art 4; International Convention on the Protection of the Rights of All Migrant Workers and Members of Their Families (adopted on 18 December 1990, entered into force on 1 July 2003) 2220 UNTS 3, Art 18; International Convention on the Elimination of All Forms of Racial Discrimination (adopted on 7 March 1966, entered into force on 4 January 1969) 660 UNTS 195, Art 5(a).

[82] See, eg: ECHR, Art 6; American Convention on Human Rights (adopted on 22 November 1969, entered into force on 18 July 1978) 1144 UNTS 123 ('ACHR'), Arts 8 and 9; African Charter on Human and Peoples' Rights (adopted on 27 June 1981, entered into force on 21 October 1986) 1520 UNTS 217 ('ACHPR'), Art 7.

[83] Decision of the Commission, Decision No 2017-05 (March 2017) para 12.

[84] Ibid, para 16.

[85] Ibid, para 27.

and/or his former business partners with a fair trial. On this basis, the Commission concluded that the proceedings against the applicant, inter alia, 'were not based on the rule of law and … lack due process'.[86] The Commission also gives considerable weight to decisions from national courts which deny the extradition of an individual (who is the subject of a red notice) on the basis of a real risk that his or her right to a fair trial would be violated upon surrender to the requesting country.[87] By contrast, where an applicant simply asserted that her right to a fair trial had been violated because 'she was never informed of any criminal case opened against her', the Commission found that her information 'was not substantiated enough to demonstrate the likelihood of a flagrant denial of her fundamental rights'.[88]

The Commission is inconsistent in how it considers evidence which addresses general conditions in a country (as opposed to evidence that is specific to the applicant). Historically, it did not consider general conditions relevant to its analysis. For instance, in Decision No 2018-03 the Commission disregarded reports from several international human rights organisations about 'structural shortcomings in the [country's] justice system, as well as systemic violations of fair trial guarantees and a lack of judicial independence' on the basis that it was only concerned with 'specific information' relating to the applicant's prosecution'.[89] It concluded that, because the trial *in absentia* of the applicant was conducted in accordance with the relevant national procedural law, the data was compliant with Article 2 of the INTERPOL Constitution.[90] However, one year later, the Commission adopted a different approach:

> … the Commission paid particular attention to the numerous reports and statements issued by reliable resources such as the [UN] High Commissioner for Human Rights and the UN Committee Against Torture, diverse foreign governments and regional entities (United States Department of State Country Reports, European Parliament) as well as various human rights organizations (Freedom House, Human Rights Watch, International Federation for Human Rights, International Commission of Jurists), which all express serious concerns over the procedural safeguards under [the country's] criminal law and document instances of witness intimidation, prosecution of defence counsel, media censorship, pressure to convict from government, lack of independence of judges, amounting to gross violations of international fair trial standards.[91]

[86] Ibid, para 35.

[87] In such decisions, INTERPOL states that extradition decisions from members do not 'directly affect the compliance of the corresponding data registered in INTERPOL's files', but it clearly attaches considerable weight to these decisions (see, eg, Decision of the Commission, Decision No 2018-03 (January 2018) para 46).

[88] Decision of the Commission, Decision No 2017-17 (October 2017) paras 30 and 40. See also: Decision of the Commission, Decision No 2018-02 (January 2018).

[89] Decision of the Commission, Decision No 2018-06 (April 2018) paras 24 and 29.

[90] Ibid, para 32.

[91] Decision of the Commission, Decision No 2019-06 (April 2019) para 31.

In this Decision, the Commission again repeated its view that it 'does not usually rely on general statements concerning the situation in a country to ground its findings' (on the basis that it is not for the Commission to 'assess a country's law enforcement of judicial system in *abstracto*'), but it also accepted that, 'in some instances where multiple international and national reliable sources all present a consistent, documented and concurring account of a situation characterized by serious human rights violations', these documents could serve to reinforce an applicant's individual allegations and support an application.[92]

This approach is the approach that the Commission must adopt if it intends to respect its obligation to act 'in the spirit of the [UDHR]' under Article 2(1) of the INTERPOL Constitution. At the same time, the Commission must assure itself that when adopting this approach it does not compromise the neutrality of the Organisation (on which, see the discussion of Article 3 in section II.C below). Best practice would be for the Commission to delineate the substantive content of the right to a fair trial before evaluating all of the evidence, both general and specific, to determine whether or not it can be said to be acting within the 'spirit' of the UDHR.

b. Right not to be Subjected to Torture or to Cruel, Inhuman or Degrading Treatment or Punishment

Article 5 of the UDHR provides that '[n]o one shall be subjected to torture or to cruel, inhuman or degrading treatment or punishment'. The right to be free from torture and other forms of ill-treatment is reflected in universal and regional human rights treaties.[93] As with the right to a fair trial, the Organisation cannot intervene in respect of an individual in any manner which would be incompatible with an individual's right not to be subjected to torture or to cruel, inhuman or degrading treatment or punishment. To do so would be contrary to Article 2(1) of the INTERPOL Constitution and Articles 2 and 11(1) of the IRPD (in addition to a breach of INTERPOL's external law obligations, as discussed in Chapter 11).

In the context of a challenge to a red notice, the CCF appears willing to defer to views of UN bodies concerning the applicant when considering a submission that alleges that the country to which the applicant is to be extradited is likely to subject him to torture or to cruel, inhuman or degrading treatment or punishment. In the case of Djamel Ktiti,[94] INTERPOL had published a red notice in respect of Ktiti based on an arrest warrant issued by Algeria accusing Ktiti of being an accomplice in drug trafficking activities. The red notice led

[92] Ibid, para 32.

[93] See, eg: ICCPR, Arts 7 and 10; ECHR, Art 3; ACHR, Art 5; ACHPR, Art 5.

[94] See: 'Interpol agrees to remove Algerian wanted person alert against French national, given real risks of torture', Redress press release (7 December 2015).

to Ktiti being arrested in Morocco in 2009. A complaint was made to the UN Committee Against Torture ('CAT') alleging that any extradition by Morocco would amount to a violation of Article 3 of the UN Convention against Torture and other Cruel, Inhuman or Degrading Treatment or Punishment ('UNCAT')[95] because the Algerian arrest warrant was based on evidence likely to have been obtained by torture, and Ktiti was likely to be tortured by the Algerian authorities upon his return. The CAT allowed the complaint, finding a violation of Article 15 of the UNCAT[96] on the facts before it, and it held that any extradition of Ktiti to Algeria would consequently violate Article 3 of the UNCAT.[97] Ktiti was therefore released by the Moroccan authorities, but he was apprehended again in Spain on the basis of the same red notice. An application was then made to the Commission for the deletion of data concerning Ktiti on the basis that the publication of a red notice was, inter alia, contrary to Article 2(1) of the INTERPOL Constitution as it 'leads INTERPOL knowingly to participate in a potential violation of international law' – ie, Articles 3 and 15 of UNCAT and the corresponding provisions of the ICCPR, in addition to regional human rights treaties and customary international law.[98] The Commission, in an unreported decision, agreed to delete the red notice and all data concerning Ktiti in its files. As discussed above, the decision can be considered as being based on a view that the conduct was not only outside the 'limits of the laws existing in different countries' but also not in the 'spirit' of the UDHR as required by Article 2(1) of the INTERPOL Constitution.

Similarly, in Decision No 2018-14, the applicant claimed, inter alia, that 'he would be exposed to a high risk of torture in prison in order to obtain coerced confessions' if extradited to the requesting country.[99] To support his assertion, he relied on a decision of the UN Human Rights Committee, which stated that the extradition of the applicant would constitute a breach of Article 7 of the ICCPR. In view of these findings, the Commission concluded that the extradition of the applicant to the relevant country would breach the prohibition on return of an individual to a country where he would be exposed 'to torture and serious violations

[95] Article 3 of the UNCAT (adopted on 10 December 1984, entered into force on 26 June 1987) 1465 UNTS 85 provides that '1. No State Party shall expel, return ("refouler") or extradite a person to another State where there are substantial grounds for believing that he would be in danger of being subjected to torture. 2. For the purpose of determining whether there are such grounds, the competent authorities shall take into account all relevant considerations including, where applicable, the existence in the State concerned of a consistent pattern of gross, flagrant or mass violations of human rights'.

[96] Article 15 of the UNCAT provides that '[e]ach State Party shall ensure that any statement which is established to have been made as a result of torture shall not be invoked as evidence in any proceedings, except against a person accused of torture as evidence that the statement was made'.

[97] *Ktiti v Morocco*, Communication No 419/2010, UN Doc CAT/C/46/D/419/2010 (26 May 2011) para 9.

[98] See: Ferstman, C and Russell, C, Letter from Redress and Fair Trials International to the CCF (26 January 2015).

[99] Decision of the Commission, Decision No 2018-14 (July 2018) para 38.

of fundamental human rights', so the processing of data was not compliant with Article 2(1) of the INTERPOL Constitution on the basis that it was not within the 'spirit' of the UDHR.[100]

Similarly, a decision of a national court denying extradition on the basis that the individual may be subject to torture or inhuman treatment if extradited is of considerable weight in any Article 2 analysis. For instance, in Decision No 2018-03, the Commission remarked that 'the conclusions drawn by Country B's independent judicial body on the risks faced by the Applicant in the case of extradition cannot be ignored by the Commission in the course of its own review', equating the rights in Articles 3 and 6 of the ECHR with that of Articles 5 and 10 of the UDHR.[101] On this basis, the Requests Chamber of the CCF concluded that the retention of data in its systems was not within the 'spirit' of the UDHR.

c. Right to Asylum from Persecution

Article 14 of the UDHR provides that individuals are conferred the right to seek and enjoy asylum from persecution.[102] The principle of *non-refoulment*, which flows from the more general right to seek asylum from persecution,[103] is enshrined in Article 33(1) of the 1951 Convention relating to the Status of Refugees ('1951 Convention').[104] It provides that '[n]o Contracting State shall expel or return ("refouler") a refugee in any manner whatsoever to the frontiers of territories where his life or freedom would be threatened on account of his race, religion, nationality, membership of a particular social group or political opinion'.[105] The principle of *non-refoulement* is well-established in a number of international treaties,[106] is widely accepted in State practice, and has the status of customary

[100] Ibid, paras 49–50.

[101] Decision of the Commission, Decision No 2018-03 (January 2018) paras 51–52. See also: Decision of the Commission, Decision No 2018-15 (July 2018).

[102] Article 14 of the UDHR reads: '1. Everyone has the right to seek and to enjoy in other countries asylum from persecution. 2. This right may not be invoked in the case of prosecutions genuinely arising from non-political crimes or from acts contrary to the purposes and principles of the United Nations'.

[103] UN High Commissioner for Refugees, 'Note on Non-Refoulement', UN Doc No EC/SCP/2 (23 August 1977) paras 2–4; Lauterpacht, E and Bethlehem, D, 'The Scope and Content of the Principle of Non-Refoulement: Opinion' in Feller, E et al (eds), *Refugee Protection in International Law* (Cambridge, Cambridge University Press, 2003) 89.

[104] Convention Relating to the Status of Refugees (adopted on 28 July 1951, entered into force on 22 April 1954) 189 UNTS 137.

[105] See: Ibid, Art 33(1). See also: UN High Commissioner for Refugees, 'Note on Non-Refoulement', UN Doc No EC/SCP/2 (23 August 1977).

[106] International Convention for the Protection of All Persons from Enforced Disappearance (adopted on 20 December 2006, entered into force on 23 December 2010) 2716 UNTS 3, Art 16; UNCAT, Art 3; Inter-American Convention on Extradition (signed on 25 February 1981, entered into force on 28 March 1992), Art 4(5); Organization of African Unity (OAU) Convention Governing the Specific Aspects of Refugee Problems in Africa (adopted on 10 September 1969, entered into force on 20 June 1974) 1001 UNTS 45, Art II(3); ACHR, Art 22(8). The principle of *non-refoulement* is also expressed in conventions concerning extradition: see European Convention on Extradition (opened for signature on 13 December 1957, entered into force on 18 April 1960) ETS No 024, Art 3(2).

international law.[107] It reflects the commitment of the international community to ensure the enjoyment of human rights for all persons, including the right to life, to freedom from torture or cruel, inhuman or degrading treatment or punishment, and to liberty and security of person. These and other rights are under threat when a refugee is returned to persecution or danger.

In light of the foregoing, it is clear that the Organisation cannot intervene in respect of an individual in any manner which would be incompatible with an individual's right to seek asylum from persecution or which fails to respect the principle of *non-refoulement*. To do so would be contrary to Article 2(1) of the INTERPOL Constitution and Articles 2 and 11(1) of the IRPD (in addition to a breach of INTERPOL's external law obligations).

The fact that INTERPOL is obligated, under both its internal law and its external law, to respect an individual's rights to asylum from persecution has been expressly acknowledged by INTERPOL in practice. On 19 May 2015, INTERPOL publicly announced a Refugee Policy (which had been in force since June 2014)[108] under which its General Secretariat would remove information in respect of an individual who has been recognised as a refugee (or is an asylum-seeker) under the 1951 Convention. Although the complete text of the Refugee Policy is not publicly available, it has been reported that, under the Refugee Policy, the processing of red notices and diffusions will not be allowed if the following conditions are met:

(1) the status of refugee or asylum-seeker has been confirmed;
(2) the notice/diffusion has been requested by the country where the individual fears persecution; and
(3) the granting of the refugee status is not based on political grounds vis-à-vis the requesting country.[109]

Logically read, these criteria are conjunctive requirements. All three must be satisfied before INTERPOL will refuse to process a red notice or diffusion. The Refugee Policy further states that, where INTERPOL denies the processing of a red notice or diffusion against a refugee:

> consideration will be given to sharing the information sent by the requesting country with the country of asylum so that the latter can reconsider its previous decision of granting the refugee status. If the country of asylum decides to revoke the refugee status

[107] UN High Commissioner for Refugees, 'Advisory Opinion on the Extraterritorial Application of *Non-Refoulement* Obligations under the 1951 Convention relating to the Status of Refugees and its 1967 Protocol' (26 January 2007) para 15; UN High Commissioner for Refugees, 'Declaration of States Parties to the 1951 Convention and/or its 1967 Protocol Relating to the Status of Refugees', UN Doc HCR/MMSP/2001/09 (16 January 2002) para 4; Allain, J, 'The *jus cogens* nature of *non-refoulement*' (2001)13 *International Journal of Refugee Law* 533–58 at 538.

[108] See: Fair Trials International, 'Strengthening INTERPOL: An Update', Annex 1 – Excerpts from INTERPOL text on the Refugee Policy (30 May 2017). The policy was approved by INTERPOL's Executive Committee at its June 2014 session.

[109] Ibid.

> based on the new information, the processing of red notices and diffusions may be allowed if it otherwise complies with INTERPOL's rules.[110]

Accordingly, the *raison d'etre* of INTERPOL's Refugee Policy has been officially stated in the following terms:

> [t]he objective of the policy is to support member countries in preventing criminals from abusing refugee status, while providing adequate and effective safeguards to protect the rights of refugees, as guaranteed under the 1951 Convention … and other applicable conventions.[111]

It might be questioned what exactly the three criteria posited in the Refugee Policy precisely entail. In that regard, three questions concerning the proper interpretation of the criteria are pertinent. First, what does it mean for an individual's status of refugee or asylum-seeker to have been 'confirmed'? Second, is it a strict requirement that the red notice or diffusion has to have been requested by the country where the individual fears persecution? Third, what does it mean for the 'granting of the refugee status' to be 'based on political grounds vis-à-vis the requesting country'?

In respect of the first criterion, INTERPOL's practice suggests that, for an individual's status as a refugee to have been confirmed, '… a refugee status document or a decision granting refugee status has been treated as sufficient evidence'.[112] While there is no publicly available information on what is required to evidence that an individual's status of asylum-seeker has been confirmed, in the authors' experience, official documentation from the country in which asylum has been requested (eg, an asylum registration card) will generally suffice. However, in certain cases, the Commission will request permission from the applicant to 'conduct verifications with the NCB host concerning the applicant's protective status'.[113]

In respect of the second criterion, it might be surmised that, although untested in practice, the requirement that the red notice or diffusion be requested by the country where the individual fears persecution is not absolute. This is because the principle of *non-refoulement* would also prohibit extradition to a country known to extradite a given individual to the country where the individual fears persecution, ie, 'indirect *refoulement*'.[114] Were it an absolute requirement that the red notice or diffusion must have been requested by the country where the individual fears persecution, INTERPOL, in refusing to delete a red notice issued by a different

[110] Ibid.

[111] Ibid.

[112] Fair Trials International, 'Strengthening INTERPOL: An Update' (30 May 2017) para 35.

[113] Letter from the CCF to an applicant (7 February 2019). A copy of this letter is in the authors' files.

[114] See, eg: UN Human Rights Committee, 'Note on the Principle of *Non-Refoulement*' (November 1997); Coleman, N, *European Readmission Policy: Third Country Interests and Refugee Rights* (Leiden, Martinus Nijhoff Publishers, 2009) 235–36, explaining that the prohibition of *refoulement* in Article 33(1) of the 1951 Convention 'is defined by a result', and that '[t]he manner in which this result comes about is irrelevant'.

member, may be complicit in that country's eventual extradition of the individual to his or her country of persecution in violation of the principle of *non-refoulment*. An interpretation of the second criterion consistent with the object and purpose of the Refugee Policy strongly militates against any such reading and suggests that a red notice or diffusion must be removed if it tempts indirect *refoulement* to an individual's country of persecution.

Finally, whilst admittedly unclear, the third criterion suggests that, where an individual is granted refugee status in light of a high-level political or diplomatic conflict between the requesting country and the country in which refugee status has been granted, this will not result in the deletion of the red notice/diffusion. This criterion is inextricably linked to the prohibition laid down by Article 3 of the INTERPOL Constitution, which, inter alia, forbids INTERPOL from undertaking any intervention or activity of a 'political … character' (discussed in section II.C below).

On 29 September 2017, the INTERPOL General Assembly adopted a resolution in light of 'the mounting concerns that dangerous criminals and terrorists might try to abuse the refugee protection system'.[115] The resolution outlines a range of measures which members are 'urged' to perform systematically in the process of examining asylum applications, including to (1) check INTERPOL's databases, (2) use the INTERPOL Information System to exchange information, and (3) inform other countries and the INTERPOL General Secretariat of a decision to deny an asylum application in light of an individual's criminal background.[116] The resolution also 'endorses the guidelines contained in Report GA-2017-86-REP-10' (which is not publicly available) and encourages members to provide the General Secretariat and the CCF with confirmation of the granting of refugee status and information on the outcome of the review of an asylum application.[117]

Practice discloses that, in a number of cases, INTERPOL has deleted red notices after being informed that the individual concerned is an asylum-seeker or has acquired refugee status. For example, a red notice concerning Rachid Mesli, a human rights lawyer who had been convicted by an Algerian court in circumstances which led Amnesty International to declare him a prisoner of conscience and the victim of an unfair trial, was deleted after a request to the CCF to apply the Refugee Policy.[118] Ochoa Urioste, the Legal Director of a Bolivian State-owned oil and gas company who had criticised the Bolivian Government and repeatedly refused to sign certain contracts which he considered illegal, sought asylum in Uruguay after Bolivia indicted him on corruption charges. A red notice was then issued upon Bolivia's request, but it was deleted after the applicant invoked

[115] Resolution No GA-2017-86-RES-9, 'INTERPOL policy on refugees', INTERPOL General Assembly, 86th session (Beijing, 2017).

[116] Ibid, 2.

[117] Ibid.

[118] Fair Trials International, 'Strengthening INTERPOL: An Update' (30 May 2017) para 31.

the Refugee Policy.[119] Similarly, a red notice in respect of Paramjeet Singh, a supporter of the Sikh's right to self-determination, was promptly deleted after he made INTERPOL aware of his refugee status in the United Kingdom ('UK').[120] These examples evince that, in practice, the Refugee Policy may itself be invoked, together with Article 2(1) of the INTERPOL Constitution and Articles 2 and 11(1) of the IRPD, to support a request for the removal of a red notice or diffusion issued against a refugee or an asylum-seeker.

An applicant, in fact, relied on his past refugee status in Decision No 2018-07, resulting in the deletion of the red notice concerning him (albeit he argued that the data processed by INTERPOL was contrary to Article 3 of the INTERPOL Constitution on political grounds, as discussed in section II.C.i below). The applicant was a journalist who was recognised as a refugee in an undisclosed country before he acquired citizenship there. He provided official documents in respect of both his past refugee status and his naturalisation. The Commission took into account Article 1(c) of the 1951 Convention (ie, the 'cessation clause') which provides that the Convention ceases to apply to an individual who has acquired a new nationality. However, the Commission took the view that although the *non-refoulement* provision did not apply *stricto sensu*, 'the factual situation leading to the earlier recognition of a well-founded fear of persecution may well continue to exist after the acquisition of a new nationality'.[121] It concluded that, in light of 'its status as a customary norm of international law', the principle of *non-refoulement* is 'of relevance to any individual who risks being subjected to serious harm or to a flagrant denial of other fundamental human rights upon return to his/her country of origin'.[122] As such, INTERPOL took the principle into account, observing that 'the most important factor' in such situations 'is to assess whether the situation which had put the individual at risk and initially justified the protective status has substantially changed'.[123] In the applicant's case, the Commission was of the view that no such substantial change had taken place and (after also considering the general context of the case) concluded that the data was not compliant with Article 3 of the INTERPOL Constitution.

B. Quality

A separate ground on which an applicant may wish to challenge data in the INTERPOL Information System is found in Article 12 of the IRPD: 'Quality'. Article 12(1) provides that '[d]ata processed in the INTERPOL Information

[119] Ibid.
[120] Ibid.
[121] Decision of the Commission, Decision No 2018-07 (April 2018) para 49.
[122] Ibid.
[123] Ibid, para 50.

System must be accurate, relevant, not excessive in relation to their purpose and up to date, to allow them to be used by National Central Bureaus, national entities and international entities'.

How does one determine whether data is 'accurate', 'relevant', 'not excessive in relation to their purpose' and 'up to date'? Unfortunately, INTERPOL has repeatedly skated over the content of Article 12(1), focusing instead on whether data is 'sufficient'. The question of whether data is 'sufficient' is, however, a separate basis on which to challenge a notice (on which, see section II.D below in the context of a red notice).[124] The confusion of the Commission in this regard is tangible in Decision No 2019-02 where an applicant challenged the quality of the data in a diffusion. In its analysis, the Commission briefly mentioned Article 12 but decided that it would 'rather centre[] its study on whether the NCB ... provided sufficient elements that would form a clear, succinct and coherent description of their (sic) criminal involvement of the Applicant in the facts underlying the case'.[125] This is, of course, an incorrect application of the IRPD. The language of 'a succinct and clear description of the criminal activities' is set out in Article 83(2)(b)(i) of the IRPD as one of the criteria that must be satisfied for the Commission to conclude that 'sufficient judicial data has been provided' to publish a red notice. It is never applicable to a diffusion, as was at issue in Decision No 2019-02. In treating the concept of 'sufficient judicial data' in Article 83(2)(b)(i) as synonymous with 'quality' in Article 12(1), the Commission was not only incorrectly applying its rules, but also implying that the 'quality' of data can only be challenged if the data submitted by the NCB is not 'clear, succinct or coherent'. Because the NCB itself had submitted differing accounts of the applicant's alleged criminal involvement, the Commission concluded that it had 'reservations regarding the quality of some of the data in accordance with Article 12'.[126] But even then, the Commission concluded the data was 'compliant with INTERPOL's rules', subject to an 'update' to describe 'accurately' the applicant's involvement in the crime.[127]

The reasoning in Decision No 2019-02 unnecessarily complicates a straightforward rule.

First, data is not 'up to date' if an applicant can adduce official documentation proving as much. For instance, in Decision No 2017-05 the applicant provided evidence that certain of the charges described in the red notice had been abandoned by the country concerned. The Commission, therefore, concluded that the data was 'not properly updated'.[128]

[124] See, eg, IRPD, Article 83(2)(b) in respect of red notices, Article 88(2)(c) in respect of blue notices, Article 89(2)(d) in respect of green notices, Article 90(2)(d) in respect of yellow notices, Article 91(2)(c) in respect of black notices, Article 92(2)(a)(iii) and (b)(iii) in respect of purple notices, and Article 93(3) in respect of orange notices.

[125] Decision of the Commission, Decision No 2019-02 (January-February 2019) para 55.

[126] Ibid, para 59.

[127] Ibid, para 68.

[128] Decision of the Commission, Decision No 2017-05 (March 2017) paras 22–36.

Second, in order to determine whether data is 'relevant', it is necessary to consider 'the general purpose for the processing of the data'.[129] The purposes for processing data vary depending on the type of intervention concerned, but are neatly summarised in Article 10(2) of the IRPD (see section II.D below in respect of the purpose of red notices). Relatedly, Article 35 of the IRPD requires that, prior to recording any data in INTERPOL's files, the NCB must be satisfied that the data is 'of interest for the purposes of international police cooperation'. In order to comply with this condition, two criteria apply: (1) the processing of data may only be carried out for a 'given, explicit purpose',[130] and (2) the data must be of an 'international nature', which is to be assessed by considering the extent to which the data may be used by entities other than the source of the data.[131] INTERPOL has interpreted the latter requirement as meaning that the data must be of 'international interest'.[132] For instance, in Decision No 2019-07, the Commission concluded that a 'petty crime', such as the theft of a mobile phone, does not meet the threshold in Article 35 of the IRPD as it is not, inter alia, 'of interest for the purpose of international police cooperation'.[133]

Third, a determination of whether data is 'not excessive in relation to their purpose' is understood by considering 'the possible actions against the person (for example sentence rendered)'.[134]

Finally, and more difficult to assess, is how the Commission approaches whether data is 'accurate'. There is limited practice available, and even those decisions which are relevant are plagued by heavy redactions. From the decisions that are available (either publicly or in the authors' files), it would appear that the Commission is willing to engage in arguments concerning accuracy where the data concerns technical information, such as identifiers. For instance, in Decision No 2017-11, the applicant argued that information in a green notice was not accurate. Most of the data he challenged could be easily verified – ie, identity particulars, his current location, previous convictions. In response, the NCB accepted that the data was incorrect, so the NCB requested INTERPOL to delete the green notice and reissue a new one. In light of this action, the Commission accepted that the new green notice was accurate.[135] In Decision No 2019-02, when faced with similar inaccuracies, the Commission concluded that the data was compliant with INTERPOL's rules, provided that the applicant's file was updated to reflect his actual level of involvement in the events described in the diffusion (ie, 'corrected' as is contemplated in Article 18 of the IRPD).

[129] Decision of the Commission, Decision No 2019-08 (July 2019) paras 68–9 (emphasis in original).
[130] IRPD, Art 10(1). See also: IRPD, Art 35(2).
[131] IRPD, Art 35(2)(b).
[132] Decision of the Commission, Decision No 2019-07 (April 2019) para 38.
[133] Ibid, paras 40–4. It came to the same conclusion in respect of Article 83(1)(a)(i) of the IRPD (which gives effect to Article 35(2) in the context of red notices).
[134] Decision of the Commission, Decision No 2019-08 (July 2019) paras 68–9 (emphasis in original).
[135] Decision of the Commission, Decision No 2017-11 (June 2017) paras 21–32.

This practice is detailed in the Commission's 2017 Activity Report: when data is 'not accurate, it does not automatically result in the deletion of the information concerned. Rather, these checks result in updates being made to INTERPOL's files, either directly by the NCBs consulted in the context of processing a request, or by the General Secretariat'.[136] It is therefore surprising that the Commission allowed technical inaccuracies to remain uncorrected in Decision No 2019-02, where the Commission concluded that 'minor discrepancies' and 'slight inaccuracies' were of 'no real consequence'.[137] The inaccuracies in this notice concerned the applicant's identity and details about his employment, neither of which the NCB addressed in its reply to the Commission.[138] The Commission's departure from its rational approach in Decision No 2019-02 and its 2017 Activity Report is not explained. Nor does it explain how an admitted inaccuracy (howsoever slight) can be married with the clear requirement in Article 12(1) that data be 'accurate'.[139]

Even more troubling is the Commission's complete unwillingness to entertain challenges which concern data that is not of a technical nature, such as data relating to the facts which underpin a charge. In such circumstances, the Commission has repeatedly stated that it 'is not empowered to conduct an investigation, to weigh evidence, to make a determination on the merits of a case or to evaluate the reliability of evidence'.[140] Rather, it views these activities as 'the function of the competent national authorities, either at trial or during an extradition hearing'.[141] Presumably, the Commission has come to this conclusion in light of Article 12(2) of the IRPD, which provides that the '[NCBs], national entities and international entities shall be responsible for the quality of the data they record and transmit in the INTERPOL Information System', and Article 63(1) of the IRPD, which stipulates that all '[NCBs], national entities and international entities about to use data processed in the INTERPOL Information System for the purposes of applying coercive measures … must ensure that these data are still accurate and relevant'.[142] It may also be comforted by Article 128(1)

[136] Report submitted by the CCF, 'Report No. 3: Activity Report of the Commission for the Control of INTERPOL's Files for 2017', GA-2018-87-REP-03 (9 October 2018) 12.

[137] Decision of the Commission, Decision No 2019-09 (July 2019) para 39.

[138] Ibid, paras 33–6.

[139] See also, by way of analogy, the right to rectification under EU law: eg, Regulation (EU) 2016/679 of the European Parliament and the Council of the European Union of 27 April 2016 on the protection of natural persons with regard to the processing of personal data and on the free movement of such data, and repealing Directive 95/46/EC (General Data Protection Regulation), Official Journal L119/1 (4 May 2016) 1–88 ('GDPR'), Art 16.

[140] Decision of the Commission (2 July 2019) para 52. A copy of this decision is in the authors' files.

[141] Ibid.

[142] See also: IRPD, Arts 11(4) and 76(2)(a). The latter provision provides that an NCB or international entity requesting a notice must ensure the quality of the data it provides in support of its request. This obligation is a continuing obligation pursuant to Article 80(2)(a) of the IRPD, which provides that the NCB or entity which originally requested a notice must 'continue to ensure that the data it has provided in the notice remains accurate and relevant'.

of the IRPD, which provides that data is 'a priori, considered to be accurate and relevant when entered by a [NCB], a national entity or an international entity into the INTERPOL Information System and recorded in a police database of the Organization'.

However, these provisions do not absolve the CCF or the General Secretariat of its obligations when data is challenged on the basis of Article 12(1) of the IRPD, and it certainly does not allow the Commission to defer to NCBs. First, it is within the exclusive power of the Requests Chamber of the CCF to 'examine and decide on requests for … deletion of … data processed in the INTERPOL Information System' on the basis of INTERPOL's rules,[143] and, in the course of examining such requests, it is the obligation of the Requests Chamber to 'examine the compliance of the processing of the data with INTERPOL's rules'.[144] Similarly, Article 22(5) of the IRPD stipulates that the General Secretariat must 'ensure that the conditions for processing data in the Organization's databases are duly observed', and Article 36 of the INTERPOL Constitution provides that the CCF must 'ensure that the processing of personal information by the Organization is in compliance with the regulations the Organization establishes in this manner'. Thus, allowing an NCB to determine whether or not data is 'accurate' is an unauthorised delegation of decision-making power contrary to Articles 28(1)(b) and 33(3) of the CCF Statute, Article 22(5) of the IRPD and Article 36 of the INTERPOL Constitution. Second, taking the NCB's views as conclusive is a breach of the requirement of independence in Article 11(2) of the CCF Statute: '[i]n the exercise of their functions, the members of the Commission shall be independent, remain free from external influence, whether direct or indirect, and neither solicit nor accept instructions from any person, body or government'. By allowing the NCB to decide on an issue that is determinative of the outcome of a request for deletion, the Commission indirectly subjects itself to external influence from the NCB instead of acting in its independent capacity when fulfilling its duty to 'examine the compliance of the processing of the data with INTERPOL's rules'.[145] Third, taking the NCB's views as conclusive is a breach of Article 2(1) of the INTERPOL Constitution and Article 11(1) of the IRPD because a decision-making body that decides only on the basis of the views of the requesting NCB is one that is lacking in independence and impartiality (as required by Article 10 of the UDHR). As a consequence, a failure to investigate adequately whether data is compliant with Article 12(1) of the IRPD, for any reason, is a clear breach of INTERPOL's internal law.

The failings of the Commission's approach in respect of Article 12(1) is palpable in two domestic cases. In *Prendi (aka Aleks Kola) v Albania*, the High Court of Justice of England and Wales made it clear that INTERPOL had failed to ensure

[143] CCF Statute, Art 28(1)(b).
[144] Ibid, Art 33(3).
[145] Ibid.

the quality of even the most basic of the data – ie, the identity of the subject of a red notice. The Court held that:

> [t]he red notice plus the addendum/corrigendum is a collection of facts in the form of the Interpol photograph, the fingerprint images and the description of Leke Prendi. But whoever made up the red notice could not speak to the truth of any of those facts directly. They all came from sources other than Interpol Tirana. There is no evidence to suggest that the person who correlated the information to make up the red notice obtained the various elements directly from the person who took the Interpol photograph, took the fingerprints, or measured Leke Prendi's height. There is no evidence about when, where or how the Interpol photograph was taken, Leke Prendi's height measured, or where the fingerprints were actually taken. The email of 9 April 2015, from Interpol Tirana, would appear to be a multiple hearsay statement of where 'the fingerprints' were 'received' in 1999 without giving any details of when, where and why the finger prints (sic) were actually taken. Thus there is nothing to demonstrate that those are, indeed, a photograph of Leke Prendi, his finger prints (sic) or even that it was his height at the relevant time.[146]

Accordingly, the UK refused to extradite Aleks Kola and the reputation of INTERPOL was severely undermined.[147] The case of *Boreh v Djibouti*[148] is even more concerning because it was demonstrated that INTERPOL renders itself liable to being deliberately misled by the requesting NCB if the INTERPOL General Secretariat is overly reliant on the evidence and statements of the NCB. In *Boreh v Djibouti*, it became clear that INTERPOL had published a red notice on the basis of false representations made by the requesting NCB. NCB Djibouti had informed INTERPOL that Boreh was implicated in a grenade attack on the evening of 3 March 2009. However, Boreh's solicitors later discovered that NCB Djibouti, Djibouti authorities and a UK solicitor had falsified the information in order to obtain a red notice to freeze and confiscate Boreh's assets. The judge made the following observation:

> [m]ysteriously given that CCF at Interpol were sent a copy of my 13 November 2014 judgment by Gibson Dunn on 8 December 2014, on 6 January 2015, CCF informed Interpol Djibouti that the Red Notice had been reinstated. As I said in the course of argument on Day 3 of the hearing, I have little doubt that if Interpol had had any idea about the material which was before this court at the present hearing, they would have withdrawn the Red Notice straight away. Following my indication that I would if necessary order Djibouti to write saying that an urgent meeting with Interpol should be convened, I understand Djibouti has taken steps to have the Red Notice lifted.[149]

[146] *Prendi (aka Aleks Kola) v Government of the Republic of Albania* [2015] EWHC 1809 (Admin), para 49 (emphasis added).
[147] Evans, M, 'High court blocks extradition of Albanian killer claiming his description does not match wanted man' *The Telegraph* (25 June 2015).
[148] *Boreh v Djibouti* [2015] EWHC 769 (Comm).
[149] Ibid, para 210 (emphasis added).

Of course, it is clear from the practice of the Commission that it would not have come to a different conclusion, even if presented with information such as that in *Boreh v Djibouti* which strongly suggested that information in its systems was fabricated. This is apparent in Decision No 2019-02 where the applicant outrightly argued that the charges were 'fabricat[ed] … by particular individuals for their personal interest'.[150] But the Commission responded that such arguments 'raise questions that more appropriately fall under the jurisdiction of national courts', and the Commission 'does not conduct investigations or fact-finding inquiries', so it 'cannot therefore conclude based on these individual allegations'. In adopting this position, and by failing to engage in any analysis whatsoever, the General Secretariat and the Commission acted in breach of their obligations under the INTERPOL Constitution and the IRPD to enforce and apply the Organisation's data processing rules.

Moreover, a failure to assess whether the data is accurate is a breach of an applicant's right to respect for private life under international law (and therefore also a breach of Article 2(1) of the INTERPOL Constitution). Article 12 of the UDHR provides that '[n]o one shall be subjected to arbitrary interference with his privacy, family, home or correspondence, nor to attacks upon his honour and reputation'. To give effect to this right, Article 12 provides that '[e]veryone has the right to the protection of the law against such interference or attacks'.[151] The language of Article 17 of the ICCPR is similar. It provides that '[n]o one shall be subjected to arbitrary or unlawful interference with his privacy' and '[e]veryone has the right to the protection of the law against such interference'. Article 8 of the ECHR, which gives effect to Article 12 of the UDHR,[152] provides that '[e]veryone has the right to respect for … private … life'.[153]

The right to respect for private life encompasses the right to respect for privacy,[154] and the protection of personal data is generally viewed as an element of the right to respect for privacy: 'the storage, use and exploitation of all kinds of private data … are … covered by the [right to respect for privacy]. … The right to be informed about the existence of personal data collection and the right to the rectification or possible deletion of false data is also protected'.[155] This was recognised

[150] Decision of the Commission, Decision No 2019-02 (January-February 2019) para 55.

[151] See also: ICCPR, Art 17; ECHR, Art 8; ACHR, Art 11; Arab Charter on Human Rights (adopted on 22 May 2004, entered into force on 15 March 2008) ('ArCHR'), Art 21.

[152] The preamble to the ECHR indicates that the ECHR was the consequence of the collective resolve of European countries 'to take the first steps for the collective enforcement of certain of the rights stated in the [UDHR]'.

[153] ECHR, Art 8(1). Interference with the right to private life is only permitted in limited circumstances (as set out in Article 8(2)).

[154] Kälin, W and Künzli, J, *The Law of International Human Rights Protection* (Oxford, Oxford University Press, 2009) 381.

[155] Ibid, 383.

by the UN Human Rights Committee in General Comment 16 concerning the right to privacy in Article 17 of the ICCPR:

> [t]he gathering and holding of personal information on computers, data banks and other devices, whether by public authorities or private individuals or bodies, must be regulated by law. … In order to have the most effective protection of his private life, every individual should have the right to ascertain in an intelligible form, whether, and if so, what personal data is stored in automatic data files, and for what purposes.[156]

The UN Human Rights Committee also added that:

> [e]very individual should also be able to ascertain which public authorities … control or may control their files. If such files contain incorrect personal data or have been collected or processed contrary to the provisions of the law, every individual should have the right to request rectification or elimination.[157]

The UN Human Rights Committee's interpretation of Article 17 of the ICCPR in General Comment 16 is consistent with its views. For example, in *Van Hulst v Netherlands*, the UN Human Rights Committee found that 'the right to privacy implies that every individual should have the right to request rectification or elimination of incorrect personal data in files controlled by public authorities'.[158]

The approach of the UN Human Rights Committee is consistent with the approach of the ECtHR. The latter has found that the protection of personal data is of fundamental importance to a person's enjoyment of his or her right to respect for private life as guaranteed by Article 8 of the ECHR.[159] In *Khelili v Switzerland*,[160] the ECtHR was presented with the following facts. During a police check in Switzerland, the police found Ms Khelili to be carrying calling cards which read '[n]ice, pretty woman, late thirties, would like to meet a man to have a drink together or go out from time to time. Tel. no. […]'.[161] Ms Khelili alleged that, following that discovery, the police entered her name in their records as a prostitute, an occupation which she consistently denied.[162] Ms Khelili requested that the word 'prostitute' be deleted from the police records but, notwithstanding her request, she continued to be listed as a 'prostitute' in police records. The ECtHR found that the retention of the word 'prostitute' in the police files breached Article 8 of the ECHR.[163] In so doing, the ECtHR found that (1) the allegation of unlawful

[156] UN Human Rights Committee, 'General Comment 16: Article 17 (Right to Privacy)', UN Doc HRI/GEN/1/Rev.9 (8 April 1988) para 10.
[157] Ibid (emphasis added).
[158] *Van Hulst v Netherlands*, Communication No 903/1999, UN Doc CCPR/C/82/D/903/1999 (1 November 2004) para 7.9.
[159] *S and Marper v United Kingdom* [2008] ECHR 1581, para 103.
[160] *Khelili v Switzerland* [2011] ECHR 195.
[161] Ibid, para 8.
[162] Ibid, para 9.
[163] Ibid, para 71.

prostitution appeared too vague and general and was not supported by concrete facts since she had never been convicted of unlawful prostitution,[164] and (2) the authorities must provide proof of the accuracy of data.[165]

The approach of the ECtHR in *Khelili v Switzerland* is consistent with EU legislation. The EU views the protection of data as a standalone fundamental right. Article 8 of the EU Charter of Fundamental Rights provides:

> (1) Everyone has the right to the protection of personal data concerning him or her.
> (2) Such data must be processed fairly for specified purposes and on the basis of the consent of the person concerned or some other legitimate basis laid down by law. Everyone has the right of access to data which has been collected concerning him or her, and the right to have it rectified.
> (3) Compliance with these rules shall be subject to control by an independent authority.

In order to respect the right to protection of personal data, the EU has implemented, inter alia, the GDPR and Directive 2016/680.[166] Although these instruments are not directly binding on INTERPOL (on which, see Chapter 6), they evidence best practice as regards the protection of personal data – a right which INTERPOL must respect in light of Article 2(1) of the INTERPOL Constitution and Article 11(1) of the IRPD. The GDPR and Directive 2016/860 set out six principles relating to the processing[167] of personal data,[168] all of which must be observed by controllers of personal data.[169] The 'accuracy principle' is one such principle, and it provides

[164] Ibid, para 66.

[165] Ibid, para 70.

[166] Directive (EU) 2016/680 of the European Parliament and of the Council of the European Union of 27 April 2016 on the protection of natural persons with regard to the processing of personal data by competent authorities for the purposes of the prevention, investigation, detection or prosecution of criminal offences or the execution of criminal penalties, and on the free movement of such data, and repealing Council Framework Decision 2008/977/JHA, Official Journal L 1919/89 (4 May 2016) 89–131.

[167] 'Processing' is defined as 'any operation or set of operations which is performed on personal data or on sets of personal data, whether or not by automated means, such as collection, recording, organisation, structuring, storage, adaptation or alteration, retrieval, consultation, use, disclosure by transmission, dissemination or otherwise making available, alignment or combination, restriction, erasure or destruction' (GDPR, Art 4(2); Directive 2016/680, Art 3(2)).

[168] 'Personal data' is defined as 'any information relating to an identified or identifiable natural person ("data subject"); an identifiable natural person is one who can be identified, directly or indirectly, in particular by reference to an identifier such as a name, an identification number, location data, an online identifier or to one or more factors specific to the physical, physiological, genetic, mental, economic, cultural or social identity of that natural person' (GDPR, Art 4(1); Directive 2016/680, Art 3(1)).

[169] For the purposes of the GDPR, 'controller' is defined as 'the natural or legal person, public authority, agency or other body which, alone or jointly with others, determines the purposes and means of the processing of personal data; where the purposes and means of such processing are determined by Union or Member State law, the controller or the specific criteria for its nomination may be provided for by Union or Member State law' (GDPR, Art 4(7)). For the purposes of Directive 2016/860, 'controller' is defined as 'the competent authority which, alone or jointly with others, determines the purposes and means of the processing of personal data; where the purposes and means of such processing are determined by Union or Member State law, the controller or the specific criteria for its nomination may be provided for by Union or Member State law' (Directive 2016/680, Art 3(8)).

that personal data 'shall be … accurate and, where necessary, kept up to date ….'[170] A controller holding personal information cannot use that information 'without taking steps to ensure with reasonable certainty that the data are accurate and up to date.'[171]

The 'accuracy principle' in the GDPR has been interpreted as requiring controllers to 'take all reasonable steps to ensure the personal data [they] hold is not incorrect or misleading as to any matter of fact.'[172] Because it may be 'impractical to check the accuracy of personal data someone else provides', controllers should 'take reasonable steps in the circumstances to ensure the accuracy of the information', and 'carefully consider any challenges to the accuracy of information.'[173] Controllers are advised:

> [w]hat is a 'reasonable step' will depend on the circumstances and, in particular, the nature of the personal data and what you will use it for. The more important it is that the personal data is accurate, the greater the effort you should put into ensuring its accuracy. So if you are using the data to make decisions that may significantly affect the individual concerned or others, you need to put more effort into ensuring accuracy. This may mean you have to get independent confirmation that the data is accurate.[174]

Moreover, even if the information source is someone the controller knows to be 'reliable', the data should be verified where, for example, 'inaccurate information could have serious consequences.'[175]

The 'accuracy principle' in Directive 2016/680, which is specifically applicable to personal data processed for law enforcement, has been interpreted as requiring a controller to take 'every reasonable step to correct inaccurate data.'[176] The controllers are required to rectify personal data that is 'inaccurate as a matter of fact' either 'when it becomes apparent, or, if an individual requests it.'[177] In fact, even if an individual contests the accuracy of personal data, 'but it is not possible to be certain about its accuracy', the controller is 'required to restrict the processing of data for the law enforcement purposes.'[178]

In failing to take any steps to ensure with any certainty that the data is accurate in respect of an applicant, the Commission (ie, INTERPOL) breaches an applicant's right to privacy and protection of data. The foregoing suggests that, at a minimum, to comply with an applicant's right to privacy and protection of

[170] GDPR, Art 5(1)(d); Directive 2016/680, Art 4(1)(d).
[171] European Union Agency for Fundamental Rights and Council of Europe, *Handbook on European data protection law*, 2018 edn (Luxembourg, Publications Office of the European Union, 2018) 127.
[172] Information Commissioner's Office, 'Guide to the General Data Protection Regulation (GDPR)' (22 May 2019) 34.
[173] Ibid, 39.
[174] Ibid, 39.
[175] Ibid, 40.
[176] Information Commissioner's Office, 'Guide to Law Enforcement' (25 April 2019) 10.
[177] Ibid, 24.
[178] Ibid, 29.

data, the Commission should independently assess whether the personal data it processes is accurate with reasonable certainty, particularly in light of the significant impact its decisions have on an individual who is the subject of a notice or diffusion. If the Commission has doubts, then it should restrict the data until those doubts can be removed.

INTERPOL has, in fact, been confronted with the argument that 'to process information that it knows or should know to be untrue, and therefore by definition inaccurate within the meaning of Article 12(1) of the IRPD', is a breach of an applicant's right to respect for private life.[179] The Commission responded as follows:

> [t]he Commission ... is not empowered to conduct an investigation, to weigh evidence, or to make a determination on the merits of a case. That is the function of the competent national authorities. The mere submission of evidence that would support a contrary account would require the Commission to evaluate the reliability of the evidence in a manner that should be undertaken at trial or an extradition hearing. Instead ... the Commission reviews whether the NCB provided sufficient information that link the wanted individual to the charges against him, and a clear description of the criminal activities in which he is accused.
>
> Therefore, the Commission finds that in this case, the NCB ... has put forth a reasonable explanation that the case materials collected refute the Applicant's contention of lack of evidentiary basis and that the national authorities have enough elements to his possible effective personal and active participation in these acts.[180]

This uncritical deference to the NCB breaches the applicant's right to a fair trial and right to an effective remedy: if the Requests Chamber cannot (or will not) assess the applicant's contentions (and evidence), the Requests Chamber is unable to determine thoroughly and effectively whether the applicant's right to respect for private life had been breached (which requires a determination on the accuracy of the data). As discussed in Chapter 11, the applicant's right to a fair trial and right to an effective remedy before the Commission is uncontroversial in light of the (counterbalancing) immunity granted to INTERPOL by France.[181] The UN Human Rights Committee has emphasised, '[a]dministrative

[179] Letter from an applicant to the CCF (29 September 2017). A copy of this letter is in the authors' files.

[180] Decision of the Commission (4 July 2018) paras 40–1. A copy of this decision is in the authors' files.

[181] See: Agreement between the International Criminal Police Organization – INTERPOL and the Government of the French Republic regarding INTERPOL's Headquarters in France (entered into force on 1 September 2009) as amended by Decree No 2016-326 of 17 March 2016 promulgating the additional protocol in the form of an exchange of letters between the Government of the French Republic and the International Criminal Police Organization – INTERPOL on the interpretation and application of Article 24 of the Agreement of 14 and 24 April 2008 regarding INTERPOL's headquarters in France (signed in Paris on 9 February 2016 and in Lyon on 12 February 2016 and entered into force on 16 February 2016), Art 5.

mechanisms are particularly required to … investigate allegations of [human rights] violations promptly, thoroughly and effectively through independent and impartial bodies'.[182]

In light of the Commission's deficient and deferential analysis in Article 12(1) challenges, the more practical approach for an applicant to adopt before the Commission is to evidence why the information is 'inaccurate' in order to colour the Commission's understanding of an alleged breach of Article 2 or Article 3 of the INTERPOL Constitution. For instance, in Decision No 2018-13, the applicant argued that charges of commercial fraud in Bahrain were 'inaccurate'. In particular, he argued that the data was inaccurate because he had received 'lawful and agreed payments of remuneration made for his benefit by virtue of his employment contract' (as opposed to payments received by fraud).[183] He emphasised that he left his employment 'with no indication that there were any outstanding issues as to his financial arrangements … connected to his employment and benefits package'.[184] In support of his claim, he submitted a copy of a 'compromise agreement' which stated that 'this agreement has been made in good faith and in recognition that there are no offences to answer'.[185] He also provided correspondence which showed that the disputed sums were 'resolved and duly paid'.[186] The Commission observed that the sums in the court decision were 'exactly the same' as those referred to in the compromise agreement,[187] to which the NCB replied that any settlement (ie, the compromise agreement) does not bar the launch of criminal proceedings.[188] This evidence should have led the Commission to find a breach of Article 12(1) of the IRPD on the basis that the data was not 'accurate' (ie, it was 'incorrect or misleading as to any matter of fact').[189] But the Commission failed to discuss Article 12 at all, instead considering whether the data was 'sufficient' for the purposes of Article 83 of the IRPD (again, erroneously conflating 'sufficient' with 'accurate'). That being said, the decision is useful because the Commission overtly relies on its 'doubts' about the quality of the data to inform its understanding of the 'political nature of the proceedings' under Article 3 of the INTERPOL Constitution, leading it to conclude that 'on balance, the data challenged are not compliant with INTERPOL's rules'.[190] This approach overcomes the Commission's unwillingness to apply properly Article 12(1) of the IRPD.

[182] UN Human Rights Committee, 'General Comment 31: The Nature of the General Legal Obligation Imposed on States Parties to the Covenant', UN Doc CCPR/C/21/Rev.1/Add.13 (26 May 2004) para 15.

[183] Decision of the Commission, Decision No 2018-13 (July 2018) paras 21 and 28.

[184] Ibid, para 23 (redaction in the original).

[185] Ibid, para 24.

[186] Ibid, para 26.

[187] Ibid, para 34.

[188] Ibid, para 35.

[189] Information Commissioner's Office, 'Guide to the General Data Protection Regulation (GDPR)' (22 May 2019) 34.

[190] Decision of the Commission, Decision No 2018-13 (July 2018) para 64.

C. Neutrality

Article 3 of the INTERPOL Constitution sets out the so-called 'neutrality' restriction upon INTERPOL's powers to act.[191] Article 3 reads in the manner of an express prohibition: '[i]t is strictly forbidden for the Organization to undertake any intervention or activities of a political, military, religious or racial character'.

As a matter of INTERPOL's internal law, the INTERPOL General Secretariat has stated that Article 3 is to be construed as if it were a treaty provision, by 'general interpretation tenets under international law', such as the general rule of treaty interpretation that a provision is to be '… interpreted in good faith in accordance with the ordinary meaning to be given to the terms of the treaty in their context and in light of its objects and purpose'.[192] The purpose of Article 3 has been explained as follows: (1) to ensure the independence and neutrality of INTERPOL as an international organisation, (2) to reflect international extradition law, and (3) to protect individuals from persecution.[193] The organs of an international organisation interpret the rules of the organisation.[194] Thus, we briefly explore how Article 3 of the INTERPOL Constitution has been interpreted by INTERPOL's organs.

A large body of interpretative guidance on Article 3 has been gradually developed by the ICPC/INTERPOL General Assembly through a catalogue of resolutions.[195] Although the focus has shifted slightly since 1956, the current

[191] See: Gottlieb, Y, 'Article 3 of Interpol's Constitution: Balancing International Police Cooperation with the Prohibition on Engaging in Political, Military, Religious, or Racial Activities' (2011) 23 *Florida Journal of International Law* 135–86 at 136–37.

[192] INTERPOL, 'Repository of Practice: Application of Article 3 of INTERPOL's Constitution in the context of the processing of information via INTERPOL's channels', 2nd edn (February 2013) ('Repository of Practice') 7, para 19 citing Article 31(1) of the VCLT.

[193] Repository of Practice, 6, para 16 citing 'Document GTI5-2008-05 prepared for the Ad Hoc Working Group on the Processing of Information'.

[194] Where an organisation's members assent or acquiesce in any such interpretation, that interpretation informs the organisation's competence to act (see: *Legality of the Use by a State of Nuclear Weapons in Armed Conflict*, Advisory Opinion [1996] ICJ Rep 66, para 19 (on the relevance of Article 31(3)(b) of the VCLT)). See further: Schermers, HG and Blokker, NM, *International Institutional Law: Unity within Diversity*, 6th revised edn (Leiden, Brill Nijhoff Publishers, 2018) 883–84, who argue that Article 31(3)(b) of the VCLT is not the foundation on which the 'practice of the organization' should be understood to rest.

[195] Resolution No AGN/43/Res/3, 'Safeguarding of International Civil Aviation', ICPC General Assembly, 43rd session (Cannes, 1951); Resolution No AGN/48/Res/8, 'Acts of Violence Committed by Organised Groups', INTERPOL General Assembly, 48th session (Nairobi, 1979); Resolution No AGN/53/Res/6, 'Violent Crime Commonly Referred to as Terrorism', INTERPOL General Assembly, 53rd session (Luxembourg, 1984); Resolution No AGN/53/RES/7, 'Application of Article 3 of the Constitution', INTERPOL General Assembly, 53rd session (Luxembourg, 1984); Resolution No AGN/63/Res/9, 'Application of Article 3 of the Constitution in the context of serious violations of international humanitarian law', INTERPOL General Assembly, 63rd session (Rome, 1994); Resolution No AGN/67/Res/12, 'Cairo declaration against terrorism', INTERPOL General Assembly, 67th session (Cairo, 1998); Resolution No AG-2006-Res-04, 'Statement to Reaffirm the Independence and political Neutrality of Interpol', INTERPOL General Assembly, 75th session (Rio de Janeiro, 2006).

approach in determining whether an intervention or activity is prohibited by Article 3 is to consider 'all relevant information and pertinent elements'[196] in accordance with Article 34(3) of the IRPD, including:

- (a) the nature of the offence, namely the charges and the underlying facts;
- (b) the status of the persons concerned;
- (c) the identity of the source of the data;
- (d) the position expressed by another [NCB] or another international entity;
- (e) obligations under international law;
- (f) the implications for the neutrality of the Organization;
- (g) the general context of the case.[197]

INTERPOL describes this as a 'comprehensive interpretative approach'.[198] Practically, it means that INTERPOL will consider anything that is logically relevant to determining whether or not a given intervention or activity is contrary to Article 3. Moreover, the Repository of Practice[199] 'requires' INTERPOL to examine and consider pertinent facts 'beyond those explicitly supplied in the request for police cooperation, such as information concerning the background for the request or how it relates to other requests'.[200]

The first criterion in Article 34(3) of the IRPD deserves closer analysis because classification of the 'nature' of an offence has received considerable attention from INTERPOL. If an offence is criminalised 'solely' due to its political, military, religious or racial nature then it is considered a 'pure' offence.[201] 'Pure' offences 'do not have any ordinary-law element' and 'are usually directed against the State and exclusively affect the public interest and cause only public wrong'.[202] INTERPOL's stance on what might be identified as a 'pure' offence has changed over the years. In 1984, the General Assembly provided a list of examples of offences which 'by their very nature' are 'pure' political, military, racial, or religious offences.[203] It was subsequently said in 2003 that the list may not be up to date and it would be 'impractical' going forward to adopt an exhaustive list of pure offences.[204] That being said, INTERPOL appears to accept that any of the examples in the 1984 list remain 'pure' offences.[205]

[196] Repository of Practice, 8, para 29.
[197] See also: Ibid, para 28.
[198] Ibid, para 29.
[199] The Repository of Practice is a guide prepared by the General Secretariat on the principles that inform the interpretation and application of Article 3 in the context of data processing.
[200] Ibid.
[201] Repository of Practice, 7, para 22.
[202] Ibid, citing Bassiouni, MC, *International Extradition: United States Law and Practice*, 5th edn (Oxford, Oxford University Press, 2007) 660–62.
[203] Ie, (1) membership of a prohibited organisation, (2) the expression of certain prohibited opinions, (3) offences involving the press, (4) insulting the authorities, (5) offences against the internal or external security of the State, (6) desertion from the armed forces, (7) treason, (8) espionage, (9) practising a prohibited religion, (10) recruitment or propaganda for particular religions, and (11) membership of a racial association (Resolution AGN/53/RES/7, 'Application of Article 3 of the Constitution', INTERPOL General Assembly, 53rd session (Luxembourg, 1984), II.1).
[204] Repository of Practice, 7, paras 23–4.
[205] Ibid, 15.

If a doubt is raised about whether it is a 'pure' offence or 'ordinary-law' offence, then INTERPOL considers whether the offence is 'relative', ie, containing political, military, religious, or racial elements, in addition to ordinary law elements. Such offences are analysed through the application of the predominance test.[206] The notion of predominance was introduced by the ICPC General Assembly in 1951 and developed by a subsequent resolution of the INTERPOL General Assembly in 1984.[207] In determining what element is predominant, INTERPOL will take into account (1) the links between the aims of the defendant and their victims, (2) the place where the action was carried out (ie, area of conflict), (3) the status of the victims, and (4) the seriousness of the offence.[208]

Previously, INTERPOL treated 'pure' offences, in addition to offences which had a 'predominant' political, military, religious or racial element, as necessarily within the scope of Article 3.[209] However, Article 34(3) of the IRPD makes it clear that the nature of the offence is only one element of at least seven to be considered in the context of an Article 3 analysis. Of course, a 'pure' political/military/religious/racial offence may be an important element in an analysis, but it cannot determine the application of Article 3. The Repository of Practice endorses this approach: 'considering that Article 3 refers to the "character" of the relevant activity, elements other than the nature of the offence ought to be taken into consideration'.[210] Unfortunately, the Commission shows no such clarity of thought, often conflating the predominance test and the approach set out in Article 34(3) of the IRPD.[211]

The following discussion explains each proscribed category within Article 3 (political, military, religious and racial) and discusses what INTERPOL's practice reveals about the content of each category. It will also consider how Article 34(3) of the IRPD has been applied, with particular emphasis on the nature of the offence, including which offences are typically considered 'pure' offences and how the predominance test has been applied by the Commission.[212]

[206] Ibid, 7, para 22.

[207] See: Resolution No AGN/20/RES/11, 'Request for international inquiries', International Criminal Police Commission ('ICPC') General Assembly, 20th session (Lisbon, 1951); Resolution No AGN/53/RES/7, 'Application of Article 3 of the Constitution', INTERPOL General Assembly, 53rd session (Luxembourg, 1984).

[208] Martha, RSJ, 'Remedies against INTERPOL: role and practice of defence lawyers' (Speech at the European Criminal Bar Association, Autumn Conference, Lyon, 6 October 2007) para 65; Resolution No AGN/53/RES/7, 'Application of Article 3 of the Constitution', INTERPOL General Assembly, 53rd session (Luxembourg, 1984), II.3. See also: Repository of Practice, 9, 'Scenario B'.

[209] Resolution No AGN/53/RES/7, 'Application of Article 3 of the Constitution', INTERPOL General Assembly, 53rd session (Luxembourg, 1984), II.1.

[210] Repository of Practice, 8, para 27.

[211] For instance, the CCF commences many decisions with the following convoluted language: '[w]ith respect to the assertion that the matter is of a political, religious or racial character, the Organization applies the predominance test, i.e., it evaluates all relevant information and pertinent elements, as provided by the rules, to determine whether the offense is of a predominantly political, religious, or racial character over its ordinary-law character'.

[212] See further: Repository of Practice, 11–46.

i. Political Character

The proscription against interventions or activities of a political character has been described by a commentator (who works at INTERPOL) to be 'the primary element aimed at guaranteeing INTERPOL's neutrality'.[213] The proscription on political interventions or activities is somewhat analogous to the political offence exception seen in extradition law. It has been said that Article 3 'introduced' the political offence exception from extradition law into INTERPOL's practice,[214] but that statement is arguably too strong. Owing to differing conceptions of what amounts to a political offence in extradition law,[215] the exception does not necessarily replicate that under Article 3. For instance, three distinct tests have emerged in analysing political offences in extradition law: (1) the French 'objective' test, (2) the Swiss 'proportionality' or 'predominance' test, and (3) the Anglo-American 'incidence' test.[216] None of these directly accord with the approach adopted by INTERPOL. An applicant would, therefore, be well-advised to resort in the first instance to INTERPOL's practice on the subject, rather than arguing by analogy with the jurisprudence of extradition law.

Considering, first, the nature of the offence, the Repository of Practice is particularly illustrative on what has been determined by INTERPOL to be a 'pure' political offence. INTERPOL has stated that certain offences against the State, such as treason,[217] espionage,[218] divulging State secrets,[219] and illegal speech against a former President of the requesting State,[220] are considered 'pure' political offences. For instance, where a diffusion was circulated for the offence of 'insulting the former President of the State', INTERPOL concluded that the offence concerned a 'purely political' crime and the INTERPOL Information System could not be used in connection with such an offence.[221] This is, as discussed above, too simplistic

[213] Gottlieb, Y, 'Article 3 of Interpol's Constitution: Balancing International Police Cooperation with the Prohibition on Engaging in Political, Military, Religious, or Racial Activities' (2011) 23 *Florida Journal of International Law* 135–86 at 153.

[214] Ibid, arguing that Article 3 'reflect[s] principles of international extradition law' and 'introduced the political offense exception into INTERPOL's practice'.

[215] See generally: Van Den Wijngaert, C, 'The Political Offence Exception to Extradition: Defining the Issues and Searching for a Feasible Alternative' (1980) 20 *Revue beige de droit international* 741–54; Cantrell, CL, 'The Political Offense Exemption in International Extradition: A Comparison of the United States, Great Britain, and the Republic of Ireland' (1997) 60 *Marquette Law Review* 777–824; DeFabo, V, 'Terrorist or Revolutionary: The Development of the Political Offender Exception and Its Effects on Defining Terrorism in International Law' (2012) 2 *American University National Security Law Brief* 69–104.

[216] See: Kielsgard, MD, 'The Political Offense Exception: Punishing Whistleblowers Abroad', *EJIL: Talk!* (14 November 2013).

[217] Repository of Practice, 8, 'Scenario A', where it is stated that '[t]he rationale for such a determination is that this act is considered to be a pure political crime in extradition practice'. See also: Repository of Practice, 21.

[218] Ibid, 21.

[219] Ibid.

[220] Ibid, 15, 'Scenario A', 'Case 2'.

[221] Ibid, 15, 'Case 1'.

an approach to Article 34(3) of the IRPD as it fails to take into account the other relevant elements, but it is an approach often adopted by INTERPOL.[222] Similarly, INTERPOL has 'consistently' viewed the offence of 'illegal emigration' as a pure political offence (since it does not involve any ordinary law crime elements), and it has refused to process data solely on the basis of this element.[223] It also refused to issue a red notice for the arrest of the former President of Honduras, Manuel Zelaya, in 2009 on the basis that the charges of 'misuse of authority; usurpation of public functions; offences against the system of government; and treason' were 'of a political nature with no ordinary-law element'.[224] That being said, there are some instances in which INTERPOL has adopted a slightly more nuanced approach. For instance, where a diffusion was circulated seeking the arrest of an individual for 'high treason', INTERPOL placed great weight on the nature of the 'purely political' offence, but also considered 'the position expressed by another [NCB]' and open-source reports that informed 'the general context of the case'.[225] Similarly, whilst INTERPOL expects that offences committed in the context of an unconstitutional seizure of power (discussed below) will almost always lead to the application of Article 3, it acknowledges that each request has to be examined on a case-by-case basis.[226]

In relation to its consideration of the other elements in Article 34(3) of the IRPD, INTERPOL has stated that if an NCB seeks the arrest and extradition of a person on a charge of murder (ie, an ordinary law offence), but the individual is the serving head of State, it would usually conclude that Article 3 applies on the basis of the 'status of the persons concerned and obligations under international law' (ie, immunity *ratione personae* of a head of State).[227] Where a red notice request was sent and a diffusion circulated by an NCB seeking the arrest and extradition of a former Prime Minister for financial crimes, INTERPOL considered that the 'status of the [persons] concerned' and 'the general context of the case' (ie, the Prime Minister had lost a recent election to the presidency and remained a major opponent to the current regime) meant that Article 3 was applicable.[228]

The latter case raises the interesting question of how INTERPOL tackles cases that concern politicians wanted by their own countries. INTERPOL has emphasised that, in such circumstances, it considers two additional elements. First, it may ask the requesting NCB to clarify whether the individual enjoys immunity from prosecution in his or her own country. Second, it may ask the NCB to provide specific evidence that the offence is of an ordinary law nature, such as

[222] See, for instance: Ibid, 21–2, 'Background', 'Case 1', 'Case 3', 'Case 4', 'Case 5'.
[223] Ibid, 33–4.
[224] 'INTERPOL will not issue Red Notice for arrest of President Manuel Zelaya', INTERPOL press release (7 July 2009).
[225] Repository of Practice, 21, 'Case 2'; IRPD, Art 34(3).
[226] Repository of Practice, 24, 'Current practice'.
[227] Ibid, 9, 'Scenario C'.
[228] Ibid, 13, 'Scenario A', 'Case 5'.

evidence of personal gain. For example, a red notice was requested by an NCB for its former President on charges of embezzlement for a series of economic decisions that severely undermined the national treasury. The General Secretariat did not publish the notice on the basis of 'the general context of the case' (ie, the previous occurrence of a *coup d'état*, which deposed the individual), the 'position expressed by … another international entity' (ie, international financial institutions) and the fact that the former President derived no personal benefit.[229]

However, there are times when INTERPOL seems to ignore Article 34(3) of the IRPD entirely, instead simply questioning if the individual was personally enriched. For instance, INTERPOL published a red notice at the request of an NCB for its country's former President on charges of corruption and illicit enrichment because the President had committed the offences 'not for political gain but rather to personally enrich himself'.[230] In another case, a former President had been charged with 'misappropriation' because, whilst serving as President of the country, he had issued an emergency decree in order to award a contract without putting it out to tender. INTERPOL requested further information and the NCB replied that the individual had personally benefited from the illegal activities. INTERPOL therefore published the red notice.[231] Both of these cases show a blindness to the elements to be examined pursuant to Article 34(3) of the IRPD. The status of the person concerned and the general context of the case should always be of paramount importance in cases where a former politician is wanted by his or her own country. This is necessary to guard against the use of the Organisation's channels to persecute individuals inappropriately. For instance, although INTERPOL initially issued a red notice in January 2015 against former President Viktor Yanukovych and his son, it subsequently deleted the notice when additional information was submitted regarding the broader context.[232]

In a recent well-reasoned decision of the Commission, it fully engaged with Article 34(3) of the IRPD when considering the political character of a red notice. In so doing, it recognised that a case may be political even if an applicant is not a current or former government official. The Commission first determined that the alleged crime was of an ordinary law nature. However, it observed there was a 'strong link' between the applicants and a leader of the opposition party in the country of the NCB that had requested the red notice.[233] The Commission was therefore of the view that the 'statuses of the Applicants

[229] Ibid, 13, 'Scenario A', 'Case 6'.

[230] Ibid, 12, 'Scenario A', 'Case 2'.

[231] Ibid, 12, 'Scenario A', 'Case 3'.

[232] See: 'Interpol cancels Red Notice concerning President Yanukovych and his son O. Yanukovych', Joseph Hage Aaronson LLP press release (3 May 2017).

[233] Decision of the Commission (2 October 2019) para 57. A copy of this decision is in the authors' files.

indicate a political element in the case by virtue of its publicized association to [a leader of the opposition] and his family'.[234] The Commission then made a number of observations regarding the 'context' of the case. First, it considered the circumstances surrounding the proceedings, in particular the 'trajectory and the context in which the charges were levied against the Applicants'.[235] It observed that, prior to the present proceedings, a national court had found that the prosecutors had acted 'palpably without authority' in respect of one of the applicants.[236] Second, it reviewed the documents provided and underlined that certain elements raised 'concern regarding possible motivations behind the proceedings'.[237] Third, it considered the mistreatment of individuals associated with the underlying criminal proceedings, including claims submitted before a national court, written testimony and national news reports.[238] Fourth, it noted that various other individuals associated with the relevant political party had also been subjected to raids, questioning or criminal proceedings.[239] In light of the foregoing, the Commission was of the view that there are some political elements in the specific context of the case and in relation to the proceedings at the national level'.[240] Next, the Commission considered whether the relevant NCB had misused INTERPOL's channels, which it held could 'exacerbate existing concerns under Article 3 of INTERPOL's Constitution, and specifically raise doubts regarding the ordinary-law character of a case'.[241] It observed that the relevant NCB had issued a diffusion in order to seek the location of the applicants, but then sought their arrest, detention and deportation, which was patently not the purpose of the diffusion. This was a 'misuse' of INTERPOL's channels and a violation of Articles 10 and 11 of the IRPD.[242] In addition, when the General Secretariat provisionally blocked the diffusion, the relevant NCB continued to circulate messages. This was also a 'misuse' of INTERPOL's channels.[243] Finally, the Commission examined 'the position expressed' by other NCBs, one of which had provided the Commission with a judgment of its national courts which found the underlying case to be of a political character. The Commission was of the view that the decision by the national court corroborated several of the claims under Article 3 which were submitted by the applicants.[244] In light of the foregoing, it concluded that the status of the applicants, the general context of

[234] Ibid.
[235] Ibid, para 59.
[236] Ibid, para 60.
[237] Ibid, para 64.
[238] Ibid, para 66.
[239] Ibid, para 69.
[240] Ibid, para 70.
[241] Ibid, para 72.
[242] Ibid, paras 73 and 75.
[243] Ibid, para 74.
[244] Ibid, para 80.

the case and the position expressed by another NCB raised concerns regarding the compliance of the data with Article 3 of the INTERPOL Constitution. On this basis, it held that offences concerning the applicants were political in character and should be deleted from INTERPOL's files. The foregoing is exemplary of how Article 34(3) of the IRPD should be employed in practice.

ii. Military Character

In the context of an intervention or activity of a 'military' character, INTERPOL has (again) devoted much of its practice and guidance to the nature of the offence, rather than considering the totality of elements set out in Article 34(3) of the IRPD. It has also adopted a similar approach to that of political offences in that it will not process data in respect of certain 'pure' military offences: ie, offences which do not constitute ordinary law crimes or violations of *ius in bello*, such as desertion and draft evasion.[245] It does so in the purported application of extradition law.[246] Thus, an NCB was informed that it could not use INTERPOL's channels to request additional information about persons who had refused military service (a criminal offence under the relevant national penal code).[247] Similarly, where an individual was charged with the offence of desertion, INTERPOL determined that the crime was 'a pure military offence that fell within the scope of Article 3'.[248]

The existence of a military context is not determinative of the application of Article 3. So, for instance, where a soldier murders a fellow soldier in peacetime, INTERPOL will generally allow the processing of data.[249] To this end, a red notice request in respect of a robbery committed by a cadet at a military institute was deemed an ordinary law crime and not of a military character (despite the fact that the arrest warrant was issued by a military court).[250] Similarly, INTERPOL allowed a request for a yellow notice (ie, an alert for a missing person) in respect of a soldier who had disappeared during his military service because the NCB assured INTERPOL that (1) his disappearance had no connection to a military conflict or operation and (2) if found alive, no criminal measures would be taken against him.[251]

Acts committed in an armed conflict pose an interesting set of questions. The general position is that an act committed in an armed conflict may not be processed in INTERPOL's channels, unless it relates to certain international

[245] Repository of Practice, 35.
[246] Ibid.
[247] Ibid, 37, 'Scenario A', 'Case 1'.
[248] Ibid, 37, 'Scenario A', 'Case 4'.
[249] Ibid, 35, 'Scenario C'. See also: Ibid, 38, 'Scenario C'.
[250] Ibid, 38, 'Scenarios A and B'.
[251] Ibid, 'Scenario C'.

crimes (as discussed below).[252] The rationale underlying the general approach, according to the Repository of Practice, is that acts committed in violation of the laws of war would not necessarily constitute a crime, and would therefore fall outside the scope of Article 2 of the INTERPOL Constitution. Alternatively, and even if such acts are considered crimes by the requesting NCB, INTERPOL is of the view that these crimes would 'generally be viewed as being committed against the external or internal security of the State' and within the scope of Article 3.[253] Thus, in one case, red notice requests were sent by an NCB in respect of individuals wanted for aggravated murder. However, the murders took place in the context of an internationally recognised armed conflict and the deaths occurred in an ambush of the opposing army. As such, the red notices were not published.[254] In another comparable case, INTERPOL determined that offences committed by military forces of one INTERPOL member against another, although amounting to murder, attempted murder, and destruction of property under the law of the victims' country, fell within Article 3.[255] Interestingly, INTERPOL later decided that, because the soldiers attacked were UN peacekeeping forces, 'the case should not be considered as an armed conflict between two INTERPOL member countries and as such did not fall within the scope of Article 3'.[256] The rationale underlying this appears to be that, in the latter situation, the act was not committed against the security of a given State, so INTERPOL's neutrality would not be compromised where the military forces of a given member perpetrate an attack on a neutral intervening entity. Presumably, this outweighed the military status of the persons concerned and the general context of an armed conflict in an Article 34(3) analysis.

With respect to international crimes, the INTERPOL General Assembly approved cooperation with the International Criminal Tribunal for the former Yugoslavia ('ICTY') in 1994,[257] thereby allowing the Organisation to consider serious international crimes. However, INTERPOL is still required to conduct

[252] See: Resolution No AG-2004-RES-16, 'Co-operation Agreement with the International Criminal Court', INTERPOL General Assembly, 73rd session (Cancun, 2004), declaring in its preamble that 'the crimes which come within the jurisdiction of the International Criminal Court also fall within the aims of the Organization as defined in Articles 2 and 3 of the Constitution'. See also: Repository of Practice, 37, which states that '… where the source [of data] is an international tribunal established by the UN Security Council acting under Chapter VII of the United Nations Charter (e.g. ICTY, ICTR) or an international tribunal acting on behalf of the international community in a similar manner (e.g. ICC acting upon a referral from the Security Council), it would be difficult to argue that the case is predominantly political or military'.

[253] Repository of Practice, 36, 'Scenario D'.

[254] Ibid, 38, 'Scenario D', 'Case 1'.

[255] Ibid, 38, 'Scenario D', 'Case 2'.

[256] Ibid.

[257] Resolution No AGN/63/RES/9, 'Application of Article 3 of the Constitution in the context of serious violations of international humanitarian law', INTERPOL General Assembly, 63rd session (Rome, 1994).

a proper analysis in accordance with Article 34(3) of the IRPD.[258] This means that the nature of certain offences, such as compelling a prisoner of war or civilian to serve in the forces of a hostile power,[259] will be considered 'pure' military offences.[260] As international criminal law has developed, INTERPOL has given more weight to its 'obligations under international law' pursuant to Article 34(3)(e) of the IRPD. In 1997, 'recognizing that genocide is a crime which is condemned by the whole international community', the INTERPOL General Assembly recommended cooperation with the International Criminal Tribunal for Rwanda.[261] The UN Security Council then called on States 'to cooperate with the International Criminal Police Organization (ICPO-Interpol) in apprehending and transferring persons indicted by the ICTY and the ICTR'.[262] In 2003, the INTERPOL General Assembly approved a cooperation agreement between INTERPOL and the Special Court for Sierra Leone,[263] and, in 2004, it approved a cooperation agreement with the International Criminal Court.[264] The preamble to the resolution which approved the ICC cooperation agreement unequivocally states that 'the crimes which come within the jurisdiction of the International Criminal Court also fall within the aims of the Organization as defined in Articles 2 and 3 of the Constitution'. In effect, this means that if the ICC requests the publication of a red notice for a crime under the Rome Statute of the ICC, the General Secretariat is of the view that the 'identity of the source of the data' (ie, the ICC) and the 'nature of the offence' (ie, a serious international crime) mean that Article 3 does not apply 'unless there is any specific doubt in relation to a particular item of data'.[265]

INTERPOL has found it more difficult to assess requests concerning serious international crimes that are sent from NCBs, as opposed to international entities. As such, and in light of the 'increase in the number of requests forwarded through INTERPOL channels concerning genocide, crimes against humanity

[258] See: Repository of Practice, 36. The report mentioned is Report AGN/63/RAP No 13 but INTERPOL has not made this report publicly available.

[259] Statute of the ICTY, Art 2(e).

[260] Gottlieb, Y, 'Article 3 of Interpol's Constitution: Balancing International Police Cooperation with the Prohibition on Engaging in Political, Military, Religious, or Racial Activities' (2011) 23 *Florida Journal of International Law* 135–86 at 157, referring to Report AGN/63/RAP No 13.

[261] Resolution No AGN/66/RES/10, 'Co-operation in searching for persons accused of serious violations of international humanitarian law committed in Rwanda and neighbouring countries between 1st October 1990 and 31st December 1994', INTERPOL General Assembly, 66th session (New Delhi, 1997).

[262] UN Security Council Resolution 1503, 28 August 2003, operative para 4.

[263] Resolution No AG-2003-RES-08, 'Co-operation Agreement between the International Criminal Police Organization – Interpol and the Special Court for Sierra Leone', INTERPOL General Assembly, 72nd session (Benidorm, 2003).

[264] Resolution AG-2004-RES-16, 'Co-operation Agreement with the International Criminal Court', INTERPOL General Assembly, 73rd session (Cancún, 2004).

[265] Repository of Practice, 9, 'Scenario D'.

and war crimes' and 'the proliferation of disputes between member countries concerning the processing of such requests', the INTERPOL General Assembly decided that the Organisation would not process requests concerning genocide, crimes against humanity and war crimes 'where the request concerns a national of another member country, and that other member country, upon being informed by the General Secretariat of the request, protests against the request within thirty days'.[266] The General Secretariat was asked to implement the resolution through the relevant procedures (as is required by Article 26(a) of the INTERPOL Constitution). It is unclear how the General Secretariat implemented this in practice, but the Repository of Practice refers to Resolution No AG-2010-RES-10 as a 'policy on war crimes' and notes that this 'policy' was applied in respect of diffusions sent by an NCB seeking the arrest of nationals of another country for, inter alia, 'crimes against the international community', which INTERPOL determined 'falls within the general category of war crimes'. In that case, because a protest was submitted in respect of the diffusions, INTERPOL concluded that the data could not be recorded in its databases.[267]

This 'policy on war crimes' is a blunt attempt to grapple with the complex law of universal jurisdiction that can arise in cases of serious international crimes.[268] A concern about the misuse of universal jurisdiction should not, however, override the proper consideration of all relevant elements pursuant to Article 34(3) of the IRPD. The 'protests' of another NCB should simply be one consideration of many (see Article 34(3)(d) which expressly provides that the Commission should consider 'the position expressed by another [NCB]') that informs INTERPOL's analysis of whether or not the relevant data complies with its rules. To make a decision on the sole basis of whether or not a member protests, allows the internal politics of a member to dictate whether or not INTERPOL will process data, thereby compromising the Organisation's neutrality.

iii. Religious Character

In order to uphold 'fundamental principles of international human rights, notably the right to freedom of religion'[269] (as reflected in Article 18 of the UDHR and in the Declaration on the Elimination of All Forms of Intolerance and of Discrimination Based on Religion or Belief),[270] and to reflect extradition law

[266] Resolution No AG-2010-RES-10, 'Co-operation with new requests concerning genocide, crimes against humanity and war crimes', INTERPOL General Assembly, 79th session (Doha, 2010).

[267] Repository of Practice, 39, 'Scenarios D and E'.

[268] See: Bassiouni, CM, 'Universal Jurisdiction for International Crimes: Historical Perspectives and Contemporary Practice' (2001) 42 *Virginia Journal of International Law* 81–162.

[269] Repository of Practice, 40.

[270] Declaration on the Elimination of All Forms of Intolerance and of Discrimination Based on Religion or Belief, proclaimed by UN General Assembly Resolution 36/55 (25 November 1981).

(such as the UN Model Treaty on Extradition),[271] INTERPOL will not undertake an intervention or activity of a 'religious' character.

In considering the 'nature of the offence', the INTERPOL General Assembly has stated that 'practising a prohibited religion', 'recruitment or propaganda for particular religions',[272] and 'belonging to a banned religious group'[273] are 'pure' religious offences. INTERPOL appears to treat the nature of these offences as the decisive element in a determination of whether data is within the scope of Article 3. For instance, a red notice request stated that the individual concerned was wanted for the offence of the 'creation, leadership, participation in religious-extremist, separatist, fundamentalist or other forbidden organization'. INTERPOL concluded that the offence was equivalent to 'membership of a religious organization', which is 'an offence of a religious character by its very nature', so the red notice was not published.[274]

INTERPOL adopts a more nuanced approach when the offence has not been identified by the INTERPOL General Assembly as being 'pure' in nature. It acknowledges, in accordance with international human rights law, that restrictions on freedom of religion can be prescribed by law if 'necessary to protect public safety, order, health or morals or the fundamental rights and freedoms of others'.[275] This adds an interesting dimension because even if INTERPOL is of the view that the nature of the offence is 'purely' religious, it may not attach much weight to this element if the restriction on the right was necessary and proportionate.[276] In respect of 'relative' offences, INTERPOL turns to the predominance test. For instance, if an NCB seeks a red notice in respect of an individual who participated in the bombing of a religious site that caused the death of civilians, it would normally conclude that the seriousness of the crime and the status of the victims prevails over the religious motivation of the individual, so the 'nature of the offence' is predominantly an ordinary law crime.[277]

[271] UN Model Treaty on Extradition (adopted by UN General Assembly on 14 December 1990, amended by UN General Assembly Resolution on 4 February 1998) Doc A/RES/45/116, A/RES/52/88, Art 3(b). The UN Model Treaty on Extradition provides that extradition can be refused if it is believed that the request was made for prosecuting or punishing a person on the basis of his or her religion. See also: Repository of Practice, 40.

[272] Resolution No AGN/53/RES/7, 'Application of Article 3 of the Constitution', INTERPOL General Assembly, 53rd session (Luxembourg, 1984), II.1.

[273] Repository of Practice, 40, fn 62, referring to Resolution No AGN/63/RES 9, 'Application of Article 3 of the Constitution in the context of serious violations of international humanitarian law', INTERPOL General Assembly, 63rd session (Rome, 1994).

[274] Ibid, 42, 'Scenario A'.

[275] See, eg: Declaration on the Elimination of All Forms of Intolerance and of Discrimination Based on Religion or Belief, proclaimed by UN General Assembly Resolution 36/55 (25 November 1981) Art 1(3); ICCPR, Art 18(3).

[276] Repository of Practice, 41.

[277] Ibid, 9, 'Scenario B'.

That being said, the Commission often struggles to apply Article 34(3) of the IRPD in the context of Article 3 of the INTERPOL Constitution, especially when the applicant fails to do so in his or her request. For instance, in Decision No 2017-15, an applicant challenged a green notice (ie, a notice to warn about a person's criminal activities) which concerned the offence of 'CRIMINAL ORGANIZATION/ASSOCIATION/GROUP'. He did so on the basis that, inter alia, 'the case is of a predominantly religious character'.[278] Unfortunately, the applicant focused solely on the 'nature of the offence'. He argued that the data registered against him is 'related to his religion, therefore religiously motivated'.[279] He explained that, after he converted to Islam, he joined many organisations and projects to help Muslims, but he was threatened many times due to his religion so he moved to another country. In response, the NCB explained that the applicant 'is still an active follower of radical Islam and continues to spread the ideas of radical Islam with a view of overthrowing the [...] order', so he 'remains a threat to public safety'.[280] The decision of the Commission leaves much to be desired. First, the Commission's approach is flawed: the Commission (again) conflated the predominance test with the approach in Article 34(3) of the IRPD.[281] Second, when it considered the 'nature of the offence', it did not apply the predominance test. It simply accepted the description of the offence provided by the NCB: 'the offence as described is of a common law character'.[282] This is plainly insufficient: as discussed in detail above in section II.B, deference to an NCB in this regard is (1) an unauthorised delegation of decision-making power contrary to Articles 28(1)(b) and 33(3) of the CCF Statute, Article 22(5) of the IRPD and Article 36 of the INTERPOL Constitution, (2) a breach of the requirement of independence in Article 11(2) of the IRPD, and (3) a breach of Article 2(1) of the INTERPOL Constitution and Article 11(1) of the IRPD. This is, presumably, why the Repository of Practice explicitly states that Article 34(3) of the IRPD 'provides for – indeed requires – the examination and consideration of pertinent facts beyond those explicitly supplied in the request for police cooperation, such as information concerning the background for the request or how it relates to other requests'.[283] Next, the Commission concluded that, because the applicant 'does not appear to be a religious leader', his status was irrelevant. It also placed emphasis on the fact that 'no NCB or other international organization has taken the position that Article 3 has been violated'.[284] Of course, this inverts the element in Article 34(3)(d) of the IRPD, which provides that INTERPOL should

[278] Decision of the Commission, Decision No 2017-15 (October 2017) para 8.
[279] Ibid, para 16.
[280] Ibid, para 20 (redaction in original).
[281] Ibid, para 32.
[282] Ibid, para 26.
[283] Repository of Practice, 8.
[284] Decision of the Commission, Decision No 2017-15 (October 2017) para 27.

examine 'the position expressed by other National Central Bureau …'. It is plainly nonsensical to attribute any weight to the silence of NCBs. Finally, the Commission remarked that 'the offence does not appear to undermine the neutrality of the Organization'.[285] It was on the basis of the foregoing that it concluded the processing of data was compliant with Article 3. Had it properly applied its rules by considering the 'identify of the source of the data' and its 'obligations under international law' and properly assessed the 'nature of the offence', the Commission may very well have come to a different conclusion.

It should be noted that cases involving freedom of religion often raise corresponding questions about freedom of expression. A challenge on the sole basis of freedom of expression would most likely be premised on the application of Article 2 of the INTERPOL Constitution. However, if the offence concerns 'the expression of certain prohibited opinions' – ie, political, military, religious or racial – the INTERPOL General Assembly has stated that these are to be considered 'pure' offences, in respect of which the Organisation cannot process data. In light of this 'long-standing practice in the application of Article 3',[286] INTERPOL diverts from international human rights law in this respect (under which the right to freedom of expression is not absolute).[287] This was, for instance, the position adopted by INTERPOL when an NCB sent red notice requests and circulated diffusions for the arrest of individuals wanted for having produced film material deemed offensive to Islam. INTERPOL considered the broadcasting of the footage the expression of an opinion related to a religious matter, so it denied the requests and deleted the data from its databases.[288]

iv. Racial Character

Like its approach to interventions or activities of a religious character,[289] INTERPOL has stated that its approach to interventions or activities of a racial character 'corresponds with fundamental principles of international human rights', notably the prohibition on racial discrimination,[290] as reflected in Article 2 of the UDHR and the International Convention on the Elimination of All Forms of Racial Discrimination.[291] INTERPOL adopts a broad interpretation of the word

[285] Decision of the Commission, Decision No 2017-15 (October 2017) para 27.

[286] Repository of Practice, 15, 'Scenario A', 'Case 3'.

[287] Eg, Article 19(3) of the ICCPR provides that freedom of expression may be 'subject to certain restrictions' as 'are provided by law and are necessary'. INTERPOL, by contrast, only makes exception if the expression could be considered hate speech or incitement to violence (Repository of Practice, 14 and 15, 'Scenario A', 'Case 3').

[288] Repository of Practice, 15, 'Scenario A', 'Case 3'.

[289] Ibid, 40.

[290] Ibid.

[291] International Convention on the Elimination of All Forms of Racial Discrimination (adopted on 21 December 1965, entered into force on 4 January 1969) 660 UNTS 195.

'racial' on the basis of the definition of 'racial discrimination' in the International Convention on the Elimination of All Forms of Racial Discrimination:

> any distinction, exclusion, restriction or preference based on race, colour, descent, or national or ethnic origin which has the purpose or effect of nullifying or impairing the recognition, enjoyment or exercise, on an equal footing, of human rights and fundamental freedoms in the political, economic, social, cultural or any other field of public life.[292]

In considering the 'nature' of certain offences, the INTERPOL General Assembly has made it clear that 'membership of a racial organization' is a 'pure' offence.[293] However, it is clear from INTERPOL's practice that the Organisation is not concerned with race per se, but rather, with racial discrimination. For instance, INTERPOL did not delete data in respect of a diffusion for an individual wanted for the crime of 'racism, minimization and approval of the genocide committed during the Second World War' because, despite the fact that the offence concerned race, it was an ordinary law crime condemned by various international instruments.[294]

INTERPOL also considers personal data revealing racial or ethnic origin 'particularly sensitive data' pursuant to Article 1(18) of the IRPD. As such, an individual can also challenge the processing of data in INTERPOL's systems on the basis of 'racial elements in the context of police work'.[295] In particular, personal data that reveals 'racial or ethnic origin' can only be processed by INTERPOL if (1) 'relevant and of particularly important criminalistic value for achieving the aims of the Organization and the purposes of the processing [of data]', and (2) 'described objectively and contain[ing] no judgment or discriminatory comments'.[296] For instance, INTERPOL concluded that the terms 'black Muslim extremist' and 'extremists of African origin believing in Islam' used by an NCB in its database were contrary to Article 3 'since a category of suspects cannot be identified by the association of a racial characteristic and a religious one'.[297] It adopts the same approach to the word 'gypsies' and does not allow NCBs to request data through its channels about individuals 'simply because they belong[] to a different ethnic group'.[298]

D. Challenges Specific to Red Notices

We have discussed three general standards of review on which to challenge the processing of data by the Organisation before the Commission – lawfulness,

[292] Ibid, Art 1(1).

[293] Resolution No AGN/53/RES/7, 'Application of Article 3 of the Constitution', INTERPOL General Assembly, 53rd session (Luxembourg, 1984), II.1.

[294] Repository of Practice, 42, 'Scenario B', 'Case 1'.

[295] Ibid, 41, 'Scenario C'.

[296] IRPD, Art 42. See also: Repository of Practice, 41.

[297] Repository of Practice, 42, 'Scenario C', 'Case 2'.

[298] Ibid, 'Case 1', 'Case 5'.

quality and neutrality. An applicant can rely on any of the foregoing arguments if applicable, no matter the form of intervention. However, there are additional provisions which are relevant to particular types of interventions. In Chapter 7, we discussed the many forms of notices available to the Organisation, including, blue, green, yellow, black, purple, orange, stolen work of art notices, and INTERPOL–UN Security Council Special Notices. NCBs and international entities can also circulate diffusions, ie, standardised requests for cooperation and alerts.

Among the notices, the red notice stands out for its impact on individuals. Red notices are published at the request of NCBs or international entities to seek the location of a wanted person and his or her detention, arrest or restriction of movement for the purposes of extradition, surrender, or similar lawful action. If an individual subject to a red notice is located (eg, at an international border), then Article 87 of the IRPD provides that the country where the person has been located must (subject to limitations deriving from national law and applicable international treaties) immediately inform the requesting NCB or international entity and the General Secretariat of the fact that the person has been located, and it may provisionally arrest the wanted person or monitor or restrict his or her movement.[299] Following this process, an extradition procedure typically takes place.

Whilst it is true that INTERPOL does not itself arrest or detain the subject of a red notice, the mere publication of a red notice is capable of impinging on, inter alia, the subject's (1) right to liberty and (2) right to freedom of movement. Indeed, when circulated via the INTERPOL Information System (which can be consulted by NCBs and authorised entities anywhere in the world), the red notice is the Organisation's most powerful tool.[300] As observed by Fair Trials International:

> [t]he Red Notice has been described as a 'wanted poster with teeth', and indeed has significant human impact. A Red Notice will be available to all NCBs and other entities connected to the I-24/7 network, which will be able to cross-check a person's name and identifiers against INTERPOL's databases. … [I]t is at each country's discretion how it acts on a Red Notice or Diffusion, but …, many countries readily arrest people on either basis.[301]

Article 3 of the UDHR (which is of particular relevance to INTERPOL in light of Article 2(1) of the INTERPOL Constitution) provides that '[e]veryone has the right to … liberty'. Article 9 of the UDHR complements Article 3. It provides that '[n]o one shall be subjected to arbitrary arrest … [or] detention'. Articles 3

[299] IRPD, Art 87(a)(ii).

[300] Semmelma, J and Munson, ES, 'INTERPOL Red Notices and Diffusions: Powerful – And Dangerous – Tools of Global Law Enforcement', *National Association of Criminal Defence Lawyers – The Champion* (2014) 28.

[301] Fair Trials International, 'Strengthening respect for human rights; strengthening INTERPOL' (18 November 2013) para 43.

and 9 of the UDHR are given effect in universal and regional treaties.[302] Most notably, Article 9(1) of the ICCPR provides that '[e]veryone has the right to liberty and security of person. No one shall be subjected to arbitrary arrest or detention. No one shall be deprived of his liberty except on such grounds and in accordance with such procedure as are established by law'. In *Diallo*, the ICJ elaborated that Article 9(1) of the ICCPR applies, in principle, to any form of arrest or detention decided upon and carried out by a public authority, whatever its legal basis and the objective being pursued.[303] An arrest or detention may be authorised by domestic law and nonetheless be arbitrary: 'the notion of arbitrariness is not to be equated with "against the law", but must be interpreted more broadly to include elements of inappropriateness, injustice, lack of predictability and due process of law, as well as elements of reasonableness, necessity and proportionality'.[304] Article 9(1) is also not confined to criminal proceedings; it applies, in principle, 'to measures which deprive individuals of their liberty that are taken in the context of an administrative procedure, such as those which may be necessary in order to effect the forcible removal of an alien from the national territory'.[305]

The right to liberty also means that anyone detained or arrested has specific rights, including:

(1) the right to be informed promptly of the reasons for the arrest or detention and the charges against him or her (including full details of the charge, such as the type of offence and elements upon which the accusation is founded);[306]
(2) the right to be brought promptly before a judge or other officer authorised by law to exercise judicial power;[307]
(3) the right to a trial within a reasonable time or to release;[308]
(4) the right to bring *habeas corpus* proceedings (ie, to challenge the legality of detention);[309] and
(5) the right to be treated with humanity and with respect to dignity.[310]

[302] See, eg, ICCPR, Art 9; ECHR, Art 5; ACHR, Art 7; ArCHR, Art 14; ACHPR, Art 6.

[303] *Case concerning Ahmadou Sadio Diallo (Republic of Guinea v Democratic Republic of the Congo)* (Merits, Judgment) [2010] ICJ Rep 639, para 77. See also: UN Human Rights Committee, 'General Comment 35: Article 9 (Liberty and security of person)', UN Doc CCPR/C/GC/35 (16 December 2014) para 5.

[304] UN Human Rights Committee, 'General Comment 35: Article 9 (Liberty and security of person)', UN Doc CCPR/C/GC/35 (16 December 2014) paras 22–3.

[305] *Case concerning Ahmadou Sadio Diallo (Republic of Guinea v Democratic Republic of the Congo)* (Merits, Judgment) [2010] ICJ Rep 639, para 77.

[306] See, eg, ICCPR, Art 9(2); ECHR, Art 5(2); ACHR, Art 7(4). This is reiterated in Article 14(3)(a) of the ICCPR and Article 6(3)(a) of the ECHR.

[307] See, eg, ICCPR, Art 9(3); ECHR, Art 5(3); ACHR, Art 7(5).

[308] See, eg, ICCPR, Art 9(3); ECHR, Art 5(3); ACHR, Art 7.

[309] See, eg, ICCPR, Art 9(4); ECHR, Art 5(4); ACHR, Art 7(6).

[310] See, eg, ICCPR, Art 10(1). This is relevant in respect of attacks on dignity that do not reach the threshold of severity of suffering required by Article 7 of the ICCPR.

The right to liberty is clearly threatened by the publication of a red notice. In practice:

> [m]any people will only discover they are subject to a Red Notice or Diffusion when they are arrested. This can be a devastating experience, as Ilya Katsnelson, a US Citizen, found out when he was arrested at gunpoint in Germany. He spent 50 days in detention before being allowed to return to Denmark. Such periods of detention are not unusual. Indeed, Henk Tepper, a Canadian potato farmer, spent a year detained in Lebanon in appalling conditions, as a result of a Red Notice issued by Algeria in connection with an allegedly substandard consignment of potatoes.[311]

The right to freedom of movement is also impacted by the publication of a red notice, a fact which has been explicitly acknowledged by the Commission on multiple occasions: '[w]hile INTERPOL correctly asserts that a Red Notice is no more than a request for cooperation with a view to extradition, it has serious consequences for the individual concerned. If the Notice is not justified, then an individual's right to freedom of movement … is unjustifiably restricted.[312] In practice:

> [a] person who knows that they are subject to a Red Notice is likely to refrain from travelling for fear of arrest and detention when passing international border points. Even within the Schengen area, the space within the European Union in which border controls are abolished, an individual may hesitate to travel for fear that contact with authorities might lead to an arrest.
>
> Many national authorities will also often refuse visas to those subject to a Red Notice, sometimes severely restricting the freedom of movement of the individual concerned. Magda Osipova (not her real name), an Israeli citizen and successful entrepreneur from Russia, has spent several years unable to visit her daughter in the US because her visa has been refused due to a Red Notice, based on fraud allegations which she maintains are the product of local corruption. She has, as a result, missed seeing her granddaughter growing up.[313]

Freedom of movement is a right guaranteed in Article 13 of the UDHR, which is of particular relevance to INTERPOL in light of Article 2(1) of the INTERPOL Constitution. Article 13 of the UDHR provides that '1. Everyone has the right to freedom of movement and residence within the borders of each State. 2. Everyone has the right to leave any country, including his own, and to return to his country'. Article 13 of the UDHR is reflected in universal and regional human

[311] Fair Trials International, 'Strengthening respect for human rights; strengthening INTERPOL' (18 November 2013) para 44.

[312] Hawkes, B, Chairman of the Commission (Speech at the 82nd INTERPOL General Assembly session, 21–24 October 2013). See also: Frayssinet, J, CCF Member and Rapporteur (Speech at the 83rd INTERPOL General Assembly session, 3–7 November 2014).

[313] Fair Trials International, 'Strengthening respect for human rights; strengthening INTERPOL' (November 2013) paras 45–6.

rights treaties.[314] Any limitation on the right to freedom of movement must be necessary and proportionate. The ICCPR expressly stipulates that the right to leave any country and move lawfully within the territory of a State cannot be subject to any restrictions 'except those which are provided by law, are necessary to protect national security, public order (ordre public), public health or morals or the rights and freedoms of others, and are consistent with the other rights recognized in the [ICCPR]'.[315] Red notices must, therefore, be issued with due regard to the principles of necessity and proportionality.

Against the foregoing background, the following sections consider a few of the most common grounds on which to challenge a red notice (aside from those grounds of general application discussed in section II.A–C above).

i. Minimum Criteria

Article 83(1) of the IRPD specifies the 'minimum criteria' that must be satisfied before a red notice may be published (and maintained)[316] by the General Secretariat. The first minimum criterion is that the offence must be 'a serious ordinary-law crime' (ie, more than an 'ordinary law crime' as required by Article 2(2) of the INTERPOL Constitution). The Commission has not been definitive about what constitutes a 'serious' ordinary law crime, but it makes an assessment based on 'the acts for which the individual is subject to data in INTERPOL's files (for example, the type of criminality or the elements characterizing his/her effective participation in the acts he/she is accused of)'.[317] To assist in this assessment, Article 83(1)(a)(i) of the IRPD specifies categories of offences for which red notices cannot be published: (1) offences that raise controversial issues in various countries relating to behavioural or cultural norms, (2) offences that relate to family/private matters, and (3) offences that originate from a violation of laws or regulations of an administrative nature or derive from private disputes, unless the criminal activity is aimed at facilitating a serious crime or is suspected of being connected to organised crime.[318] The General Secretariat keeps an updated (non-exhaustive) list of specific offences that fall within these categories.[319]

The phrase 'controversial issues' in Article 83(1)(a)(i) of the IRPD is broad and allows the Commission to exercise discretion. For instance, in a child abduction case, the Commission was of the view that 'parental child abduction'

[314] Eg, ICCPR, Art 12; Protocol No 4 to the ECHR, Art 2; ACHR, Art 22; ACHPR, Art 12.

[315] ICCPR, Art 12(3).

[316] IRPD, Art 81(3)(c).

[317] Decision of the Commission, Decision No 2019-08 (July 2019) paras 68–9 (emphasis in original).

[318] See also: Smith, A, 'Interpol red notices – another small step towards transparency?' *The Law of Nations* (22 May 2017): 'the [CCF] examines carefully the evidence adduced by a country in support of a notice, in order to determine the merits of a defence argument to the effect that the notice has been issued in response to a civil rather than a criminal dispute'.

[319] IRPD, Art 83(1)(a)(i).

offences are not necessarily 'controversial offences', even though some countries will not act upon a red notice issued for this type of offence. However, in most child abduction cases, the Commission will not publish a red notice on the basis that it concerns 'family/private matters'. That being said, the Commission is of the view that, if there is a 'violent context in which the abduction took place' then the offence is neither 'controversial' nor a 'family/private' matter, but in the realm of a 'serious ordinary-law crime'.[320] In response to a decision by the Commission on this basis, an applicant submitted an application for revision which included evidence that the abduction did not take place in a 'violent context' and a judicial decision which showed that he had been granted custody by the courts in one member country (whereas his spouse had been granted custody in the courts of another member country). The Commission was, therefore, of the view that the case concerned 'a dispute between member countries, which derives from competing and contradicting national court decisions'.[321] The Commission concluded that it was 'not the appropriate forum to address situations of competing custodial disputes' and deleted the red notice on the basis that it was an offence related to 'private family matters' for the purposes of Article 83(1)(a)(i).[322]

The third category of offences, 'offences that originate from a violation of laws or regulations of an administrative nature or derive from private disputes, unless the criminal activity is aimed at facilitating a serious crime or is suspected of being connected to organized crime', has been the subject of a number of decisions of the Commission. In Decision No 2018-04, the applicant challenged a red notice on grounds of, inter alia, non-compliance with Article 83(1)(a)(i) of the IRPD.[323] The applicant argued that the alleged criminal activity upon which the notice was founded 'derives from a private commercial dispute' and allegations of criminality only occurred as 'retaliation' for arbitration proceedings.[324] The Commission, considering the 'genuine nature of the dispute', concluded that the information provided by the NCB in response to the applicant's request was 'imprecise', and the link between the applicant and the alleged criminal activities was not properly clarified.[325] As is common in complex cases, the Commission did not make a conclusive pronouncement on compliance with Article 83(1)(a)(i), but concluded that all of the elements of the case, including its 'doubts identified on the link of the case with a private dispute', meant that the data was not compliant with its rules.[326]

[320] Decision of the Commission (29 March 2017). A copy of this decision is in the authors' files.
[321] Decision of the Commission (31 January 2018) para 41. A copy of this decision is in the authors' files.
[322] Ibid, para 42.
[323] Decision of the Commission, Decision No 2018-04 (January 2018) para 14.
[324] Ibid, paras 14 and 23.
[325] Ibid, paras 42–3.
[326] Ibid, para 64.

Unhelpfully, the Commission is inconclusive on whether a criminal act perpetrated in the course of a commercial relationship can be identified as being 'criminal' in itself for the purposes of Article 83(1)(a)(i) of the IRPD. It might be suggested that the answer, on first principles, is 'yes'. If a given allegation of, for example, fraud or bribery in the course of a commercial relationship would ordinarily attract the involvement of 'criminal police authorities', there seems to be no reason why the act of publishing a red notice in relation to such an act would be inconsistent with the aim in Article 2(1) of the INTERPOL Constitution of ensuring the 'widest possible mutual assistance between all criminal police authorities'. Consequently, it might be said that INTERPOL impliedly possesses the power to issue such red notices, and that Article 83(1)(a)(i) should be read as a specification, and not a modification, of its competence, instructively demonstrating the doctrines of speciality and implied powers at work.

In Decision No 2018-03, the CCF questioned whether a red notice based on the offence of 'uttering unfunded cheques' was compliant with Article 83(1)(a)(i).[327] The CCF reasoned that, although the offence of 'uttering unfunded cheques' was a criminal offence in the country requesting the red notice, such acts would 'probably not be recognized as an extraditable offence in many other national systems, where the lack of dual criminality would prevent national authorities to act upon requests for police cooperation based on this offence'.[328] It also considered Article 35 of the IRPD which provides that, prior to the recording of data in a police database, the NCB must ensure that the data is 'of interest for the purposes of international police cooperation'.[329] The Commission was of the view that, because many countries would consider the inability to pay a debt or to fulfil a contractual obligation as a civil matter simpliciter, the publication of a red notice for an offence of 'uttering unfunded cheques' 'may not, in most instances, lead in practice to actual international police co-operation'.[330] Although the CCF chose (again) to consider the entire case before coming to a conclusion (merely observing that the foregoing 'raised reservations as to the compliance of the data challenged'),[331] the principle of law to be gleaned from the CCF's reasoning is that, were an offence not regarded as a criminal offence by a sufficient number of INTERPOL's members, data processing activities with respect to such offences would fall outside INTERPOL's competence. That being said, in another case, the Commission was of the view that, where an applicant was convicted of the same criminal acts in five different cases involving different amounts of unfunded cheques, it 'may illustrate a fraudulent scheme or fraud'.[332]

[327] Ibid, para 4.
[328] Ibid, para 29.
[329] See also: Article 83(1)(a)(iii) of the IRPD which states that the request must be of interest for the purposes of international police cooperation.
[330] Decision of the Commission, Decision No 2018-03 (January 2018) para 30.
[331] Ibid, para 31.
[332] Decision of the Commission, Decision No 2018-02 (January 2018) para 32.

In more recent decisions, INTERPOL has adopted a slightly more nuanced stance in respect of unfunded cheques. First, it appears that the INTERPOL General Secretariat has set a 'minimum threshold' for whether it will even consider the publication of a red notice for unfunded cheques: a total amount of at least US$10,000 (a rather arbitrary number) or 'the issuance of multiple cheques on several occasions in a repetitive manner, regardless of the amount of the cheques'.[333] Second, the Commission has also acknowledged the legal basis on which it refuses to issue red notices for unfunded cheques, eg, Article 11 of the ICCPR.[334] It was on this basis that the Commission decided in Decision No 2019-01 that 'the mere act of issuing an unfunded cheque where no criminal intent has been demonstrated does not meet the criteria of a "serious ordinary-law crime"' and recommended that the red notice be deleted.[335]

The second minimum criterion that must be satisfied is that (1) if the person is sought for prosecution, a red notice will only be published if the conduct constituting the offence is punishable by a maximum deprivation of liberty of at least two years (or a more serious penalty), or (2) if the person is sought to serve a sentence, he/she must be 'sentenced to at least six months' imprisonment and/or there [must be] at least six months of the sentence remaining to be served'.[336]

The General Secretariat can override both minimum criteria (ie, a serious ordinary law crime and the penalty threshold) if it considers that the publication of the red notice would be of 'particular importance to international police cooperation'.[337] However, it is difficult to imagine many circumstances in which this would be justified. If the request to publish a red notice contains several offences, the red notice may be published for all offences provided that at least one offence satisfies the minimum criteria in Article 83(1)(a) of the IRPD (and the other conditions for publishing a red notice are met).[338]

ii. Minimum Data

Article 83(2) of the IRPD specifies the 'minimum data' that must be provided before a red notice may be published (and maintained)[339] by the General Secretariat. The identity particulars that must be provided are set out in Article 83(2)(a). Of course, an applicant can and should challenge a red notice if his or her identity particulars are incorrect. However, this is more likely to result

333 Decision of the Commission, Decision No 2019-01 (January-February 2019) para 10.

334 Article 11 of the ICCPR provides that '[n]o one shall be imprisoned merely on the ground of inability to fulfil a contractual obligation'.

335 Decision of the Commission, Decision No 2019-01 (January-February 2019) para 10.

336 IRPD, Art 83(1)(a)(ii).

337 Ibid, Art 83(1)(b).

338 Ibid, Art 83(1)(c).

339 Ibid, Art 81(3)(c).

in the correction of the data (on which, see section II.B above), rather than the wholesale deletion of the red notice.

More pertinent is Article 83(2)(b) of the IRPD which requires that 'sufficient judicial data' be provided. 'Judicial data' includes a 'summary of facts of the case, which shall provide a succinct and clear description of the criminal activities of the wanted person, including the time and location of the alleged criminal activity'.[340] Pursuant to Article 83(2)(b)(i), in early 2017, the Commission elaborated that the summary of facts in a red notice must provide '[c]oncrete elements characterizing effective participation of an individual to the acts he is accused of'.[341] It rowed back slightly from this position a few months later, requiring only sufficient information 'to indicate the possible effective and personal participation of the Applicant to the criminal acts of which he was accused'.[342] In the latter decision, an applicant had challenged the publication of a red notice on the basis of, inter alia, a lack of evidentiary basis. The Commission observed that, in the red notice, the 'key element' concerning the applicant's possible intent to commit the criminal activity in question was not indicated, the main person the applicant was accused of conspiring with had not been interrogated, and the investigation showed a chain of events 'based on assumptions'.[343] It observed that these elements 'raised doubts' as to the 'sufficiency of elements of effective participation', and it ultimately concluded that the data was not compliant with INTERPOL's rules.[344] In another decision, Decision No 2019-09, the Commission was of the view that 'potential minor discrepancies … are insignificant for the general coherence of the summary of facts, which is necessarily and by nature an abridged and concise statement and which cannot reflect comprehensively the whole factual context of the case'.[345] The Commission is clearly correct in noting that the summary is not intended to be comprehensive, but it can hardly be said that a summary is 'succinct and clear' if the information is incorrect.

Judicial data also includes the charge(s), the law(s) covering the offence, the maximum penalty possible, sentence imposed or sentence remaining to be served, and reference to a valid arrest warrant or judicial decision having the same effect.[346] In Decision No 2017-01, the applicant argued that there was simply no charge on which to base the red notice. In response to questions from the Commission, the requesting NCB replied that enquiries against the accused were ongoing and extradition proceedings had not been undertaken. In light of this information, the Commission concluded that the red notice was 'premature' and the red notice

[340] Ibid, Art 83(2)(b)(i).

[341] Decision of the Commission, Decision No 2017-01 (March 2017) para 12.

[342] Decision of the Commission, Decision No 2017-14 (October 2017) para 31 (emphasis added). See also: Decision of the Commission, Decision No 2018-01 (January 2018) which appears to either concern the exact same facts and issues or replicate Decision No 2017-14 (October 2017) with slightly different material redacted.

[343] Decision of the Commission, Decision No 2017-14 (October 2017) paras 30–5.

[344] Ibid, paras 35 and 71.

[345] Decision of the Commission, Decision No 2019-09 (July 2019) para 39.

[346] IRPD, Art 83(2)(b)(ii)–(v).

was deleted.[347] The CCF has also stated that, although the IRPD only requires a 'reference' to a valid arrest warrant in Article 83(2)(b)(v), it views receipt of a copy of the arrest warrant as an essential condition in order to independently assess 'whether information concerning the legal basis of searches for people recorded in INTERPOL's files was accurate and up-to-date'.[348] The CCF has revealed the reason for its diligence: it has found that, upon insisting on receipt of a copy of the relevant arrest warrant, some NCBs cancelled their requests on the basis that the arrest warrant was no longer valid.[349]

The requirement of a valid arrest warrant in the context of a red notice request is indispensable because a red notice is published in order to seek the location of a wanted person and his/her detention, arrest or restriction of movement for the purposes of extradition, surrender, or similar lawful action.[350] As discussed above, the mere publication of a red notice threatens the right to liberty of the person concerned, and the general approach under international human rights law is that persons may be arrested, detained or otherwise deprived of their liberty only on grounds established by law.[351] The principle of lawfulness is breached, for example, where the production of an arrest warrant is prescribed by law, but a person is arrested without a warrant. For example, in *Luyeye Magana ex-Philibert v Zaire*, the UN Human Rights Committee stated that Zaire's arrest and detention of Luyeye Magana ex-Philibert 'without any warrant of arrest or summons' had subjected him to arbitrary arrest and detention.[352]

The IRPD only contains limited procedural safeguards in this respect. Article 84 provides that a requesting NCB must provide assurances that:

(1) the authority which issued the arrest warrant or handed down the judicial decision has the necessary power;
(2) the red notice request has been coordinated with the relevant authorities responsible for extradition, and assurances have been given that extradition will be sought upon arrest of the person, in conformity with national laws and/or the applicable bilateral and multilateral treaties;
(3) if the arrest warrant has not been issued by a judicial authority, the laws of the requesting country or the rules governing the operation of the international entity provide for a mechanism of appeal before a judicial authority.[353]

When INTERPOL's rules and practices are contrasted with that which is required under international human rights law, it is clear that INTERPOL does not

[347] Decision of the Commission, Decision No 2017-01 (March 2017) para 28.
[348] CCF, 'Annual Activity Report of the CCF for 2011', CCF/83/12/d382, para 72.
[349] Ibid, para 74.
[350] Contrast with the purpose of a blue notice, see: Decision of the Commission, Decision No 2018-10 (April 2018) para 44.
[351] UDHR, Arts 3 and 9; ICCPR, Art 9; ECHR, Art 5; ACHR, Art 7; ArCHR, Art 14; ACHPR, Art 6.
[352] *Luyeye Magana ex-Philibert v Zaire*, Communication No 90/1981, UN Doc CCPR/C/OP/2 (21 July 1983) para 7.2.
[353] IRPD, Art 84(1)–(3).

adequately protect the subjects of red notices from arbitrary arrest or detention, or unjustified restrictions on their freedom of movement.

First, to ensure the principle of lawfulness is not breached, INTERPOL's rules should require the provision of a valid arrest warrant to INTERPOL before it publishes a red notice (ie, it should not be best practice alone). If INTERPOL publishes and/or maintains a red notice that is demonstrably not underpinned by a valid arrest warrant, INTERPOL will prima facie breach an individual's right to freedom of movement (and, therefore, also breach Article 2(1) of the INTERPOL Constitution). Indeed, in the context of INTERPOL's publication and maintenance of a red notice despite the prohibition of double jeopardy in EU law, the Administrative Court of Wiesbaden noted that:

> [i]f Interpol, despite the prohibition of double jeopardy, does not refrain from transmitting the data of the red notice to all the Member States and does not ensure that the data is erased without delay, the referring court has considerable doubts regarding the reliability under data protection law of the International Organisation 'Interpol'. This unreliability ultimately leads to the question of whether, due to the lack of appropriate safeguards at Interpol, the Member States should not refrain entirely in this respect from cooperating with Interpol, as this is the only way of safeguarding freedom of movement within the context of European Union … As there is quite clearly no coordination of red notices within the EU and in the absence of a uniform regulatory framework, the freedom of the citizens of the Member States can only be ensured through withdrawal from Interpol.[354]

In addition, if INTERPOL publishes a red notice, but the arrest warrant underpinning the red notice is invalid, it may have implications for INTERPOL's obligation not to aid or assist in the commission of an internationally wrongful act. By way of background, in extradition proceedings between two countries, the requesting country remains responsible for ensuring the valid legal basis for detention in the requested country, as observed by the ECtHR in *Stephens v Malta (No 1)*: '[b]y setting in motion a request for the applicant's detention pending extradition, the responsibility lay with Malta to ensure that the arrest warrant and extradition request were valid as a matter of Maltese law, both substantive and procedural'.[355] This approach to responsibility aligns with

[354] *WS v Federal Republic of Germany*, Case C-505/19, 'Request for a preliminary ruling' (3 July 2019) para 27.

[355] *Stephens v Malta (No 1)* [2009] ECHR 663, para 52. This approach is also recognised in other areas of international law. Compare, in this regard, the reasoning applied by the International Tribunal for the Law of the Sea ('ITLOS') in *The M/V "Norstar" Case (Panama v Italy)*: '[i]n the view of the Tribunal, the above facts and circumstances indicate that, while the arrest of the *M/V "Norstar"* took place as a result of judicial cooperation between Italy and Spain, the Decree of Seizure and the request for its enforcement by Italy were central to the eventual arrest of the vessel. It is clear that without the Decree of Seizure, there would have been no arrest … Accordingly, the Tribunal finds that the dispute before it concerns the rights and obligations of Italy and that its decision would affect the legal interest of Italy (*The M/V "Norstar" Case (Panama v Italy)* (Preliminary Objections, Judgment of 4 November 2016) ITLOS Reports 2016, paras 165 and 167).

the finding by the ICJ in the *Arrest Warrant* case that the 'mere international circulation' of an arrest warrant could constitute a violation of the requesting country's international obligations.[356] Thus, if an individual is deprived of his liberty pursuant to an invalid arrest warrant with the aid and assistance of a red notice published by INTERPOL, INTERPOL may have aided and assisted in the commission of an internationally wrongful act.

Second, Article 84(3) of the IRPD is problematic because INTERPOL should only accept arrest warrants issued by judicial authorities. This is, for instance, the approach adopted in the EU in the context of a European arrest warrant ('EAW').[357] The EAW system entails a 'dual level of protection for procedural rights and fundamental rights': that is, judicial protection must be provided at the first level, at which a national arrest warrant is adopted, and judicial protection must be afforded at the second level, at which an EAW is issued.[358] Advocate General Campos Sánchez-Bordona has explained that the EAW 'must be based on a national arrest warrant ('NAW') issued by a judicial authority in the strict sense'.[359] The reason for this approach is to ensure that the authority which issues the national arrest warrant and the EAW is 'capable of exercising its responsibilities objectively, taking into account all incriminatory and exculpatory evidence, without being exposed to the risk that its decision-making power be subject to external directions or instructions'.[360] Of course, in some countries, police authorities and prosecutors are empowered by law to order the arrest or detention of a person in certain circumstances (eg, to prevent an individual from committing an offence or to prevent a suspect from fleeing). However, as established by EU legislation and jurisprudence, an arrest warrant issued by a police authority or public prosecutor cannot underpin an EAW. This is because arresting or detaining a person in his or her place of residence is significantly less harmful than arresting and transferring a person away from his or her home, job and family.[361] By the same logic, an arrest warrant issued by a judicial authority, in the strict sense, should always underpin an INTERPOL red notice, especially because INTERPOL does not offer any judicial protection when it issues a red notice.

Article 84(3) of the IRPD is also problematic from a practical perspective. It provides that INTERPOL will accept an arrest warrant issued by a non-judicial authority where 'the laws of the requesting country … provide for a mechanism of

[356] *Arrest Warrant of 11 April 2000 (Democratic Republic of the Congo v Belgium)* (Judgment) [2002] ICJ Rep 3, para 71.

[357] Council Framework Decision of 13 June 2002 on the European arrest warrant and the surrender procedures between Member States (2002/584/JHA), Art 6.

[358] *Bob Dogi v Hungary*, Case C-241/15, ECLI:EU:C:2016:385, para 56.

[359] Opinion of Advocate General Campos Sánchez-Bordona, Joined Cases C-566/19 PPU and C-626/19 PPU, ECLI:EU:C:2019:1012, para 65.

[360] *Minister for Justice and Equality v OG and PI*, Joined Cases C-508/18 and C-82/19 PPU, ECLI:EU:C:2019:456, para 74.

[361] See: Fair Trials International, 'Beyond Surrender: Putting human rights at the heart of the European Arrest Warrant' (28 June 2018).

appeal before a judicial authority'. However, in some countries, an individual can only appeal an arrest warrant issued by a non-judicial authority if present in the relevant country (ie, after extradition). In early 2017, a national of the Kingdom of the Netherlands was arrested in Venezuela on the basis of a red notice published by INTERPOL at the request of the NCB in Curaçao. The applicant subsequently submitted a request to the Commission in which he argued, inter alia, that the Public Prosecutor's Office in Curaçao, which had issued an arrest warrant against him, was not independent from the executive. He also emphasised that there was no possibility for him to appeal the arrest warrant issued by the Public Prosecutor's Office until he was in Curaçao. The requesting NCB submitted that (1) the Public Prosecutor's Office was independent, and (2) once arrested in Curaçao, the applicant would be brought before a judge within two days and have access to all available legal avenues under Curaçao's law to challenge the arrest warrant and his pre-trial detention. The requesting NCB's explanations were deemed sufficient by the Commission.[362] The applicant spent 21 months in detention before he was extradited to Curaçao. However, during his detention in Venezuela neither the lawfulness of his detention nor the lawfulness of the arrest warrant was reviewed because he was not physically in Curaçao. Curaçao's unwillingness to review the lawfulness of his detention or the lawfulness of the arrest warrant prolonged the applicant's detention. It is, of course, accepted that an individual detained with a view to extradition can be detained even though it is not reasonably considered necessary.[363] However, there must be sufficient guarantees against arbitrariness.[364] If the applicant's prolonged detention was arbitrary, it is arguable that INTERPOL aided and assisted the Kingdom of the Netherlands in the commission of an internationally wrongful act.[365]

The failings in INTERPOL's rules are exacerbated by the approach of the Commission when an applicant challenges the validity of an arrest warrant. The plain reading of Article 83(2)(b)(v) suggests that, if an applicant is able to show that the arrest warrant which underpins the notice is invalid, then the red notice should be deleted on the basis that the data is not compliant with INTERPOL's rules. However, INTERPOL has proved unwilling to engage with questions concerning whether the arrest warrant is valid, particularly where the NCB that requested the red notice confirms the validity of the arrest warrant. It defers entirely to the NCB. This occurred in a recent request to the Commission. The applicant, in addition to reasoned submissions, provided an expert opinion from a retired judge of the highest court in the country that had issued the arrest warrant. The judge explained why the arrest warrant issued against the applicant was issued in violation of national law. In the Commission's consultations with the relevant

[362] Decision of the Commission (27 October 2017). A copy of this decision is in the authors' files.
[363] *Chahal v United Kingdom* [1996] ECHR 54, para 112.
[364] Ibid, para 119.
[365] Curaçao is a constituent part of the Kingdom of the Netherlands.

NCB, the NCB 'confirmed the validity of the proceedings and … arrest warrant'.[366] The Commission concluded that '*a priori*, the explanations provided by the NCB were sufficient to clarify the situation and that the information provided by the Applicant was not sufficient to establish that the arrest warrant based on which the Notice was issued is not valid'.[367] If evidence from a respected jurist of the relevant country was not persuasive, it is difficult to foresee on what grounds an applicant could forcefully challenge the validity of an arrest warrant.

When an arrest warrant issued by a non-judicial authority is challenged, the Commission is simply of the view that it must be 'particularly attentive to the quality of the elements characterizing his/her active involvement in the acts of which he/she is accused'.[368] It is puzzling that the Commission does not acknowledge that an arrest warrant issued by, for instance, a prosecutor's office controlled by the executive may not provide adequate procedural safeguards. The Commission adopts this approach despite the fact that UN Human Rights Committee, the ECtHR and the Court of Justice of the EU each recognise that prosecuting authorities can lack impartiality and independence.[369]

In light of the foregoing difficulties, to facilitate the best possible challenge on the basis of the criteria in Article 83(2)(b) of the IRPD (and to overcome the deference of the Commission to the requesting NCB), it is suggested that applicants should adduce documentation from other members of INTERPOL, particularly from the courts of other members, which suggest the data is not 'sufficient'. For instance, the CCF held that where 'three INTERPOL member countries have successfully now declined to cooperate on this case, due to issues linked to the evidentiary basis and the coherence of the accusations, which have not been addressed or clarified by the … authorities', this raised 'serious concerns as to the overall coherence of the charges and as to the effective personal participation of the Applicant and his father … to criminal acts, hindering the possibility of actual international police cooperation'.[370] In light of these new concerns, the Commission found the data not to be compliant with its rules. The Commission was, however, less receptive to evidence of a settlement in a civil case that concerned the same issues in the criminal case, observing that 'civil matters indeed do not have a systematic bearing on criminal matters, especially when they are rendered in another jurisdiction'.[371]

[366] Decision of the Commission (2 July 2019) para 27. A copy of this decision is in the authors' files.
[367] Ibid, para 36.
[368] CCF, 'Annual Activity Report of the CCF for 2011', CCF/83/12/d382, para 72.
[369] See, for instance: UN Human Rights Committee, *Vladimir Kulomin v Hungary*, Communication No 521/1992, UN Doc CCPR/C/50/D/521/1992 (6 May 1992) para 11.3; *Huber v Switzerland* [1990] ECHR 25; *Minister for Justice and Equality v OG and PI*, Joined Cases C-508/18 and C-82/19 PPU, ECLI:EU:C:2019:456.
[370] Decision of the Commission, Decision No 2019-06 (April 2019) paras 39 and 41 (redactions in original).
[371] Decision of the Commission, Decision No 2019-08 (July 2019) para 59.

iii. Purpose of a Red Notice

Notices and diffusions are published on the basis of explicit purposes. The purposes vary depending on the type of intervention concerned, but are summarised in Article 10(2) of the IRPD. A red notice may only be published 'in order to seek the location of a wanted person and his/her detention, arrest or restriction of movement for the purpose of extradition, surrender, or similar lawful action'.[372] The Commission has emphasised that the purpose 'is not to obtain the transfer of the person in order to assist in an investigation or give evidence in proceedings'.[373] If the purpose of the red notice has been achieved, then the red notice should be cancelled by the General Secretariat.[374]

Many applicants argue that, where a country refuses to extradite (or the country would, in theory, because it does not extradite its own nationals) then the purpose has been achieved and the red notice should be deleted. This argument has little impact with the Commission. In Decision No 2018-04, the Attorney General of Country B declined the extradition request from Country A on the basis that the dual criminality criteria were not satisfied in the case. The Commission was of the view that, because 'Country A's authorities have established their willingness to seek the Applicant's extradition, wherever this would be a legally available option … the specific situation in Country B would not preclude Country A's authorities from later requesting the extradition of the Applicant from a different country where he could be arrested'.[375] Similarly, when Jordan refused to extradite an applicant, the Commission observed that such a rejection is an 'insufficient reason for the revocation of the Red Notice', and its refusal to extradite 'does not in itself challenge that the Notice has yet to achieve its purpose, and which may indeed be achieved in the future within the limits of lawful police search'.[376]

Relatedly, the General Secretariat is required to cancel a notice under Article 81(3)(d) of the IRPD if the NCB or international entity that requested the notice 'obtains data allowing it to carry out the required action but has not taken any steps to this end and, after being consulted, has not provided reasonable grounds for its lack of action'.[377] The principal mischief that Article 81(3)(d) is intended to address was articulated by the CCF in its Annual Activity Report of 2009: '[w]hen processing individual requests, the Commission found that some countries did not appear to seek the extradition of the subjects of red notices issued at their request, although there was significant evidence to show that the

[372] IRPD, Art 82. See also: IRPD, Art 10(2)(a).
[373] Decision of the Commission, Decision No 2017-01 (March 2017) para 29.
[374] IRPD, Art 81(3)(a).
[375] Decision of the Commission, Decision No 2018-04 (January 2018) para 54.
[376] Decision of the Commission, Decision No 2019-07 (April 2019) paras 22–4.
[377] IRPD, Art 81(3)(d). It is to be noted that the application of Article 81(3)(d) of the IRPD is not confined to red notices but applies to all notices.

countries concerned knew in which countries concerned the requesting party was residing'.[378]

Thus, pursuant to Article 81(3)(d) of the IRPD, the General Secretariat is obligated to cancel a red notice unless the requesting NCB can demonstrate that (1) it did not obtain data allowing it to take steps to carry out the 'required action', (2) it has taken steps to carry out the 'required action' or (3) it has reasonable grounds for not taking steps to carry out the 'required action'. The 'required action' in the context of a red notice is 'extradition, surrender or similar lawful action' (ie, action to achieve the purpose of the red notice). Naturally, a member country cannot seek 'extradition, surrender or similar lawful action' in respect of an alleged criminal if it does not know the location of the individual sought. In this sense, the initial data that must be obtained by an NCB for the purposes of Article 81(3)(d) of the IRPD is the location of the individual sought. The Commission has made it clear that the NCB will not be deemed to know the applicant's location unless it has been 'confirmed' by an INTERPOL member.[379] It is not sufficient for the applicant or the applicant's counsel to inform the NCB of the applicant's location.

If the requesting NCB obtains the location of the subject of the red notice from an INTERPOL member, it must then perform the 'required action'. In particular, Article 87(b) of the IRPD specifies that the requesting NCB:

> shall act immediately once it has been informed that the person has been located in another country and, in particular, shall ensure the swift transmission – within the time limits defined for the case in question – of data and supporting documents requested by the country where the person was located or by the General Secretariat.

Article 81(3)(d) does permit exceptions to compliance with Article 87(b). It provides that the General Secretariat is not obligated to cancel a red notice if the requesting NCB can demonstrate that it has 'reasonable grounds' for not taking steps to carry out the required action. In one such case, the applicant was the subject of a red notice requested by the NCB in Country A. He was detained and arrested in Country B on the basis of that red notice. Country B, in accordance with Article 87(a)(i) of the IRPD, acted 'immediately' to inform Country A that the applicant had been located, and it requested that Country A request extradition within the shortest possible time frame. Country A acknowledged receipt and provided assurances that it would take steps to do so. However, when Country A had not requested the applicant's extradition within one month, the Court of Appeal in Country B ordered the applicant's release. The applicant therefore requested deletion of the red notice on the basis that

[378] CCF, 'Annual Activity Report of the CCF in 2009', CCF/77/12/d303, para 37.
[379] Decision of the Commission (2 July 2019) para 68. A copy of this decision is in the authors' files.

Country A had not complied with its obligations in Article 87(b) of the IRPD and that, as a consequence, the General Secretariat was obligated to cancel the red notice (provided Country A did not have reasonable grounds for its lack of action). The Commission conducted enquiries with the NCB in Country A to elicit whether there were any such reasonable grounds, but when the NCB did not reply 'in a timely manner', the General Secretariat deleted the red notice.[380] It therefore remains to be seen exactly what grounds will be considered 'reasonable' for not taking steps to carry out the required action.

In concluding this section, and as emphasised at the outset of this chapter, we note that there are 135 provisions in the IRPD alone and dozens of grounds on which data in the INTERPOL Information System can be challenged. The foregoing section focused on three general standards of review applicable to all types of data processed in the INTERPOL Information System – lawfulness, quality and neutrality – before considering provisions specific to red notices. It is likely that a number of these provisions will be invoked in any successful request to the Commission.

III. Regulation of Employment Relations

The employment relationship between the Organisation and its staff is beyond the prescriptive and adjudicatory jurisdiction of any national legal order.[381] However, despite the fact that Article 30 of the INTERPOL Constitution is clear about the international nature of employment within INTERPOL, for a significant period of time, the Organisation had not expressed this reality very clearly. The Organisation did not have its own staff rules and it relied on French labour and social institutions to provide social security. Moreover, the Organisation did not declare which law applied to its employment contracts. The conceptual confusion about the Organisation's legal position on this matter became apparent during a number of labour disputes involving the Organisation in the 1980s. Initially, the Organisation argued that the French Labour Courts were not competent, but it presented no defence against the rebuttal that such a position created a legal vacuum. The Organisation therefore acquiesced to the findings of the French Labour Courts.[382]

[380] Letter from the CCF to an applicant (9 July 2019). A copy of this letter is in the authors' files.

[381] See: Martha, RSJ, *Tax Treatment of International Civil Servants* (Leiden, Martinus Nijhoff Publishers, 2010) 16–20; Germond, L, *Les principes généraux selon le Tribunal administratif de l'O.I.T.* (Paris, Editions A. Pedone, 2009) 18–9.

[382] Seidl-Hohenveldern, I, 'Avis concernant l'incompétence des tribunaux nationaux pour régler des litiges opposant l'Organisation Internationale de Police Criminelle – Interpol à ses agents' (26 May 1986).

However, this acquiescence did not mean that the Organisation's employment relations were subject to national laws. As discussed in Chapter 6, international administrative tribunals have often declared that the laws of a Member State, whether statutory or judicial, do not govern international organisations or any of their organs. Otherwise, the organisation's operations could be encumbered by the numerous entanglements generated by the domestic laws and judgments of its members.[383] It was not until 1986 – following an extensive legal opinion by Professor Seidl-Hohenveldern[384] – that Article 53 of the INTERPOL General Regulations was adopted in order to prescribe and clarify that the Organisation shall promulgate staff regulations.

The Organisation now has Staff Regulations,[385] Staff Rules (which were approved by the Executive Committee in furtherance of the Staff Regulations) (collectively, the 'Staff Manual')[386] and Staff Instructions (which are issued by the Secretary General). These rules specify the basic conditions of employment and the basic duties and rights of INTERPOL staff members. INTERPOL has also accepted the jurisdiction of the Administrative Tribunal of the International Labour Organization ('ILOAT') in respect of appeals.[387] In Judgment 1080, the ILOAT summarised the Organisation's position with respect to its employees:

> [i]t is true that things are more complex in that for some years where there were no Staff Regulations and the status of Interpol staff under French law was unclear. The complainants see breach of their acquired rights in the failure to reckon their termination indemnities according to French practice and the requirements of the collective agreement applicable to them by virtue of their status in law at the date of recruitment.
>
> Their plea might succeed if INTERPOL had agreed to apply French law and subscribed to the collective agreement they rely on. But they do not cite any text that would bear out their thesis, whether it be their contracts of appointment, or any provision of INTERPOL's rules, or any individual decision taken under the French legislation they want the Organization to apply.

[383] See, for instance, the position adopted by the World Bank Administrative Tribunal in *de Merode v The World Bank*, Decision No 1 (5 June 1981) para 36; *Mould and others v International Bank for Reconstruction and Development*, Decision No 210 (14 May 1999) paras 23–4; *Cissé v International Bank for Reconstruction and Development*, Decision No 242 (26 April 2001) para 23; *Rodriguez-Sawyer v International Bank for Reconstruction and Development*, Decision No 330 (13 May 2005) para 14; *Aida Shekib v International Bank for Reconstruction and Development*, Decision No 358 (3 February 2007).

[384] Seidl-Hohenveldern, I, 'Avis concernant l'incompétence des tribunaux nationaux pour régler des litiges opposant l'Organisation Internationale de Police Criminelle – Interpol à ses agents' (26 May 1986).

[385] The Staff Regulations are an appendix to the INTERPOL General Regulations [I/GREG/GA/1956/(2019)].

[386] Staff Manual [II.C/SREG/GA/1987(2006)] [II.C/SRUL/EC/1988(2019)].

[387] See: Staff Manual, Reg 13.4.

> The conclusion of the passage in their submissions about the collective agreement is not that Interpol should apply it to them but that it shows up the amounts of their indemnities as too low. Whether they are pleading breach of the law or of their acquired rights their reasoning fails because it is at odds with the already cited principle that international organisations are independent.[388]

As at 31 January 2020, the ILOAT had considered 20 complaints filed by employees or former employees against INTERPOL.

[388] *Mr OB v International Criminal Police Organization (Interpol)*, ILOAT, Judgment No 1080 (1991) para 13.

9

Internal Law Disputes

The Commission for the Control of INTERPOL's files ('CCF' or 'Commission') is an independent body within the International Criminal Police Organization ('INTERPOL' or the 'Organisation') with the principal mandate to 'ensure that the processing of personal information by the Organization is in compliance with the regulations the Organization establishes in this matter'.[1] The Commission's competence and powers are further specified in Article 3 of the Statute of the Commission for the Control of INTERPOL's Files ('CCF Statute').[2]

The Requests Chamber of the Commission is specifically vested with powers to 'examine and decide on requests for access to, or correction and/or deletion of, data processed in the INTERPOL Information System' (eg, red notices), and to make decisions binding on the Organisation.[3] The references to 'the regulations the Organization establishes' and to 'INTERPOL's rules' in Article 36 of the INTERPOL Constitution and Articles 3(1)(a) and 33(3) of the CCF Statute indicate that the Requests Chamber is charged primarily with applying the internal law of the Organisation (although the rules do not explicitly state that the Requests Chamber is only required to apply INTERPOL's internal law). This means that proceedings before the CCF do not concern, for instance, the guilt or innocence of the subject of INTERPOL's interventions:

> the function of the Commission is to review whether the processing of data in INTERPOL's files meets INTERPOL's applicable legal requirements in accordance with Article 36 of INTERPOL's Constitution. The Commission is not empowered to conduct an investigation, weigh evidence, or make a determination on the merits of a case. That is the function of the competent national authorities.[4]

Similarly, the Requests Chamber has remarked that it has a 'limited fact-finding role' and does not sit in 'a manner akin to that in which a domestic appellate court re-examines the actions of a domestic court of first instance'.[5]

[1] INTERPOL Constitution, Art 36. The history of the CCF is discussed in Chapter 8 and the structure of the CCF is discussed in Chapter 7.

[2] CCF Statute [II.E/RCIA/GA/2016].

[3] Ibid, Arts 3(1)(c), 28(1)(b) and 38(1).

[4] Decision of the Commission, Decision No 2017-02 (March 2017) para 23. This is a common refrain in decisions of the Commission. See also: Decision of the Commission, Decision No 2018-02 (January 2018) para 10: 'Article 3(1)(a) and Article 33(3) of the Statute of the Commission establish that the powers of the Commission are limited to controlling whether the processing of data in INTERPOL's files meets INTERPOL's applicable legal requirements'.

[5] Decision of the Commission, Decision No 2018-02 (January 2018) para 37.

Challenges to INTERPOL's data processing, therefore, take the form of 'requests' submitted pursuant to Article 30 of the CCF Statute. In addition to requests for access to data in the INTERPOL Information System, individuals may request that data processed in the INTERPOL Information System is corrected or deleted on grounds of inconsistency with INTERPOL's internal law.[6] The INTERPOL Information System includes all structured material resources and software used by the Organisation – the databases, communications infrastructure, etc – to process data through INTERPOL's channels in the context of international police cooperation.[7] Where the processing of data is *ultra vires*, the processing is a nullity and void *ab initio*.[8]

This chapter is concerned with the procedural mechanisms that an individual or entity must rely on to challenge data processed in the INTERPOL Information System before the CCF. The substantive grounds on which an individual or entity could mount such a challenge are considered in detail in Chapter 8.

I. Proceedings before the CCF

A. The Parties

i. The Applicant

Only the subjects of data in the INTERPOL Information System can be party to proceedings before the CCF.[9] 'Data' is defined as:

> any item of information, irrespective of its source, pertaining to constituent elements of ordinary-law crimes, the investigation and prevention of such crimes, the prosecution of the offenders and punishment of the offences, and any information pertaining to missing persons and unidentified dead bodies.[10]

[6] CCF Statute, Art 29.

[7] See the definition of 'INTERPOL Information System' in Article 1(4) of INTERPOL's Rules on the Processing of Data [III/IRPD/GA/2011(2019)] ('IRPD').

[8] *Certain Expenses of the United Nations (Article 17, paragraph 2, of the Charter)* (Advisory Opinion) [1962] ICJ Rep 151, 222 (Separate Opinion of Judge Morelli); Higgins, R et al (eds), *Oppenheim's International Law: United Nations*, Vol I (Oxford, Oxford University Press, 2017) 353–54.

[9] The CCF remarked in 2015 that the profile of the requesting parties has changed over the years. It used to deal directly with individuals wanted for offences like murder, drug trafficking or other ordinary law crimes. Now, the Commission frequently processes requests concerning politicians, former heads of State or government, or businessmen wanted for fraud offences who are represented by law firms specialising in data protection and/or in requesting deletion of data registered in INTERPOL's files (CCF, 'Activity Report of the CCF for 2015 (1986–2016)', CCF/96/12/d461, para 76).

[10] IRPD, Art 1(2). 'Personal data', which is a type of 'data', is data about 'an identified natural person or a person who may be identified by means that may reasonably be used' (IRPD, Art 1(3)). The CCF has remarked that 'an identifiable person is one who can be identified, directly or indirectly, in particular by reference to a name or label, an identification number (eg, travel document), or to one or more factors specific to his/her physical identity (eg, fingerprints, DNA)' (CCF, 'Activity Report of the CCF for 2015 (1986–2016)', CCF/96/12/d461, para 52).

The ability to submit a request to the CCF in relation to data processed in the INTERPOL Information System is specifically granted by Article 18(1) of the IRPD: '[a]ny person or entity shall be entitled to submit directly to the Commission for the Control of INTERPOL's Files a request for access to, or correction and/or deletion of data processed in the INTERPOL Information System concerning that person or entity'. Article 29(1) of the CCF Statute is drafted in similar terms: '[a]ny person or entity' has the 'right to submit directly to the Commission a request for access to, or correction and/or deletion of, data processed in the INTERPOL Information System and concerning that person or entity'. As such, in order to have standing before the Commission, a person or entity must be the subject of 'data' in the INTERPOL Information System (ie, data must 'concern' the person or entity). It is, therefore, insufficient to be indirectly impacted. For instance, a company cannot submit a request to the CCF if its employee is the subject of data processed in the INTERPOL Information System (eg, a red notice), even if that data interferes with the company's operations and finances (eg, by impacting its reputation).

That being said, a strict interpretation of the rules does suggest that victims of crimes can make a request on the basis of Article 29(1) of the CCF Statute and Article 18(1) of the IRPD where they can be identified by reasonable means. INTERPOL, in fact, recognises that victims' data is processed in the INTERPOL Information System.[11] For instance, it is feasible that a victim of a violent or sexual crime might wish to make a request for deletion of data where he or she can be identified in the summary of facts in a red notice. The victim could argue that the processing of data is not compliant with, for instance, his or her right to respect for private life (on which, see Chapter 8) and there is no legitimate law enforcement aim in the processing of such data. On this basis, the victim of a crime could argue for the deletion of the data pertaining to him or her in the INTERPOL Information System. It is, however, difficult to imagine a situation in which such a request would result in the deletion of the entire red notice. It is more likely that the Commission would (or, at least, should) delete any identifying information about the victim, whilst preserving the underlying red notice against the accused. This is the best approach from a policy perspective as it balances the interests of the victim with the interests of the Organisation and the National Central Bureau ('NCB') concerned.

ii. The Respondent

As far as the responding party is concerned, INTERPOL's rules and practice are confused. On the one hand, INTERPOL's rules indicate that the responding party before the CCF is the INTERPOL General Secretariat; on the other hand, recent practice indicates that the CCF deems the relevant NCB the responding party.

[11] See Article 40 of the IRPD which sets out '[a]dditional conditions for recording data on persons who are victims or witnesses'. See also: IRPD, Art 44(1)(f).

As a matter of construction, when proceedings are brought before the CCF, the cause of action is necessarily against the General Secretariat (rather than against the NCB at whose request the General Secretariat intervenes). In other words, applications to the CCF call into question the General Secretariat's actions. The General Secretariat must be regarded as the respondent because it is the executive arm of INTERPOL, responsible for the general administration of the INTERPOL Information System.[12] Article 22(5) of the IRPD stipulates that the General Secretariat:

> shall manage the processing of data in the INTERPOL Information System and ensure that the conditions for processing data in the Organization's databases are duly observed. It shall put in place the tools for managing data and access to the System. It shall perform a management role when conducting spot checks and resolving processing incidents.

Article 74(2) of the IRPD further elaborates on the role of the General Secretariat in respect of notices:

> [i]n particular, it is responsible for:
>
> (a) checking the compliance of all notice requests with the present Rules and publishing, as soon as possible, any notice requests it deems to be in compliance;
> (b) simultaneously recording any published notices in a database of the Organization for direct consultation by National Central Bureaus, national entities and international entities according to the access rights they have been granted;
> (c) translating any notices into the Organization's working languages according to the directives decided upon by the General Assembly;
> (e) assisting National Central Bureaus and international entities in the event of a positive query result;
> (f) ensuring that published notices continue to comply with the conditions for their publication and are regularly assessed by the National Central Bureau or international entity that requested their publication. To that end, the General Secretariat shall review published notices on a regular basis and shall consult the National Central Bureaus and international entities that requested their publication, as well as the other National Central Bureaus.[13]

The General Secretariat must also cancel any notice that no longer meets the conditions for publication.[14] With respect to red notices, Article 86 of the IRPD expressly requires a legal review by the General Secretariat 'prior to their publication to ensure compliance with INTERPOL's Constitution and Rules, in particular with Articles 2 and 3 of INTERPOL's Constitution'. As a consequence, when the object of the proceedings at the CCF is, for instance, the cancellation of a red notice, the very fact that a red notice was published means that the Commission is actually being asked to review the conduct of the General Secretariat, ie, to

[12] IRPD, Art 22(1).
[13] See also: IRPD, Art 77(1)–(2).
[14] Ibid, Art 81(3)(c).

examine whether the General Secretariat breached its obligations set out above. Indeed, in filing such an application, the applicant is challenging the conduct of the General Secretariat, not the conduct of the NCB concerned.

It appears, however, that the Commission treats the respondent as the NCB at whose request the General Secretariat processed and/or published the data. The procedural oddity of this situation is evident: again, and it is worth repeating, the impugned conduct (ie, the processing and/or publication of the data) is that of the General Secretariat, not the requesting NCB. This approach is all the more perplexing when one considers that a successful application leads the General Secretariat to modify its conduct (ie, to correct or delete the data), not the requesting NCB. It also perpetuates the misconception that member countries are abusing the system,[15] when, in fact, it is the General Secretariat which is failing to exercise diligence when processing and/or publishing data in the INTERPOL Information System, particularly with respect to red notices.

B. Admissibility

As noted above, it is the Requests Chamber which is competent to 'examine and decide on requests for access to, or correction and/or deletion of, data in the INTERPOL Information System'.[16] It also has the exclusive power to decide on its competence to process such requests.[17] A request must be submitted to the Requests Chamber by the applicant or a 'duly authorised representative'[18] (or 'legal representative').

The Requests Chamber will first examine the admissibility of the request.[19] A request is admissible if it complies with the specific criteria set out in Rule 30 of the 2019 Operating Rules of the Commission ('2019 Operating Rules').[20] That is, the request must (1) include an original letter sent by post and signed by the applicant[21] which explains the purpose of the request, (2) be written in Arabic, English, French or Spanish, (3) come from the person or entity that it concerns (or a duly authorised representative or legal representative),[22] (4) be

[15] Eg, Mackinnon, A, 'The Scourge of the Red Notice: How some countries use Interpol to go after dissidents and debtors', *Foreign Policy* (3 December 2018).

[16] CCF Statute, Arts 3(1)(c) and 28(1)(b).

[17] Ibid, Art 28(1)(a).

[18] Ibid, Art 30(2).

[19] Ibid, Art 32.

[20] See: CCF Operating Rules, CCF/107/d488 (1 February 2019), Rule 30.

[21] In practice, the CCF will accept an original letter signed by the applicant's duly authorised representative or legal representative.

[22] If the applicant is represented by a duly authorised representative, the request must be accompanied by an original power of attorney signed by the applicant authorising the representative to access any information recorded in INTERPOL's files; if the applicant is represented by a legal representative, the request must be accompanied by a written declaration or certificate (2019 Operating Rules, Rule 30(1)(c)–(d)).

accompanied by a non-redacted identity document,[23] and, (5) if the request is for correction and/or deletion of information, set out the reasons for the request with a summary of supporting arguments, making specific reference to any relevant attached documents (translated into either Arabic, English, French or Spanish).[24]

If further information is required to determine the admissibility of the request, the Requests Chamber will invite the applicant to submit any missing or additional information, but it will cease consideration of the request whilst the information is outstanding.[25] It may, but is not required to, continue to examine the request if the missing or additional information is submitted at a later date.[26] However, if the Requests Chamber determines that the request is 'unreasonable' (eg, because it is repetitive) or not within its competence, then it can refrain from any further action, including replying to the applicant who submitted the request.[27]

The Requests Chamber will inform the applicant of its decision on admissibility at the earliest opportunity and no later than one month from receipt of the request by the Commission.[28] If the request is declared inadmissible, in whole or in part, the Requests Chamber must explain the reasons to the applicant.[29] If the Requests Chamber determines that the request is admissible, it will send a letter notifying the applicant of this decision, detailing the procedure it will follow. Its first action will be to determine whether any data concerning the applicant is being processed in the INTERPOL Information System.[30] The second step is dictated by the type of request: ie, a request for access, pre-emptive/provisional measures, correction or deletion, or an application for revision – each of which is discussed in turn below. In all circumstances, the Requests Chamber will examine the request on the basis of written submissions, although hearings can be held if the Requests Chamber deems it necessary.[31]

C. Requests for Access

Article 29(1) of the CCF Statute and Article 18(1) of the IRPD provide that one of the functions of the Requests Chamber is to receive requests from any person

[23] If the applicant is an 'entity', the request must include the entity's full name, date of incorporation or registration, official registration number (if any) and official address (2019 Operating Rules, Rule 30(1)(g)). The request must also be accompanied by documents showing that the individual who lodged the application on behalf of the entity has standing or authority to represent the entity (for example, an extract from the Chamber of Commerce register or minutes of the governing body) (2019 Operating Rules, Rule 30(1)(f)).

[24] 2019 Operating Rules, Rule 30(1)(h).

[25] Ibid, Rule 30(2).

[26] Ibid, Rule 30(3).

[27] Ibid, Rule 30(4).

[28] CCF Statute, Art 32(1); 2019 Operating Rules, Rule 31(3).

[29] CCF Statute, Art 32(3); 2019 Operating Rules, Rule 31(4).

[30] CCF Statute, Art 33(1).

[31] Ibid, Art 36; 2019 Operating Rules, Rule 28.

wishing to access data processed in the INTERPOL Information System. In practice, an individual will often seek access as a first step to understand if, and if so what, data has been processed in the INTERPOL Information System. He or she can then decide whether to send a subsequent request to block, correct and/or delete data. It is good practice to seek the following in any request for access: (1) confirmation or denial of the existence of data,[32] (2) a description of the data processed, (3) the purpose of the processing of the data, (4) the legal basis for the processing of the data, and (5) a copy of the data, including the 'summary of facts of the case'.[33]

The Requests Chamber must decide on a request for access within four months from the date on which the request was declared admissible.[34] It can extend this time period, but any extension must be (1) reasonable, (2) promptly communicated to the General Secretariat, the source of the data and the applicant, and (3) reasoned.[35] The final decision on a request for access must be provided to the applicant within one month from the date on which it was adopted by the Requests Chamber.[36] The Requests Chamber will respond to a request for access in one of five ways: it will (1) neither confirm nor deny that data exists in the INTERPOL Information System, (2) confirm data exists but withhold access, (3) confirm data exists but provide only limited access, (4) confirm data exists and provide full access, or (5) confirm that no data exists in the INTERPOL Information System.

Although an applicant has a prima facie right of access to data in the INTERPOL Information System concerning him or her,[37] the source of the data (eg, an NCB) often has an interest in not disclosing either the existence or contents of the data. One of the main tasks of the Requests Chamber is, therefore, to 'protect the interests of the parties, while preserving at the same time the essence of an adversarial procedure in order to provide an effective remedy'.[38]

The fact that there is an absence of data in the INTERPOL Information System is itself a form of information, and the fact that no data is recorded does not

[32] Compare: Directive (EU) 2016/680 of the European Parliament and of the Council of 27 April 2016 on the protection of natural persons with regard to the processing of personal data by competent authorities for the purposes of the prevention, investigation, detection or prosecution of criminal offences or the execution of criminal penalties, and on the free movement of such data, and repealing Council Framework Decision 2008/977/JHA, Official Journal L 119/89 (4 May 2016) 89–131, Art 14; Regulation (EU) 2016/679 of the European Parliament and of the Council of 27 April 2016 on the protection of natural persons with regard to the processing of personal data and on the free movement of such data, and repealing Directive 95/46/EC (General Data Protection Regulation), Official Journal L 119/1 (4 May 2016) 1–88, Art 15(1).

[33] Article 83(2)(b)(i) of the IRPD provides that judicial data provided to INTERPOL for publication of a red notice must include a 'summary of facts of the case, which shall provide a succinct and clear description of the criminal activities of the wanted person, including the time and location of the alleged criminal activity'.

[34] CCF Statute, Art 40(1).

[35] Ibid, Art 40(3).

[36] Ibid, Art 41(3).

[37] Ibid, Art 35(1).

[38] Decision of the Commission, Decision No 2018-07 (April 2018) para 24. See also: CCF, 'Activity Report of the CCF for 2015 (1986–2016)', CCF/96/12/d461, para 99.

necessarily mean that the person is not of interest to any of the members of the Organisation. INTERPOL is a voluntary organisation, so members do not have to share information with INTERPOL concerning ongoing investigations. If no data concerning the applicant is being processed at the time the request is examined, the Requests Chamber may decide on appropriate measures[39] (on which, see section I.D below).

Where data concerning the applicant is in the INTERPOL Information System, the Requests Chamber must 'consult' the source of the data before disclosing the information to the applicant.[40] The Requests Chambers has interpreted this as a requirement to seek the authorisation of the source of the data.[41] It might be said that this interpretation gives the source of the data – typically an NCB – more power than the CCF Statute envisions in Article 35(2). It also cuts across the presumption of accessibility in favour of the applicant in Article 35(1) of the CCF Statute – ie, '[i]nformation connected with a request shall be accessible to the applicant and the source of the data', subject to the restrictions, conditions and procedures set out in Article 35 (discussed below). The Requests Chamber's interpretation of Article 35 of the CCF Statute is likely informed by Article 7(1) of the IRPD, which provides that NCBs and international entities[42] 'shall retain, at all times, control over the processing of their data'.[43] However, Article 7(1) is concerned with the control of an NCB or international entity over the processing of its data in INTERPOL's databases by other NCBs, international entities or private entities;[44] it is not relevant to proceedings at the CCF and an applicant's right of access.[45]

The communication of information may be restricted at the decision of the Requests Chamber, on its own initiative or at the request of the source of the data, the General Secretariat or the applicant, for one or more of the following grounds: (1) to protect public or national security or to prevent crime, (2) to protect the

[39] CCF Statute, Art 33(2).

[40] Ibid, Art 35(2).

[41] Letter from the CCF to an applicant (25 January 2019). A copy of this letter is in the authors' files.

[42] Article 27 of the IRPD permits the Organisation, whenever it considers it desirable, to establish relations with international entities in order to collaborate with them on data processing, so long as such cooperation is consistent with the aims and objects of the Organisation. An 'international entity' is 'any international, intergovernmental or non-governmental organization which fulfils an international public interest mission, which has concluded an agreement with the Organization on the exchange of data and which has been granted direct or indirect access to a part of the INTERPOL Information System by the Organization' (IRPD, Art 1(9)).

[43] IRPD, Art 7(1).

[44] Article 28 of the IRPD permits the Organisation to establish relations with private entities wishing to cooperate with it on data processing matters, insofar as it is relevant to the accomplishment of the Organisation's aims. A 'private entity' is 'any legal person governed by private law such as a business, company, commercial association or a not-for-profit organization, not covered by the category of international entities, which has concluded an agreement with the Organization on the exchange of data, and in particular, on the processing of data in the INTERPOL Information System' (IRPD, Art 1(10)).

[45] This is evidenced by the distinct access restrictions (established in Article 7(1) and set out in Article 58 of the IRPD) that an NCB or international entity may impose on 'other National Central Bureaus, international entities or private entities' (IRPD, Art 58(1) (emphasis added)).

confidentiality of an investigation or prosecution, (3) to protect the rights and freedoms of the applicant or third parties, and/or (4) to enable the Commission or the Organisation to properly discharge its duties. If a restriction on disclosure is requested, it must be justified and the request must specify whether some information, such as summaries, may be provided.[46] The Commission has observed that restrictions on the basis of Article 35(3) of the CCF Statute are exceptions to the general principle of communication of information and bear consequences on the rights of the parties; therefore, Article 35(3) must be interpreted strictly.[47] Such restrictions must be necessary and proportionate to the stated purpose, and the Requests Chamber 'must be allowed unlimited access to the information concerned in order to make an effective determination'.[48] In analysing the justification for restriction, the Requests Chamber also considers, inter alia, the general context of the case, the other avenues available to the applicant to obtain access to the information at the national level, the potential violation of other rules or international obligations, and the 'possible risks for INTERPOL'.[49]

Article 35(3) of the CCF Statute makes it clear that the Requests Chamber is not bound to acquiesce to requests to restrict information. The Requests Chamber must undertake its own independent analysis and only the Requests Chamber can decide that information connected with a request shall not be accessible – ie, 'the communication of information may be restricted at the decision of the Requests Chamber'.[50] Unfortunately, the Requests Chamber has failed, in some instances, to exercise its own discretion. For instance, in response to a request for access submitted by an applicant, the CCF simply responded that 'the [NCB] in [the relevant country] has restricted the communication of any information including the existence or absence of data concerning [the applicant] in the INTEPROL Information System'.[51]

This type of blanket restriction is incompatible with an applicant's due process rights (even in circumstances where the CCF has come to its own decision). Indeed, it can plausibly be argued that an applicant must be granted full access to the data concerning him or her in the INTERPOL Information System.[52] Without such

[46] CCF Statute, Art 35(4).

[47] Decision of the Commission, Decision No 2018-07 (April 2018) para 25.

[48] Ibid.

[49] Ibid.

[50] CCF Statute, Art 35(3). See also: *Gaskin v United Kingdom* (1989) 12 EHRR 36, para 49, where the European Court of Human Rights observed that a system which grants (determinative) controlling rights to the source of the data would only be in conformity with the principle of proportionality 'if it provides that an independent authority finally decides whether access has to be granted in cases where a contributor fails to answer or withholds consent'.

[51] Letter from the CCF to an applicant (11 October 2018). A copy of this letter is in the authors' files.

[52] See: Ausloos, J and Dewitte, P, 'Shattering one-way mirrors – data subject access rights in practice', 8 *International Data Privacy Law* (2018) 7: '[f]irst and foremost, the right of access constitutes an essential first step toward the exercise of other prerogatives granted to data subjects. … Neither rectification or erasure of personal data, nor blocking or objecting to the processing of personal data seem easy or even possible unless the data subject knows exactly what data the controller processes and how'.

access, an applicant cannot (1) assess the lawfulness of the data in accordance with Article 11(1) of the IRPD, (2) assess the adequacy of the data in accordance with Article 12(1) of the IRPD, or (3) overcome the immense hurdle of the presumption of accuracy of the data.[53] It renders an applicant defenceless.

The right of access is especially important when the applicant's basic rights are at stake: 'when restrictive measures are taken against individuals that have a serious impact on their fundamental rights, human rights law requires that the individuals are given a minimum of information on the grounds for these measures so that they can defend themselves'.[54] When INTERPOL takes restrictive measures against an applicant (eg, by issuing a red notice), it is obvious that the applicant's basic rights (including the right to freedom of movement[55] and the right not to be arbitrarily arrested or detained[56]) may be seriously impacted.[57] This is recognised by the CCF itself: 'certain data-processing operations might infringe upon people's basic rights'.[58] It is for this reason that the approach in Decision No 2018-07 is surprising. The applicant submitted a request to the Commission for access to the data concerning him in the INTERPOL Information System after he was directly affected by the processing of data in the INTERPOL Information System (ie, he was detained and exposed to extradition proceedings on the basis of a red notice). The NCB opposed any disclosure and sought an absolute restriction on the communication of information to the applicant, without reference to any of the grounds mentioned in Article 35(3) of the CCF Statute. The NCB also did not consent to any counterbalancing measures (such as the provision of a redacted summary, or a minimum of information, or even confirmation of the existence of the data). The Commission, therefore, concluded that the restriction was not justified, and the NCB had not demonstrated the relevance and proportionality of the requested restriction.[59] However, despite its patent dissatisfaction with the lack of justification provided by the NCB, the Commission decided, in reliance on Article 35(4) of the CCF Statute, that 'such improper justification would not lead to the disclosure of the data concerned without the consent of

[53] IRPD, Art 128(1).

[54] Fabritius, B, 'Abusive use of the INTERPOL system: the need for more stringent legal safeguards', Committee on Legal Affairs and Human Rights, Parliamentary Assembly of the Council of Europe, Doc No 14277 (29 March 2017) para 24.

[55] Universal Declaration of Human Rights, Art 13.

[56] Ibid, Art 9. In the *Iran Hostages* case, the International Court of Justice determined that '[w]rongfully to deprive human beings of their freedom … is in itself manifestly incompatible … with the fundamental principles enunciated in the Universal Declaration of Human Rights' (*United States Diplomatic and Consular Staff in Tehran* (Judgment) [1980] ICJ Rep 3, para 91).

[57] It will be recalled that INTERPOL must act in accordance with the spirit of the Universal Declaration of Human Rights (see: INTERPOL Constitution, Art 2(1)). See Chapter 8 for a discussion of how a red notice can impinge on an individual's right to freedom of movement and right not to be arbitrarily arrested or detained.

[58] Frayssinet, J, Member of the CCF and Rapporteur, 'Annual Activity Report of the CCF for 2013' (Speech to the INTERPOL General Assembly, 83rd session, Monaco, 2014).

[59] Decision of the Commission, Decision No 2018-07 (April 2018) paras 27–30.

the NCB'.[60] This indicates that the Commission either opted for deference to the NCB or erroneously concluded that it was bound to give effect to the NCB's request, in either case, acting to the detriment of the applicant's due process rights.

It should also be mentioned that restrictions on the communication of information under Article 35 of the IRPD are not only relevant to requests for access: the source of the data, the General Secretariat and the applicant can request that the communication of information connected with any type of request be restricted. For instance, the applicant could request restrictions when it does not want certain information in a request for deletion conveyed to the source of the data. In Decision No 2018-07, the applicant requested that the Commission not communicate certain information to the NCB on the basis of Article 35(3)(c) of the CCF Statute (ie, to protect his rights). The Commission was of the view that, in light of the 'sensitive nature' of the arguments in his request, and considering his allegations of a politically motivated prosecution and his past protective status, the restrictions sought were justified. The Commission was also of the view that it was proportional because it could still transmit questions to the NCB, which was the source of the data, without raising the specific content in the applicant's request, so it granted the applicant's request for a restriction.[61]

D. Requests for Pre-Emptive/Provisional Measures

As mentioned above, if no data is being processed when the request for access is examined, the CCF has the power to 'decide on appropriate measures, taking into consideration confidentiality requirements'.[62] The phrase 'appropriate measures' is extremely broad. It can, therefore, be utilised by an applicant to seek an opportunity to present his or her views prior to the processing of any data in respect of him or her in the INTERPOL Information System (including on the INTERPOL public website) and to ask the Requests Chamber to take appropriate pre-emptive measures. This may be useful if an applicant fears that data concerning him or her may be processed in the INTERPOL Information System because an INTERPOL member has commenced an investigation or outrightly acknowledged that it will seek the assistance of INTERPOL (eg, if an applicant fears that a red notice is forthcoming). An applicant must specifically request pre-emptive measures if he or she wishes to take advantage of this provision.

If data is being processed in the INTERPOL Information System, then an applicant can seek provisional measures pursuant to Article 37(1) of the CCF Statute: '[a]t any time during the proceedings, the Requests Chamber may decide on provisional measures to be taken by the Organization in relation to the processing

[60] Ibid, para 30.
[61] Ibid, para 26.
[62] CCF Statute, Art 33(2).

of the data concerned'. A commonly sought provisional measure is a block on the data in the INTERPOL Information System pending a determination of the applicant's request for deletion. In order to obtain provisional measures, the applicant must raise a doubt regarding compliance with the conditions for data processing. The authority of the Requests Chamber to decide on provisional measures supplements the General Secretariat's obligation to 'take all appropriate steps to prevent any direct or indirect prejudice … data may cause' to the individual concerned in the event that a doubt arises regarding compliance with the conditions for data processing.[63] This means that, in practice, the applicant must identify the following in order to obtain provisional measures: (1) the conditions for data processing which may be in breach (see Chapter 8 for a discussion of the substantive grounds on which an applicant might rely), and (2) the prejudice the data may cause to the applicant. Provisional measures ordered by the Requests Chamber are implemented in accordance with the procedure specified in Article 41 of the CCF Statute[64] (as discussed in detail below in section I.G).

E. Requests for Correction and/or Deletion

In addition to the foregoing, applicants regularly seek the correction and/or deletion of data in the INTERPOL Information System.[65] Very often such requests indulge in the argument that there is no evidence that the applicant has committed the crime referred to in the notice or diffusion. This argument is not the right argument because the Requests Chamber is primarily charged with applying the internal law of the Organisation. In other words, for a request to correct or delete data to be successful it must be supported by arguments derived from INTERPOL's rules. This is made explicit in Article 33(3) of the CCF Statute: 'if the request is for correction or deletion, the Requests Chambers shall examine the compliance of the processing of the data with INTERPOL's rules'. It is also noteworthy that Article 128(1) of the IRPD establishes a rebuttable presumption in favour of the NCBs that '[d]ata are … considered to be accurate and relevant when entered by [the NCBs] … into the INTERPOL Information System and recorded in a police database of the Organization.' It follows from the above that, in order to prevail, a requesting party must present well-argued submissions and supporting evidence to demonstrate a lack of compliance with INTERPOL's conditions for data processing.[66]

The Requests Chamber must decide on a request for correction and/or deletion within nine months from the date on which the request was declared admissible.[67]

[63] IRPD, Art 129(1).
[64] CCF Statute, Art 37(2).
[65] Ibid, Art 29(1); IRPD, Art 18(1).
[66] Martha, RSJ, 'Remedies against INTERPOL: role and practice of defence lawyers' (Speech at the European Criminal Bar Association, Autumn Conference, Lyon, 6 October 2007) para 41.
[67] CCF Statute, Art 40(2).

It can extend this time period, but any extension must be (1) reasonable, (2) promptly communicated to the General Secretariat, the source of the data and the applicant, and (3) reasoned.[68]

F. Applications for Revision

Despite the fact that there is no opportunity to appeal, there is the opportunity to apply for 'revision' of a decision of the Requests Chamber under Article 42 of the CCF Statute. However, the ability to seek revision is limited. An application for revision may be made only when (1) it is based on the discovery of a fact, (2) such fact could have led the Requests Chamber to a different conclusion if it had been known when it took the previous decision on access, correction or deletion, and (3) the application for revision is made within six months of the discovery of the fact.[69]

In Decision No 2019-06, the applicant submitted an application for revision in light of the fact that national authorities had rejected a mutual legal assistance request concerning the same criminal case which underpinned the red notice. The Commission was of the view that the authorities' refusal to cooperate in this circumstance did constitute a new fact which could not have been communicated to the Commission in the previous request.[70] If an application for revision is admissible, the Commission will study the new fact in addition to the information provided by the parties in the previous request.

G. Effect of Findings

Unlike the decisions of most first instance national courts, the decisions of the Requests Chamber are final and binding on the Organisation.[71] Decisions must also be reasoned and contain, inter alia, 'a summary of the proceedings, the submissions of the parties, a statement of the facts, the application of INTERPOL's rules, an analysis of legal arguments, and operative parts'.[72]

The written decision of the Requests Chamber must be provided to the General Secretariat within one month from the date on which the decision was made,[73] and the General Secretariat must implement a decision within one month from the date on which it was received, unless further clarifications are needed for the implementation of the decision.[74] If further clarifications are needed, the General

[68] Ibid, Art 40(3).
[69] Ibid, Art 42(1).
[70] Decision of the Commission, Decision No 2019-06 (April 2019) paras 16–23.
[71] CCF Statute, Art 38(1); 2019 Operating Rules, Rule 19(2).
[72] CCF Statute, Art 38(2).
[73] Ibid, Art 41(1).
[74] Ibid, Art 41(2).

Secretariat must proceed with the implementation of its decision within one month from the date on which the clarifications are received.[75] The General Secretariat must promptly notify the Commission of the implementation of its decision.[76] The Requests Chamber must notify the applicant and the source of the data of the implementation of its decision by the General Secretariat and provide its written decision to the applicant and the source of the data promptly and no later than one month from the date on which the Requests Chamber received notification of implementation by the General Secretariat.[77] When providing its written decision to the applicant and the source of the data, the Requests Chamber may do so subject to 'confidentiality requirements and restrictions'.[78] In practice, decisions may be heavily redacted, and to the detriment of the applicant. For instance, in a recent decision of the Requests Chamber, the legal arguments of the NCB were 'RESTRICTED' in their entirety, making it impossible for the applicant to examine the veracity of its legal arguments.[79] The General Secretariat must also promptly notify the Organisation's members who had received the data of any corrections or deletions.[80]

The Requests Chamber also has the power to decide on other appropriate remedies (ie, other than to correct or delete the data) if it finds that the data has not been processed in accordance with INTERPOL's rules.[81] To this end, where an applicant is successful in obtaining the deletion of data from the INTERPOL Information System, the General Secretariat provides an applicant with a certificate stating as much. It is typically addressed 'TO WHOM IT MAY CONCERN' and states that '[t]he General Secretariat of the International Criminal Police Organization-INTERPOL hereby certifies that, as of today, […], born on […], is not subject to an INTERPOL Notice or diffusion'. The certificate is dated and stamped by the Office of Legal Affairs of the General Secretariat. The certificate is helpful if, for instance, a country has downloaded but not updated information from the INTERPOL Information System and detained the applicant on the basis of outdated information. This certificate can be provided to the relevant country to explain that data concerning the applicant should no longer be in the INTERPOL Information System.

In the event that the General Secretariat does not observe the Requests Chamber's findings, the Commission may bring the matter to the Executive Committee, which is constitutionally empowered to supervise the execution of the decisions of

[75] Ibid.

[76] Ibid.

[77] Ibid, Art 41(3).

[78] Ibid, Art 38(3). Article 38(3) does not define or designate 'confidentiality requirements and restrictions' but, at a minimum, it is likely a reference to the 'restrictions on disclosure' set out in Article 35 of the CCF Statute (discussed above).

[79] Decision of the Commission (31 January 2018) paras 45–6, 56–8, 67 and 73. A copy of this decision is in the authors' files.

[80] CCF Statute, Art 41(4).

[81] Ibid, Art 39(2).

the General Assembly and the work of the Secretary General.[82] The issue before the Executive Committee in such a case is not the merits of the Commission's findings, but the fact that the General Secretariat refuses to correct a situation found by the Requests Chambers (which is constitutionally endowed by the General Assembly to issue decisions that are final and binding on the Organisation)[83] to be in contravention of a rule (or rules) established by the General Assembly.[84] The General Secretariat's refusal to implement fully a decision of the Requests Chamber is a violation of Article 26(a) of the INTERPOL Constitution, which requires the General Secretariat to put into application the decisions of the General Assembly.

II. Re-Examination by the General Secretariat

One of the key contemporary issues for the administrative justice system is the reconsideration of administrative decisions. Reconsideration is a feature of a system of administrative redress whereby a subject who is aggrieved by a decision of a public authority may have that decision reviewed internally before pursuing redress in an external forum. In some cases, the subject may be able to request reconsideration on the basis of the merits of the decision alone. However, it is more common that reconsideration is only available where the authority concerned becomes aware of information that could have caused it to adopt a different decision (either of its own volition or due to a request by the subject).[85]

In the case of INTERPOL, Article 128 of the IRPD can reasonably be interpreted as providing a procedure through which the INTERPOL General Secretariat can reconsider whether the processing of data is compliant with INTERPOL's rules. Although the term of art used in the IRPD is 'examination', the structure of Article 128 indicates that the process can be considered a re-examination by the General Secretariat. Re-examination by the General Secretariat is a logical dimension of its responsibilities as the executive organ of the Organisation. As discussed above in section I.A.ii, the General Secretariat is responsible for the general administration of the INTERPOL Information System.[86] It has the responsibility of managing the processing of data in the INTERPOL Information System and,

[82] INTERPOL Constitution, Art 22(a) and (d).

[83] CCF Statute, Art 38(1). See also: INTERPOL Constitution, Art 36.

[84] This is not appreciated by either Schöndorf-Haubold (Schöndorf-Haubold, B, 'The Administration of Information in International Administrative Law – The Example of Interpol – Part I/II' (2008) 9 *German Law Journal* 1719–52) or by De Wet (De Wet, E, 'Holding International Institutions Accountable: The Complementary Role of Non-Judicial Oversight Mechanisms and Judicial Review' (2008) 9 *German Law Journal* 1987–2011).

[85] On reconsideration of administrative decisions generally, see: Cowan, D et al, 'Reconsidering Mandatory Reconsideration' (2017) *Public Law* 215–34; Thomas, R and Tomlison, J, 'Current issues in administrative justice: Examining administrative review, better initial decisions, and tribunal reform', Economic and Social Research Council (November 2016); Bress, D, 'Administrative Reconsideration' (2005) 91 *Virginia Law Review* 1737–93.

[86] IRPD, Art 22(1).

most importantly, ensuring that the conditions for processing data in INTERPOL's databases (which contain, inter alia, notices and diffusions) are duly observed.[87] In practice, the General Secretariat considers that data is 'accurate and relevant when entered by a National Central Bureau, a national entity or an international entity into the INTERPOL Information System and recorded in a police database of the Organization'.[88]

If a doubt subsequently arises regarding compliance with the conditions for data processing, it is incumbent upon the General Secretariat to remove that doubt by re-examining whether the processing of the data is compliant with INTERPOL's rules.[89] In so doing, it must obtain clarifications and/or supplementary data from the NCB concerned.[90] According to Article 128(4) of the IRPD, the General Secretariat must draw a conclusion following such a re-examination. If it concludes that the processing of data complies with its rules, then it 'validates' the recording of the data and deems the re-examination procedure 'closed'.[91] It will then notify the relevant NCB of the same.[92] If it does not so conclude, then it 'shall take any other appropriate steps to ensure that these conditions have actually been met'.[93] In this regard, Article 128(4)(b) of the IRPD specifically envisages that the General Secretariat will 'correct' or 'delete' the data to ensure compliance.

By way of example, the General Secretariat initiated the re-examination procedure in *AMIA I* (which is discussed in Chapters 8 and 10). In *AMIA I*, the General Secretariat had published red notices at the request of NCB Buenos Aires against 12 Iranian nationals for allegedly participating in the bombing of the Asociación Mutual Israelita Argentina building. The General Secretariat subsequently suspended (by way of a provisional measure) all 12 red notices following a finding of the Argentinean judiciary that the judge who had issued the arrest warrants was to be removed for judicial misconduct. In other words, the General Secretariat re-examined its decision to publish the red notices when a doubt arose regarding compliance with the conditions for data processing, and, in the course of that re-examination, suspended the red notices by way of a provisional measure.[94]

Re-examination by the General Secretariat thus corresponds to its continuing obligation to ensure that data processing is consistent with the Organisation's rules. This means that, even if the Commission has considered the question of compliance with the conditions for data processing in respect of the relevant data, it does

[87] Ibid, Art 22(5).
[88] Ibid, Art 128(1).
[89] Ibid, Art 128(2).
[90] Ibid.
[91] Ibid, Art 128(4).
[92] Ibid, Art 128(5).
[93] Ibid, Art 128(3).
[94] The General Secretariat did not complete its re-examination because the dispute was settled pursuant to Article 24 of the Rules on the Processing of Information for the Purposes of International Police Cooperation (the predecessor provision to Article 135 of the IRPD). Further information can be found in Chapter 10.

not suspend the General Secretariat's continuing obligations to do the same. In other words, the General Secretariat's continuing obligations exist independently. In its 2012 Annual Activity Report to the INTERPOL General Assembly, the CCF confirmed the same:

> [t]he Commission emphasized that the General Secretariat remains responsible for ensuring that the Rules on the Processing of Data which the Organization had adopted are observed (Article 22.5 of the [I]RPD), even if an item of information were the subject of a complaint to the Commission. As such, there are no rules or procedures which could be interpreted as suspending that obligation while a complaint is being processed and preventing the General Secretariat from taking any appropriate steps (updating, blocking, withdrawing an item of information from the INTERPOL website, deleting data), including when an item of information is recorded directly by an NCB.[95]

This idea is now reflected in Article 28(2)(c) of the CCF Statute, which states that nothing in the Statute shall prevent 'the General Secretariat from blocking, correcting or deleting, in accordance with INTERPOL's rules, data processed in the INTERPOL Information System'.

Technically, the foregoing provisions mean that, in case of an adverse decision by the Requests Chamber, an applicant should be able to make representations for re-examination to the General Secretariat. However, whereas re-examination by the General Secretariat was once a standard feature of the Organisation's practice, in recent years, the General Secretariat has tended to defer entirely to the CCF. The Commission's comment in its 2012 Annual Activity Report (as set out above) is a reminder to the General Secretariat that its deference is ill-conceived.

[95] CCF, 'Annual Activity Report of the CCF for 2012', CCF/86/12/d419, para 96.

10

Challenges by National Central Bureaux

I. Legal Framework

Members of an international organisation are generally understood to have the right to challenge the lawfulness of institutional acts of the organisation,[1] despite the presumption that acts of an international organisation directed at the fulfilment of its purposes are not *ultra vires* the organisation (ie, beyond its powers).[2] In the context of the International Criminal Police Organization ('INTERPOL' or the 'Organisation'), the General Assembly adopted Article 135 of INTERPOL's Rules on the Processing of Data ('IRPD')[3] to enable members to resolve institutional disputes that arise in connection with the application of the IRPD. In so doing, the General Assembly (which is the 'body of supreme authority' in the Organisation,[4] responsible for applying the INTERPOL Constitution)[5] endowed the Executive Committee and, in certain cases, itself with the power to settle such disputes with finality.

Article 135(1) of the IRPD provides that '[d]isputes that arise in connection with the application of the present Rules should be solved by concerted consultation. If this fails, the matter may be submitted to the Executive Committee and, if necessary, to the General Assembly'. Article 135(2) of the IRPD states that '[a]ll national entities shall be represented in the settlement of disputes by their National Central Bureaus [('NCBs')]'. In practice, disputes under Article 135 of the IRPD arise between two NCBs or between an NCB and the General Secretariat.

Where the dispute is between two NCBs, the dispute is, in effect, a dispute between governments. There are both advantages and disadvantages to this

[1] Schermers, HG and Blokker, NM, *International Institutional Law*, 6th revised edn (Leiden, Brill Nijhoff Publishers, 2018) 916–17; Cannizzaro, E and Palchetti, P, '*Ultra Vires* Acts of International Organizations' in Klabbers, J and Wallendahl, Å (eds), *Research Handbook on the Law of International Organizations* (Gloucester, Edward Elgar Publishing, 2011) 365–97 at 387; Osieke, E, 'The Legal Validity of Ultra Vires Decisions of International Organizations' (1983) 77 *American Journal of International Law* 239–56 at 240–41.

[2] *Certain Expenses of the United Nations (Article 17, paragraph 2, of the Charter)* (Advisory Opinion) [1962] ICJ Rep 151, 168.

[3] IRPD [III/IRPD/GA/2011(2019)]. Article 135 replaced Article 24 of the Rules on the Processing of Information for the Purposes of International Police Cooperation and covers the same types of disputes as its predecessor.

[4] INTERPOL Constitution, Art 6.

[5] Ibid, Arts 8(d) and 44. See also: Seyersted, F, *Common Law of International Organizations* (Leiden, Martinus Nijhoff Publishers, 2008) 248–49.

reality. The main disadvantage is that a pure police matter may be influenced by the international political climate and diplomatic relations between the governments that sit behind the disputing NCBs. The main advantage is that governments normally prefer to seek a negotiated settlement of their differences, rather than have recourse to third-party dispute settlement.[6] Therefore, in practice, when an NCB first challenges the use of INTERPOL's channels by another NCB, the General Secretariat normally consults both parties separately in an effort to resolve the dispute. At this stage, the role of the General Secretariat is that of a mediator and conciliator. It often happens that, on further clarification, the challenging NCB drops its complaint. Of course, the reverse also occurs, ie, the requesting NCB revokes its request or accepts that the General Secretariat should delete any relevant data.

In the event that the disputing NCBs fail to settle their dispute at the stage of concerted consultation (sometimes due to uncompromising positions reflective of the relations between the two governments), the matter 'may' be submitted to the Executive Committee.[7] Use of the word 'may' indicates that the Executive Committee can decide that it should not be seised of a dispute. This prospect provides the General Secretariat with valuable ammunition for dealing with the disputing parties and induces them to adopt a more compromising attitude. Where the matter is submitted to the Executive Committee, this is normally done by the INTERPOL Secretary General, and the submission is based on a report with recommendations of the INTERPOL General Counsel (which the INTERPOL Secretary General may or may not endorse).[8] Before the Executive Committee, the disputing NCBs present their cases.[9] At any point in time while a dispute is pending before the Executive Committee, the Executive Committee may decide to 'appoint a rapporteur or create a consultative body from among its members' and/or 'consult external experts who will report back to the Executive Committee'.[10] The Executive Committee is not bound by the opinion of the experts.[11] The Executive Committee may either issue a final decision on the matter or it may decide to submit the dispute for consideration and a final decision to the General Assembly.[12] A decision to refer a dispute to the General Assembly must be done on an exceptional basis and requires a two-thirds

[6] Anderson, D, 'Negotiation and Dispute Settlement' in Evans, MD (ed), *Remedies in International Law: The Institutional Dilemma* (Oxford, Hart Publishing, 1998) 111–22 at 112.

[7] IRPD, Art 135(1).

[8] 'INTERPOL's Procedures for the Handling of Article 24 Disputes Between Member Country National Central Bureaus (NCBs)', INTERPOL press release (7 March 2007).

[9] In the past, disputing NCBs have been invited to make written submissions to the Executive Committee and to have their delegates participate in the Executive Committee meeting (see: 'INTERPOL's Procedures for the Handling of Article 24 Disputes Between Member Country National Central Bureaus (NCBs)', INTERPOL press release (7 March 2007)).

[10] Resolution No GA-2017-86-RES-05, 'Settlement of disputes under Article 135 of the INTERPOL's Rules on the Processing of Data', INTERPOL General Assembly, 86th session (Beijing, 2017).

[11] Ibid.

[12] Ibid.

majority vote by the Executive Committee.[13] In other words, there is no automatic right of appeal from the Executive Committee to the General Assembly. In the exceptional case where a dispute is referred to the General Assembly, the dispute will be decided by simple majority;[14] unsurprisingly, the vote is likely to be heavily influenced by the prevailing international political climate.

Finally, it bears mentioning that the General Secretariat is of the view that Article 135 of the IRPD cannot be invoked by an NCB either pre-emptively or after the relevant data has been deleted from the INTERPOL Information System. This became clear in June 2020 in the case concerning Alex Nain Saab Morán. In May 2019, NCB Caracas requested concerted consultations within the framework of Article 135 of the IRPD in connection with Saab and others.[15] On 25 July 2019, the United States ('US') charged Saab with money laundering in connection with a scheme to pay bribes to take advantage of the Bolivarian Republic of Venezuela's government-controlled exchange rate.[16] On 12 June 2020, Saab was arrested and detained in the Republic of Cabo Verde, allegedly pursuant to a red notice requested by the US in June 2020.[17] After the arrest of Saab in Cabo Verde, NCB Caracas again sought to invoke Article 135. On 25 June 2020, the General Secretariat addressed the requests from NCB Caracas of May 2019 and June 2020. The General Secretariat stated that Article 135 cannot be invoked pre-emptively (hence the request of NCB Caracas in May 2019 could not operate to preclude the publication of a red notice in respect of Saab at a later date) and the General Secretariat need not facilitate concerted consultations because the red notice in respect of Saab had been cancelled.[18] There is, however, reason to question the wisdom of the General Secretariat's view that Article 135 cannot be invoked pre-emptively by an NCB. It is arguable that, had the General Secretariat engaged in concerted consultations further to the request of NCB Caracas in May 2019, any decision to publish a red notice against Saab would have been a more informed decision.

II. Examples

In practice, the vast majority of disputes between two NCBs (or between an NCB and the General Secretariat) are settled without any public knowledge. However,

[13] Ibid.

[14] INTERPOL Constitution, Art 14.

[15] 'Prisão de Alex Saab Morán. Cabo Verde envolvido numa grave encrenca jurídica e diplomática', *Santiago Magazine* (26 June 2020).

[16] US Department of Justice, 'Two Colombian businessmen charged with money laundering in connection with Venezuela bribery scheme' (25 July 2019).

[17] 'Venezuela demands release of businessman connected to Maduro', *Associated Press* (15 June 2020).

[18] 'Prisão de Alex Saab Morán. Cabo Verde envolvido numa grave encrenca jurídica e diplomática', *Santiago Magazine* (26 June 2020).

four high-profile disputes have entered the public domain. Each of these will be considered in turn. Two of the four disputes relate to the bombing of the Asociación Mutual Israelita Argentina ('AMIA') building in Buenos Aires in 1994.

The first dispute, *AMIA I* (which is also discussed in Chapters 8 and 9), derives from the publication of red notices by the INTERPOL General Secretariat at the request of NCB Buenos Aires in November 2003 against 12 Iranian nationals for allegedly participating in the bombing of the AMIA building. In January 2004, NCB Tehran challenged the General Secretariat's publication of the red notices on the ground that they were issued in violation of the INTERPOL Constitution and INTERPOL's rules because of alleged irregularities concerning the Argentinean investigating judge, Judge Galeano (including the bribery of a main witness).[19] The dispute could not be resolved by concerted consultations, so it was submitted to the Executive Committee. NCB Tehran and NCB Buenos Aires adduced additional information and presented their reasons for, respectively, challenging and requesting the publication of the red notices. In a unanimous decision, the Executive Committee ordered the General Secretariat to cancel the 12 red notices (in spite of the argument put forward by NCB Buenos Aires that it considered that any defects associated with the arrest warrants signed by Judge Galeano were cured by subsequent letters from Argentina stating that it still considered the red notices valid). NCB Buenos Aires appealed the decision of the Executive Committee, but the decision was subsequently endorsed by the General Assembly.[20]

In 2006/2007, news of INTERPOL and the AMIA bombing entered the public domain again (in what became known as *AMIA II*). In November 2006, NCB Buenos Aires requested the General Secretariat to publish red notices against nine individuals (eight Iranian nationals and one Lebanese national) who allegedly participated in the bombing of the AMIA building. The request of NCB Buenos Aires followed a re-examination of the prosecutor's case and the issuance of new arrest warrants (by a judge other than Judge Galeano). NCB Tehran challenged NCB Buenos Aires on its request for the publication of the red notices. In March 2007, the Executive Committee unanimously authorised the General Secretariat to publish six of the nine red notices on the basis that 'the reasons for having the Red Notices cancelled in 2005 were not present in 2007'. NCB Tehran appealed, so the publication of the red notices was temporarily suspended. The decision of the Executive Committee was subsequently endorsed by the General Assembly at its 76th session, and the six red notices were published.[21]

[19] Following a finding of the Argentinean judiciary in September 2004 that Judge Galeano should be removed for judicial misconduct, the General Secretariat suspended (by way of a provisional measure) the red notices in October 2004.

[20] 'Argentinean Red Notices for Iranian officials cancelled', INTERPOL press release (27 September 2005).

[21] 'INTERPOL General Assembly upholds Executive Committee decision on AMIA Red Notice dispute', INTERPOL press release (7 November 2007).

The third dispute concerns a former Prime Minister of Kazakhstan, Akezhan Kazhegeldin.[22] Kazhegeldin was the Prime Minister of Kazakhstan from 1994 to 1997. He was subsequently sought by Kazakhstan on charges of abuse of his official position, tax evasion and illegal possession of arms. On 12 July 2000, Kazhegeldin was arrested by the Italian authorities pursuant to a red notice published by the General Secretariat at the request of NCB Astana (as it was then known). The next day, the International League of Human Rights publicly expressed its concern over Kazhegeldin's arrest and the red notice issued by the General Secretariat on the basis that these acts 'constitute serious violations of agreed international norms'.[23] Following a request by Kazhegeldin's lawyer, the General Secretariat deleted the red notice on the basis that the use of INTERPOL's channels in this regard was a violation of Article 3 of the INTERPOL Constitution.[24] NCB Astana brought the matter to the attention of the Executive Committee, which unanimously affirmed the General Secretariat's decision. NCB Astana then requested the General Assembly, at its 71st session in Yaoundé, Cameroon in 2002, to reverse the decisions of the Executive Committee and the General Secretariat. On 23 October 2002, the General Assembly voted, by a 46–38 simple majority with 23 abstentions, to reinstate the red notice.[25] Subsequently, on 24 October 2002, the General Secretariat issued a red notice against Kazhegeldin.[26]

The fourth and final dispute concerns Zsolt Tamás Hernádi, the Chairman and Chief Executive Officer of Magyar Olaj-és Gázipari Részvénytársaság[27] Plc ('MOL'). Hernádi is wanted by the Croatian authorities for 'offering a bribe' to the then Prime Minister of Croatia, Ivo Sanader, to enable MOL to obtain a substantial stake in INA (Croatia's leading oil and gas company) and gain management rights of INA.[28] A red notice was published against Hernádi on 2 October 2013.[29] Shortly after the publication of the red notice, Hernádi submitted a request to the

[22] For background, see: Both, CR, 'International Police Force or Tool for Harassment of Human Rights Defenders and Political Adversaries: INTERPOL's rift with the human rights community' (2002) 8 *ILSA Journal of International & Comparative Law* 35761.

[23] 'International League for Human Rights voices its concern: Arrest of Mr Kazhegeldin constitutes serious violations of international norms', Public letter from the President of the International League for Human Rights to the Italian Minister of Justice (13 July 2000).

[24] 'INTERPOL Drops Arrest Warrant against Kazakhstani Opposition Leader', *Eurasianet* (26 June 2002).

[25] Resolution No AG-2002-RES-18, 'Request for Review from the Kazakhstan NCB concerning the Kazhegeldin Case (Article 3)', INTERPOL General Assembly, 71st session (Yaoundè, 2002).

[26] 'INTERPOL re-issue of red notice on former Kazakhstan PM', INTERPOL press release (24 October 2002).

[27] 'Hungarian Oil and Gas Company' (authors' translation).

[28] On 30 December 2019, Hernádi was found guilty of 'offering a bribe' to Ivo Sanader by a Croatian court and sentenced to two years' imprisonment. He was convicted and sentenced in Croatia, despite living in Hungary, where he has fought extradition to Croatia.

[29] Office of Legal Affairs, Report No 21, 'Dispute between NCB Zagreb and NCB Budapest concerning the re-publication of a red notice', AG-2016-RAP-21, INTERPOL General Assembly, 85th session (Bali, 2016), para 1.

Commission for the Control of INTERPOL's Files ('CCF'). The General Secretariat provisionally blocked the red notice whilst his case was being considered by the CCF. In February 2015, the General Secretariat reinstated the red notice (for reasons not publicly available). The red notice was suspended again by the General Secretariat in November 2015 at the request of the CCF while it was considering Hernádi's case. In December 2015, the CCF concluded that the red notice complied with INTERPOL's rules. However, in an unusual decision, the Office of Legal Affairs of the General Secretariat ('Office of Legal Affairs') decided that it would only reinstate the red notice if additional conditions were satisfied (eg, if Croatia took full responsibility for reimbursing the possible legal expenses that INTERPOL could encounter in possible external actions brought by Hernádi).[30]

In September 2016, the Ambassador of Hungary to France approached the General Secretariat. In a meeting held at the General Secretariat at the Ambassador's request, the Ambassador expressed Hungary's reservations about the possible reinstatement of the red notice against Hernádi. Hungary's position was made official in a joint letter signed by the Hungarian Minister of Justice and the Hungarian Minister of Foreign Affairs and Trade ('Hungarian Ministers'), which was sent to the INTERPOL Secretary General on 26 September 2016. The Hungarian Ministers explicitly requested the permanent deletion of the red notice. In support of their request, they mentioned the importance of MOL to the Hungarian economy and the harm caused to Hernádi. The Hungarian Ministers further detailed the criminal proceedings that took place in Hungary in the case and concluded that the ongoing proceedings in Croatia were in breach of the *non bis in idem* principle (as provided for in the legislative framework of the European Union ('EU')[31]).[32]

On 3 October 2016, NCB Zagreb sent a message to the INTERPOL President and the members of the Executive Committee asking that the red notice be unblocked.[33] In addition, in response to the letter sent by the Hungarian Ministers, the Croatian Minister of Justice, the Minister of Foreign and European Affairs, and the Minister of Interior ('Croatian Ministers') sent a letter to the INTERPOL Secretary General and the INTERPOL President on 14 October 2016. In their letter, the Croatian Ministers expressed their view that the letter from the Hungarian Ministers had been sent with the sole intention of delaying the proceedings and exerting political pressure on INTERPOL.[34]

[30] Ibid, para 2 and app 1.

[31] According to the principle of *non bis in idem* in EU law, no one shall be liable to be tried or punished again in criminal proceedings for an offence for which he or she has already been finally acquitted or convicted within the EU in accordance with the law.

[32] Office of Legal Affairs, Report No 21, 'Dispute between NCB Zagreb and NCB Budapest concerning the re-publication of a red notice', AG-2016-RAP-21, INTERPOL General Assembly, 85th session (Bali, 2016), para 3.

[33] Ibid, para 5.

[34] Ibid, para 4.

In conformity with Article 135(1) of the IRPD, the General Secretariat initiated concerted consultations between NCB Zagreb and NCB Budapest, which took place on 19 October 2016 at the General Secretariat in Lyon, France. No agreement was reached, so the matter was referred to the Executive Committee for consideration. Both NCBs were invited to make written submissions and present their positions to the Executive Committee during its 190th session on 6 November 2016 in Bali.[35] The decision of the Executive Committee was unequivocal: '[t]he General Secretariat shall immediately delete the red notice … and all data concerning [Hernádi] recorded in INTERPOL's databases, and shall refrain from processing any data concerning [him] in relation to this case', and 'NCB Zagreb may not use INTERPOL's channels … in relation to this case'.[36] In addition, the Executive Committee called upon NCB Zagreb and NCB Budapest to resolve amicably any existing dispute related to the case through bilateral discussions or by referring the dispute to the mechanisms put in place by the EU. The Executive Committee further decided that '[i]f the dispute is solved by a competent EU body in favour of Croatia, NCB Zagreb may request the Executive Committee to reconsider the publication of the red notice'.[37]

NCB Zagreb appealed the decision of the Executive Committee to the General Assembly. In Report No 21, submitted to the 85th session of the General Assembly on 7 November 2016, the Office of Legal Affairs provided the General Assembly with an overview of the dispute and invited the General Assembly to 'confirm' the decision of the Executive Committee.[38] The decision of the Executive Committee was endorsed by the General Assembly in November 2016, and the red notice was deleted.

On 16 May 2017, the Zagreb County Court requested a preliminary ruling under Article 267 of the Treaty on the Functioning of the European Union from the Court of Justice of the EU ('CJEU'). The Zagreb County Court referred five questions to the CJEU, including questions related to the principle of *non bis in idem*.[39] On 25 July 2018, the CJEU responded that the principle of *non bis in idem* did not apply to the specific factual matrix relevant to Hernádi.[40] After the decision of the CJEU, NCB Zagreb requested that the Executive Committee reconsider the publication of the red notice against Hernádi. The Executive Committee considered this request and determined that the processing of data was permitted. A new red notice was therefore published in November 2018.[41]

The foregoing cases demonstrate that, where the dispute is ostensibly a dispute between an NCB and the General Secretariat (eg, *AMIA I* and *Kazhegeldin*), as

[35] Ibid, para 8.
[36] Ibid, para 9.
[37] Ibid, para 9.
[38] Ibid, para 12.
[39] *AY (Mandat d'arrêt – Témoin)*, Case C-268/17, ECLI:EU:C:2018:602, para 20.
[40] Ibid, para 64.
[41] Ilic, I and Szakacs, G, 'Interpol renews arrest warrant for MOL's CEO, Croatia says', *Reuters* (Zagreb, 17 November 2018).

opposed to a dispute ostensibly between two NCBs (eg, *AMIA II* and *Hernádi*), the prospects of the General Assembly aligning with the NCB are higher. In such disputes, the technical arguments that motivate the General Secretariat to publish, block or delete data can be difficult to relay in the politically charged environment of a General Assembly session, and it is easy to portray the General Secretariat as a stubborn bureaucracy that seeks to impose its will on the members of the Organisation. In an effort to avoid showdowns between the General Secretariat and an NCB before the General Assembly (or indeed the Executive Committee), the General Secretariat will often process the impugned data in the INTERPOL Information System subject to the caveat that the case is under review. The effect of such a caveat is that (many) NCBs will not use the impugned data for the purposes of international police cooperation which, in turn, provides the General Secretariat with some leverage for resolving the dispute.

Furthermore, although *AMIA I*, *AMIA II*, *Kazhegeldin* and *Hernádi* indicate that members tend to intervene only on behalf of their own nationals, Article 135 of the IRPD does not embrace the 'nationality of claims' rule. In general international law, the 'nationality of claims' rule requires that, in principle, if the claimant State cannot establish the nationality of the claim, the claim is inadmissible because of the absence of any legal interest on its part.[42] However, this rule does not apply in the context of INTERPOL because its members have a right – and interest – in supervising and challenging acts *ultra vires* the Organisation (an international organisation that they willed into existence). The members of INTERPOL have a common interest in ensuring that the political neutrality of the Organisation is preserved[43] and that the Organisation abides by its commitment to observe the spirit of the Universal Declaration of Human Rights.[44]

This conclusion is borne out by lesser known cases where notices were challenged by members whose nationals were not the subject of the relevant notices. The most striking example arose in 1950. After hijacking two aircrafts and landing them in Allied-occupied Germany, Czechoslovakian nationals requested political asylum in the US and were granted asylum. In the meantime, Czechoslovakia requested the publication of red notices in respect of the Czechoslovakian nationals, and the General Secretariat acceded to the request. J Edgar Hoover, then Director of the Federal Bureau of Investigation, which represented the US

[42] *Panevezys-Saldutiskis Railway* (Judgment) [1939] PCIJ Series A/B No 76, 16. However, there are a number of exceptions to this principle (see: Crawford, J, *Brownlie's Principles of Public International Law*, 9th edn (Oxford, Oxford University Press, 2019) 676).

[43] See Article 3 of the INTERPOL Constitution and Resolution No AG-2006-RES-04, in which the General Assembly resolved to '[c]all upon the General Secretariat as well as the member countries to consult with one another or with any intergovernmental institution contemplating to take measures which would interfere with the Organization's neutrality and independence' (Resolution AG-2006-RES-04, 'Statement to Reaffirm the Independence and Political Neutrality of Interpol', INTERPOL General Assembly, 75th session (Rio de Janeiro, 2006), operative para 4).

[44] See Article 2(1) of the INTERPOL Constitution and the analysis of the International Court of Justice in the context of the Convention against Torture at paragraph 68 in *Questions relating to the Obligation to Prosecute or Extradite (Belgium v Senegal)* (Judgment) [2012] ICJ Rep 422.

in the International Criminal Police Commission ('ICPC') (the prior name of INTERPOL), asserted that the ICPC should not have published the red notices because of its constitutional prohibition on political interventions. He therefore took the (rather extreme) decision to withdraw the US from the ICPC.[45] Fortunately, more recent experiences suggest that a carefully managed dispute settlement procedure, such as that envisaged in Article 135 of the IRPD, is likely to produce an outcome that carries the necessary legitimacy to avoid such a dramatic turn of events.

[45] Fooner, M, *INTERPOL: Issues in World Crime and International Criminal Justice* (New York, Plenum Press, 1989) 24, 41.

11

External Law and Responsibility

In Chapter 8, it was explained that the sources of the legal obligations of the International Criminal Police Organisation ('INTERPOL' or the 'Organisation') can be divided into two broad categories: internal law (which includes INTERPOL's constituent instrument) and external law. Chapter 8 considered the internal law of the Organisation. This chapter is concerned with the external law and responsibility of the Organisation.

I. External Legal Order[1]

International organisations are bound by international agreements to which they are party and 'general rules of international law'.[2] This is not a controversial proposition: the International Criminal Tribunal for the former Yugoslavia,[3] the Court of Justice of the European Communities ('CJEC')/Court of Justice of the European Union ('CJEU')[4] and national courts[5] have all reached similar conclusions.

[1] There are different views on the operation of domestic laws in respect of international organisations. For an in-depth discussion, see: Seyersted, F, *Common Law of International Organizations* (Leiden, Martinus Nijhoff Publishers, 2008) 441–585. This book does not engage with this discussion, save to note that there are examples of international organisations considering themselves subject to contractual and non-contractual obligations under domestic law.

[2] *Interpretation of the Agreement of 25 March 1951 between the WHO and Egypt* (Advisory Opinion) [1980] ICJ Rep 73, para 37. The International Court of Justice ('ICJ') has also used the expression 'general international law' (see, eg: *Accordance with International Law of the Unilateral Declaration of Independence in respect of Kosovo* (Advisory Opinion) [2010] ICJ Rep 403, paras 78–84; *Pulp Mills on the River Uruguay (Argentina v Uruguay)* (Judgment) [2010] ICJ Rep 14, paras 53–66 and 204–05).

[3] Eg, *Prosecutor v Blagoje Simić et al* (Decision on the Prosecution Motion under Rule 73 for a Ruling concerning the Testimony of a Witness) (27 July 1999) Case No IT-95-9, para 42.

[4] Eg, *Yassin Abdullah Kadi and Al Barakaat International Foundation v Council of the European Union and Commission of the European Communities*, Joined Cases C-402/05 P & C-415/05 P, [2008] ECR I-6351, para 291; *Western Sahara Campaign UK v Commissioners for Her Majesty's Revenue and Customs and Secretary of State for Environment, Food and Rural Affairs*, Case C-266/16, ECLI:EU:C:2018:118, para 47. Prior to the entry into force of the Treaty of Lisbon on 1 December 2009, the CJEU was known as the CJEC.

[5] Eg, *Nacci v Bari Institute of the International Centre for Advanced Mediterranean Agronomic Studies*, Italian Court of Cassation (8 June 1994) 114 ILR 540, 544; *Supreme Headquarters Allied Powers Europe and Allied Joint Force Command Headquarters v Supreme Site Services GmbH, Supreme Fuels GmbH & Co KG and Supreme Fuels Trading FZE*, Court of Appeal of 's-Hertogenbosch, Judgment No 200.216.570_01 (10 December 2019) para 6.7.9.1.

This proposition is also reflected in the practice of international organisations, including legal opinions of secretariats[6] and resolutions of the United Nations ('UN') Security Council.[7] While there is a lack of discussion in the jurisprudence of the ICJ on the meaning of the expressions 'general rules of international law' and 'general international law', the expressions should be understood to include customary international law of a universal (or almost universal) character (rather than customary international law of a local character)[8] and general principles of law.[9] In other words, and as detailed below, international organisations, such as INTERPOL, are bound by international agreements to which they are party, customary international law and general principles of law.

With respect to international agreements, international organisations may, pursuant to their constituent instruments, enter into treaty relationships with other international organisations and States. By way of example, and as discussed in Chapter 7, INTERPOL has entered into international agreements with the UN[10] (and several of its specialised agencies)[11] and a number of INTERPOL members.[12]

With respect to customary international law, it is acknowledged that many rules of customary international law will not be relevant to international

[6] Eg, Secretariat of the UN Industrial Development Organization ('UNIDO'), 'United Nations sanctions against Iraq – Shipment of equipment to a project in Iraq – *Force majeure*' in *United Nations Juridical Yearbook* (1990), Part Two, Chapter VI, 311; Legal Adviser of the UNIDO, 'Internet e-mail message memorandum to a UNIDO Industrial Development Officer concerning partnership with [Company] in a UNIDO project in [State]' in *United Nations Juridical Yearbook* (2014), Part Two, Chapter VI, 350.

[7] Eg, UN Security Council Resolution 841, 16 June 1993, operative para 9.

[8] See: *Case concerning Right of Passage over Indian Territory* (Merits) [1960] ICJ Rep 6, 39; *Columbian-Peruvian asylum case* (Judgment) [1950] ICJ Rep 266, 276.

[9] *Certain Activities Carried Out by Nicaragua in the Border Area (Costa Rica v Nicaragua) and Construction of a Road in Costa Rica along the San Juan River (Nicaragua v Costa Rica)* [2015] ICJ Rep 665, 842, para 16 (Separate Opinion of Judge *ad hoc* Dugard): '[w]hat meaning then is to be attached to the term "general international law" … ? … Certainly it includes both customary international law and general principles of law within the meaning of Article 38 (1)(c) and (d) of the Court's Statute'; Verdirame, G, *The UN and Human Rights: Who Guards the Guardians* (Cambridge, Cambridge University Press, 2011) 71: '[t]he most plausible interpretation is that [the expressions "general rules of international law" and "general international law"] are shorthand for customary international law of universal or quasi-universal applicability and for general principles of law'. See also: Benvenisti, E, *The Law of Global Governance* (The Hague, Brill, 2014) 99.

[10] Cooperation Agreement between the United Nations and the International Criminal Police Organization (INTERPOL) (signed on 8 July 1997) 1996 UNTS 391.

[11] Eg, Cooperation Agreement between the International Criminal Police Organization – INTERPOL and the United Nations Educational, Scientific and Cultural Organization (signed on and entered into force on 5 October 1999) 2085 UNTS 445.

[12] Eg, Agreement between the International Criminal Police Organization – INTERPOL and the Government of the French Republic regarding INTERPOL's Headquarters in France (entered into force on 1 September 2009) as amended by Decree No 2016-326 of 17 March 2016 promulgating the additional protocol in the form of an exchange of letters between the Government of the French Republic and the International Criminal Police Organization – INTERPOL on the interpretation and application of Article 24 of the Agreement of 14 and 24 April 2008 regarding INTERPOL's headquarters in France (signed in Paris on 9 February 2016 and in Lyon on 12 February 2016, entered into force on 16 February 2016).

organisations because they have no territorial waters, no nationals, etc.[13] However, it is difficult to conceive of many international organisations whose activities do not engage (at least some of) the rules of customary international law relating to the protection of fundamental human rights. In *Rwamakuba*, Trial Chamber III of the International Criminal Tribunal for Rwanda ('ICTR') found that, as a 'special kind of subsidiary organ of the UN Security Council', the ICTR was obligated 'to grant an effective remedy' to an accused or former accused.[14] To reach this conclusion, Trial Chamber III reasoned as follows. First, it found that the right of an individual to an effective remedy forms part of customary international law.[15] Second, it found that 'the United Nations, as an international subject, is bound to respect rules of customary international law, including those rules which relate to the protection of fundamental human rights'.[16] That there exists a relationship between the right of an individual to an effective remedy and an obligation on subjects of international law to respect that right appears unimpeachable. In the *Tehran Hostages* case, the United States correctly spoke of '[t]he existence of … fundamental rights for all human beings … and the existence of a corresponding duty on the part of every State [ie, a subject of international law] to respect and observe them'.[17]

Thus, even if an international organisation is not a party to a human rights treaty, the international organisation will be bound by any rule contained in customary international law.[18] It is, therefore, not surprising that the International Law

[13] It is worth noting that, in its work on the 'identification of customary international law', the International Law Commission ('ILC') was not concerned with the issue of whether international organisations are bound by customary international law. Rather, the ILC was only concerned with 'the way in which the existence and content of rules of customary international law are to be determined' (Report of the ILC on the work of its seventieth session (30 April 2018 – 1 June 2018 and 2 July 2018 – 10 August 2018), 'Draft conclusions on identification of customary international law, with commentaries', UN Doc A/73/10 (2018) 119, Conclusion 1).

[14] *The Prosecutor v André Rwamakuba* (Decision on Appropriate Remedy) (31 January 2007) Case No ICTR-98-44C-T, para 49. In this case, Mr Rwamakuba sought an effective remedy for the violation of his right to legal assistance.

[15] Ibid, paras 40–5.

[16] Ibid, para 48.

[17] *United States Diplomatic and Consular Staff in Tehran (United States of America v Iran)*, Memorial of the Government of the United States of America (12 January 1980) 182 (emphasis added).

[18] See: UN Secretariat, 'Secretary-General's Bulletin: Observance by United Nations forces of international humanitarian law', UN Doc ST/SGB/1999/13 (6 August 1999) s 3. This is also recognised in the ILC Draft Articles on the Responsibility of International Organizations ('DARIO'). Article 4 of the DARIO provides the elements of an internationally wrongful act. It requires that the conduct objected to be attributable to an international organisation under international law and that it constitutes a breach of an obligation that exists under international law for that organisation. In the Commentary, it is stated that the obligation may result either from a treaty binding the international organisation or from any other source of international law applicable to the organisation ('Draft articles on the responsibility of international organizations, with commentaries' in *Yearbook of the International Law Commission* (2011) Vol II, Part Two, 53, Commentary to Art 4, para 2). Article 4 should be read alongside Article 10, which defines the existence of a breach of an international obligation without regard to the origin or character of the obligation concerned. In the Commentary, it is stated that an international obligation may be established 'by a customary rule of international law, by a treaty or by a

Association's Committee on the Accountability of International Organisations found that:

> [h]uman rights obligations, which are increasingly becoming an expression of the common constitutional traditions of States, can become binding upon IO-s in different ways: through the terms of their constituent instruments; as customary international law; or as general principles of law or if an IO is authorised to become a party to a human rights treaty. The consistent practice of IO-s points to a recognition of this. Moreover, certain human rights obligations may have attained the status of peremptory norms.[19]

There is, of course, nothing objectionable about subjecting international organisations to customary international law (and, in particular, customary human rights law). If the international community permitted States to create international organisations as a means to flout these fundamental rules, the whole international legal system would quickly disintegrate. Furthermore, the capacity of international organisations to operate on the international plane entails their capacity to contribute (within the scope of their activities) to customary international law (ie, law-making capacity).[20] It would be curious if international organisations were not bound by the rules in which they played a role in creating.

INTERPOL has (explicitly and implicitly) recognised that it is subject to customary international law on at least three occasions. First, the Organisation is one of 12 international organisations to have ratified the 1986 Vienna Convention on the Law of Treaties between States and International Organizations or between International Organizations ('VCLT-IO').[21] The VCLT-IO is 'an international agreement governed by international law' which is tailored to international organisations 'as subjects of international law distinct from States'.[22] The VCLT-IO explicitly affirms that disputes should be settled in conformity with 'the principles of justice and international law' and that 'the rules of customary international law will continue to govern questions not regulated by the provisions of the present Convention'.[23] Second, in its comments and observations of 9 February 2005 to

general principle applicable within the international legal order' ('Draft articles on the responsibility of international organizations, with commentaries' in *Yearbook of the International Law Commission* (2011) Vol II, Part Two, 63, Commentary to Art 10, para 2).

[19] International Law Association, 'Accountability of International Organisations', Final Report (2004) 22. See also: Cogen, M, 'Human Rights, Prohibition of Political Activities and the Lending Policies of the World Bank and the International Monetary Fund' in Chowdhury, SR, Denters, EMG and de Waart, PJIM (eds), *The Right to Development in International Law* (Dordrecht, Martinus Nijhoff Publishers, 1992) 379–96 at 387.

[20] Report of the ILC on the work of its seventieth session (30 April 2018 – 1 June 2018 and 2 July 2018 – 10 August 2018), 'Text of the draft conclusions on identification of customary international law, with commentaries', UN Doc A/73/10 (2018) 130, Conclusion 4(2).

[21] As of 31 January 2020, the VCLT-IO was not in force. The VCLT-IO will enter into force upon its ratification by 35 States.

[22] VCLT-IO, preamble and Art 2(1)(a).

[23] Ibid, preamble.

the ILC on practice relevant to the topic of the responsibility of international organisations, INTERPOL stated that '[t]he obligations resting upon international organizations by virtue of their constituent instruments and the secondary law of international organizations are international legal norms in the same way as the obligations from the treaties to which an organization may be a party and other applicable rules of customary international law'.[24] Third, INTERPOL's public website previously stated that:

> the principles enshrined in the Universal Declaration of Human Rights have been widely considered to have attained the status of customary international law. The obligation in the Universal Declaration of Human Rights – to ensure a minimum level of respect for an individual's most essential rights stemming from his existence as a human being – is not only limited to states; it extends to actors on the international scene as well.[25]

With respect to general principles of law, there is ample evidence to indicate that international organisations are bound by three categories of general principles of law.

First, there are general principles existing in *foro domestico* of States. The most prominent examples are found in the jurisprudence of the CJEC from the late 1960s/1970s according to which certain fundamental rights, as articulated in the domestic constitutional law of the Member States of the European Communities and the European Convention on Human Rights ('ECHR'),[26] were regarded as general principles of law binding on the European Communities.[27]

Second, there are general principles of international law. For instance, the CJEU has had regard to 'the general international-law principle of the relative effect of treaties', according to which 'treaties do not impose any obligations, or confer any rights, on third States without their consent'.[28]

Third, there are general principles of law common to all international organisations. General principles of law common to all international organisations exist independently of constituent instruments of international organisations.[29]

[24] ILC, 'Comments and observations received from Governments and international organizations', UN Doc A/CN.4/556 (12 May 2005) 30 and 43–4.

[25] INTERPOL, 'Human rights', 6 October 2016, available at: http://web.archive.org/web/20161006081133/http://www.interpol.int/About-INTERPOL/Legal-materials/Human-rights.

[26] Convention for the Protection of Human Rights and Fundamental Freedoms (adopted on 4 November 1950, entered into force on 3 September 1953) 213 UNTS 221.

[27] Eg, *Erich Stauder v City of Ulm, Sozialamt*, Case C-29/69, [1969] ECR 419; *Internationale Handelsgesellschaft mbH v Einfuhr-und Vorratsstelle für Getreide und Futtermittel*, Case C-11/70, [1970] ECR 1125; *J Nold, Kohlen- und Baustoffgroßhandlung v Commission of the European Communities*, Case C-4/73, [1974] ECR 491.

[28] Eg, *Council of the European Union v Front populaire pour la libération de la saguia-el-hamra et du rio de oro (Front Polisario)*, Case C-104/16 P, ECLI:EU:C:2016:973, para 100.

[29] Institut de Droit International, 'The Law Applicable to Joint International State or Quasi-State Enterprises of an Economic Nature' (28 August 1985) Art 5(3). See also: *Mirella et al v Secretary-General of the United Nations*, Judgment No UNDT/2017/099 (29 December 2017), para 107 (although this judgment was vacated on 29 June 2018 by the UN Appeals Tribunal).

These general principles of law have been repeatedly invoked by international administrative tribunals.[30]

II. Responsibility

A. General Framework

Today, international organisations are one of the most prominent non-State actors on the international plane. They perform many functions traditionally performed by States, including, for example, maintaining peace and security (eg, the UN), attaining the highest possible level of health (eg, the World Health Organization), providing financial assistance (eg, the World Bank), and facilitating international police cooperation (eg, INTERPOL). In performing these functions, international organisations encounter difficult choices. Should the World Bank finance a coal-fired power plant where there is evidence that the use of the power plant will lead to environmental damage? Should the UN end a peacekeeping operation where there is evidence to suggest that, in so doing, a genocidal conflict will occur? Should INTERPOL publish and maintain a red notice at the request of a member where there is evidence that the member will torture the relevant individual upon his extradition? These questions raise issues concerning the (potential) responsibility of international organisations.

As subjects of international law which are bound by obligations under international agreements to which they are party and 'general rules of international law', international organisations possess the capacity to breach those obligations, ie, commit internationally wrongful acts ('*aktive Deliktsfähigkeit*'),[31] and they are responsible under international law for breaches of those obligations. This was recognised by the ICJ in *Cumaraswamy* in which it held that the UN 'may be required to bear responsibility for the damage arising' from 'acts performed by the UN or by its agents acting in their official capacity'.[32] It was also recognised

[30] A portion of these general principles are general principles of international civil service law. Methodologically, it is clear that these principles are not derived from the internal law of one international organisation, but, rather, they are shared by all international organisations (see, eg: *In re Touré*, where the Administrative Tribunal of the International Labour Organization ('ILOAT') relied on the Advisory Opinion in *Reparation for Injuries* (which sets out principles of general application to all agents of an organisation, not only staff members) to identify 'the duty of protection and assistance to which every international organisation owes its officials under a general principle of international civil service law' (*In re Touré*, ILOAT, Judgment No 3141 (2012) para 43)).

[31] On the capacity of international organisations to commit internationally wrongful acts ('*aktive Deliktsfähigkeit*'), see: Meng, W, 'Internationale Organisationen im völkerrechtlichen Deliktsrecht' (1985) 45 *Zeitschrift für ausländisches öffentliches Recht und Völkerrecht* 324–57; von Arnauld, A, *Völkerrecht* (Heidelberg, CF Müller GmbH, 2012) 150–51.

[32] *Difference Relating to Immunity from Legal Process of a Special Rapporteur of the Commission on Human Rights* (Advisory Opinion) [1999] ICJ Rep 62, para 66.

by UN Secretary-General Boutros-Ghali in a 1996 report to the UN General Assembly:

> [t]he international responsibility of the United Nations for the activities of United Nations forces is an attribute of its international legal personality and its capacity to bear international rights and obligations. It is also a reflection of the principle of State responsibility – widely accepted to be applicable to international organizations – that damage caused in breach of an international obligation and which is attributable to the State (or to the Organization), entails the international responsibility of the State (or of the Organization) and its liability in compensation.[33]

The ILC drew on this reasoning in its work on the responsibility of international organisations.[34] As with the law of treaties, the issue of responsibility of States was addressed first, and the issue of responsibility of international organisations was addressed later, with the ILC Articles on the Responsibility of States for Internationally Wrongful Acts ('ARS') offering a 'source of inspiration'.[35] In 2011, the ILC adopted a set of articles on the responsibility of international organisations (ie, the DARIO).[36] The UN General Assembly subsequently took 'note' of the DARIO.[37]

The structure of the DARIO broadly replicates the structure of the ARS. Careful consideration of the DARIO, against the background of the reports of Special Rapporteur Gaja and the ILC reports, reveals that, although many of the articles in the DARIO are similar to the articles in the ARS, these similarities are not the consequence of a mechanical replica of text or 'a presumption that solutions applying to states are generally applicable to international organizations' but, rather, 'the result of an analysis of the available materials'.[38]

[33] Report of the UN Secretary-General, 'Administrative and budgetary aspects of the financing of the United Nations peacekeeping operations: financing of the United Nations peacekeeping operations', UN Doc A/51/389 (20 September 1996) para 6.

[34] 'Draft articles on the responsibility of international organizations, with commentaries' in *Yearbook of the International Law Commission* (2011) Vol II, Part Two, 52, Commentary to Art 3, para 1.

[35] Report of the ILC Working Group, 'The responsibility of international organizations: scope and orientation of the study', UN Doc A/CN.4/L.622 (6 June 2002) para 14.

[36] 'Draft articles on the responsibility of international organizations, with commentaries' in *Yearbook of the International Law Commission* (2011) Vol II, Part Two, 46–105.

[37] UN General Assembly, 'Responsibility of international organisations', UN Doc A/RES/66/100 (27 February 2012) operative para 3.

[38] Fifth report on responsibility of international organizations by Special Rapporteur Giorgio Gaja, UN Doc A/CN.4/583 (2 May 2007) para 2. See also. Sixth report on responsibility of international organizations by Special Rapporteur Giorgio Gaja, UN Doc A/CN.4/597 (1 April 2008) para 5; Scovazzi, T, 'Within and Beyond *Mutatis Mutandis*', in Ragazzi, M (ed), *Responsibility of International Organizations: Essays in Memory of Sir Ian Brownlie* (Leiden, Martinus Nijhoff Publishers, 2013) 121–32 at 130. In his book on the analogy between States and international organisations, Bordin compellingly argues that the ILC's extension of rules from States to international organisations through the use of analogy should not be dismissed, without more, as *de lege ferenda* or 'progressive development' of the law. Bordin's work confirms that the ILC was not on the wrong path when it viewed the two categories of international legal subjects as falling under common principles or when it saw 'little' or 'no reason' to distinguish between them (Bordin, FL, *The Analogy between States and International Organizations* (Cambridge, Cambridge University Press, 2019)).

In the context of INTERPOL and the (implicit) suggestion of some that INTERPOL's members are responsible for its internationally wrongful acts, certain elements of the law of responsibility merit brief attention. These elements pertain to the law of attribution and the relationship between the responsibility of international organisations and the responsibility of their members.

With respect to the law of attribution, conduct consisting of an act or omission that may be attributed to an international organisation includes that of any of its organs, as well as that of its 'agents'.[39] These 'agents' may be its officials, as well as other persons acting for the organisation on the basis of functions conferred by an organ.[40] In *Reparation for Injuries*, the ICJ stated that it understood the word 'agent' in 'the most liberal sense, that is to say, any person who, whether a paid official or not, and whether permanently employed or not, has been charged by an organ of the Organization with carrying out, or helping to carry out, one of its functions – in short, any person through whom it acts'.[41] In *Cumaraswamy*, as noted above, the ICJ held that the UN 'may be required to bear responsibility for the damage arising' from 'acts performed by the UN or by its agents acting in their official capacity'.[42] This view is not confined to the UN. In a decision of 30 October 1996, the Swiss Federal Council found that '*[e]n règle générale, sont imputables à une organisation internationale les actes ou omissions de ses organes de tout rang et de toute nature et de ses agents dans l'exercice de leurs compétences*'.[43] Furthermore, *ultra vires* acts of an organ or agent will be attributable to the organisation where the organ or agent acts in an official capacity and within the overall functions of the organisation[44] – eg, an act performed by an organ within the scope of the

[39] 'Draft articles on the responsibility of international organizations, with commentaries' in *Yearbook of the International Law Commission* (2011) Vol II, Part Two, 55, Art 6(1).

[40] Ibid, Commentary to Art 6, para 2.

[41] *Reparation for Injuries Suffered in the Service of the United Nations* (Advisory Opinion) [1949] ICJ Rep 174, 177. In *Mazilu*, the ICJ noted that '[i]n practice, according to the information supplied by the Secretary-General, the United Nations has had occasion to entrust missions – increasingly varied in nature – to persons not having the status of United Nations officials' (*Applicability of Article VI, Section 22, of the Convention on the Privileges and Immunities of the United Nations* (Advisory Opinion) [1989] ICJ Rep 177, para 48).

[42] *Difference Relating to Immunity from Legal Process of a Special Rapporteur of the Commission on Human Rights* (Advisory Opinion) [1999] ICJ Rep 62, para 66.

[43] 'As a rule, one attributes to an international organization acts and omissions of its organs of all rank and nature and of its agents in the exercise of their competences' (authors' translation) (Decision of the Swiss Federal Council, VPB 61.75 (30 October 1996) para 4). See also: 'Draft articles on the responsibility of international organizations, with commentaries' in *Yearbook of the International Law Commission* (2011) Vol II, Part Two, 55, Commentary to Art 6, paras 1–4.

[44] 'Draft articles on the responsibility of international organizations, with commentaries' in *Yearbook of the International Law Commission* (2011) Vol II, Part Two, 60, Art 8. The UN Office of Legal Affairs advised in 1974 that tortious acts committed by members of a UN Emergency Force during their off-duty periods could be recognised as engaging the responsibility of the UN if the acts were closely related to the functions of the UN Emergency Force member, such as the use of a government-issued weapon (Report of the ILC, 'Responsibility of international organizations: Comments and observations received from international organizations', UN Doc A/CN.4/637/Add.1 (17 February 2011) 15).

functions of the organisation as a whole will be attributable to the organisation even if the act is performed by the wrong organ as a matter of internal distribution of functions.[45]

With respect to the relationship between the responsibility of international organisations and the responsibility of their members, Article 3 of the DARIO provides that '[e]very internationally wrongful act of an international organization entails the international responsibility of that organization'. Article 3 must be read alongside relevant practice which indicates that, generally, a State that is a member of an international organisation may not incur responsibility for the internationally wrongful act of that organisation.[46] In the International Tin Council ('I.T.C.') litigation, Lord Kerr (then sitting in the Court of Appeal of England and Wales) said that he could not:

> find any basis for concluding that it has been shown that there is any rule of international law, binding upon the member States of the I.T.C., whereby they can be held liable – let alone jointly and severally – in any national court to the creditors of the I.T.C. for the debts of the I.T.C. resulting from contracts concluded by the I.T.C. in its own name.[47]

Lord Kerr's view was affirmed by the House of Lords of the United Kingdom ('UK'). In the House of Lords, in respect of an alleged rule of international law imposing on sovereign States and members of an international organisation 'joint and several liability for the default of the organisation in the payment of its debts unless the treaty which establishes the international organisation clearly disclaims any liability on the part of the members', Lord Templeman found that '[n]o plausible evidence was produced of the existence of such a rule of international law before or at the time of [the Sixth International Tin Agreement] in 1982 or thereafter'.[48] The views of Lord Kerr and Lord Templeman in the I.T.C. litigation were echoed in a resolution adopted by the Institut de Droit International in 1995: 'there is no general rule of international law whereby States members are, due solely to their membership, liable, concurrently or subsidiarily, for the obligations of an international organization of which they are members'.[49] The positions of Lord Kerr, Lord

[45] *Certain Expenses of the United Nations (Article 17, paragraph 2, of the Charter)* (Advisory Opinion) [1962] ICJ Rep 151, 168.

[46] See: Akande, D, 'International Organizations' in Evans, MD (ed), *International Law*, 5th edn (Oxford, Oxford University Press, 2018) 227–58 at 244.

[47] *JH Rayner (Mincing Lane) Ltd v Department of Trade and Industry and others and related appeals; Maclaine Watson & Co Ltd v Department of Trade and Industry* [1988] 3 WLR 1033 (CA), 1095. The I.T.C. litigation arose as a consequence of the failure of the I.T.C. to fulfil its obligations under several contracts.

[48] *JH Rayner (Mincing Lane) Ltd v Department of Trade and Industry; Maclaine Watson & Co Ltd v Department of Trade and Industry; Maclaine Watson & Co Ltd v International Tin Council; TSB England and Wales v Department of Trade and Industry; Amalgamated Metal Trading Ltd v International Tin Council* [1989] 3 WLR 969 (HL), 983.

[49] Institut de Droit International, 'The Legal Consequences for Member States of the Non-Fulfilment by International Organizations of their Obligations toward Third Parties' (1 September 1995), Art 6(a).

Templeman and the Institut de Droit International rightly led Special Rapporteur Gaja to conclude that 'only in exceptional cases could a State that is a member of an international organization incur responsibility for the internationally wrongful act of that organization'.[50] Of course, that is not to say that the existence of parallel responsibility of other subjects of international law (eg, States) is excluded where an international organisation is responsible for an internationally wrongful act in the same set of circumstances. It clearly is not.[51]

B. The Responsibility of International Organisations in Practice

With the foregoing preliminary observations on the framework for responsibility in mind, we now explore how INTERPOL could conceivably commit internationally wrongful acts in connection with the circulation of information about wanted persons. The following hypothetical will assist in this exercise.

On 1 September 2017, the INTERPOL General Secretariat published a red notice against Heracles at the request of the National Central Bureau ('NCB') of Rosmarus in relation to allegations of money laundering. On 4 January 2018, Heracles requested the Requests Chamber of the Commission for the Control of INTERPOL's Files ('Requests Chamber') (the internal body responsible for deciding on requests in respect of data processed in the INTERPOL Information System) to order the General Secretariat to delete the red notice in respect of him. In his request, Heracles argued that there was a real risk that he would be tortured in Rosmarus and provided the Requests Chamber with evidence (in the form of witness statements) that members of his family (who are co-accused in Rosmarus) had been tortured upon their detention in Rosmarus. Heracles also requested the Requests Chamber to afford him an oral session. On 2 August 2018, the Requests Chamber informed Heracles that it had rejected his request to delete the red notice. In rejecting Heracles' request, the Requests Chamber:

(1) found that it does not enter into a searching inquiry designed to confirm or refute the validity of proceedings in a manner akin to that in which a domestic appellate court would re-examine the actions of domestic courts;
(2) found that it is not empowered to conduct an investigation, weigh evidence or make a determination on the merits of a case;
(3) found that, as it was able to make a determination on each of Heracles' claims on the basis of the elements available to it, an oral session was not necessary;

[50] Fourth report on responsibility of international organizations by Special Rapporteur Giorgio Gaja, UN Doc A/CN.4/564 and Add. 1–2 (28 February 2006, 12 April 2006, 20 April 2006) para 96. Such exceptional circumstances are envisaged in Part Five of the DARIO.

[51] 'Draft articles on the responsibility of international organizations, with commentaries' in *Yearbook of the International Law Commission* (2011) Vol II, Part Two, 53, Commentary to Art 3, para 6.

(4) informed Heracles that it had (a) engaged in *ex parte* communications with the INTERPOL General Secretariat, (b) refused to share the substance of the *ex parte* communications with Heracles, and (c) made a decision on the substance of the *ex parte* communications without providing Heracles an opportunity to respond to the information relayed by the General Secretariat;
(5) relied on information and evidence provided by NCB Rosmarus, but refused to share this information and evidence (either before or after making its decision) with Heracles because of security concerns cited by NCB Rosmarus; and
(6) stated that its decision is binding and there is no opportunity to appeal either the substance of its decision or any procedural irregularities in the proceedings.[52]

On 1 September 2018, Heracles flew from Urusus to Larmastan. Upon entering Larmastan, Heracles was arrested by the Larmastan authorities on the basis of the red notice. Subsequently, on 1 February 2019, Heracles was extradited from Larmastan to Rosmarus. From 2 February 2019 to 3 April 2019, Heracles was physically tortured in Rosmarus by the Rosmarus authorities. Since 6 April 2019, Heracles has been detained in solitary confinement, and no trial date has been set.

The decision of INTERPOL to publish and maintain a red notice against Heracles, alongside the treatment of Heracles in Rosmarus, raises questions concerning INTERPOL's responsibility under international law. In particular, INTERPOL must respect Heracles' customary international law rights (eg, afford Heracles a fair trial and an effective remedy), and it must not aid or assist Rosmarus in the commission of internationally wrongful acts (eg, aid or assist Rosmarus in the commission of torture or cruel, inhuman or degrading treatment or punishment).

i. *Right to a Fair Trial and Right to an Effective Remedy*

The right to a fair trial forms part of customary international law.[53] Fair trial guarantees can be found in most universal[54] and regional[55] human rights treaties.

[52] While the example concerning Heracles is fictional, the authors have been privy to decisions of the Requests Chamber which, together, exhibit (expressly or impliedly) the foregoing reasoning.

[53] See: *Prosecutor v Zlatko Aleksovski* (Judgment) (24 March 2000) Case No IT-95-14/1-A, para 104; *Prosecutor v Clément Kayishema and Obed Ruzindana* (Judgment) (1 June 2001) Case No ICTR-95-1-A, para 51; UN Human Rights Committee, 'General Comment No. 29: States of Emergency (Article 4)', UN Doc CCPR/C/21/Rev.1/Add.11 (31 August 2001) para 11; Henckaerts, J-M and Doswald-Beck, L, *Customary International Humanitarian Law* (Cambridge, Cambridge University Press, 2009) Vol I, Rule 100, 352.

[54] See, eg: International Covenant on Civil and Political Rights (adopted on 16 December 1966, entered into force on 23 March 1976) 999 UNTS 171 and 1057 UNTS 407 ('ICCPR'), Art 14; Convention on the Rights of the Child (adopted on 20 November 1989, entered into force on 2 September 1990) 1577 UNTS 3, Art 4; International Convention on the Protection of the Rights of All Migrant Workers and Members of Their Families (adopted on 18 December 1990, entered into force on 1 July 2003) 2220 UNTS 3, Art 18; International Convention on the Elimination of All Forms of Racial Discrimination (adopted on 7 March 1966, entered into force on 4 January 1969) 660 UNTS 195, Art 5(a).

[55] See, eg: ECHR, Art 6; American Convention on Human Rights (adopted on 22 November 1969, entered into force on 18 July 1978) 1144 UNTS 123 ('ACHR'), Arts 8 and 9; African Charter on Human

Two fair trial guarantees, which are applicable to both civil and criminal proceedings, are of particular importance in this context: the right to equality before courts and tribunals[56] and the right to a fair hearing.[57] These rights ensure equality of arms, ie, the same procedural rights are to be provided to all parties unless distinctions are based on law and can be justified on objective and reasonable grounds, not entailing actual disadvantage or other unfairness.[58] The essence of equality of arms is that each side should be given the opportunity to challenge all arguments and evidence put forward by the other side.[59]

The right to an effective remedy also forms part of customary international law.[60] This right is well established and can be found in many universal and regional human rights treaties.[61] The right to an effective remedy 'directs international organisations in their dealings with … non-state entities beyond the first level of accountability; the right … include[s] both the "procedural right of effective access" and "the substantive right to a remedy"'.[62]

In the now famous string of *Kadi* judgments, the CJEC/CJEU considered the steps that the institutions of the European Community ('EC')/European Union ('EU') (ie, an international organisation) are required to take when imposing restrictive measures on an individual in order to comply with an individual's rights to a fair trial and an effective remedy. These rights were considered in the form of the 'principle of effective judicial protection'.[63] The *Kadi* judgments demonstrate the type of steps that INTERPOL should have taken in order to comply with Heracles' rights to a fair trial and an effective remedy.

and Peoples' Rights (adopted on 27 June 1981, entered into force on 21 October 1986) 1520 UNTS 217 ('ACHPR'), Art 7.

56 ICCPR, Art 14(1). See also: Shah, S, 'Detention and Trial' in Moeckli, D, Shah, S and Sivakumaran, S (eds), *International Human Rights Law* (Oxford, Oxford University Press, 2018) 252–77 at 267.

57 ICCPR, Art 14(1); ECHR, Art 6(1); ACHR, Art 8(1).

58 UN Human Rights Committee, 'General Comment No 32, Article 14: Right to equality before courts and tribunals and to a fair trial', UN Doc CCPR/C/GC/32 (23 August 2007) para 13.

59 Ibid. See also: Shah, S, 'Detention and Trial' in Moeckli, D, Shah, S and Sivakumaran, S (eds), *International Human Rights Law* (Oxford, Oxford University Press, 2018) 252–77 at 267.

60 See: Wellens, K, *Remedies against International Organisations* (Cambridge, Cambridge University Press, 2002) 17; Shelton, D, *Remedies in International Human Rights Law*, 2nd edn (Oxford, Oxford University Press, 2006) 238. Indeed, the right of access to justice (which captures elements of the right to an effective remedy) has been recognised as a peremptory norm of general international law (ie, a norm from which no derogation is permitted) (*Washington Julio Efrain Cabrera v Comisión Técnica Mixta de Salto Grande*, CSJN, Fallos 305: 2150 (5 December 1983); *Case of Goiburú et al v Paraguay* (Merits, Reparations and Costs, 22 September 2006) IACHR Series C No 153, para 131; *Case of La Cantuta v Perú* (Merits, Reparations and Costs, 29 November 2006) IACHR Series C No 162, para 160).

61 See, eg: ICCPR, Art 2(3); ECHR, Art 13; ACHR, Art 25. See also: UDHR, Art 8.

62 Wellens, K, *Remedies against International Organisations* (Cambridge, Cambridge University Press, 2002) 17–8.

63 '[T]he principle of effective judicial protection is a general principle of Community law stemming from the constitutional traditions common to the Member States, which has been enshrined in Articles 6 and 13 of the [ECHR], this principle having furthermore been reaffirmed by Article 47 of the Charter of fundamental rights of the European Union' (*Yassin Abdullah Kadi and Al Barakaat International Foundation v Council of the European Union and Commission of the European Communities*, Joined Cases C-402/05 P & C-415/05 P, [2008] ECR I-6351, para 335).

The *Kadi* cases were brought in response to a number of UN Security Council resolutions under Chapter VII of the UN Charter that were designed to combat terrorist threats to international peace and security. The resolutions provide for, inter alia, the freezing of assets of organisations, entities or individuals ('Persons') identified by the UN Sanctions Committee[64] and whose names are included in a consolidated list ('Consolidated List'). When States propose names of Persons to the UN Sanctions Committee to be included in the Consolidated List ('Proposing States') they have to provide a statement of case setting out the basis for that listing, including supporting documents that can be provided to the UN Sanctions Committee.[65] The UN Sanctions Committee must in turn produce a summary of the reasons for including the Person on the Consolidated List ('Summary of Reasons').[66] At the level of the EC, Member States considered that additional action was required to implement the UN Security Council resolutions, and the Council of the EU adopted a series of regulations providing for, amongst other matters, the freezing of assets of Persons identified by the UN Sanctions Committee.

On 17 October 2001, Mr Yassin Abdullah Kadi ('Kadi') was identified by the UN Sanctions Committee as being an individual associated with Usama bin Laden and the Al-Qaeda Network, and his name was listed on the Consolidated List. In the EC, Kadi's name was added to the list in Annex I to Council Regulation (EC) No 467/2001 by Commission Regulation (EC) No 2062/2001. Kadi's name was subsequently listed in Annex I to Council Regulation (EC) No 881/2002,[67] which imposed specific restrictive measures directed against persons associated with Usama bin Laden, the Al-Qaeda Network and the Taliban.

On 18 December 2001, Kadi brought an action seeking the annulment, initially, of Council Regulation 467/2001 and Commission Regulation 2062/2001 and, then, of Council Regulation 881/2002, insofar as those regulations concerned him. The Court of First Instance dismissed the action.[68] On appeal, the Grand Chamber set aside the judgment of the Court of First Instance and annulled Council Regulation 881/2002, insofar as it concerned Kadi, save that the Grand Chamber held that the effects of the regulation would be maintained for a maximum period of three months to allow the Council of the EU to remedy the infringements identified.[69] In short, the Grand Chamber found that:

(1) the obligations imposed by an international agreement cannot have the effect of prejudicing the constitutional principles of the Treaty establishing the EC

[64] The UN Sanctions Committee was established pursuant to UN Security Council Resolution 1267, 15 October 1999.

[65] UN Security Council Resolution 1735, 22 December 2006, operative para 5.

[66] UN Security Council Resolution 1822, 30 June 2008, operative paras 12–3.

[67] Council Regulation (EC) No 467/2001 was repealed on 29 May 2002 by Council Regulation (EC) No 881/2002 (at which time Commission Regulation (EC) No 2062/2001 was also impliedly repealed).

[68] *Kadi v Council and Commission*, Case T-315/01, [2005] ECR II-3649.

[69] *Yassin Abdullah Kadi and Al Barakaat International Foundation v Council of the European Union and Commission of the European Communities*, Joined Cases C-402/05 P & C-415/05 P, [2008] ECR I-6351, paras 372–76.

(including the principle that all EC acts must respect fundamental rights), and there was no basis for an act adopted by the EC, such as Council Regulation 881/2002, to have immunity from review;[70]

(2) the EC courts must ensure the full review of the lawfulness of all EC acts in light of fundamental rights, including where such acts are designed to implement UN Security Council resolutions;[71]

(3) the effectiveness of judicial review means that the competent EC authority is bound to communicate the grounds for the contested listing decision to the Person and to provide the Person with the opportunity to be heard in that regard;[72]

(4) since the Council of the EU had neither communicated to Kadi the evidence relied on against him to justify the restrictive measures imposed on him nor afforded him the right to be informed of that evidence within a reasonable period after those measures were enacted, Kadi had not been in a position to effectively make known his point of view in that regard, with the consequence that the rights of defence and the right to effective judicial review had been infringed;[73] and

(5) for the same reasons set out in (4) above, Kadi's fundamental right to respect for property had been infringed.[74]

On 21 October 2008, the Chairman of the UN Sanctions Committee authorised the disclosure of the Summary of Reasons to Kadi and, on 22 October 2018, the Summary of Reasons was also communicated to the European Commission. The European Commission gave Kadi until 10 November 2008 to comment on those reasons and to provide it with any information that he might consider relevant before it took its final decision as to whether to maintain his listing in Annex I to Council Regulation 881/2002. On 10 November 2008, Kadi sent his comments to the European Commission along with supporting evidence. On 28 November 2008, the European Commission adopted Commission Regulation (EC) No 1190/2008, which amended Annex I of Council Regulation 881/2002 to include Kadi's details. Commission Regulation 1190/2008 entered into force on 3 December 2008. On 8 December 2008, the European Commission responded to Kadi's comments.

On 26 February 2009, Kadi brought an action for annulment of Commission Regulation 1190/2008. On 30 September 2010, the General Court gave judgment and annulled Commission Regulation 1190/2008 insofar as it concerned Kadi.[75] The European Commission, the Council of the EU and the UK appealed the judgment of the General Court to the Grand Chamber and sought to have it set aside.

[70] Ibid, paras 283–85, 299, 303–04, 306–08.
[71] Ibid, para 326.
[72] Ibid, paras 336–41.
[73] Ibid, paras 345–50.
[74] Ibid, paras 369–71.
[75] *Yassin Abdullah Kadi v European Commission*, Case T-85/09, [2010] ECR II-5177.

On 18 July 2013, the Grand Chamber dismissed the appeal.[76] In so doing, the Grand Chamber provided detailed guidance on the intensity of review required by a decision-maker and the rights of the Person that must be respected.

With respect to the procedural steps to be taken by the competent EU authority, the Grand Chamber set out the following steps to be taken before a Person could be listed, or a Person's listing could be maintained, in Annex I of Council Regulation 881/2002. First, it recognised that the UN Security Council has been endowed by the UN members with the primary responsibility for the maintenance of international peace and security, and the EU authority must take due account of the terms and objectives of UN Security Council resolutions and the relevant obligations under the UN Charter. As a consequence, where the UN Sanctions Committee has decided to list the name of a Person on the Consolidated List, the EU authority must take the decision to list the Person, or maintain the Person on the list, in Annex I of Council Regulation 881/2002 on the basis of the Summary of Reasons provided by the UN Sanctions Committee.[77]

Second, respect for the rights of the defence and the right to effective judicial protection requires the EU authority to disclose to the Person concerned the evidence against him which is available to that authority and which it relied on in making its decision and, when that disclosure takes place, to ensure that the Person is placed in a position in which he may effectively make known his views on the grounds advanced against him.[78] These two steps must be implemented prior to any decision to maintain a listing.[79]

Third, when comments are made by a Person, the EU authority is under an obligation to carefully and impartially examine whether the reasons in the Summary of Reasons are well founded in light of those comments and any exculpatory evidence so provided. In that context, it is for the EU authority to assess whether it is necessary to seek the assistance of the UN Sanctions Committee (or through that committee, the Proposing State) in order to obtain the disclosure of information or evidence to enable it to discharge its duty of careful and impartial examination.[80]

Fourth, 'without going so far as to require a detailed response to the comments made by the [Person] …, the obligation to state reasons … entails in all circumstances … that that statement of reasons identifies [to] the [Person], specific and concrete reasons why the competent authorities consider that the [Person] must be subject to restrictive measures'.[81]

With respect to the approach to be taken by EU courts in the event that the Person challenges the lawfulness of the decision to list or maintain the listing, the

[76] *European Commission and others v Yassin Abdullah Kadi*, Joined Cases C-584/10 P, C-593/10 P & C-595/10 P, ECLI:EU:C:2013:518.

[77] Ibid, paras 106–07.

[78] Ibid, paras 111–12.

[79] Ibid, para 113.

[80] Ibid, paras 114–15.

[81] Ibid, para 116.

Grand Chamber found that the EU courts must determine whether an EU authority has complied with the procedural steps set out above.[82] The EU courts must also ensure that the decision to list or maintain the listing of a Person was taken on a sufficiently solid factual basis. That entails a verification of the factual allegations in the Summary of Reasons which underpins the decision, with the consequence that judicial review cannot be restricted to an assessment of the abstract cogency of the Summary of Reasons.[83] To that end, it is for the EU courts, where necessary, to request the EU authority to produce information/evidence relevant to such an examination, irrespective of whether it is confidential.[84] There is no requirement on the EU authority to produce all the information/evidence underlying the Summary of Reasons, but it is necessary that the information/evidence produced supports the reasons relied on against the Person concerned.[85] If the EU authority 'finds itself unable to comply with the request', it is the duty of the EU courts to base their decision on the material which has been disclosed to them. If that material is insufficient to allow a finding that a reason for the decision is well founded, the EU courts shall disregard that reason as a possible basis for the decision to list or maintain a listing.[86] If the EU authority provides the relevant information/evidence requested, the EU courts must then assess the probative value of that information/evidence in the circumstances of the particular case and in light of any observations submitted in relation to them by, among others, the Person concerned and determine whether the facts alleged are made out in light of that information/evidence.[87]

The Grand Chamber acknowledged that security concerns might preclude the disclosure of some information/evidence to the Person concerned, but it did not accept that this was a reason not to provide the information/evidence to the EU courts. Where there are security concerns, it is for the EU courts to apply techniques which accommodate both the security concerns and the need to guarantee sufficiently to an individual respect for his procedural rights (such as the right to be heard and the requirement for an adversarial process).[88] To that end, it is for the EU courts to determine whether the reasons relied on by the EU authority for not disclosing the information/evidence to the Person concerned are well founded. If the EU courts conclude that the reasons given do not preclude disclosure, or at the very least partial disclosure, of the information/evidence concerned, it shall give the EU authority the opportunity to make such disclosure to the Person concerned. If the EU authority does not disclose that information/evidence, in

[82] Ibid, para 118.

[83] Ibid, para 119.

[84] Ibid, para 120. This is because it is the task of the relevant EU authority to establish, in the event of challenge by the Person, that the reasons relied on against the Person concerned are well founded, and not the task of the Person to adduce evidence that those reasons are not well founded (at para 121).

[85] Ibid, para 122.

[86] Ibid, para 123.

[87] Ibid, para 124.

[88] Ibid, para 125.

whole or in part, the EU courts shall not take that material into account when examining the lawfulness of the contested measure.[89] If the reasons relied on by the EU authority do preclude disclosure to the Person concerned of information/evidence produced to the EU courts, an appropriate balance has to be struck between the requirements attached to the right to effective judicial protection and those flowing from the security concerns. In order to strike such a balance, it is legitimate to consider possibilities such as the disclosure of a summary outlining the information's content or the evidence in question. It is for the EU courts to assess whether and to what extent the failure to disclose confidential information/evidence to the Person concerned and his consequential inability to submit his observations are such as to affect the probative value of the confidential evidence.[90]

The decision of the Grand Chamber on 18 July 2013 in *Kadi* serves to demonstrate, by comparison, the questionable nature of the treatment meted out to Heracles by the General Secretariat (in publishing and maintaining the red notice) and the Requests Chamber (in considering Heracles' request to delete the red notice). As set out above, the right to a fair trial prescribes that the same procedural rights are provided to all parties unless distinctions are based on law and can be justified on objective and reasonable grounds, not entailing actual disadvantage or other unfairness, and the right to an effective remedy demands a procedural right of effective access. It is difficult to see how the approach of either organ of INTERPOL in respect of Heracles can be considered consistent with his rights to a fair trial and an effective remedy. Applying the framework developed by the Grand Chamber on 18 July 2013 in *Kadi*, it might be said that INTERPOL should have proceeded as follows.

First, the General Secretariat should have disclosed to Heracles the evidence against him which it relied on to publish the red notice, and it should have ensured that Heracles was in a position to have effectively made known his views on this evidence. The General Secretariat should then have carefully and impartially examined whether the reasons for the red notice were well founded in light of comments made by Heracles and any exculpatory evidence provided by him. In that context, it was for the General Secretariat to assess whether it was necessary to seek the assistance of NCB Rosmarus in order to obtain the disclosure of information or evidence to enable it to discharge its duty of careful and impartial examination. The General Secretariat should also have provided specific and concrete reasons to Heracles for its decision to publish a red notice.

Second, the Requests Chamber should have determined whether the General Secretariat had complied with the steps set out above. The Requests Chamber should also have determined whether the decision of the General Secretariat to publish a red notice against Heracles was taken on a sufficiently solid factual basis. This entails a verification of the factual allegations in the summary of facts in a

[89] Ibid, paras 126–27.
[90] Ibid, paras 128–29.

red notice, with the consequence that the review cannot be restricted to an assessment of the abstract cogency of the summary of facts. To that end, it was for the Requests Chamber, where necessary, to request the General Secretariat to produce information/evidence relevant to such an examination. If the General Secretariat was unable to comply with the request, it was the duty of the Requests Chamber to base its decision as to whether the decision to publish a red notice was taken on a sufficiently solid factual basis solely on the material which had been disclosed to it. If that material was insufficient to allow a finding that a reason for the publication of the red notice was well founded, the Requests Chamber should have disregarded that reason as a possible basis for the decision to publish the red notice. If the General Secretariat provided the relevant information/evidence requested, the Requests Chamber should have assessed the probative value of that information/evidence in the circumstances of the case and in light of any observations submitted by Heracles to determine whether the facts alleged were made out in light of that information/evidence. In addition, the Requests Chamber should have assessed whether the reasons relied on for not disclosing information/evidence to Heracles (eg, security concerns) were well founded: if not well founded, the Requests Chamber should not have taken that information/evidence into account; if well founded, the Requests Chamber should have considered possibilities for limited disclosure.

The foregoing breaches were compounded by the Requests Chamber's failure to organise an oral session. An oral session would have afforded Heracles the opportunity to rebut the presumption in INTERPOL's rules that the representations made by NCB Rosmarus are accurate.[91] In particular, an oral session would have permitted a more complete assessment of the background to the circumstances underpinning the red notice, and allowed Heracles to air his evidence and challenge the information/evidence provided by NCB Rosmarus and the General Secretariat.

Finally, INTERPOL should have provided Heracles with a forum to complain about any breaches of his due process rights.

In considering the treatment afforded to Heracles by the Requests Chamber, it is apt to recall the language of the General Claims Commission in *B.E. Chattin (United States) v United Mexican States*:

> [n]either during the investigations nor during the hearings in open court was any such thing as an oral examination or cross-examination of any importance attempted. It seems highly improbable that the accused have been given a real opportunity during the hearings in open court, freely to speak for themselves. It is not for the Commission to endeavor to reach from the record any conviction as to the innocence or guilt of Chattin and his colleagues; but even in case they were guilty, the Commission would render a

[91] See: INTERPOL's Rules on the Processing of Data [III/IRPD/GA/2011(2019)], Art 128(1): '[d]ata are, a priori, considered to be accurate and relevant when entered by a National Central Bureau, a national entity or an international entity into the INTERPOL Information System and recorded in a police database of the Organization'.

> bad service to the Government of Mexico if it failed to place the stamp of its disapproval and even indignation on a criminal procedure so far below international standards of civilization as the present one.[92]

ii. Right not to be Subjected to Torture or Cruel, Inhuman or Degrading Treatment or Punishment (in the Context of Aid and Assistance)

There is little doubt that the right not to be subjected to torture or cruel, inhuman or degrading treatment or punishment forms part of customary international law.[93] The right to be free from torture and other forms of ill-treatment is reflected in universal and regional human rights treaties.[94] In torturing Heracles, Rosmarus breached this right.

Thus, the question arises as to whether the publication and maintenance of the red notice by INTERPOL can be considered aid and/or assistance to Rosmarus in the commission of an internationally wrongful act. In raising this question, the authors note that other international organisations accept that, in certain circumstances, they are internationally responsible where they provide aid and assistance to a State which commits an internationally wrongful act. For example, on 12 October 2009, the UN Legal Counsel provided the following advice:

> [the UN Organization Mission in the Democratic Republic of the Congo] may not lawfully provide logistic or 'service' support to any [Armed Forces of the Democratic Republic of the Congo ('FARDC')] operation if it has reason to believe that the FARDC units involved are violating … [international humanitarian, human rights or refugee law]. … [T]his follows directly from the Organization's obligations under customary international law.[95]

The advice of the UN Legal Counsel is sound. In the context of State-to-State aid and assistance, the ICJ has found that the responsibility for '"aid or assistance" furnished by one State for the commission of a wrongful act by another

[92] *B.E. Chattin (United States) v United Mexican States* (Award, 23 July 1927) IV RIAA 282, 292.

[93] See: *Prosecutor v Anto Furundžija* (Judgment) (10 December 1998) Case No IT-95-17/1-T, para 153; *Al-Adsani v United Kingdom* (2002) 34 EHRR 11, para 61; *Case of Maritza Urrutia v Guatemala* (Merits, Reparations and Costs, 27 November 2003) IACHR Series C No 103, para 92; *Questions relating to the Obligation to Prosecute or Extradite (Belgium v Senegal)* (Judgment) [2012] ICJ Rep 422, para 99; UN Human Rights Committee, 'General Comment No 24: General comment on issues relating to reservations made upon ratification or accession to the Covenant or the Optional Protocols thereto, or in relation to declarations under Article 41 of the Covenant', UN Doc CCPR/C/21/Rev.1/Add.6 (11 November 1994) para 8; Henckaerts, J-M and Doswald-Beck, L, *Customary International Humanitarian Law* (Cambridge, Cambridge University Press, 2009) Vol I, Rule 90, 315.

[94] See, eg: ICCPR, Art 7; ECHR, Art 3; ACHR, Art 5; ACHPR, Art 5.

[95] Internal document issued on 12 October 2009 by the UN Legal Counsel (O'Brien, P, 'Note to Mr. Le Roy' (12 October 2009), Attachment to Ms O'Brien's Note of 12 October 2009, para 12). This document was published in *The New York Times* on 9 December 2009.

State' is part of customary international law.[96] This customary rule is reflected in Article 16 of the ARS[97] and, as regards international organisations, in Article 14 of the DARIO.[98]

Whilst there remains debate on particular aspects of the law precluding an international organisation from aiding or assisting a State in the commission of an internationally wrongful act,[99] an argument that INTERPOL aided and assisted Rosmarus in the commission of an internationally wrongful act could be made with a certain degree of confidence. Such an argument could be articulated as follows.

First, INTERPOL provided aid and assistance, in the literal sense, to Rosmarus. Aid and assistance can take any form,[100] and, in Heracles' case, INTERPOL published and maintained a red notice which led to Heracles' arrest by the Larmastan authorities and his extradition to Rosmarus where he was tortured.

Second, INTERPOL's aid and assistance significantly contributed to Rosmarus' internationally wrongful act.[101] In this respect, the 'key question to be asked is whether a given action or omission made it easier for another State or international organisation to commit its wrongful act'.[102] The publication and maintenance of a red notice by INTERPOL made it easier for Rosmarus to torture Heracles because the red notice served to locate Heracles so that he could be extradited to Rosmarus.

Third, the international obligation breached by Rosmarus (ie, the customary international law obligation not to subject individuals to torture or cruel, inhuman or degrading treatment or punishment) also binds INTERPOL.[103]

[96] *Application of the Convention on the Prevention and Punishment of the Crime of Genocide (Bosnia and Herzegovina v Serbia and Montenegro)* (Judgment) [2007] ICJ Rep 43, para 419.

[97] Ibid, para 420.

[98] 'Draft articles on the responsibility of international organizations, with commentaries' in *Yearbook of the International Law Commission* (2011) Vol II, Part Two, 66, Commentary to Art 14, para 1.

[99] Reinisch, A, 'Aid or Assistance and Direction and Control between states and International Organizations in the Commission of Internationally Wrongful Acts' (2010) 7 *International Organizations Law Review* 63–77 at 66–73.

[100] Crawford, J, *State Responsibility: The General Part* (Cambridge, Cambridge University Press, 2013) 402; Jackson, M, *Complicity in International Law* (Oxford, Oxford University Press, 2015) 153.

[101] 'Draft articles on the responsibility of international organizations, with commentaries' in *Yearbook of the International Law Commission* (2011) Vol II, Part Two, 66, Commentary to Art 14, para 4. In paragraph 5 of its Commentary to Article 16 of the ARS, the ILC explained that '[t]here is no requirement that the aid or assistance should have been essential to the performance of the internationally wrongful act; it is sufficient if it contributed significantly to that act.'

[102] Lanovoy, V, *Complicity and its Limits in the Law of International Responsibility* (Oxford, Hart Publishing, 2016) 185.

[103] As explained in section I above, INTERPOL is bound by customary international law. See: 'Draft articles on the responsibility of international organizations, with commentaries' in *Yearbook of the International Law Commission* (2011) Vol II, Part Two, 66, Commentary to Art 14, para 5; Crawford, J, *State Responsibility: The General Part* (Cambridge, Cambridge University Press, 2013) 409; Jackson, M, *Complicity in International Law* (Oxford, Oxford University Press, 2015) 162: '[w]here the rule is one of customary international law, both parties will most likely be bound by the obligation'.

Fourth, INTERPOL had knowledge of, or was wilfully blind to, the circumstances of Rosmarus' internationally wrongful act.[104] In challenging the red notice on 4 January 2018 before the Requests Chamber, Heracles had argued that there was a real risk that he would be tortured in Rosmarus and provided the Requests Chamber with evidence (in the form of witness statements) that members of his family (who are co-accused in Rosmarus) had been tortured upon their detention in Rosmarus.

Fifth, and finally, INTERPOL intended, by the aid and assistance given, to facilitate the occurrence of Rosmarus' internationally wrongful act.[105] 'Intent' in this context 'does not require the assisting state to desire that the unlawful conduct be committed. Nor does the assisting state have to be in common cause with the principal. Knowledge or virtual certainty that the recipient state will use the assistance unlawfully is capable of satisfying the intent element …, whatever the assisting state's desire or purpose'.[106]

In the next chapter, Chapter 12, we will consider the principal mechanism through which INTERPOL can be held responsible for breaches of its external law.

[104] 'Draft articles on the responsibility of international organizations, with commentaries' in *Yearbook of the International Law Commission* (2011) Vol II, Part Two, 66, Commentary to Art 14, para 3; Jackson, M, *Complicity in International Law* (Oxford, Oxford University Press, 2015) 162.

[105] 'Draft articles on the responsibility of international organizations, with commentaries' in *Yearbook of the International Law Commission Yearbook* (2011) Vol II, Part Two, 66, Commentary to Art 14, para 4.

[106] Moynihan, H, 'Aiding and Assisting: Challenges in Armed Conflict and Counterterrorism', Chatham House Research Paper (November 2016) 24. Moynihan is, of course, considering State-to-State assistance, but there is no logical reason why her understanding of 'intent' does not apply in the context of international organisation-to-State assistance.

12

External Law Disputes

Chapter 11 explained that the International Criminal Police Organization ('INTERPOL' or the 'Organisation') is responsible for breaches of its external law. This chapter is concerned with the principal mechanism through which INTERPOL can be held responsible by a private party for breaches of its external law. In seeking to hold INTERPOL responsible for breaches of its external law, a private party will seek remedies provided by general international law.

The discussion in this chapter takes place against the background of the rights of private parties under customary international law to a fair trial and an effective remedy.[1] The significance of the latter has not been lost on INTERPOL: '[t]he protection of INTERPOL is closely linked to the protection of the rights of the requesting parties. If an applicant is not provided with an effective remedy, INTERPOL might be exposed to challenges to its immunity from potential lawsuits brought before national jurisdictions'.[2]

I. Immunity from Jurisdiction and Adequate Alternative Dispute Settlement Systems

Most domestic laws operate in respect of international organisations in the same manner as they do in respect of other subjects within the domestic jurisdiction of States. However, adjudication of the laws is limited by the immunity from jurisdiction granted to almost every international organisation.[3]

For most international organisations, immunity from jurisdiction is expressly provided in the constituent instrument or in a special convention or agreement.[4]

[1] On which, see Chapter 11.

[2] Vajić, N, Chairman of the CCF, 'Annual Activity Report of the CCF for 2015' (Speech to the INTERPOL General Assembly, Bali, 9 November 2016) para 22.

[3] Even if there is no immunity from jurisdiction, the entitlement to immunity from enforcement is generally broader (Higgins, R et al (eds), *Oppenheim's International Law: United Nations*, Vol I (Oxford, Oxford University Press, 2017) 441).

[4] Eg, Convention on the Privileges and Immunities of the United Nations (adopted on 13 February 1946, entered into force on 17 September 1946) 1 UNTS 15 and 90 UNTS 327 (corrigendum to UNTS Vol 1), s 2; Convention on the Privileges and Immunities of the Specialized Agencies (approved on 21 November 1947, entered into force on 2 December 1948) 33 UNTS 261, s 4;

Even without such express provision, national courts may grant an international organisation immunity, for example, pursuant to a rule of customary international law granting immunity to all international organisations.[5]

Various reasons have been proffered as to why an international organisation requires immunity from jurisdiction. First, there 'is the danger of prejudice or bad faith in the national courts',[6] although prejudice would not necessarily be in bad faith.[7] Second, an international organisation is in 'need of protection against baseless actions brought from improper motives or by the numerous cranks, fanatics or cantankerous persons who may conceive that they have a duty to compel the organization to take some particular step or that they have suffered wrong at its hands'.[8] Third, it is undesirable to allow 'the courts of particular members to determine, quite possibly in different senses, the legal effects of acts performed in the exercise of the organization's functions'.[9] While these three reasons provide some understanding as to why an international organisation requires immunity from jurisdiction, none fully captures the quintessence of why. The fundamental reason why an international organisation requires immunity from jurisdiction is to protect its independence.[10] Immunity from jurisdiction ensures that domestic

Headquarters Agreement between the Organization of American States and the Government of the United States of America (signed on and entered into force on 14 May 1992) ('OAS Treaty'), Art IV.

[5] Eg, in 1985, the Dutch Supreme Court found that '[i]t must be assumed that even in cases where there is no treaty [in which privileges and immunities are conferred upon international organisations] it follows from unwritten international law that an international organization is entitled to the privilege of immunity from jurisdiction on the same footing as generally provided for in the treaties referred to above' (*Spaans v Iran-United States Claims Tribunal*, Supreme Court of the Netherlands (20 December 1985) 94 ILR 321, para 3.3.4). See also: *Eckhardt v European Organization for the Safety of Air Navigation (Eurocontrol) (No 2)*, District Court of Maastricht (12 January 1984) 94 ILR 331, 337–38; *Supreme Headquarters Allied Powers Europe and Allied Joint Force Command Headquarters Brunssum v Supreme Site Services GmbH, Supreme Fuels GmbH & Co KG and Supreme Fuels Trading FZE*, Court of Appeal of 's-Hertogenbosch, Judgment No 200.216.570_01 (10 December 2019) para 6.7.9.1. The decisions of the Dutch courts reflect the 'majority view', according to which 'international organizations enjoy absolute immunity from legal proceedings even if no express treaty provision is applicable' (Reinisch, A, *International Organizations before National Courts* (Cambridge, Cambridge University Press, 2000) 146). This view is also reflected in Higgins, R et al (eds), *Oppenheim's International Law: United Nations*, Vol I (Oxford, Oxford University Press, 2017) 553. However, for a contrasting view, see: Wood, M, 'Do International Organizations Enjoy Immunity under Customary International Law?' in Blokker, NM and Schrijver, NJ (eds), *Immunity of International Organizations* (Brill Nijhoff Publishers, Leiden, 2015) 29–60.

[6] Wood, HM, 'Legal Relations between Individuals and a World Organization of States' (1944) 30 *Transactions of the Grotius Society* 141–64 at 143–44.

[7] Schermers, HG and Blokker, NM, *International Institutional Law*, 6th revised edn (Leiden, Brill Nijhoff Publishers, 2018) 1079.

[8] Wood, HM, 'Legal Relations between Individuals and a World Organization of States' (1944) 30 *Transactions of the Grotius Society* 141–64 at 144.

[9] Ibid.

[10] Higgins, R et al (eds), *Oppenheim's International Law: United Nations*, Vol I (Oxford, Oxford University Press, 2017) 559; Bekker, PHF, *The Legal Position of Intergovernmental Organizations: A Functional Necessity Analysis of Their Legal Status and Immunities* (Dordrecht, Martinus Nijhoff Publishers, 1994) 99–103; Reinisch, A, *International Organizations before National Courts* (Cambridge, Cambridge University Press, 2000) 233–35.

courts, and other domestic actors, cannot interfere unilaterally in the operations of an organisation. International organisations, such as INTERPOL, are established to carry out functions in the common interests of their members. An international organisation can only fully operate in the common interest of all members if it is not subject to the jurisdiction of any individual member. Thus, today, it is generally recognised that international organisations require immunity from jurisdiction to be able to perform their functions with independence,[11] and this immunity is founded on the principle of functional necessity.[12]

In INTERPOL's case, the various headquarters agreements and ad hoc conference-hosting agreements provide INTERPOL with immunity from jurisdiction. Of these agreements, the agreement with France is the most consequential.[13] Article 5 of the Headquarters Agreement provides that:

> 1. The Organization shall enjoy immunity from legal process, except in the cases specified below:
>   (a) the waiver expressly results from clauses in a contract;
>   (b) a civil claim for damages arising from an accident caused by a motor vehicle belonging to the Organization or used on its behalf, or from a violation of road traffic regulations involving a motor vehicle belonging to the Organization or used on its behalf;
>   (c) a counter claim directly linked to proceedings begun as a main action by the Organization.
> 2. The Organization may expressly waive its immunity from legal process in certain cases.

[11] Along with an international organisation's immunity from jurisdiction, the immunity of persons who perform functions in connection with the international organisation, as well as the inviolability of the premises of the organisation and of persons connected with it and the exemption from taxation granted to the organisation and its officials, guarantee the independence of the organisation when it performs its functions.

[12] Higgins, R, *Problems & Process: International Law and How We Use it* (Oxford, Clarendon Press, 1994) 93: '[d]oes the *imperii/gestionis* distinction apply to international organizations? … To suggest that this distinction has any relevance to organizations is to assimilate them to states, which is not correct. Their basis of immunity is different. The relevant test under general international law is whether an immunity from jurisdiction to prescribe is necessary for the fulfilment of the organization's purposes'. In this respect, it is clear that the decision of the Supreme Court of the United States in *Jam et al v International Financial Corp*, (586 U.S. ___ 2019) ('*Jam*') is inconsistent with general international law. In *Jam*, the Supreme Court of the United States decided that international organisations enjoy the same restrictive immunity from suit as that enjoyed by foreign governments under the Foreign Sovereign Immunities Act of 1976.

[13] INTERPOL's headquarters is in Lyon, France. The Agreement between the International Criminal Police Organization – INTERPOL and the Government of the French Republic regarding INTERPOL's Headquarters in France (entered into force on 1 September 2009) ('Headquarters Agreement') was amended in 2016 by Decree No 2016-326 of 17 March 2016 promulgating the additional protocol in the form of an exchange of letters between the Government of the French Republic and the International Criminal Police Organization – INTERPOL on the interpretation and application of Article 24 of the Agreement of 14 and 24 April 2008 regarding INTERPOL's headquarters in France (signed in Paris on 9 February 2016 and in Lyon on 12 February 2016, entered into force on 16 February 2016) ('Additional Protocol').

Article 5 must be read alongside the preamble to the Headquarters Agreement, which provides that INTERPOL and France '[d]esir[e] to define, on the territory of the French Republic, the … immunities of [INTERPOL] which are necessary for the exercise of its functions and the achievement of its aims'.

The immunity granted to INTERPOL under Article 5 of the Headquarters Agreement cannot be considered in isolation. In the period from 1999 to 2007, there were a series of cases at the European Court of Human Rights and in Council of Europe Member States in which the courts demonstrated a willingness to question the immunity of international organisations where the international organisations failed to provide adequate alternative dispute settlement systems. The seminal cases were *Waite and Kennedy v Germany* and *Beer and Regan v Germany*.[14] In these cases, the European Court of Human Rights found that:

> where States establish international organisations in order to pursue or strengthen their cooperation in certain fields of activities, and where they attribute to these organisations certain competences and accord them immunities, there may be implications as to the protection of fundamental rights. It would be incompatible with the purpose and object of the Convention, however, if the Contracting States were thereby absolved from their responsibility under the Convention in relation to the field of activity covered by such attribution. It should be recalled that the Convention is intended to guarantee not theoretical or illusory rights, but rights that are practical and effective. This is particularly true for the right of access to the courts in view of the prominent place held in a democratic society by the right to a fair trial …
>
> For the Court, a material factor in determining whether granting [the European Space Agency] immunity from German jurisdiction is permissible under the Convention is whether the applicants had available to them reasonable alternative means to protect effectively their rights under the Convention.[15]

Following *Waite and Kennedy* and *Beer and Regan*, domestic courts in Belgium,[16] France[17] and Italy[18] proved willing to question the immunity of international

[14] These cases are discussed in more detail in Chapter 8.

[15] *Waite and Kennedy v Germany* [1999] ECHR 13, paras 67–8. See also: *Beer and Regan v Germany* [1999] ECHR 6, paras 57–8. However, see the much later case of *Stichting Mothers of Srebrenica and others v The Netherlands* [2013] ECHR 739, paras 163–64: '[a]s the applicants rightly pointed out, in *Waite and Kennedy* … – as in *Beer and Regan* … – the Court considered it a "material factor", in determining whether granting an international organisation immunity from domestic jurisdiction was permissible under the Convention, whether the applicants had available to them reasonable alternative means to protect effectively their rights under the Convention. In the present case it is beyond doubt that no such alternative means existed either under Netherlands domestic law or under the law of the United Nations. … It does not follow, however, that in the absence of an alternative remedy the recognition of immunity is *ipso facto* constitutive of a violation of the right of access to a court'.

[16] *Siedler v Western European Union*, Brussels Labour Court of Appeal (17 September 2003) *Journal des Tribunaux* (2004) 617. The decision of the Labour Court of Appeal was upheld by the Court of Cassation in 2009 (*Siedler v Western European Union*, Belgian Court of Cassation (21 December 2009) ILDC 1625 (BE 2009)).

[17] *Banque Africaine de Développement v MA Degboe*, French Court of Cassation (25 January 2005) 132 *Journal du droit International* (2005) 1142.

[18] *Drago v International Plant Genetic Resources Institute*, Italian Court of Cassation (19 February 2007) ILDC 827 (IT 2007).

organisations where the international organisations had failed to provide individuals with reasonable alternative means to protect effectively their rights.[19]

II. Article 24 of the Headquarters Agreement

Naturally, the foregoing jurisprudence forced INTERPOL to reflect on the prospect of a French court denying INTERPOL immunity in the context of a claim by a private party that INTERPOL has, for example, breached its obligations to provide a fair trial and an effective remedy. In an effort to exclude the possibility of a French court unilaterally determining the adequacy of the alternative means provided by the Organisation, and with inspiration from Article VIII of the OAS Treaty,[20] INTERPOL agreed to the inclusion of Article 24(1) and (3) in the Headquarters Agreement. Article 24(1) of the Headquarters Agreement provides that:

> [u]nless the Parties in the dispute decide otherwise, any dispute between the Organization and a private party shall be settled in accordance with the Optional Rules for Arbitration between International Organizations and Private Parties of the Permanent Court of Arbitration [('Rules')] by a tribunal composed either of one or three members appointed by the Secretary General of the Permanent Court of Arbitration. …

Three preliminary observations can be made regarding Article 24(1).

[19] Long before *Waite and Kennedy*, *Beer and Regan* and the decisions of domestic courts in Belgium, France and Italy, the Supreme Court of Argentina had found that, when a treaty containing immunity from domestic legal process is not paired with alternative means to settle disputes, the treaty provision granting immunity is invalid on the basis of a breach of the peremptory norm of general international law on the right of access to justice (*Washington Julio Efrain Cabrera v Comisión Técnica Mixta de Salto Grande*, CSJN, Fallos 305: 2150 (5 December 1983)). See also: *Duhalde v Organización Panamericana de la Salud – Organización Mundial de la Salud – Oficina Sanitaria Panamericana*, CSJN, Fallos 322: 1905 (31 August 1999).

[20] Martha, RSJ, 'International Financial Institutions and Claims of Private Parties: Immunity Obliges' in Cisse, H, Bradlow, DD and Kingsbury, B (eds), *The World Bank Legal Review, Volume 3: International Financial Institutions and Global Legal Governance* (2012) 93–131 at 129. Article VIII, Section 1 of the OAS Treaty provides that '[w]ithout prejudice to the immunities conferred by the [International Organizations Immunities Act] or this Agreement, the Organization shall make provisions for appropriate modes of settlement of disputes for which jurisdiction would exist against a foreign government under Section 1605(a)(2)-(6) of the United States Foreign Sovereign Immunities Act of 1976 ("FSIA"), as amended, and as to which the Organization is a party and asserts immunity under Section 1 of Article IV of this Agreement …'. Article VIII, Section 2 of the OAS Treaty provides that '[i]n the event that the parties to a dispute to which this Article applies cannot agree upon a mode of settlement, the following provisions shall apply: (a) Except as provided in subparagraph (b) of this Section, the appropriate mode of settlement shall be binding arbitration in accordance with the procedures of the American Arbitration Association or the Inter-American Commercial Arbitration Commission, at the election of the Organization; provided, however, that no arbitrator or arbitration tribunal shall have authority to issue an order that a court or other judicial authority is precluded from issuing under the IOTA with respect to the property, archives, or officials of the Organization. (b) Small claims shall be resolved in accordance with the procedures established in Annex C, which may be changed from time to time by agreement of the parties …'.

First, Article 24(1) does not simply provide a mechanism to resolve disputes arising in connection with the Headquarters Agreement: Article 24(1) states that any dispute between the Organisation and a private party shall be settled in accordance with the Rules. In this regard, Article 24(1) is to be contrasted with Article 24(2) of the Headquarters Agreement which provides that '[u]nless the Parties decide otherwise, any dispute between the Government of the French Republic and the Organization concerning the interpretation or application of the present Agreement … shall be submitted to an arbitral tribunal … in conformity with the Optional Rules for Arbitration involving International Organizations and States of the Permanent Court of Arbitration'.

Second, Article 24(1) extends to any dispute deriving from the Organisation's external law, including any dispute deriving from private law (contractual or otherwise).[21]

Third, the construction of Article 24(1) is different to the construction of the dispute settlement clauses typically found in investment treaties. In investment treaties, an investor is typically presented with a choice of fora to which he can submit his dispute. For example, Article 9(2) of the Agreement on encouragement and reciprocal protection of investments between the Republic of Panama and the Kingdom of the Netherlands envisages that a disgruntled Panamanian investor may submit a dispute to a competent court of the Kingdom of the Netherlands or to the International Centre for Settlement of Investment Disputes for settlement by arbitration. By contrast, Article 24(1) provides a default mechanism whereby disputes between the Organisation and a private party must be settled in accordance with the Rules unless otherwise agreed.

Article 24(1) must be read alongside Article 24(3) of the Headquarters Agreement. Prior to 16 February 2016, Article 24(3) provided that:

> [t]he procedure specified in [Article 24(1)] shall not be applicable to disputes whose origins lie in the application or interpretation of the Organization's Constitution or its appendices.

By including this provision in the Headquarters Agreement, INTERPOL sought to ensure that a tribunal constituted under the Rules could not interfere with its constitutional autonomy. With effect from 16 February 2016, following an amendment by way of the Additional Protocol, Article 24(3) provides that:

> [t]he procedure specified in [Article 24(1)] shall not be applicable to disputes whose origins lie in the application or interpretation of the Organization's Constitution or its appendices, including those disputes relating to the processing of data in INTERPOL's Information System and those relating to the employment conditions of the Organization's officials.

[21] It is interesting that the Rules (which prescribe in Article 33(1) that the arbitral tribunal shall have regard, where appropriate, to the general principles governing the law of international organisations and to the rules of general international law in resolving the dispute) were designated as the procedural rules to govern arbitrations under Article 24(1) and not, for example, the International Chamber of

In short, the Additional Protocol added the words 'including those disputes relating to the processing of data in INTERPOL's Information System and those relating to the employment conditions of the Organization's officials' to Article 24(3). While the Additional Protocol added clarity to the kind of disputes that are carved out of the procedure prescribed by Article 24(1), it is doubtful that the Additional Protocol altered the scope of the carve-out. Rather, use of the word 'including' indicates that disputes relating to the processing of data in the INTERPOL Information System and disputes relating to the employment conditions of the Organisation's officials are two categories of disputes whose origins lie in the application or interpretation of the INTERPOL Constitution or its appendices.

In Chapters 8 and 11, the authors explained that the sources of INTERPOL's legal obligations can be divided into two broad categories: internal law (which includes INTERPOL's constituent instrument and its appendices) and external law (eg, international agreements, customary international law of a universal (or almost universal) character and general principles of law). The distinction between internal law and external law is of supreme importance in the context of Article 24(1) and (3) of the Headquarters Agreement. Prima facie, an alleged breach of the Organisation's internal law will constitute a dispute 'whose origins lie in the application or interpretation of the Organization's Constitution or its appendices'. On the other hand, prima facie, an alleged breach of the Organisation's external law (eg, an alleged breach of an individual's rights to a fair trial and an effective remedy)[22] will not constitute a dispute 'whose origins lie in the application or interpretation of the Organization's Constitution or its appendices'. Of course, in a given case, there may be a coincidence of obligations incumbent upon INTERPOL under its internal and external law. For instance, an individual could allege that INTERPOL officials tortured him. Such an allegation would engage Article 2(1) of the INTERPOL Constitution[23] (ie, the Organisation's internal law) and INTERPOL's obligation under customary international law not to subject individuals to torture (ie, the Organisation's external law). Where such a coincidence arises, a tribunal constituted in accordance with Article 24(1) of the Headquarters Agreement would have jurisdiction to consider whether INTERPOL breached its obligations under its external law, but it would not have jurisdiction (as a consequence of Article 24(3)) to consider whether INTERPOL breached its obligations under its internal law. The partial award of the arbitral tribunal in the *BIS Shares Repurchase* case supports this distinction. It will be recalled from Chapter 8 that the *BIS Shares Repurchase* case concerned the recall of privately held shares in the Bank for International

Commerce Arbitration Rules, as was the preference of Grosse (Grosse L, 'L'accord de siège de 2008 entre la France et INTERPOL' (2008) 54 *Annuaire Français de Droit International* 615–28 at 624).

[22] On which, see Chapter 11.

[23] Article 2(1) of the INTERPOL Constitution provides that one of INTERPOL's aims is '[t]o ensure and promote the widest possible mutual assistance between all criminal police authorities within the limits of the laws existing in the different countries and in the spirit of the "Universal Declaration of

Settlements ('BIS') (an international organisation). The *BIS Shares Repurchase* arbitral tribunal observed that:

> [t]he legality of the repurchase has been contested principally under the Statutes of the Bank and secondarily under principles of international law regarding expropriation. In the first case, the question is whether the modification of the Statutes, assuming conformity with principles of international law, was carried out in accordance with Articles 57 and 58 of the Statutes. ... If that question is answered in the affirmative, the validity of the modification must still be examined under principles of international law.[24]

From the foregoing, it is clear that, generally speaking, a private party would be ill-advised to bring a claim against INTERPOL before a French court on the basis that it has breached its external law. A French court would likely point to INTERPOL's immunity from legal process and the prospect of pursuing a claim under Article 24(1) of the Headquarters Agreement. Of course, if a private party is obstructed from pursuing a claim under Article 24(1) of the Headquarters Agreement, it could conceivably point to the recognition of the right of access to justice as a peremptory norm of general international law and test INTERPOL's immunity in a French court.

Human Rights'". Article 5 of the Universal Declaration of Human Rights provides that '[n]o one shall be subjected to torture or to cruel, inhuman or degrading treatment or punishment.'

[24] *Partial Award on the lawfulness of the recall of the privately held shares on 8 January 2001 and the applicable standards for valuation of those shares* (Partial Award of 22 November 2002) XXIII RIAA 183, para 142.

Appendix 1

The Constitution of the International Criminal Police Commission, 1923

En considération que la lutte contre les criminels internationaux ne peut être effectuée avec succès qu'au moyen d'une coopération étroite des autorités de police de tous les Etats cultivés, le congrès International de police s'assemblant à VIENNE en Septembre 1923 a décidé de fonder une 'COMMISSION INTERNATIONALE DE POLICE CRIMINELLE', dont l'activité commencera de suite.

Le congrès établit en outre les statuts suivants pour cette commission:

ARTICLE 1

Le but de la 'Commission Internationale de la Police Criminelle' est:

a) la garantie et le perfectionnement de la plus large assistance réciproque entre toutes les autorités de police selon les lois des divers états;
b) la création et le perfectionnement de toutes les dispositions et organisations qui sont aptes à favoriser la lutte contre les criminels.

ARTICLE 2

La 'Commission Internationale de la Police Criminelle' a son siège à VIENNE, tant que le congrès ne désignera pas une autre ville.

ARTICLE 3

Les membres de la 'Commission Internationale de la Police Criminelle' seront élus par le Congrès Internationale de Police assemblé en ce moment à VIENNE de telle manière que chaque état soit représenté au moins par un délégué.

Les gouvernements des états qui ne sont pas représentés à ce Congrès International de Police seront invités à désigner leurs représentants.

De plus, tous les candidats, desquels on peut attendre une aide efficace pour le but de la Commission, peuvent être admis comme membres. La majorité des membres de la Commission décide de leur admission.

ARTICLE 4

Les présidents, resp. Sous-présidents du dernier congrès ou de la dernière assemblée de la commission sont chargés de la direction et représentation de la 'Commission Internationale de Police criminelle'.

ARTICLE 5

Un comité administratif, composé de cinq rapporteurs et d'un secrétaire est adjoint au président pour les affaires. Deux de ces rapporteurs et le secrétaire seront élus parmi les fonctionnaires des autorités de la sureté publique de l'état, auquel appartient le président de la Commission.

Le comité administratif est élu avec majorité par les membres de la commission du milieu de celle-ci et exerce sa fonction jusqu'à la prochaine assemblée de la Commission.

Si les affaires l'exigent le président est autorisé, pour causes extraordinaires de nommer quelques rapporteurs de plus.

ARTICLE 6

Pour se mettre en relation avec le président les membres de la commission nomment un correspondant de chaque état n'étant pas déjà représenté dans le comité administratif par un rapporteur.

ARTICLE 7

Les propositions des membres sur des objets concernant la compétence de la commission sont à adresser par écrit au président, qui au besoin les assigne aux rapporteurs pour la révision.

L'assemblée de la commission décide de telles proportions.

ARTICLE 8

Chaque année la commission sera convoquée par le président à une séance ordinaire. L'ordre du jour proposé sera communiqué en même temps.

ARTICLE 9

La présence d'au moins la moitié des membres ainsi que la pluralité des voix est nécessaire pour prendre des résolutions.

En cas d'urgence, si la commission n'est pas assemblée, le président a le droit de faire prendre des résolutions par écrit.

ARTICLE 10

La Commission Internationale de la Police Criminelle décide avec majorité des changements et suppléments de ces statuts.

Appendix 2

The Constitution of the International Criminal Police Commission, 1939

ARTICLE 1

Le but de la 'Commission Internationale de Police Criminelle' est défini par les principes suivants:

a) La Commission assume la garantie et le développement de l'assistance mutuelle la plus large entre toutes les Polices criminelles dans le cadre des lois qui régissent les divers Etats;
b) La Commission assume le souci de la création et du développement de toutes les institutions capables de contribuer efficacement à la répression de la criminalité.

Sont à considérer comme telles institutions, sauf extension ultérieure:

1. Le bureau central international pour la répression des contrefaçons de billets de banque, chèques et d'autres valeurs;
2. Le journal 'Sûreté Publique Internationale';
3. Le service de renseignements concernant les malfaiteurs internationaux (Contrôle international): le répertoire international des recherches judiciaires: le répertoire international des individus réputés généralement dangereux;
4. La transmission internationale des empreintes digitales et des photographies de malfaiteurs internationaux;
5. Le bureau central international pour la répression des falsifications de passeports.

ARTICLE 2

La 'Commission Internationale de Police Criminelle' décide de siéger à Vienne tant que l'assemblée plénière n'aura pas désigné une autre résidence.

ARTICLE 3

La 'Commission Internationale de Police Criminelle' se compose:

a) *des membres effectifs*, qui seront délégués par leur gouvernement; ces membres ne seront pas soumis à élection;
b) *des membres extraordinaires*, qui seront élus à la majorité des deux tiers des voix, lors d'une session ordinaire.

Toutefois, ne pourront être présentées que les candidatures des personnes:

1. qui ont rendu des réels services à la Commission;
2. qui, par leurs connaissances techniques ou scientifiques, ou bien par les fonctions qu'ils exercent, sont susceptibles d'apporter une aide précieuse aux travaux de la Commission.

Le nom de tout candidat présenté, suivant paragraphe 2 ci-dessus, devra être communiqué deux mois avant la session, en outre, s'il s'agit d'un fonctionnaire public en activité, ce dernier devra produire au préalable l'autorisation de son gouvernement.

Seuls les membres ont le droit de prendre part aux sessions de la Commission: les membres effectifs sont, de plus, autorisés à s'y faire accompagner d'un assistant (secrétaire ou interprète), ainsi que d'experts en la matière à discuter. De tels experts et assistants pourront être présents à toutes sessions et délibérations à l'exception de celles ou il s'agit de la gestion de la Commission. Seuls les membres effectifs pourront participer au vote. Les membres fondateurs, élus en 1923 par le Congrès international de police, restent membres de la Commission, pourvu que leur Gouvernement n'y s'élève d'objections. Il en est de même, en règle générale, pour ce qui concerne les membres extraordinaires.

ARTICLE 4

La Commission élit sa Présidence à la majorité des deux tiers des voix.

La présidence se compose du Président et de six Vice-Présidents, dont l'un sera le délégué du pays qui organise la session suivante.

Le Président sera élu pour cinq ans.

Il est rééligible.

Les Vice-Présidents seront élus pour deux ans. Après ce terme ils pourront être remplacés, mais ils sont rééligibles. Les renouvellements se font tous les ans par moitié.

Si plusieurs Vice-Présidents ont plus de deux années de fonction, les sortants seront désignés par la voie du sort.

ARTICLE 5

Le Président sera assisté, outre des Vice-Présidents, d'un Comité administratif composé de neuf rapporteurs ordinaires, deux rapporteurs permanents et d'un secrétaire général.

Les deux rapporteurs permanents et le secrétaire général seront choisis par le Président. Toutefois, leur désignation sera approuvée par les membres de la majorité absolue des voix. Ils exerceront leur mandat jusqu'à l'expiration de celui du Président.

Les neufs rapporteurs ordinaires seront élus pour deux ans et réélus selon le mode indiqué pour les Vice-Présidents.

Pour des affaires extraordinaires, le Président pourra désigner d'office un ou plusieurs autres rapporteurs.

Le Président, les Vice-Présidents, et rapporteurs ordinaires devront être choisis parmi les membres délégués par leur gouvernement. Il ne pourra être désigné plus d'un Vice-Président par pays.

Le président, Vice-Présidents, rapporteurs, secrétaire général et membres pourront, en raison des services exceptionnels rendus à la « Commission Internationale de Police Criminelle » être autorisés, à la majorité des 2/3 voix, à conserver le titre honorifique de leurs fonctions.

ARTICLE 6

Les membres adresseront les propositions appartenant au domaine des travaux de la Commission directement au Président et par écrit; le Président remettra, le cas échéant, ces communications aux rapporteurs chargés de les étudier.

Les résolutions relatives à ces propositions seront prises en assemblée plénière de la Commission.

ARTICLE 7

Le Président convoquera la Commission annuellement pour une session ordinaire.

Cette convocation sera faite par lettre accompagnée de l'ordre du jour prévu.

Le Comité administratif se réunit au besoin mais au moins une fois par an.

Il est convoqué à cet effet par le Président de la Commission. Les membres extraordinaires ne peuvent pas se faire représenter aux séances.

ARTICLE 8

Les décisions sont prises à majorité simple.

Le Président peut exiger un vote par écrit en cas urgents si la Commission n'est pas réunie à cette date.

Appendix 3

The Constitution of the International Criminal Police Commission, 1946

ARTICLE 1

1. La Commission Internationale de Police Criminelle a pour but d'assurer et de développer une assistance officielle réciproque la plus large de toutes les autorités de police criminelle dans le cadre des lois existant dans les différents Etats, d'établir et de développer toutes les institutions capables de contribuer efficacement à la répression des crimes et délits de droit commun *à l'exclusion rigoureuse de toute affaire présentant un caractère politique, religieux ou racial.*
2. L'organe exécutif de la Commission Internationale de Police Criminelle est le Bureau Central International. Il y a un caractère permanent. Sous réserve d'extension, ses attributions sont les suivantes:
   a) La centralisation des renseignements pour la lutte contre la falsification de monnaies, papiers de valeurs et documents;
   b) L'édition de la Revue Internationale de Police Criminelle, avec le supplément *contrefaçons et falsifications*, où l'on se bornera à attirer l'attention sur les nouvelles émissions et sur les falsifications d'accord avec les Instituts d'émission et les autorités judiciaires saisies – *à l'exclusion de noms de personnes arrêtées, recherchées ou soupçonnées*;
   c) Le service de renseignements relatifs aux malfaiteurs internationaux, le répertoire international des recherches judiciaires, le répertoire international des individus ayant commis des crimes et des délits importants de droit commun sur le plan international;
   d) La transmission internationale d'empreintes digitales et photographiques de malfaiteurs internationaux.

ARTICLE 2

1. Le siège de la Commission Internationale de Police Criminelle est fixé par l'assemblée plénière de la Commission. Ce siège doit être établi dans les pays où se trouve le Bureau Central International. C'est là que se trouvera le Secrétaire général responsable du contrôle de ce Bureau.
2. Les services de police criminelle, membres de la Commission Internationale, mettent leur activité à la disposition de cette Commission et du Bureau Central International.

ARTICLE 3

1. La Commission Internationale de Police Criminelle est composée:
   a) des membres effectifs soit les membres délégués par leur Gouvernement auprès de la Commission. Ces membres ne sont pas soumis à élection;
   b) des membres extraordinaires, soit les membres élus à la majorité des deux tiers des voix au cours d'une assemblées plénière. Ces membres devront toujours avoir l'approbation de leur Gouvernement.
2. Seules les personnes suivantes peuvent être candidates au titre de membre extraordinaire:
   a) celles qui ont rendu à la Commission des services effectifs ou
   b) celles qui, en considération de leurs connaissances techniques ou scientifiques ou des fonctions qu'elles assument, sont censées devoir promouvoir de façon estimable les activités de la Commission.
3. Le nom du candidat présenté en vertu du deuxième alinéa de ce paragraphe doit être modifié deux mois avant la réunion. Il doit, en outre, présenter l'approbation préalable de son Gouvernement.
4. N'aura droit de vote qu'un seul délégué effectif par pays.
5. Les membres fondateurs élus par le Congrès International de la Police Criminelle en 1923 demeurent membres de la Commission, pour autant que leur Gouvernement n'y mette pas obstacle. La même remarque vaut en général pour les membres extraordinaires.
6. Seuls les membres ont le droit de participer aux assemblées de la Commission. Un membre effectif peut cependant se faire assister d'un adjoint (secrétaire ou interprète), ainsi que d'experts. Ces experts ou adjoints peuvent assister à toutes les réunions ou délibérations, sauf à celles au cours desquelles il sera traité de la gestion interne de la Commission.

ARTICLE 4

1. la Commission élit sa présidence aux deux tiers des voix. La présidence se compose d'un président et de 7 vice-présidents. En outre le délégué du pays qui organise la réunion suivante, peut être désigné comme vice-président.
2. Le président est élu pour 5 ans. Il est rééligible. Les vice-présidents sont élus pour deux ans. Ils sont également rééligibles.

ARTICLE 5

1. Le président sera assisté de 3 rapporteurs généraux et d'un secrétaire général, qui constitueront le Comité Exécutif. Le Comité Exécutif est chargé sous la responsabilité du Président, de l'exécution de toutes les mesures prises par l'Assemblée, du contrôle du Bureau Central International et de toutes les institutions de la Commission, ainsi que de la préparation des sessions (assemblée plénières).
2. Le Comité Exécutif peut avoir recours aussi à un collègue de dix rapporteurs choisis parmi les membres de la Commission pour l'examen de toutes les questions à soumettre à l'assemblée et pour l'élaboration des rapports concernant ces questions.
3. Pour ces tâches spéciales, le Président choisira parme les rapporteurs ceux qui devront établir le rapport d'ensemble sur la matière.
4. Les rapporteurs généraux et le Secrétaire général sont présentés par le Président et élus par l'assemblée pour

une période de cinq ans. Toutefois, à l'expiration du mandat du Président, il y a lieu à nouvelle nomination sur la proposition du nouveau Président.

5. Les membres du Comité Exécutif devront, autant que possible, appartenir à des Etats différents, mais le Secrétaire général appartiendra de préférence au pays où est établi le siège de la Commission.
6. Les rapporteurs sont élus pour deux ans et seront réélus selon le mode indiqué pour les Vice-Présidents.
7. Le Président, les Vice-Présidents, les Rapporteurs généraux et les Rapporteurs seront élus parmi les membres des divers pays, sans qu'un même pays puisse avoir en même temps un Président et un Vice-Président ou plus d'un Vice-président.
8. En raison des services extraordinaires rendus à la C.I.P.C., les Présidents, Vice- Présidents, Rapporteurs généraux, Secrétaire général et Rapporteurs pourront être autorisés aux deux tiers des voix à conserver le titre honorifique de leur fonction.
9. Les mandats au sein de la Commission ne peuvent être conférés qu'aux membres effectifs.

ARTICLE 6

1. Les propositions des membres relatives à des affaires relevant des activités de la Commission doivent être présentées par écrit au Président qui les fait parvenir, s'il y a lieu, aux rapporteurs chargés de les étudier. En principe, ces propositions doivent parvenir au Président quatre mois avant la date de la réunion ou assemblée, ce qui lui permettra de comprendre ces propositions dans l'ordre du jour de l'assemblée de la Commission, un mois au moins avant la date de celle-ci.
2. Les résolutions relatives à ces propositions seront prises en assemblée plénière de la Commission.

ARTICLE 7

1. Le Président convoquera la Commission au moins une fois par an en indiquant autant que possible les points faisant l'objet de l'ordre du jour.
2. Le Comité Exécutif et le Collège des Rapporteurs seront réunis par le Président en cas de besoin.

ARTICLE 8

Les décisions sont prises à la majorité simple des voix, à l'exception des cas prévus dans les paragraphes précédents où les deux tiers des voix ont été requis, à l'exception des cas prévus dans les paragraphes précédents où les deux tiers des voix ont été requis. Lorsque la réunion n'est pas convoquée, le Président a le droit, dans les cas urgents, de faire adopter une décision par écrit. Toutefois, dans ce cas, le nombre des suffrages émis doit être égal ou supérieur aux deux tiers des membres ayant assisté à la session précédente.

ARTICLE 9

Les précédents statuts entrent en vigueur le 4 juin 1946 et les anciens statuts sont abrogés.

Appendix 4

The Constitution and General Regulations of the ICPO-INTERPOL, 1956

Constitution of the ICPO-INTERPOL

REFERENCES

The Constitution of the ICPO-INTERPOL adopted by the General Assembly at its 25th session (Vienna - 1956).

Articles 35 and 36 modified at the 31st session (Madrid - 1962).

Articles 2, 15, 16 and 19 modified at the 33rd session (Caracas - 1964).

Article 17 modified at the 46th session (Stockholm - 1977).

Article 1 modified at the 53rd session (Luxembourg - 1984).

Articles 11 and 12 modified at the General Assembly's 66th session (New Delhi - 1997).

At the 77th session (St Petersburg - 2008), the following amendments were made to the Constitution: Article 5 was amended, Articles 34–37 concerning the Advisers were combined in Articles 34 and 35; a new heading "THE COMMISSION FOR THE CONTROL OF FILES" was added and certain provisions concerning the Commission inserted in Articles 36 and 37.

Articles 28 and 29 modified at the 86th session (Beijing - 2017).

GENERAL PROVISIONS

Article 1

The Organization called the "INTERNATIONAL CRIMINAL POLICE COMMISSION" shall henceforth be entitled: "THE INTERNATIONAL CRIMINAL POLICE ORGANIZATION- INTERPOL". Its seat shall be in France.

Article 2

Its aims are:

(1) To ensure and promote the widest possible mutual assistance between all criminal police authorities within the limits of the laws existing in the different countries and in the spirit of the "Universal Declaration of Human Rights";
(2) To establish and develop all institutions likely to contribute effectively to the prevention and suppression of ordinary law crimes.

Article 3

It is strictly forbidden for the Organization to undertake any intervention or activities of a political, military, religious or racial character.

Article 4

Any country may delegate as a Member to the Organization any official police body whose functions come within the framework of activities of the Organization.

The request for membership shall be submitted to the Secretary General by the appropriate governmental authority. Membership shall be subject to approval by a two-thirds majority of the General Assembly.

STRUCTURE AND ORGANIZATION

Article 5

The International Criminal Police Organization-INTERPOL shall comprise:

- The General Assembly
- The Executive Committee
- The General Secretariat
- The National Central Bureaus
- The Advisers
- The Commission for the Control of Files

THE GENERAL ASSEMBLY

Article 6

The General Assembly shall be the body of supreme authority in the Organization. It is composed of delegates appointed by the Members of the Organization.

Article 7

Each Member may be represented by one or several delegates; however, for each country there shall be only one delegation head, appointed by the competent governmental authority of that country.

Because of the technical nature of the Organization, Members should attempt to include the following in their delegations:

(a) High officials of departments dealing with police affairs,
(b) Officials whose normal duties are connected with the activities of the Organization,
(c) Specialists in the subjects on the agenda.

Article 8

The functions of the General Assembly shall be the following:

(a) To carry out the duties laid down in the Constitution;
(b) To determine principles and lay down the general measures suitable for attaining the objectives of the Organization as given in Article 2 of the Constitution;
(c) To examine and approve the general programme of activities prepared by the Secretary General for the coming year;
(d) To determine any other regulations deemed necessary;
(e) To elect persons to perform the functions mentioned in the Constitution;
(f) To adopt resolutions and make recommendations to Members on matters with which the Organization is competent to deal;
(g) To determine the financial policy of the Organization;
(h) To examine and approve any agreements to be made with other organizations.

Article 9

Members shall do all within their power, in so far as is compatible with their own obligations, to carry out the decisions of the General Assembly.

Article 10

The General Assembly of the Organization shall meet in ordinary session every year. It may meet in extraordinary session at the request of the Executive Committee or of the majority of Members.

Article 11

(1) The General Assembly may, when in session, set up special committees for dealing with particular matters.
(2) It may also decide to hold regional conferences between two General Assembly sessions.

Article 12

(1) At the end of each session, the General Assembly shall choose the place where it will meet for its next session.
(2) The General Assembly may also decide where it will meet for its session in two years' time, if one or more countries have issued invitations to host that session.
(3) If circumstances make it impossible or inadvisable for a session to be held in the chosen meeting place, the General Assembly may decide to choose another meeting place for the following year.

Article 13

Only one delegate from each country shall have the right to vote in the General Assembly.

Article 14

Decisions shall be made by a simple majority except in those cases where a two-thirds majority is required by the Constitution.

THE EXECUTIVE COMMITTEE

Article 15

The Executive Committee shall be composed of the President of the Organization, the three Vice- Presidents and nine Delegates.

The thirteen members of the Executive Committee shall belong to different countries, due weight having been given to geographical distribution.

Article 16

The General Assembly shall elect, from among the delegates, the President and three Vice-Presidents of the Organization.

A two-thirds majority shall be required for the election of the President; should this majority not be obtained after the second ballot, a simple majority shall suffice.

The President and Vice-Presidents shall be from different continents.

Article 17

The President shall be elected for four years. The Vice-Presidents shall be elected for three years. They shall not be immediately eligible for reelection either to the same posts or as Delegates on the Executive Committee.

If, following the election of a President, the provisions of Article 15 (paragraph 2) or Article 16 (paragraph 3) cannot be applied or are incompatible, a fourth Vice-President shall be elected so that all four continents are represented at the Presidency level.

If this occurs, the Executive Committee will, for a temporary period, have fourteen members. The temporary period shall come to an end as soon as circumstances make it possible to apply the provisions of Articles 15 and 16.

Article 18

The President of the Organization shall:

(a) Preside at meetings of the Assembly and the Executive Committee and direct the discussions;
(b) Ensure that the activities of the Organization are in conformity with the decisions of the General Assembly and the Executive Committee;
(c) Maintain as far as is possible direct and constant contact with the Secretary General of the Organization.

Article 19

The nine Delegates on the Executive Committee shall be elected by the General Assembly for a period of three years. They shall not be immediately eligible for re-election to the same posts.

Article 20

The Executive Committee shall meet at least once each year on being convened by the President of the Organization.

Article 21

In the exercise of their duties, all members of the Executive Committee shall conduct themselves as representatives of the Organization and not as representatives of their respective countries.

Article 22

The Executive Committee shall:

(a) Supervise the execution of the decisions of the General Assembly;
(b) Prepare the agenda for sessions of the General Assembly;
(c) Submit to the General Assembly any programme of work or project which it considers useful;
(d) Supervise the administration and work of the Secretary General;
(e) Exercise all the powers delegated to it by the Assembly.

Article 23

In case of resignation or death of any of the members of the Executive Committee, the General Assembly shall elect another member to replace him and whose term of office shall end on the same date as his predecessor's. No member of the Executive Committee may remain in office should he cease to be a delegate to the Organization.

Article 24

Executive Committee members shall remain in office until the end of the session of the General Assembly held in the year in which their term of office expires.

THE GENERAL SECRETARIAT

Article 25

The permanent departments of the Organization shall constitute the General Secretariat.

Article 26

The General Secretariat shall:

(a) Put into application the decisions of the General Assembly and the Executive Committee;
(b) Serve as an international centre in the fight against ordinary crime;
(c) Serve as a technical and information centre;
(d) Ensure the efficient administration of the Organization;
(e) Maintain contact with national and international authorities, whereas questions relative to the search for criminals shall be dealt with through the National Central Bureaus;
(f) Produce any publications which may be considered useful;
(g) Organize and perform secretariat work at the sessions of the General Assembly, the Executive Committee and any other body of the Organization;
(h) Draw up a draft programme of work for the coming year for the consideration and approval of the General Assembly and the Executive Committee;
(i) Maintain as far as is possible direct and constant contact with the President of the Organization.

Article 27

The General Secretariat shall consist of the Secretary General and a technical and administrative staff entrusted with the work of the Organization.

Article 28

The appointment of the Secretary General shall be proposed by the Executive Committee and approved by the General Assembly for a period of five years. The Secretary General may be re-appointed only once, for a further period of five years, but must lay down office on reaching the age of sixty-five. The Secretary General may be allowed to complete the term of office on reaching the age of sixty-five but shall not hold office beyond the age of seventy.

The Secretary General must be chosen from among persons highly competent in police matters.

In exceptional circumstances, the Executive Committee may propose at a meeting of the General Assembly that the Secretary General be removed from office.

Article 29

The Secretary General shall engage and direct the staff, administer the budget, and organize and direct the permanent departments, according to the directives decided upon by the General Assembly or Executive Committee.

The Secretary General shall submit to the Executive Committee or the General Assembly any propositions or projects concerning the work of the Organization.

The Secretary General shall be responsible to the Executive Committee and the General Assembly.

The Secretary General shall have the right to take part in the discussions of the General Assembly, the Executive Committee and all other dependent bodies.

In the exercise of his or her duties, the Secretary General shall represent the Organization and not any particular country.

Article 30

In the exercise of their duties, the Secretary General and the staff shall neither solicit nor accept instructions from any government or authority outside the Organization. They shall abstain from any action which might be prejudicial to their international task.

Each Member of the Organization shall undertake to respect the exclusively international character of the duties of the Secretary General and the staff, and abstain from influencing them in the discharge of their duties.

All Members of the Organization shall do their best to assist the Secretary General and the staff in the discharge of their functions.

NATIONAL CENTRAL BUREAUS

Article 31

In order to further its aims, the Organization needs the constant and active co-operation of its Members, who should do all within their power which is compatible with the legislations of their countries to participate diligently in its activities.

Article 32

In order to ensure the above cooperation, each country shall appoint a body which will serve as the National Central Bureau. It shall ensure liaison with:

(a) The various departments in the country;
(b) Those bodies in other countries serving as National Central Bureaus;
(c) The Organization's General Secretariat.

Article 33

In the case of those countries where the provisions of Article 32 are inapplicable or do not permit of effective centralized co-operation, the General Secretariat shall decide, with these countries, the most suitable alternative means of co-operation.

THE ADVISERS

Article 34

On scientific matters, the Organization may consult "Advisers". The role of the Advisers shall be purely advisory.

Article 35

Advisers shall be appointed for three years by the Executive Committee. Their appointment will become definite only after notification by the General Assembly.

They shall be chosen from among those who have a world-wide reputation in some field of interest to the Organization.

An Adviser may be removed from office by decision of the General Assembly.

THE COMMISSION FOR THE CONTROL OF FILES

Article 36

The Commission for the Control of Files is an independent body which shall ensure that the processing of personal information by the Organization is in compliance with the regulations the Organization establishes in this matter.

The Commission for the Control of Files shall provide the Organization with advice about any project, operation, set of rules or other matter involving the processing of personal information.

The Commission for the Control of Files shall process requests concerning the information contained in the Organization's files.

Article 37

The members of the Commission for the Control of Files shall possess the expertise required for it to accomplish its functions. Its composition and its functioning shall be subject to specific rules to be laid down by the General Assembly.

BUDGET AND RESOURCES

Article 38

The Organization's resources shall be provided by:

(a) The financial contributions from Members;
(b) Gifts, bequests, subsidies, grants and other resources after these have been accepted or approved by the Executive Committee.

Article 39

The General Assembly shall establish the basis of Members' subscriptions and the maximum annual expenditure according to the estimate provided by the Secretary General.

Article 40

The draft budget of the Organization shall be prepared by the Secretary General and submitted for approval to the Executive Committee.

It shall come into force after acceptance by the General Assembly.

Should the General Assembly not have had the possibility of approving the budget, the Executive Committee shall take all necessary steps according to the general outlines of the preceding budget.

RELATIONS WITH OTHER ORGANIZATIONS

Article 41

Whenever it deems fit, having regard to the aims and objects provided in the Constitution, the Organization shall establish relations and collaborate with other intergovernmental or nongovernmental international organizations.

The general provisions concerning the relations with international, intergovernmental or nongovernmental organizations will only be valid after their approval by the General Assembly.

The Organization may, in connection with all matters in which it is competent, take the advice of nongovernmental international, governmental national or non-governmental national organizations.

With the approval of the General Assembly, the Executive Committee or, in urgent cases, the Secretary General may accept duties within the scope of its activities and competence either from other international institutions or organizations or in application of international conventions.

APPLICATION, MODIFICATION AND INTERPRETATION OF THE CONSTITUTION

Article 42

The present Constitution may be amended on the proposal of either a Member or the Executive Committee.

Any proposal for amendment to this Constitution shall be communicated by the Secretary General to Members of the Organization at least three months before submission to the General Assembly for consideration.

All amendments to this Constitution shall be approved by a two-thirds majority of the Members of the Organization.

Article 43

The French, English and Spanish texts of this Constitution shall be regarded as authoritative.

Article 44

The application of this Constitution shall be determined by the General Assembly through the General Regulations and Appendices, whose provisions shall be adopted by a two-thirds majority.

TEMPORARY MEASURES

Article 45

All bodies representing the countries mentioned in Appendix I shall be deemed to be Members of the Organization unless they declare through the appropriate governmental authority that they cannot accept this Constitution. Such a declaration should be made within six months of the date of the coming into force of the present Constitution.

Article 46

At the first election, lots will be drawn to determine a Vice-President whose term of office will end a year later.

At the first election, lots will be drawn to determine two Delegates on the Executive Committee whose term of office will end a year later, and two others whose term of office will end two years later.

Article 47

Persons having rendered meritorious and prolonged services in the ranks of the ICPC may be awarded by the General Assembly honorary titles in corresponding ranks of the ICPO.

Article 48

All property belonging to the International Criminal Police Commission are transferred to the International Criminal Police Organization.

Article 49

In the present Constitution:

- "Organization", wherever it occurs, shall mean the International Criminal Police Organization;
- "Constitution", wherever it occurs, shall mean the Constitution of the International Criminal Police Organization;
- "Secretary General" shall mean the Secretary General of the International Criminal Police Organization;
- "Committee" shall mean the Executive Committee of the Organization;
- "Assembly" or "General Assembly" shall mean the General Assembly of the Organization;
- "Member" or "Members" shall mean a Member or Members of the International Criminal Police Organization as mentioned in Article 4 of the Constitution;
- "delegate" (in the singular) or "delegates" (in the plural) shall mean a person or persons belonging to a delegation or delegations as defined in Article 7;

- "Delegate" (in the singular) or "Delegates" (in the plural) shall mean a person or persons elected to the Executive Committee in the conditions laid down in Article 19.

Article 50

This Constitution shall come into force on 13 June 1956.

****

APPENDIX 1:

LIST OF STATES TO WHICH THE PROVISIONS OF ARTICLE 45 OF THE CONSTITUTION SHALL APPLY

Argentina, Australia, Austria, Belgium, Brazil, Burma, Cambodia, Canada, Ceylon, Chile, Colombia, Costa Rica, Cuba, Denmark, Dominican Republic, Egypt, Eire, Finland, France, Federal German Republic, Greece, Guatemala, India, Indonesia, Iran, Israel, Italy, Japan, Jordan, Lebanon, Liberia, Libya, Luxembourg, Mexico, Monaco, Netherlands, Netherlands Antilles, New Zealand, Norway, Pakistan, Philippines, Portugal, Saar, Saudi Arabia, Spain, Sudan, Surinam, Sweden, Switzerland, Syria, Thailand, Turkey, United Kingdom of Great Britain and Northern Ireland, United States of America, Uruguay, Venezuela, Yugoslavia.

****

General Regulations of the ICPO-INTERPOL

REFERENCES

The General Regulations of the ICPO-INTERPOL adopted by the General Assembly at its 25th session (Vienna – 1956).

Articles 46 and 50 modified at the 31st session (Madrid – 1962).

Articles 41 and 58 modified at the 33rd session (Caracas – 1964).

Article 58 modified at the 36th session (Kyoto – 1967).

Articles 52 and 56 modified at the 37th session (Teheran – 1968).

Article 40 modified at the 43rd session (Cannes – 1974).

Article 58 modified at the 44th session (Buenos Aires – 1975).

Article 41 modified at the 46th session (Stockholm – 1977).

Article 53 modified at the 52nd session (Cannes – 1983).

At the 54th session (Washington – 1985), the General Regulations were modified as follows: Article 51, rewritten; Article 53 became Article 52; a new Article 53 was added; Articles 52, 54, 55, 56 and 57 were rescinded and Articles 58 to 60 were renumbered 54 to 56.

The English version of Article 53 was modified at the 56th session (Nice – 1987); the expression "Staff Rules" was replaced by "Staff Regulations".

Article 52 modified at the 57th session (Bangkok – 1988). This article, as amended in 1988, was abrogated by the General Assembly at its 65th session (Antalya – 1996) and replaced by a new Article 52 which will enter into force on 1st July 1997.

Articles 35, 36 and 37 modified at the General Assembly's 66th session (New Delhi – 1997).

Article 54 amended by the General Assembly during its 68th session (Seoul – 1999).

Article 43 amended at the 82nd General Assembly session (Cartagena de Indias – 2013).

Article 44 amended at the 83rd General Assembly session (Monaco – 2014).

Article 44 amended at the 86th General Assembly session (Beijing – 2017).

Articles 39 and 52 amended at the 88th General Assembly session (Santiago – 2019).

Article 1

These General Regulations and Appendices have been adopted in accordance with Article 44 of the Constitution of the Organization.

Should there be any differences between the two, the Constitution shall prevail.

GENERAL ASSEMBLY:
PLACE – DATE – CONVENING

Article 2

The General Assembly shall meet every year in ordinary session.

Article 3

Any Member may, on behalf of its country, invite the Assembly to meet on the territory of that country.

If this is impossible, the meeting shall be held at the seat of the Organization.

Article 4

Any such invitation should be sent to the President before the beginning of the debates of the Assembly.

Article 5

If the Executive Committee considers that circumstances are unfavourable to the meeting of the Assembly in the place fixed at its previous session, it may decide on another place.

Article 6

The President shall fix the date when the Assembly is to meet after consulting the authorities of the inviting country and the Secretary General.

Article 7

The date and place having been decided upon, the notices convening Members shall be sent not less than four months in advance by:

(a) The inviting country to the other countries, through diplomatic channels;
(b) The Secretary General to the various Members of the Organization.

Article 8

The following may be invited to be present at meetings as observers:

(a) Police bodies which are not members of the Organization;
(b) International organizations.

The list of observers shall be drawn up by the Executive Committee and should be approved by the inviting country.

The observers mentioned in § (a) shall be jointly invited by the inviting country and the Secretary General, while those mentioned in § (b) only by the Secretary General, after agreement of the Executive Committee and of the inviting country.

AGENDA

Article 9

The provisional agenda of the meeting shall be drawn up by the Executive Committee and communicated to Members not less than 90 days before the opening of the session.

Article 10

The provisional agenda shall include:

(a) The report of the Secretary General on the work of the Organization;
(b) The Secretary General's financial report and the draft budget;
(c) The general programme of activities proposed by the Secretary General for the coming year;
(d) Items whose inclusion has been ordered at the previous session of the Assembly;

(e) Items proposed by Members;
(f) Items inserted by the Executive Committee or the Secretary General.

Article 11

Any Member may, thirty days before the opening of the session, request that an item be added to the agenda.

Article 12

Before the opening meeting of the Assembly, the Executive Committee shall form the provisional agenda and the supplement to the agenda into a final agenda in the order of the urgency and priority of the items. The items left over from the previous session shall be deemed to take priority over the items suggested for the coming session.

Article 13

In so far as is possible, Members shall receive, thirty days before the opening meeting of the session, the information necessary for the examination of reports and items on the agenda.

EXTRAORDINARY SESSIONS

Article 14

Extraordinary sessions shall be held, in principle, at the seat of the Organization.

An extraordinary session shall be convened, after assent has been given by the President, by the Secretary General as soon as possible and not less than thirty days and no more than ninety days after the request has been made.

Article 15

In principle, the agenda of an extraordinary session may only include the object for its convening.

DELEGATIONS AND VOTING

Article 16

Members shall notify the Secretary General as early as possible of the composition of their delegations.

Article 17

The General Assembly shall make its decisions in plenary session by means of resolutions.

Article 18

Subject to Article 52 of the General Regulations, each country represented has one vote.

Voting shall be performed by the head of the delegation or some other delegate.

The representative of one Member may not vote for another Member.

Article 19

The decisions of the Assembly shall be taken by a simple majority, except where otherwise provided by the Constitution.

Article 20

The majority shall be decided by a count of those persons present and casting an affirmative or negative vote. Those who abstain may justify their attitude.

When the Constitution requires a "majority of the Members" the calculation of this majority shall be based on the total number of the Members of the Organization, whether they are represented or not at the session of the Assembly.

Article 21

Voting shall be done by single ballot, except where a two-thirds majority is required.

In the latter case, if the required majority is not obtained the first time, a second vote shall be taken.

Article 22

Voting shall be done by show of hands, record vote or secret ballot.

At any time a delegate may request a record vote to be taken except in cases where a secret ballot is required by the Constitution.

Article 23

Persons composing the Executive Committee shall be elected by secret ballot.

If two candidates obtain the same number of votes, a second ballot shall be taken. If this is not decisive, lots shall be drawn to determine which shall be chosen.

Article 24

Resolutions may be voted on paragraph by paragraph, on the request of any delegate. In such a case, the whole shall subsequently be put to the vote.

Only one complete resolution shall be voted on at one time.

Article 25

When an amendment to a proposal is moved, the amendment shall be voted on first.

If there are several amendments, the President shall put them to the vote separately, commencing with the ones furthest removed from the basis of the original proposal.

CONDUCT OF BUSINESS

Article 26

Meetings of the Assembly and the committees shall not be public, unless otherwise decided by the Assembly.

Article 27

The Assembly may limit the time to be allowed to each speaker.

Article 28

When a motion is under discussion, any Member may raise a point of order and this point of order shall be immediately decided by the President.

Should this be contested, any delegate may appeal to the Assembly, which shall immediately decide by a vote.

Article 29

If, during the discussions, a speaker moves the suspension or adjournment of the meeting or the debates, the matter shall immediately be put to the vote.

Article 30

A delegate may at any time move the closure of the debates. Two speakers opposed to the closure may then speak, after which the Assembly shall decide whether to accede to the motion.

Article 31

The Assembly may not vote on a draft resolution unless copies of it in all the working languages have been distributed.

Amendments and counter-proposals may be discussed immediately unless a majority of Members request that written copies of them shall be distributed first.

When a draft resolution has financial consequences, the Executive Committee shall be requested to give its opinion and the discussions postponed.

Article 32

The Secretary General or his representative may intervene in the discussions at any moment.

SECRETARIAT

Article 33

Summary records of the debates of the Assembly in the working languages shall be distributed as soon as possible.

Article 34

The Secretary General shall be responsible for the secretariat work of the Assembly; for this purpose he shall engage the necessary personnel and direct and control them.

COMMITTEES

Article 35

(1) At each session, the Assembly shall form such committees as it deems necessary. On the proposal of the President, it shall allocate work relative to the various items on the agenda to each committee.

(2) When it decides to create a regional conference, the General Assembly shall delegate to the latter the power to fix the date, place and conditions of its meetings, taking into account the proposals of member countries. If the regional conference does not take the appropriate decisions, the General Assembly shall take them.

Article 36

(1) Each committee shall elect its own chairman. Each committee member shall have the right to vote. Meetings of the committees shall be subject to the same rules as the plenary sessions of the Assembly.

(2) The provisions of paragraph 1 of the present Article shall also apply to regional conferences.

Article 37

(1) The chairman of each committee or a reporter nominated by it shall render a verbal account of its work to the Assembly.

(2) The chairmen of regional conferences may also transmit recommendations made by the conferences to the General Secretariat which shall be responsible for co-ordinating any proposed resolutions to be submitted to the General Assembly.

Article 38

Unless otherwise decided by the Assembly, any committee may be consulted between sessions.

The President, after consultation with the Secretary General, may summon a committee to meet.

THE EXECUTIVE COMMITTEE

Article 39

At the end of the ordinary session the Assembly shall fill such vacancies on the Executive Committee as exist, by election of persons chosen amongst the delegates put forward by Members whose voting rights have not been suspended under Article 52 of the General Regulations.

Article 40

At the beginning of each session the General Assembly shall elect at least three heads of delegations who will form the "Election Committee".

They shall scrutinize the nominations they receive to determine whether they are valid and submit the list of these nominations in alphabetical order to the Assembly.

They shall also act as tellers.

Article 41

If, for any reason whatsoever, the President can no longer perform his duties either during or between sessions, his place shall temporarily be taken by the senior Vice-President.

Should all the Vice-Presidents be absent, the duties of President shall provisionally devolve upon a Delegate of the Executive Committee designated by the other members of the Executive Committee.

GENERAL SECRETARIAT

Article 42

The Assembly shall elect a Secretary General by secret ballot for a term of office of five years.

The candidate for the post of Secretary General shall be proposed by the Executive Committee.

Article 43

The Secretary General should be or have been a police official.

Article 44

The five-year term of office of the Secretary General shall commence at the end of the incumbent's term of office and terminate at the end of the General Assembly session held in the year in which his term of office expires.

The Secretary General's term of office shall terminate on completion of the prescribed five-year period provided for in Article 28 of the Constitution, or in the event of the Secretary General's resignation, death, removal from office, or upon reaching the age limit as specified in Article 28 of the Constitution.

The Executive Committee shall determine the Secretary General's conditions of employment.

Article 45

Should the Secretary General be unable to carry out his duties, these shall be performed in the interim by the highest-ranking official in the General Secretariat, provided the Executive Committee has no objection.

THE ADVISERS

Article 46

Advisers may be individually or collectively consulted on the initiative of the Assembly, the Executive Committee, the President or the Secretary General. They may make suggestions of a scientific nature to the General Secretariat or the Executive Committee.

Article 47

At the request of the General Assembly, the Executive Committee or the Secretary General, reports or papers on scientific matters may be submitted to the Assembly by Advisers.

Article 48

Advisers may be present at meetings of the General Assembly as observers and, on the invitation of the President, may take part in the discussions.

Article 49

Several Advisers may be nationals of the same country.

Article 50

The Advisers may meet when convened by the President of the Organization.

BUDGET – FINANCE – PERSONNEL

Article 51

The Financial Regulations shall lay down rules governing:

- the determination of statutory contributions and payment conditions,
- the preparation, approval, implementation and control of the budget,
- the organization of an accounting system and the keeping, control and approval of the accounts,
- the procurement of works, supplies and services and the control of contracts, and shall also contain all relevant general provisions concerning the Organization's financial management.

Article 52

(1) Any Member that has not paid its statutory contributions to the Organization for the current financial year and the previous financial year shall have no vote in the General Assembly, other than votes taken on amendments to the Organization's Constitution.

(2) The Secretary General shall send a written notification to any Member that has failed to pay its statutory contributions to the Organization. The notification shall draw attention to the sanctions applied and the supporting measures established by the General Secretariat to encourage timely payment of contributions due. The Secretary General shall accordingly inform the Executive Committee and, where relevant, the General Assembly.

(3) The General Assembly may, nevertheless, decide to waive the suspension of voting rights at its discretion, if the item has been added to the agenda of the session of the General Assembly.

Article 53

The Staff Regulations shall specify the staff members of the Organization to which they apply, and lay down the rules and procedures governing their management. These rules shall specify the basic conditions of employment and the basic duties and rights of the staff members.

LANGUAGES

Article 54

(1) The working languages of the Organization shall be Arabic, English, French and Spanish.

(2) During General Assembly sessions, any delegate may speak in another language provided he makes arrangements for the interpretation of his speeches into one of the languages mentioned in paragraph 1 of this Article. Any request submitted by a group of countries for simultaneous interpretation of a language other than those mentioned in paragraph 1 of this Article must be sent, at least four months before the opening of the General Assembly session, to the Secretary General who will state whether such interpretation will be technically feasible.

(3) Countries wishing to apply the special provisions in paragraph 2 of this Article may do so only if they have undertaken to provide adequate administrative facilities and to meet all expenses involved.

MODIFICATION OF THE GENERAL REGULATIONS

Article 55

These Regulations and their Appendices may be modified at the request of any Member so long as the suggested modification has been sent to the General Secretariat at least 120 days before the opening of the following session. The Secretary General shall circulate this proposal at least 90 days before the session of the General Assembly.

The Secretary General may propose a modification to the General Regulations or their Appendices by circulating his proposal to Members at least 90 days before the session of the General Assembly.

During the session, in case of urgent necessity, any modification of the Regulations or their Appendices may be placed before the Assembly provided a written proposal to this effect be submitted jointly by three Members.

Article 56

The General Assembly shall take a decision on the proposed modification of the Regulations or their Appendices after consultation with an "ad hoc" committee composed of three delegates elected by the Assembly and two persons appointed by the Executive Committee.

This committee shall also be consulted on any proposal for the modification of the Constitution.

Appendix 5

Statement to Reaffirm the Independence and Political Neutrality of INTERPOL, 2006

The ICPO-Interpol General Assembly, meeting in Rio de Janeiro, Brazil, from 19 to 22 September 2006 at its 75th session:

RECALLING that the Organization was created in 1923, under the name of the INTERNATIONAL CRIMINAL POLICE COMMISSION (ICPC), and that its constituent instrument was revised in 1939 and in 1946;

RECALLING that in 1955 it was felt necessary to revise the constituent instrument of the Organization, in order to ensure and strengthen its position as an independent and neutral intergovernmental organization;

NOTING that, to this end, during the 25th session of the General Assembly of the ICPC, held in Vienna from 7–13 June 1956, the new Constitution of the International Criminal Police Organization (ICPO-Interpol) was adopted in 1956, in which the following elements are included:

(a) The Organization as a standing intergovernmental organization rather than a committee (Art. 1), with its own organs (Art. 5), and with a life of its own, independent of the countries which gave birth to it;
(b) The prohibition on engaging in any activities of a political, military, racial or religious nature (Art. 3);
(c) The freedom of member countries to appoint their delegates to the GA (composition delegations (Art. 7);
(d) The independence of the Executive Committee (Art. 21);
(e) The independence of the General Secretariat (Art. 30);
(f) The duty of collaboration and creation of NCBs (Art. 31);

WELCOMES THE FACT that the Organizations' independence has been confirmed by courts and that tribunals in member countries have recognized that the Organization has an existence separate from its member countries, and, in particular, that the International Labour Organization's Administrative Tribunal (ILOAT) has expressly ruled that the Organization is an independent international organization, which is not subject to any national law;

WELCOMES also the recognition of the Organization as an international legal person by other intergovernmental organizations, particularly by the United Nations;

NOTES, however, that over the last 50 years it became evident that it was necessary to undertake steps to preserve the independence and neutrality of the Organization, which include measures:

- To establish data protection rules, and to create the Commission for the Control of Interpol's Files in order to avoid interference by national data protection bodies,
- To establish its own Staff Regulations pursuant to Article 53 of the General Regulations and adhere to the jurisdiction of the ILOAT in order to avoid being subjected to national labour laws and labour courts;

EXPRESSES concern that despite the relative success of the Constitution in preserving the neutrality and independence of the Organization, the Organization faces continuous challenges, which lately have taken the following forms:

- Measures affecting the member countries' freedom to compose delegations to statutory meetings of the Organization;
- Measures affecting the independence of the staff members seconded to the General Secretariat;
- Measures affecting the independence of the members of the Executive Committee;
- Measures affecting the venue of sessions of statutory bodies.

RESOLVES to:

1. Confirm the principles of neutrality and independence enshrined in Interpol's Constitution;
2. Thank the member countries and intergovernmental organizations for helping the Organization to uphold these principles;
3. Call upon all member countries and intergovernmental organizations to respect the independence and neutrality of either the Organization itself, the Executive Committee, or the General Secretariat;
4. Call upon the General Secretariat as well as the member countries to consult with one another or with any intergovernmental institution contemplating to take measures which would interfere with the Organization's neutrality and independence;
5. Task the Executive Committee and the Secretary General to continue to take all steps necessary to ensure the neutrality and independence of the Organization as set forth in the provisions of the Constitution and to report to the General Assembly as to the concrete steps taken in this regard.

INDEX